# QUICK ESCAPES

## in the
## Pacific Northwest

"A valuable guide for travelers whose time is tight, *Quick Escapes* covers both the big name attractions and lesser known spots that locals love.

"Its two- and three-day itineraries are packed with suggestions for sightseeing, hiking, shopping, lodging, and getting a good meal. *Quick Escapes* takes the work out of wandering."

Vickie Nelson, senior editor
*Northwest Travel*

"This guide is full of tips on what to see and do on weekend trips around Seattle, Portland, and Vancouver, British Columbia."

*Los Angeles Daily News*

D0972941

Second Edition

# QUICK
# ESCAPES

## in the
## Pacific Northwest

### 40 Weekend Trips from
### Portland, Seattle, and Vancouver, B.C.

*by*

*Marilyn McFarlane*

A Voyager Book

The Globe Pequot Press

Old Saybrook, Connecticut

**Photo Credits**
P. 31: Dick Powers; pp. 39, 127, 173: courtesy Washington State Tourism Division; p. 61: courtesy Fort Vacouver National Historic Site; p. 68: courtesy Washington County Visitors Association; p. 93: courtesy of McKenzie River Rafting Company; p. 100, 254: Gary Brettnacher; p. 118: John Parkhurst; p. 152: George White, courtesy Salish Lodge; p. 158: courtesy Leavenworth Chamber of Commerce; p. 166: courtesy North Cascades National Park Service; p. 186: Art Hupy; p. 197: Doug Plummer, Courtesy Turtleback Farm Inn; p. 269: courtesy Whistler Resort Association; p. 288: courtesy Smiles Photography, Vancouver, B.C.; p. 306: Norm and Diane Perrault. All other photos by the author.

**Library of Congress Cataloging-in-Publication Data**

McFarlane, Marilyn.
    Quick escapes in the Pacific Northwest : 40 weekend trips from Portland, Seattle, and Vancouver, B.C. / by Marilyn McFarlane. — 2nd ed.
        p.      cm.
    "A voyager book."
    Includes index.
    ISBN 1-56440-283-5
F852.3.M38  1994
917.9504'43—dc20                                                  93-29768
                                                                 CIP

Manufactured in the United States of America
Second Edition/Fourth Printing

# Contents

Introduction ........................................................................ **vii**

**PORTLAND ESCAPES** ........................................................... **1**
   *Map* ........................................................................... *2–3*
  1. Columbia River to Astoria ..................................... 4
  2. Seaside to Lincoln City ......................................... 12
  3. Eugene-Florence-Newport ..................................... 22
  4. Mount Hood Loop .................................................. 31
  5. Around Mount St. Helens ...................................... 39
  6. Covered Bridges of Oregon .................................... 46
  7. Columbia River Gorge: Oregon ............................. 54
  8. Columbia River Gorge: Washington ...................... 61
  9. Oregon Wine Country ............................................ 68
 10. John Day Fossil Beds to Shaniko ........................... 76
 11. Oregon City/Salem Loop Trip ............................... 84
 12. McKenzie River Highway ...................................... 93
 13. Central Oregon ..................................................... 100
 14. Long Beach Peninsula .......................................... 108

**SEATTLE ESCAPES** ............................................................. **115**
   *Map* ....................................................................... *116–17*
  1. Strait of Juan de Fuca ........................................... 118
  2. The Hoh River Valley, Olympic Peninsula .......... 127
  3. Central Kitsap and Hood Canal ........................... 132
  4. Vashon Island ...................................................... 138
  5. Whidbey Island, Fidalgo Island .......................... 144
  6. Snoqualmie Falls and Fall City ........................... 152
  7. Leavenworth to Ellensburg .................................. 158
  8. North Cascades .................................................... 166
  9. Mount Rainier Loop ............................................ 173
 10. North Kitsap Peninsula ........................................ 180
 11. Skagit County ...................................................... 186
 12. Gig Harbor .......................................................... 192
 13. Orcas Island ........................................................ 197
 14. San Juan Island ................................................... 204

**VANCOUVER ESCAPES** ............................................... **211**
   *Map*........................................................................ *212–13*
  1. South Vancouver Island ........................................ 214
  2. Vancouver Island: Northeast Coast ..................... 221
  3. Vancouver Island: West Shore ............................. 230
  4. Strathcona and Hornby ........................................ 238
  5. The Gulf Islands ................................................. 245
  6. Langdale to Lund ................................................ 254
  7. Salt Spring Island ............................................... 263
  8. Whistler .............................................................. 269
  9. The Okanagan .................................................... 276
 10. Southeastern Vancouver Island .......................... 288
 11. Bellingham and Lummi Island ........................... 298
 12. Lake Whatcom/Mount Baker .............................. 306

**Index** ...................................................................... **315**

**About the Author** ................................................... **325**

# Introduction

This guide to brief getaways from Portland, Seattle, and Vancouver is intended for longtime residents, newcomers to the Pacific Northwest, and visitors passing through—anyone who's eager to explore the recreational wonderland that lies beyond the three major cities of the region.

When you want to travel scenic byways and discover their hidden treasures, take this book with you. It will lead you to well-known spots that no tourist should miss and will uncover hideaways that only the local folk know.

The guide provides fully detailed itineraries, much like a customized, organized tour. But they are suggestions only! Don't try to do everything listed on each trip, or you'll feel too rushed to enjoy yourself. Pick and choose among the activities, and plan to return for those you missed.

At the end of each chapter, **There's More** provides more reasons to come back. **Special Events** follows, to help you choose the festivals you want to attend. **Other Recommended Restaurants and Lodgings** gives concise descriptions of good places to eat and stay other than those included in the itinerary. Finally, **For More Information** tells you who to contact to obtain maps and learn about the area you're visiting.

The itineraries are designed as auto tours, but public transport, walking, and bicycling are viable alternatives in many cases. I recommend using them whenever you can.

Consider traveling in the off-season, rather than the high-use summer months. The weather is mild in spring and fall, though rains are frequent. Winter has its own appeal, with the crowds gone and the landscape spare or clad in white.

Facilities for the handicapped are mentioned where appropriate.

Rates and fees are not specifically stated, as they often change, but you may assume that most costs are reasonable. If a place seemed unusually expensive (or amazingly inexpensive), I have so indicated. Museums usually charge a nominal admission fee or request a donation.

Distances are approximate and are expressed in miles (and in kilometers in the Vancouver, B.C., section). American standard spelling is used throughout, except for Canadian place-names.

Make reservations in advance at hotels and inns whenever possible. Some are very small, and rooms fill quickly, especially during the busy season.

The following is a list of standard equipment you'll probably need on your escapes:

Raingear (in the Northwest, the weather is unpredictable)
Jacket
Sturdy walking shoes
Daypack
Water bottle
Insect repellent
Camera
Binoculars

A great deal of effort has gone into making this book as accurate as possible, but places do change. If you wish to suggest a correction or a special find that should be included in a future edition, please let me know. I'll be glad to investigate. Meanwhile, enjoy your mini-vacations—all forty of them.

Marilyn McFarlane
Portland, Oregon

---

The prices and rates listed in this guidebook were confirmed at press time. We recommend, however, that you call establishments before traveling to obtain current information.

Maps provided at the beginning of each section are for reference only and should be used in conjunction with a road map. Distances indicated are approximate.

# Portland Escapes

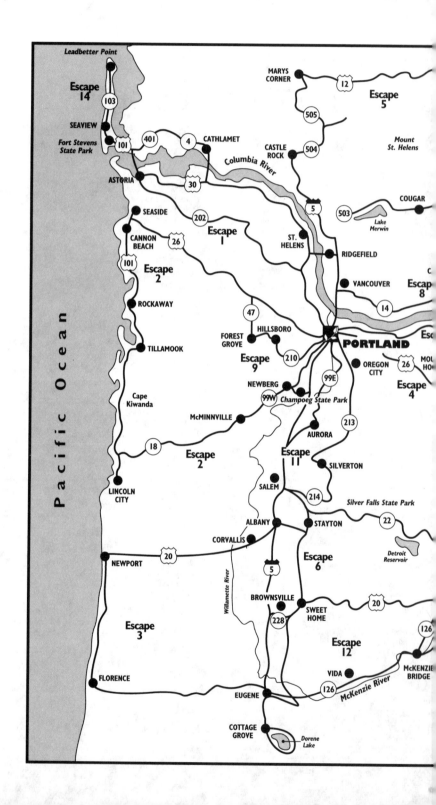

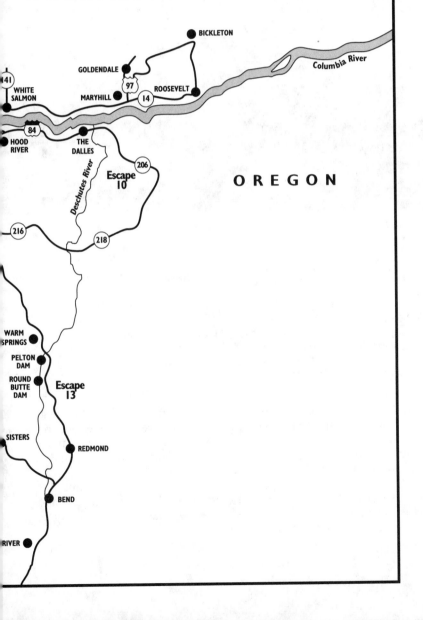

# PORTLAND ESCAPES

WASHINGTON

BICKLETON

GOLDENDALE

97

WHITE
SALMON

MARYHILL

ROOSEVELT

14

Columbia River

84

HOOD
RIVER

THE
DALLES

206

Escape
10

Deschutes River

OREGON

216

218

WARM
SPRINGS

PELTON
DAM

ROUND
BUTTE
DAM

Escape
13

SISTERS

REDMOND

BEND

RIVER

# Columbia River to Astoria

A gill-netter leaves Astoria harbor to cross the bar at the mouth of the Columbia River.

## The Explorers' Route

### 2 NIGHTS

Columbia River views • Sandy beaches • Pioneer museums
Pastoral island • Historic town • Early explorers' fort • Fishing, hiking
Canoeing, kayaking • Wildlife refuge

The broad, 1,000-mile Columbia River, the largest river in the West that flows into the Pacific, has always drawn travelers. Native Americans paddled its waters in canoes. Robert Gray, a sea captain from Boston in search of the fur trade, crossed the treacherous bar in an 83-foot sloop in 1792.

The Lewis and Clark expedition came from the East, exploring the great river's environs. Other explorers followed, along with fur trappers and traders, fishers, and loggers. Settlers swarmed in, establishing communities along the Columbia's shores.

A three-day loop trip northwest from Portland provides vivid reminders of those not-so-long-ago days, spiced with dramatic river views and glimpses of wildlife.

# Day 1

## Morning

Drive north from Portland on U.S. Route 30, the Columbia Highway, 30 miles to one of Oregon's oldest settlements, **St. Helens.** The drowsy town's 10-block historic district edges the riverbank, centering on a grassy plaza and park.

Between the plaza and the river is a handsome, Georgian Revival courthouse. Built of local basalt in 1915, it's now a museum (open Friday and Saturday afternoons) displaying pioneer artifacts. Next to the courthouse is **Columbia View Park,** an excellent vantage point for watching pleasure boats on the river. The two-acre park has an old-fashioned gazebo, a brick viewing platform, picnic tables, and boat facilities.

If you missed breakfast, stop in at the **St. Helens Cafe,** 2 blocks from the plaza. Since 1915 the cafe has been serving bountiful meals in a down-home, friendly atmosphere.

A 3-mile system of bicycle paths connects each school and the city park; and a 1-mile wooded path, the **Rutherford Parkway,** joins St. Helens with neighboring **Columbia City.**

In Columbia City, follow the signs to **Caples House Museum.** Built amid orchards above the river by the first doctor in the area, Charles Caples, it's furnished in late nineteenth-century style and is open to the public.

Continue angling northwest on Route 30, passing farms and conifer forests until you reach **Clatskanie,** 34 miles from St. Helens. If you're interested in historic homes, tour **Flippen House,** a restored and furnished Queen Anne home that dates from the turn of the century.

**Westport,** 12 miles farther down the river, is a good spot to slip your canoe or kayak into the water and paddle the quiet, willow-shaded byways and sloughs that fringe the Columbia.

Board the twelve-car ferry, which departs every hour from 5:00 A.M. to 11:00 P.M. for **Puget Island.** The ten-minute ride will take you to a bucolic world far from city stress.

*Lunch:* Picnic on the little beach near the ferry landing on Puget Island, or continue on to Cathlamet and **Birnies Retreat,** 83 Main Street (206) 795-3432. Low prices, 1960s decor, good soups, Cajun cookery.

Puget Island has miles of quiet country roads that are ideal for bicycling. The roads wind past quaint churches, grazing sheep, tidy dairy farms with rose-covered fences, and whitewashed barns.

Fish for salmon and steelhead at the public beach, bird-watch (look for Canada geese and swans), or beachcomb.

Follow the main road across the island to the bridge that takes you to **Cathlamet, Washington,** a peaceful logging and fishing community established in 1846. Visit the **Wahkiakum County Historical Museum** (open 1:00 to 4:00 P.M.) to see how the early pioneers, loggers, fishers, and farmers lived. The museum has a **walking-tour map** of the town's historical sites: a pioneer church, settlers' homes, and a cemetery.

Descend a slope to the sheltered harbor and **Elochoman Slough Marina** to watch the sturdy gill-netters come and go, reminders of the region's fishing heritage. This is one of the few full-service marinas on the lower Columbia.

As you pass the **old salmon cannery building,** it's easy to imagine long-ago workers, most of them Chinese immigrants, flicking fish into cans. The cannery building dates from 1859 and is the last of its kind in the area. It was used as a location for the film *Come See the Paradise.*

At the nearby **Columbian White-tailed Deer Refuge,** an endangered species is increasing its numbers. You might spy elk and other wildlife, too, as you bicycle or walk the wooded paths of the 5,200-acre refuge.

Travel west on State Route 4 to **Skamokawa,** one of the early river settlements, now a National Historic District. **Redmen Hall,** an old-fashioned schoolhouse from 1894, is open to the public on summer weekends. **The River Life Interpretive Center** here tells the history of the area. **Vista Park,** on the Columbia shore, is a worthy stop for its broad river views. The park has picnic facilities, tennis courts, showers, and campsites for recreational vehicles.

Now turn inland with the road as it rises toward the forested, occasionally logged-off hills. You'll catch glimpses of the river as it flows the last few miles of its long journey toward the Pacific.

As you approach **Grays River,** a short detour will take you to **Grays River salmon hatchery** and a **covered bridge,** the last such bridge on a public road in Washington.

When you reach Route 401, turn south and drive 12 miles to the high toll bridge that spans the wide, choppy river mouth. Cross the 4-mile bridge into Oregon. You've arrived in **Astoria,** the first European-American settlement in the Northwest.

In this rainwashed, fish-rich, hilly corner, John Jacob Astor set up his fur-trading post in 1811 and built a stockade called Fort Astoria. Fishing, logging, and canning drew more newcomers, many from Finland. By 1900 Astoria was the largest city in the state. It's still a sizable port and fishing town, keenly aware of its historic position and Scandinavian heritage.

Start your exploration of Astoria on **Coxcomb Hill.** Here a mural, spiraling up **Astoria Column,** depicts historical highlights. Climb the 125-foot column's 166 steps, and you'll be rewarded with a sweeping view of the city, the long bridge, the hills of Washington, and the thundering Pacific as it rolls to meet the oncoming river.

On the way to your night's lodging, stop at the **Fort Astoria log stockade.** The replica, a National Historical Landmark, is at Fifteenth and Exchange streets.

*Dinner:* **Ship Inn,** 1 Second Street, Astoria. (503) 325–0033. Casual dining on the water. Watch the ship traffic as you feast on tender, crisply battered fish-and-chips.

*Lodging:* **Rosebriar Hotel,** 636 Fourteenth Street, Astoria. (503) 325–7427. Large, Classic Revival home restored as stylish hotel. Mahogany furniture, fireplaces, television, phones.

# Day 2

## Morning

*Breakfast:* A full breakfast is included in the room rate at Rosebriar Hotel.

A must-see in Astoria is the **Columbia River Maritime Museum.** The ultramodern waterfront facility has one of the finest displays of nautical memorabilia in the country. Early sailing vessels, a river steamer wheelhouse, and World War II submarine periscopes are among its exhibits. One of the last of the West Coast lightships, the *Columbia,* lies at the wharf, restored and open for tours.

After your museum tour, stop at **Josephson's Smokehouse,** 106 Marine Drive. The smooth, flavorful, alder-smoked seafood produced here is shipped all over the world—there's none better. Buy a package of salmon; combine it with a beverage, bagels or French bread, and maybe some cream cheese and fruit, and you're prepared for the day's picnic.

Take U.S. Highway 101 6 miles south of Astoria to **Fort Clatsop National Memorial.** The reproduction of the fort used by the Lewis and Clark expedition during the wet winter of 1805–1806 has a recently enlarged visitors' center, interpretive displays, and two theaters. Buckskin-clad rangers demonstrate skills that were required of the explorers—tanning hides, curing jerky, making candles, and loading muzzles are a few.

Follow the coastal road to the northwesternmost tip of the state and

**Fort Stevens State Park.** A military reservation was built here during the Civil War to guard the river mouth from Confederate attack. Now it's a 3,800-acre park with campgrounds, bicycle and hiking trails, beaches, and an interpretive center.

Stroll the beach and you'll see, poking up from the sand, remnants of the *Peter Iredale,* a ship wrecked near here in 1906. Artifacts from the ship are on display in the **Clatsop County Heritage Museum,** Sixteenth and Exchange streets.

*Lunch:* Picnic at Fort Stevens. That wonderful smoked salmon will taste even better in this briny setting of sea-washed air and rumbling surf.

## Afternoon

Return the few miles to Astoria, and park at **Flavel House,** 441 Eighth Street. This ornate Queen Anne mansion was built in 1883 for a river pilot. It's one of the numerous Astoria homes that prosperous sea captains and merchants built in the late 1800s.

Homes on the hills above the river escaped a 1922 fire that burned much of the town. One that was preserved from the flames was Flavel House, now a museum operated by the Clatsop County Historical Society. Touring the furnished home will give you a glimpse into the lives of the well-to-do of a former day.

Purchase a **walking-tour map** in the museum; it will guide you to more than seventy gracious old homes bearing markers that explain their historical status. Astoria is a good walking town. There are some steep hills, but distances are easy to manage.

As you stroll, you might check a few shops and galleries. **The Edge** exhibits contemporary paintings and sculptures; **Michael's Antiques and Art Gallery** features Oriental and Victorian antiques and the works of Pacific Northwest artists.

You can dress in the style of your favorite decade at **Persona Vintage Clothing,** 100 Tenth Street. The intriguing shop has an extensive collection of period wear, including hats, beaded bags, jewelry, linens, and laces.

Tenth Street is home to the **Ricciardi Gallery,** the perfect place to relax with a cup of espresso and a toothsome pastry while you survey the works of regional artists. The works include paintings, ceramics, fabric art pieces, carved wood, and jewelry.

At **Shallon Winery,** 1598 Duane Street, taste unusual wines—cranberry, peach, berry, and lemon are a few.

*Dinner:* **Columbian Cafe,** 1114 Marine Drive, Astoria. (503) 325–2233. Richly flavored soups and vegetarian and seafood crepes; lively, offbeat atmosphere. Open Wednesday, Thursday, and Friday.

*Lodging:* Rosebriar Hotel.

# Day 3

## Morning

*Breakfast:* Rosebriar Hotel.

If you missed touring the Maritime Museum, take this opportunity to marvel at an extraordinary tribute to seafarers.

Drive southeast on Route 202 for 27 miles, along the Klaskanine River, to **Jewell Wildlife Management Area.** Pull out the binoculars, for you're likely to see a herd of Roosevelt elk. The huge, majestic animals often graze unconcernedly by the roadside. This is the only refuge of its kind in the state.

Continue on through the green, rolling hills, crossing and recrossing the Nehalem River, to the hamlets of **Jewell** and **Mist.** Stop at the old-fashioned general store in Mist for a touch of plank-floored, small-town nostalgia. Then follow Route 47 south through the forest to the turnoff to **Scappoose.**

*Lunch:* **The Wayside,** 50316 Columbia River Highway, Scappoose. (503) 543–9984. Longtime country cafe 2 miles south of town, completely rebuilt in 1990. Small, smoky bar/lounge and cheery little restaurant specializing in fish-and-chips. A local favorite.

## Afternoon

Turn south on Route 30 and return to Portland. If you have time, detour across the **Sauvie Island Bridge** for freshly picked produce (in season) from island farms and a visit to the historic **Bybee House** and the **Sauvie Island Wildlife Area.**

# There's More

**Boating.** St. Helens Sailing Club sponsors weekly sailboat races on the Columbia River, April to August.

Kayak and canoe in the quiet sloughs around the Columbian White-tailed Deer Refuge, Cathlamet. You can paddle in protected waters from Cathlamet to Skamokawa.

**Fishing.** Catch steelhead from Puget Island beaches; fish from the jetties of Astoria.

**Deep-sea fishing.** Astoria Charters, 333 Industry, Astoria, OR 97103. (503) 325–0990. Excursions for Pacific salmon, sturgeon, and tuna.

Olson's Charters, Hammond Marina, Hammond, OR 97121. (503) 861–2668.

**Sand Island.** The only marine park in Oregon, an island across the channel from St. Helens. Docks, campsites, nature trails.

# Special Events

**Late April.** Great Astoria Crab and Seafood Festival, Astoria, OR. Carnival, wine tastings, arts and crafts, quantities of Dungeness crab.

**Mid-June.** Port of Fun, St. Helens, OR. Parades, music, vendors, auto cruise-in, carnival, beer garden.

**Mid-June.** Scandinavian Midsummer Festival, Astoria, OR. Traditional Scandinavian dancing in authentic costumes, music, contests, foods, parades, queen's ball, entertainment, a hex bonfire, decorated Midsummer Pole.

**July.** Bald Eagle Day, Cathlamet, WA. Parade, street dancing, flea market, food booths.

**Mid-August.** Astoria Regatta, Astoria, OR. Downtown parade, boat parade, fireworks, tours of historic homes, boat races.

**Late November.** St. Lucia Festival of Lights, Astoria, OR. Christmas lighting, Scandinavian folk dancing, traditional crowning of Lucia Bride.

# Other Recommended Restaurants and Lodgings

## St. Helens, Oregon

McIntire's Delicatessen, 1845 Columbia Boulevard. (503) 397–1021. Sandwiches, special desserts, cheesecake.

The Klondike, 71 Cowlitz Street. (503) 397–4297. Old-time tavern, known for seafood.

## Clatskanie, Oregon

Hump's Restaurant, 85 North Nehalem. (503) 728–2626. Riverside setting, on the Clatskanie. Steaks, seafood, cheesecake, pies. Open 7:00 A.M. to 10:00 P.M.

## Cathlamet, Washington

Country Keeper Bed and Breakfast Inn, 61 Main Street, P.O. Box 35. (206) 795–3030. Five guest rooms in historic hillside home. Polished woods, inlaid floors, antiques, and ruffles. Full breakfast served.

Gallery Bed and Breakfast, 4 Little Cape Horn. (206) 425–7395. Contemporary, art-filled home overlooking river, 5 miles east of town on Route 4. Full breakfast.

Pizzaz, 297 East State Route 4. (206) 795–3146. Pizza, sandwiches, barbecued ribs.

Rat Tap Tavern, on the waterfront. (206) 795–3581. Local hangout at the edge of the river. Chili, beer, fish-and-chips.

## Skamokawa, Washington

Duck Inn, Route 4. (206) 795–3655. On a bluff above Skamokawa Creek. Popular steak and seafood house, where locals go to dine.

## Astoria, Oregon

Astoria Inn Bed & Breakfast, 3391 Irving Avenue. (503) 325–8153. Restored Victorian home on a hillside. Three comfortable rooms, library, television, full breakfast included.

Franklin Street Station, 1140 Franklin Avenue. (503) 325–4314. Walking distance from downtown. Tastefully furnished home with antique reproductions and modern comforts. Full breakfast.

Columbia River Inn, 1681 Franklin Avenue. (503) 325–5044. Victorian home restored as charming bed and breakfast with pink and lace decor. Quiet neighborhood, friendly innkeeper.

Grandview Bed and Breakfast, 1574 Grand Avenue. (503) 325–0000. Airy, attractive rooms in a turn-of-the-century home on a hillside above town. Warm hospitality.

# For More Information

St. Helens Chamber of Commerce, 174 South Columbia Highway, St. Helens, OR 97051. (503) 397–0685.

Lower Columbia Economic Development Council, P.O. Box 98, Skamokawa, WA 98647. (206) 795–3996.

Astoria Chamber of Commerce, 111 West Marine Drive, P.O. Box 176, Astoria, OR 97103. (503) 325–6311.

# Seaside to Lincoln City

Haystack Rock at Cannon Beach is one of the world's largest monoliths.

## A Coastal Panorama

———————————— 2 OR 3 NIGHTS ————————————

Rural countryside · Wide sandy beaches · Ocean views · Hiking
Kite flying · Fishing · Boutiques · Art galleries
Fine dining · Fishing · Fresh seafood

More visitors come to the northern Oregon coast than to any other part of the state. Yet despite the strollers, kiteflyers, picnickers, surfers, and driftwood collectors, it seldom feels crowded. In the off-season, yours may be the only footprints on a wide, smooth, sandy beach, and the only sounds you hear will be the hiss of the surf and the cries of gulls.

This getaway covers the stretch of coastline from Seaside to Lincoln City and encompasses a variety of shoreline pleasures.

# Day 1

## Morning

Drive northwest on U.S. Route 26, which cuts through a valley of rich farmland before rising into the forests of the coastal mountain range.

At **Camp 18,** west of Elsie (about 55 miles from Portland), stop for coffee or, if you've skipped breakfast, a whopping "Logger's Breakfast." The hand-built log restaurant museum was constructed in the early 1970s by Gordon Smith as a monument to loggers. The ridge pole in the Camp 18 dining room is 85 feet long and weighs 25 tons. The 500-pound doors are hand carved; ax handles form door pulls. Carved figures include an eagle, a logger, Smokey the Bear, and Big Foot.

A few miles farther, watch for a sign on the right to the **largest Sitka spruce tree** in the United States. The giant tree is a short distance off the highway.

Continue on Route 26 to **Seaside** (80 miles from Portland), a resort town that bustles with conventions, tourist traffic, souvenir shops, and arcades. It has secluded, quiet corners as well.

To get your bearings and an impression of both town and shore, stroll the 2-mile-long **Promenade** that borders the beach. You'll see kites flying, children building castles, volleyball games on the sand, and surf waders—unless the weather is stormy. In that case, everyone will be indoors reading by the fire, watching the wind whip waves high and the spindrift fly. Or they'll be downtown shopping.

Seaside's main thoroughfare, Broadway, has been spruced up and partially closed to vehicles and now boasts dozens of thriving shops and a lively atmosphere. Check **The Weary Fox,** a gallery in Sand Dollar Square, for paintings, sculpture, jewelry, and Oriental art. **Seaside Guild of Artists,** in Heritage Square, displays works of local artists.

*Lunch:* **Dooger's,** 505 Broadway, Seaside. (503) 738-3773. Justifiably famous for its rich, flavorsome clam chowder. Top off your lunch with a slice of German chocolate cake at **Harrison's Bakery.**

## Afternoon

Drive Highway 101 south 6 miles to **Cannon Beach,** a festive little community with a gorgeous setting. Cannon Beach gets its name from the cannon that swept ashore after a shipwreck in 1846. Replicas of the cannon stand sentinel at either end of town.

There are several access points to the beach, and parking is free in public lots and on the street. Stairs descend from the bluff to the shore. This is a near-perfect, 7-mile stretch of sand for strolling, building castles, playing ball games, and wading in the surf. **Haystack Rock,** a 235-foot-high monolith that is a wildlife refuge, looms just off-shore, surrounded by other rock formations. Waves billow and crash against them, tossing great plumes of white spray.

At low tide, you may find **nature interpreters** at Haystack, telling visitors about intertidal life and nesting birds on the wildlife refuge. The interpreters supply binoculars and spotting scopes and explain what to look for.

If you want to swim, check the colored flags by the lifeguard tower. Red means a dangerous surf; yellow urges caution. A lifeguard is on duty during the summer.

More than any other coastal community, Cannon Beach is known for its **art galleries and shops,** a happy combination of fine art, T-shirts, handicrafts, souvenirs, cards, kites, natural-fiber clothing, and good bookstores. Most are on Hemlock, the main street, with others lining the side streets.

Look for top-quality artworks in The Weary Fox, White Bird, Haystack Gallery, and Hannen Stained Glass. Buy Amish folk art at Country Shores and European woolens and lace at Aagensen's Imports. Gepetto's sells intriguing toys, and El Mundo has a wide selection of stylish clothing and hats.

Midafternoon, stop in **Cannon Beach Cookie Company,** 239 North Hemlock, for coffee and an oversize cookie.

Step into **The Wine Shack** to taste domestic and imported wines (tastings on Saturdays, 1:00 to 5:00 P.M.).

*Dinner:* **Cafe de la Mer,** 1287 South Hemlock Street, Cannon Beach. (503) 436–1179. Expensive, but the food is superb, the service prompt, and the atmosphere congenial. Recently expanded, but retains a warm and inviting ambience.

If you choose to dine elsewhere, less extravagantly, reserve part of the evening for the **Coaster Theater,** at 108 North Hemlock. Professional performances include plays, concerts, ballet and modern dance, and musical revues.

*Lodging:* **The Waves,** P.O. Box 3, Cannon Beach, OR 97110. (503) 436–2205. Twenty-three unit complex above the beach, in the heart of town and close to everything. Various styles of rooms and cottages; some have kitchens, fireplaces, and views.

# Day 2

## Morning

*Breakfast:* Cook for yourself, or eat at **Lazy Susan Cafe,** 126 North Hemlock Street, Cannon Beach. (503) 436–2816. A cheery cafe on two levels, in a brick courtyard off the main street. Rich coffee, crisp waffles, and generous omelets. A popular, usually crowded spot.

Drive south from Cannon Beach on U.S. Highway 101, along the wooded coastline to **Arch Cape** and **Oswald West State Park.** Park in the lot and walk the ½-mile path that leads through groves of fir and cedar trees to a protected beach with tide pools. Next to it is **Cape Falcon,** a headland honeycombed with trails that wind through salal and wild roses out to rocky cliffs. Cormorants fly above the waves that hurl against this rugged shore.

Farther south, Highway 101 rises and curves around the west side of **Neahkahnie Mountain.** The views are stunning. From high on the mountainside you can see for miles down the undulating coast, where forested headlands meet wide beaches and the constant surf. A trail leads to even more panoramic viewing points at the summit of Neahkahnie, 1,600 feet high. Legend has it that the mountain hides buried treasure from a seventeenth-century Spanish shipwreck.

Continuing on Highway 101, you'll come to the turnoff to **Manzanita,** a quiet community with a nine-hole golf course, numerous summer homes, and a couple of excellent restaurants.

From Manzanita, the highway turns slightly inland as you drive south to **Nehalem,** a hillside village above the **Nehalem River.** The low-key fishing community, where fading cabins line the banks of the river, has in recent years gained a reputation as an **art and antiques center.**

At Shepherd Gallery you can purchase pottery, paintings, and handcrafted gold jewelry; find furniture at Pete's Antiques. More than forty dealers have shops in Nehalem Antique Mall and in Nehalem Trading Post. Three Village Gallery has fine-quality artworks: Robert Bateman's wildlife paintings, hand-carved decoys, and southwestern Indian blankets and jewelry are examples.

Enjoy a cup of cappuccino and buy a bottle of Oregon wine at **River Gallery.** Then continue south on 101, passing through **Wheeler,** on Nehalem Bay. The village is home to retirees and a favored headquarters for fishing and crabbing.

**Rockaway Beach,** a few miles south, is a resort town with an emphasis on family recreation. There are volleyball nets on the beach (balls can be rented at the minimarket), a kite shop, and an arcade with video games, pizza, and popcorn. Bowling and miniature golf are available. **Spring Lake Park,** on the south end of town, offers paddleboats, bumper boats, hot tubs at the edge of the lake, and RV spaces.

Rockaway has retained its character in places like **Stucks Hardware,** on Main Street. Once a pool hall and house of ill repute run by "Redhead Ruby," it became the Sea Hag Tavern in the 1930s. Oldtimers say a stream ran under the building and a person could fish for trout through a hole in the floor. Since the 1940s the place has been a hardware store, now including gift items and souvenirs.

Go to **Jean's Sugar Shack** for homemade, hand-dipped candies. Jean's delectable chocolates are made and sold in a former church that was built in the 1930s.

Don't miss **Flamingo Jim**'s (in fact, it's almost impossible to miss) for its amazing array of lawn decorations—deer, seagulls, frogs, ducks, owls, gnomes, and raccoons are just a few. While you're scouting for whimsical finds, check **Trash 'n Treasures,** also on Main Street. It's a mixture of antiques, collectibles, and junk.

From Rockaway, drive 3 miles south to **Garibaldi.** The little town tucked against the northern curve of Tillamook Bay is known for its deep-sea fishing charters and fresh seafood outlets.

Follow the shore of **Tillamook Bay** south to **Bay City.** Stop here at **Hayes Oysters** for fresh oysters; then continue for 5 more miles on Highway 101, which turns inland toward Tillamook.

**Tillamook** is dairy country, where cows graze in lush pastures along the roadside. Dairy farms were established here in the mid-1800s by Swiss settlers, who began the milk and cheese heritage that continues today.

The small town of 3,000 people lies 8 miles inland from the ocean, south of **Tillamook Bay.** It was named for a large tribe of Salish Indians, the Killamooks (one of many spellings).

*Lunch:* **Blue Heron French Cheese Company,** 2001 Blue Heron Drive. (503) 842–8281. Blue-and-white former dairy barn north of Tillamook, off Highway 101. Deli sells soups and sandwiches; try the Blue Heron Classic, with smoked turkey and brie.

## Afternoon

At the Blue Heron Cheese Company, taste Oregon wines and Blue Heron's own brie, as well as other cheeses and regional products, and buy top-quality items in the gift shop.

The nearby **Tillamook Cheese Factory** is one of Oregon's most visited sites. There's a self-guided tour that takes you through the plant, which produces forty-five million pounds of cheese a year. The tour ends in a gift shop, deli, and ice cream counter .

You can learn about local history at the **Pioneer Museum,** 2106 Second Street, located in Tillamook's former courthouse, built in 1905. The engrossing museum has three well-lighted floors of exhibits showing life as it was a century ago on the Oregon coast. There are pioneer tools and clothing; a replica of the treehouse lived in by Joe Champion, the area's first white settler; a collection of carriages; and dozens of animals and birds of the region. The natural history display reaches far afield, showing mounted rhino horns, a leopard, elephant tusks, and an ashtray made from a rhino's foot—curious trophies from a former day, when few considered the fate of endangered species.

Leaving Tillamook, drive south toward the quiet resort community of **Neskowin.** Here the land rises to form **Cascade Head,** one of Oregon's great treasures of nature.

To climb the Head's wooded, grassy trails, which are maintained by The Nature Conservancy, is to experience the best the coast has to offer. Misty in rain and fog, shadow dappled in sun, the forests of spruce, hemlock, and alder open to wide meadows covered with Queen Anne's lace and wild cucumber vines in spring. From the meadows, 700 feet above the foamy surf, you can hear barking sea lions and see the mouth of the Salmon River as it joins the sea. The Pacific is a blue panorama to the horizon.

South of Cascade Head is **Lincoln City,** a long sprawl of commercial development on a slope beside a beautiful beach. Spend the rest of the afternoon strolling the beach, flying a kite, or browsing in the shops of this major resort town.

See a thousand music boxes at Nelscott Gift Shop; admire seashells from around the world at Pacific Originals; find seascapes at several **art galleries.** Buy a hand-painted, concrete seagull or puffin for your front yard at the **Seagull Factory,** and local crafts and imports at The Red Cock. Sip cappuccino while you read at **Cafe Roma,** a combined coffee shop and bookstore.

Lincoln City is becoming a center for antique dealers; numerous **antiques shops** line the highway. Check Rocking Horse Mall, in a historic building, and the displays in Abbington's Antiques, where a white Persian cat reigns.

At the intersection of Highway 101 and East Devils Lake Road is a $13 million development of forty-five factory outlet stores. This complex, **Factory Stores at Lincoln City,** sells name brand goods at discount prices.

*Dinner:* **Bay House,** 5911 Southwest Highway 101, Lincoln City. (503) 996–3222. Fine continental dining south of town, with a view of Siletz Bay. Expensive for this area, but one of the best on the coast.

*Lodging:* **The Hideaway,** 810 Southwest Tenth, Lincoln City, OR 97367. (503) 994–8874. Quiet, cottage-style lodgings on a bluff above the beach. Kitchens, fireplaces, sun-decks, ocean views.

# Day 3

## Morning

*Breakfast:* In your own dining nook at The Hideaway (groceries available at several nearby stores).

After a morning beach walk, drive south ½ mile to Drift Creek Road and follow it to the end. Turn right, and go ¼ mile farther to the **Drift Creek Covered Bridge**—the oldest covered bridge in Oregon (1914).

Return to Highway 101 and drive for a mile to Immonen Road, and turn left. Down this shady, wooded road you'll find two studios tucked among the ferns. First is **Mossy Creek,** a shop carrying the wares of local potters. Farther on is quaint **Alder House,** where you can watch glassblowers at work and buy exquisite pieces of glass workmanship.

Return to Lincoln City, and head north on Route 101 to the junction with Route 18 at **Otis.** The fields around this tiny community are dotted with yellow in spring, when the skunk cabbage and daffodils bloom.

*Lunch:* **Otis Cafe,** Route 18 in Otis. (503) 994-2813. A cozy, casual eatery famed for its down-home atmosphere and good cooking. Hamburgers and pies are sensational. Even the *New York Times* likes the Otis Cafe.

### Afternoon

Take Route 18 east through the forests of the Coast Range and the Van Duzer Corridor to the open country of the Willamette Valley. Redwinged blackbirds flash by as you pass nurseries and orchards, fields and vineyards, on your way to join Highway 99W, which will take you into Portland.

# There's More

**Morning Star II,** on the grounds of the Tillamook Cheese Factory. This vessel is a replica of a schooner that was built in 1854 to transport goods when road travel was hazardous or non-existent in this area.

**World War II blimp hangars.** The world's largest freestanding wooden structures stand south of Tillamook on Highway 101. Built to house coastal surveillance blimps, they're now used for manufacturing lighter-than-air craft. The facilities are not open for tours, but the doors are often open.

**Bear Creek Artichokes.** Eleven miles south of Tillamook on Highway 101, this roadside stand offers, in season, plentiful herbs, fresh produce, artichoke plants, honey, and flowers. (503) 398–5411.

**Munson Creek Falls.** The highest falls (266 feet) in the Coast Range are 9 miles south of Tillamook and 2 miles east of Highway 101. Trails lead to upper and lower falls.

**Fishing.** Fish for steelhead, chinook, and trout in the Kilchis, Wilson, Trask, Nestucca, and Salmon rivers. Catch trout, perch, and bass in Devils Lake. Find perch, crab, and flounder in Siletz Bay. Surf fish for perch, or arrange a deep-sea charter. Check with local tackle stores.

**Golf.** Hawk Creek Golf, Neskowin (9 holes) (503) 392–4120. Neskowin Beach Golf, Neskowin (9 holes) (503) 392–3377. Alderbrook Golf Course, Tillamook (18 holes) (503) 842–6413.

**Salt Cairn,** Seaside. Replica of salt cairn used by the Lewis and Clark expedition to extract salt from seawater.

**Whale watching.** Any bluff along the coast provides a vantage point for sighting gray whales on their migratory journeys. Cascade Head and Road's End Wayside, north of Lincoln City, are favorite spots. Whales are spotted all year long, but November to April are the likeliest months, and January, when about thirty whales per hour move along the coast, is the peak. The best views are usually seen in the early morning, when the sea is calm and there is no glare from the sun.

**Oregon Coastline Express.** Scenic train rides along the coast, between Tillamook and Wheeler. (503) 842–2768.

**Three Capes Scenic Drive.** From Tillamook, a coastal road leads to headlands with hiking trails, a wildlife refuge, the village of Oceanside, state parks, and a lighthouse.

# Special Events

**Early May.** Spring Kite Festival, Lincoln City. Kite-flying extravaganza and contest. Awards for most unusual, most amusing, best children's, and best stunt kites, among others.

**June.** Sandcastle Days, Cannon Beach. Granddaddy of sand-sculpture contests, with international entries and cash prizes.

**June.** Dairy Parade and Rodeo, Tillamook. Band marches, Swiss polkas, clowns, food booths, golf tournament, music.

**Mid-July.** Nehalem Arts Festival, Nehalem. Outdoor exhibition of arts and crafts by artists from around the West. Food booths, strolling musicians.

**July and August.** Robert Gray Historical Pageant, Tillamook. Celebrates first American landing on Pacific Coast. Captain Robert Gray arrived on the site of Tillamook County in 1788.

**Mid-July through August weekends.** Lewis and Clark Historical Pageant, Seaside. Re-creation of the 1804–1806 Lewis and Clark expedition.

**Mid-August.** Tillamook County Fair. Dairy show, livestock exhibitions, carnival, horse racing, grandstand shows.

# Other Recommended
# Restaurants and Lodgings

## Seaside

Beachwood Bed-and-Breakfast, 671 Beach Drive. (503) 738–9585. A block from the beach and promenade. Antiques, lace, woodsy garden, full breakfast. Three rooms.

Shilo Inn, 30 North Promenade. (503) 738–9571 or (800) 222–2244. Large, well-run motel facing the beach. Restaurant, swimming pool.

## Cannon Beach

Cannon Beach Hotel, 1116 South Hemlock. (503) 436–1392. Attractive European-style hotel with nine rooms. Gracious furnishings, phones, television, fireplace in lobby. Light breakfast included. Short walk to beach.

## Manzanita

Arbors in Manzanita, 78 Idaho. (503) 368–7055. Charming, English-style cottage a block from the beach. Two guest rooms, flower gardens, full breakfast.

Inn at Manzanita, 67 Laneda. (503) 368–6754. Luxury inn a short walk from the sea. Some ocean views. Stylish pastels, natural wood, light and airy. All units have two-person spas.

Blue Sky Cafe, 154 Laneda. (503) 368–5712. Fresh seafood, pasta, beef, chicken, all prepared with savory herbs and sauces.

Jarboe's, 137 Laneda. (503) 368–5113. Noted for innovative and superb cuisine.

## Wheeler

Nina's Italian Pizzeria and Restaurant, Highway 101. (503) 368–6592. Italian dishes, pastas, excellent pizza. Lounge 'and view of the bay.

## Garibaldi

Hill Top House, 617 Holly Avenue, P.O. Box 538. (503) 322–3221. Bed-and-breakfast with three rooms, panoramic view of docks, bay, and ocean. Full breakfast.

## Tillamook

Shilo Inn, 2515 North Main. (503) 842–7971 or (800) 222–2244. Sixty-eight-unit motel south of cheese factory on Highway 101. Pool, sauna, laundromat, kitchenettes. Wheelchair accessible.

Blue Haven Inn, P.O. Box 1034. (503) 842–2265. Gracious bed-and-breakfast home south of Tillamook. Attractive gardens, three guest rooms. Full breakfast in formal dining room.

## Cloverdale

Sandlake Country Inn, 8505 Galloway Road. (503) 965–6745. Restored historic farmhouse 16 miles southwest of Tillamook (in Sandlake). The ultimate in bed-and-breakfast country charm. Full breakfast served.

## Netarts Bay

Terimore Motel, 5105 Crab Avenue. (503) 842–4623. Ocean- and bay-view units with kitchens and fireplaces. Housekeeping cottages with one or two bedrooms.

Wee Willie's, Whiskey Creek Road. (503) 842–6869. Cafe overlooking bay. Noted for its health-conscious menu. Fish-and-chips, burgers, crab sandwiches, blackberry pie.

## Hebo

Hogie Jo's, Route 22. (503) 392–3355. Casual cafe with excellent Mexican food on weekends.

## Lincoln City

Kyllo's, 1110 Northwest First Court. (503) 994–3179. Bright, festive beachside restaurant at D River Wayside. Imaginative decor, ocean-views, good seafood, very popular.

Lighthouse Restaurant and Brewery, Lighthouse Square. (503) 994–7238. Brewery tours, chowder, chili, and sandwiches in a two-story, fern-filled restaurant with atrium.

Palmer House, 646 Northwest Inlet. (503) 994–7932. Light, bright, contemporary bed-and-breakfast with three guest rooms, one with ocean view and fireplace. One block to beach.

Spyglass Inn, 2510 SW Dune Avenue. (503) 994–2785. Hilltop home with spectacular ocean views, balconies, books, privacy. Full breakfast.

# For More Information

Seaside Chamber of Commerce, 7 North Roosevelt, P.O. Box 7, Seaside, OR 97138. (503) 738–6391 or (800) 444–6740.

Cannon Beach Chamber of Commerce, 207 North Spruce, P.O. Box 64, Cannon Beach, OR 97110. (503) 436–2623.

Tillamook Chamber of Commerce, 3705 Highway 101 North, Tillamook, OR 97141. (503) 842–7525.

Lincoln City Visitors and Convention Bureau, 801 Southwest Highway 101, Lincoln City, OR 97367. (503) 994–8378 or (800) 452–2151.

# Eugene-Florence-Newport

A former railroad depot houses a popular Eugene restaurant.

## City Culture and Coastal Beauty

———————————— 2 NIGHTS ————————————

College campus • Wineries • Rugged coastline • Fine dining
Sand dunes • Marine life • Rhododendrons • Ocean views • Aquarium

This three-day tour gives you a sampling of some of the best that an Oregon city and the Oregon coastline have to offer visitors. From the restaurants, shopping, and cultural events of Eugene to the rocky coast where waves crash and spray, the variety is exhilarating.

## Day 1

**Morning**

Travel south on I–5 100 miles to **Eugene,** and stop at the Eugene-

Springfield Convention and Visitors Bureau, 305 West Seventh Avenue, for maps and brochures. Check the calendar for concerts and events taking place at the **Hult Center for the Performing Arts;** if the evening's attraction appeals, call for reservations. The Hult Center hosts top artists from around the world in its 2,500-seat, acoustically ideal concert hall. The Eugene symphony, ballet, and opera perform on this stage. In June and July the internationally renowned Oregon Bach Festival takes place. Plan on an early dinner if you're attending the theater.

Next, drive north on Lincoln Street to **Skinner Butte Park** and go to the top of the butte where you'll have, on a clear day, panoramic views of the city, the Willamette River flowing through town, the surrounding green hills and fields, and the mountain on the horizon. Walk through the rose garden and along tree-shaded paths in this grassy park that was named for the first homesteader in the area; then head back downtown to the **Market District.**

There are dozens of shops to browse through in the district, but the main complex is **Fifth Street Public Market**. Once a feed mill, it's now a collection of interesting specialty stores selling clothing, gift items, kitchenware, arts and crafts, and foods from around the world. **Casablanca,** a good lunch spot, has Middle Eastern dishes, and **Terry's Diner** serves hamburgers and malteds in a 1950s atmosphere.

*Lunch:* **Mekala's,** Fifth Street Public Market. (503) 342–4872. Good Thai food, hot and spicy or not, as you request, and homemade coconut ice cream. Windows overlook the flower-filled courtyard of the market.

## Afternoon

A short distance from downtown Eugene, the **University of Oregon** covers 250 acres and is an arboretum with more than 2,000 varieties of trees. The university, the city's largest employer, enrolls about 20,000 students. Its lovely grounds are graced with nineteenth-century and modern buildings and outdoor sculpture.

Next to the library, on Fourteenth and Kincaid streets, is the **Museum of Art.** Its highly respected collection of Asian art is well worth a tour. There are other exhibits and a gift shop as well. (Open afternoons in summer, Wednesday to Sunday.) Also on campus is the **Museum of Natural History,** which displays fossils and animals and artifacts from prehistoric Oregon.

If there is time, take a stroll through **Hendricks Park,** 2 miles southeast of the campus. Don't miss it in the spring, when the rhododendron displays are magnificent. Thousands of the colorful plants bloom in this park, which also has paths, secluded benches, and picnic areas.

*Dinner:* **Cafe Zenon,** 898 Pearl Street. (503) 343–3005. Controlled hubbub in a busy slice of Eugene life. Outdoor tables when weather permits. Variety of ethnic cuisines, always interesting.

*Lodging:* **Campus Cottage,** 1136 East Nineteenth. (503) 342–5346. Bed-and-breakfast in a 1920s home near University of Oregon campus. Three well-furnished rooms, hospitable innkeeper, good conversation.

# Day 2

## Morning

*Breakfast:* Early morning coffee and then full breakfast at Campus Cottage. Fresh-baked scones with jam, fruit, juice, and an egg dish.

Head west on Highway 126. In 12 miles you'll reach **Fern Ridge Lake,** a 4.5-mile-long reservoir that is popular for sailing, power boating, and water skiing. Shortly after the lake and Peninsula Park, you'll come to a **wildlife viewing area**. The wetlands and marshes here provide shelter to a variety of birds and animals.

Continue on to Territorial Highway and turn left toward the Veneta business district and **Hinman Vineyards,** 27012 Briggs Hill Road. Hinman, established in 1979 in the foothills of the Coast Range, is a brick winery with graceful arches and a tower. Tastings are offered and a picnic area on the landscaped grounds is available.

If you turn right instead of left on Territorial Highway, you'll be headed for Elmira and **Forgeron Vineyard**, 89697 Sheffler Road. This small, family-owned winery is next to groves of fir trees at the end of a mile-long lane.

Continuing on Highway 126 you'll drive through Noti, a timber town where piles of logs are stacked higher than the buildings. The road winds up into the Coast Range, through dense forest where the tree trunks seem to be made of moss, they're so velvety green. In spring, the dogwood blossoms float creamy white against the dark firs, and in fall the maples and alders show yellow, brown, and red.

At the confluence of the Siuslaw River and Wild Cat Creek, watch for a **covered bridge** that was built in 1925. The pretty white bridge, a charming addition to the landscape, is easy to miss in summer because it's hidden behind the foliage. Take a sharp right at Whittaker Creek turnoff, pass under Highway 126, and you will see the bridge.

Continue on 126 to **Florence,** at the mouth of the Siuslaw River, and follow the signs to **Old Town.** The historic bayfront here offers quaint shops, boutiques, and restaurants by the harbor, home of a small fishing fleet. It won't take long to look around the area. Check the kite shop, buy a souvenir, have a cappuccino, and head for the dunes.

The **Oregon Dunes National Recreation Area** is a 47-mile stretch of sand dunes, encompassing some 32,000 acres. Walking in these undulating, desert-like hills is an experience not to be missed. South of Florence is **Jesse M. Honeyman State Park,** with convenient access to the dunes. Here a high hill, a favorite spot for climbing and sliding on the sand, meets the edge of a watery gem, Cleawox Lake.

About 10 miles south of Honeyman is the **Oregon Dunes Overlook,** where you can see the dunes from boardwalks and viewing platforms. A short trail leads into the dunes, and interpretive signs explain the natural features such as evergreen islands, beach grass, wildlife, and little lakes. The overlook is wheelchair accessible.

*Lunch:* **Cottage Restaurant and Tea Shop,** 239 Maple Street. (503) 997–8890. In this quaint blue cottage, you'll find the best of English cookery: shepherd's pie, soups, and good sandwiches. You can eat in the garden on sunny days.

## Afternoon

Leaving Florence, drive north on U.S. Highway 101 to **Darlingtonia Wayside.** Walk the boardwalk here for a look at the exotic-looking cobra lilies growing in the marsh. These plants are carnivorous, luring insects down a tube lined with nectar.

Continue north for 10 miles to **Sea Lion Caves** and take the elevator down to the caves where Steller sea lions dwell (there is an admission fee). You can get a close look at the only wild breeding colony of the sea lions on the coast, as well as postcard views of **Heceta Head lighthouse** to the north. Pigeon guillemots and Brandt's cormorants nest by the thousands in the area and can be seen from a path along the cliff.

As you drive north on 101 along the coast, you'll pass miles of smooth, uncrowded beach. Stop at any parking area to explore the shoreline; all the beaches are open to the public by state law. A park with a sandy cove, lawns, and picnic tables lies at the base of the cliff where the picturesque Heceta Head lighthouse stands.

Along the way are landmarks such as Devil's Elbow, Devil's Churn, Muriel O. Ponsler Memorial Wayside, and Captain Cook's Chasm. At **Cape Perpetua,** you can enjoy panoramic views up and down the coast. Check at Cape Perpetua Visitors' Center for exhibits and information. Walk the trails on this massive basaltic headland to see old-growth forest, tide pools, shell mounds, and chasms of turbulent foam.

When you reach **Yachats** (Ya-hots), you're in a charming seaside town nestled between the Coast Range forests and the Pacific Ocean—the perfect spot for a quiet getaway. Visit the **Little Log Church,** a tiny church built in 1927 and now open as a historical museum.

*Dinner:* **La Serre,** Second and Beach streets, Yachats. (503) 547–3420. Greenery, windows, and skylights give this highly rated restaurant a garden atmosphere. Fresh seafood, tasty salads.

*Lodging:* **Shamrock Lodgettes,** Highway 101, Yachats. (503) 547–3312. Log cabins on sloping lawns above the beach at the mouth of the Yachats River.

# Day 3

## Morning

*Breakfast:* **New Morning Coffeehouse,** Fourth Street, Yachats. (503) 547–3848. Warm, light-filled, inexpensive eatery serving good pastries and coffee. Outdoor terrace, light lunches.

Drive north on Highway 101 to **Waldport** and stop at the **Alsea Bay Bridge Interpretive Center.** Once the bay was spanned by a classic 1937 bridge; it was replaced in 1991 and the interpretive center was opened to provide information and displays on bridge history, early road development, and the settlement of the Alsea Bay area.

A few miles north of Waldport, as you approach Seal Rock, you'll see a sign for Art on the Rocks. Stop here for a look at the works of local and international artists in jewelry, paintings, and photography. Semiprecious stones are sold as well.

The heart of the Seal Rock community is a collection of shops clustered near the **General Store.** Near here is **Granny's Country Store,** which is filled with antiques and collectibles—lots of nice glass and china. Next door is another intriguing shop called Antiques, etc.

Don't miss a browse through **Trade Bead Gallery,** which has an outstanding collection of ancient and modern beads from all over the world. Even if you're not excited about beads, you'll be fascinated by the information provided on the displays of rare trade beads.

Choose something sweet at Fudge, which sells ice cream and luscious, handmade candies, and see the carved items at Seal Rock Wood Works. Tour Sea Gulch, if you're interested in chainsaw sculpture. This is a western-and-hillbilly theme park, with some 400 red cedar carvings.

At **Ona Beach State Park,** on the estuary of Beaver Creek, there are picnic tables on the well-landscaped, wooded grounds.

Paved paths curve to a bridge that crosses the creek and leads to a wide, sandy beach with driftwood. Restrooms in the park have wheelchair access.

Continuing north, before crossing the high bridge over Yaquina Bay into Newport, stop at the new **Oregon Coast Aquarium.** The state-of-the-art facility replicates the dunes, rocky pools, cliffs, and caves of coastal Oregon. Marine creatures native to the area live in pools and tanks that resemble their wild habitat. You'll see octopi, tufted puffins, seals, sea otters, and a tank of lavender-pink jellyfish floating through the water in elegant dance. There's also a touch tank of starfish and other tidepool creatures. (Open daily except Christmas.)

The **Mark O. Hatfield Marine Science Center** is nearby, with more displays of Northwest sea life. The Center is part of Oregon State University's educational and research program and offers classes, workshops, and field trips.

*Lunch:* **Canyon Way Restaurant and Bookstore,** 1216 Canyon Way SW. (503) 265–8319. Imaginative entrees, seafood, salads. Deli with sandwiches to go, espresso, and outdoor terrace, plus a good bookstore and gift shop.

## Afternoon

Tour the **Old Bay Front**, where you can watch the fishing boats come and go, buy souvenirs, and, if tourist attractions appeal, see the Wax Works, Undersea Gardens, and Ripley's Believe It Or Not. Alternatively, you might take a two-and-a-half-hour **whale watching trip** or go crabbing in the bay with Newport Tradewinds (503–265–2101). The company also offers longer trips for deep-sea fishing.

Turn east on U.S. 20, a byway that follows Elk Creek to **Toledo.** If you have the time, stop at the Michael Gibbons Gallery and Studio to view the noted artist's landscape paintings. The gallery is in a former church rectory at 40 Northeast Alder (503) 336–2797.

Continue on Route 20 to Chitwood, where you'll see an old-fashioned **covered bridge,** and on through the wooded hills and farmlands of the Willamette Valley to I–5. Turn north to take the freeway to Portland.

# There's More

**Dorris Ranch,** South Second Street and Dorris Avenue, Springfield. (503) 726–4335. The nation's first filbert orchard, now a living history farm on 250 acres. Tours every second and fourth Saturday, April through November. Nominal admission fee.

**Drift Creek Wilderness,** Waldport. Pocket wilderness in Siuslaw National Forest, contains some of the last of the coastal old-growth forest. Maps ($2.00) available at Waldport Ranger Station (503) 563–3211.

**Gwynn Creek Trail,** Cape Perpetua. Easily accessible and beautiful walk from Cape Perpetua Visitors' Center. Climbs Gwynn Creek

Canyon, through old-growth stands of Douglas fir and Sitka spruce. Full loop, 6.5 miles.

**Golf.** Oakway Golf Course, Eugene. (503) 484–1927. Executive 18-hole course, no tee times required. Florence Golf Club, Florence. (503) 997–3232. Nine-hole course by the sand dunes, "Oregon's biggest sand trap." Sandpines Golf Course, Florence. (503) 997–1937. New 18-hole course, one of Lane County's largest, built on sand dunes. Open year-round.

**Hiking, running, canoeing, whitewater rafting.** All are available in or near Eugene. Check with the visitors' bureau for specific places and arrangements.

**Lane County Ice,** Lane County Fairgrounds, Eugene. (503) 687–4421. Full-size arena ice rink, open daily.

**Lively Park Swim Center,** 6100 Thurston Road, Springfield. (503) 726–2752. Indoor water fun in surf of 4-foot waves, 136-foot open flume water slide. Spa, kiddy pool.

**Saturday Market,** High Street, Eugene. Near the Market District, an outdoor array of booths—a great place to stroll and shop on a Saturday between April and late December.

**Siuslaw River cruises** aboard the *Westward Ho!,* a half-scale replica of a sternwheeler that once plied the Columbia River. Frontier theme, costumes, entertainment, dinner cruises. (503) 268–4017. One-hour tours depart from Old Town dock in Florence.

**Yaquina Bay paddlewheeler excursion.** Dining and cruises aboard an old-fashioned paddlewheel boat. (503) 265–BELL.

# Special Events

**Late February.** Seafood and Wine Festival, Newport.

**March.** Dune Mushers Mail Run, Horsfall Beach to Florence. Dog sled teams run 72 miles through sand dunes.

**June.** Oregon Bach Festival, Eugene. Two weeks of music by world-famous performers. Concerts, workshops, lectures, dance.

**Mid-July.** Oregon Country Fair, Veneta. Arts and crafts in the woods near Eugene. Food, music.

**Summer.** Eugene Festival of Musical Theater, Hult Center for the Performing Arts, Eugene. (503) 345–0028. Community and professional productions of American musicals.

**Mid-October.** Florence Fall Festival, Florence. "Fabulous fifties" theme for a clam chowder cook-off, mushroom hunt, dances, entertainment, and arts and crafts fair.

# Other Recommended
# Restaurants and Lodgings

## Elmira

McGillivray's Log Home, 88680 Evers Road. (503) 935–3564. Oversize log home in the country with two spacious guest rooms. Full breakfast, private baths.

## Eugene

(See Portland Escapes Six and Twelve for more Eugene recommendations.)

Oregon Electric Station, 27 East Fifth. (503) 485–4444. Red-brick restaurant in Market District. Lunch, dinner, and Sunday brunch in antique railroad car, three lounges, live jazz.

Pookie's Bed 'n Breakfast, 2013 Charnelton Street. (503) 343–0383. Two guest rooms in nicely restored 1918 home. Residential neighborhood, close to downtown and campus, full or continental breakfast included.

## Florence

Johnson House Bed and Breakfast, 216 Maple Street. (503) 997–8000. Historic home turned top-quality bed-and-breakfast. Six rooms plus a charming little cottage.

Windward Inn, 3757 Highway 101 North. (503) 997–8243. Wood-paneled restaurant with fireplaces and warm, relaxed atmosphere. Local seafood, steak, homemade breads, and pastries.

## Newport

Sylvia Beach Hotel, 267 Northwest Cliff. (503) 265–5428. Unique hotel on a cliff above Nye Beach, with rooms dedicated to and furnished in accordance with various authors. Restaurant, library, gift shop, ocean views.

The Whale's Tale, 452 Bay Boulevard SW. (503) 265–8660. On the bayfront. Known for flavorful omelets and poppyseed pancakes. Light fare and seafood entrees, all prepared with care.

## Seal Rock

Blackberry Inn, 6575 Pacific Coast Highway 101 SW. (503) 563–2259. Bed-and-breakfast with casual charm. Three immaculate rooms, country furnishings, decks, hot tub, full breakfast. On two-and-a-half acres of pine trees. Beach access nearby.

Yuzen, 1011 Coast Highway 101 NW. (503) 563–5833. Highly reputed Japanese cuisine. Casual atmosphere, booths and tables, Japanese decor.

## Yachats

(There are numerous lodgings in the Yachats area; these are in or very close to town.)

Adobe Resort, 1555 Highway 101. (503) 547–3141. Popular resort at the edge of a rocky shore. Restaurant, lounge, great views.

Burd's Nest Inn, 664 Yachats River Road. (503) 547–3683. Unusual bed-and-breakfast with three attractive rooms and a lively atmosphere. Eclectic art, friendly innkeepers.

# For More Information

Eugene-Springfield Convention and Visitors' Bureau, 305 West Seventh, Eugene, OR 97440. (503) 484–5307 or (800) 547–5445.

Florence Area Chamber of Commerce, 270 Highway 101, Florence, OR 97439. (503) 997–3128.

Yachats Area Chamber of Commerce, 441 Highway 101, Yachats, OR 97498. (503) 547–3530.

Greater Newport Chamber of Commerce, 555 Coast Highway SW, Newport, OR 97365. (503) 265–8801 or (800) 262–7844.

# Mount Hood Loop

The stern-wheeler *Columbia Gorge* navigates the majestic Columbia River.

## Circling Oregon's Highest Peak

_____ 1 NIGHT _____

Evergreen forests · Waterfalls · Lakes and streams · Highest point in Oregon
Scenic overlooks · Hiking trails · Year-round skiing · Historic lodge
Fruit orchards · Columbia River · Stern-wheeler cruise

From Portland, Mount Hood's peak is a familiar presence, looming 60 miles away on the eastern horizon behind hazy, blue-green foothills. At 11,235 feet, its summit is the highest point in Oregon.

Circling around this massive, broad-shouldered volcano takes you through some of the state's most spectacular scenery, from the lush green fir forests west of the Cascade Range to the ponderosa pines, ranchlands, and acres of orchards on the east. On the mountain's north side, the wide Columbia River flows westward, fed by streams from Hood's snowfields.

A two-day loop tour is a satisfying excursion into this world of natural wonder. This itinerary, designed as a summer trip, combines vigorous recreation with restful sight-seeing. It takes you up on the mountain, into the orchards, and out on the water. With a few changes, you can enjoy many of its features in winter, substituting ski slopes or groomed trails for forest walks.

# Day 1

## Morning

From Portland take U.S. Route 26 east toward **Sandy.** If you missed breakfast, stop to eat at **Charbo's,** 36641 Highway 26, (503) 668-7323, in the Sandy Marketplace. Homemade pastries and hearty breakfasts are served here.

Five-and-a-half miles east of Sandy, stop at the Oregon Candy Farm to appease your sweet tooth. For more than fifty years the candymakers, who began their enterprise in Portland, have been selling handmade chocolates and other candies. Watch the candy-making process through glass windows in the factory weekdays from 9:00 A.M. to 5:00 P.M. and weekend afternoons (503–668–5066).

Continue on Route 26 to **Welches.** At **Northwest Delicafe,** a cafe, bakery, and delicatessen in the Welches shopping center, purchase lunch-to-go. The sandwiches are generously filled; cookies and muffins are home baked. Also in the shopping center are a bookstore, a fly-fishing shop, a ski-rental shop, and a grocery market.

The road, much of it recently widened, rises from here into Mount Hood's foothills, cutting through the forests of fir and hemlock, passing summer homes and ski cabins, to **Zigzag** (18 miles east of Sandy). In the Zigzag ranger station, pick up maps and trail information.

Take the **Lolo Pass** road north from Zigzag about 4 miles to Road N12. Turn right and follow the signs to the trailhead for **Ramona Falls**.This point is about 8 miles from the highway. The 5½-mile (round trip) trail crosses the **Sandy River** and ascends gradually through forestland and open sandy slopes above the river canyon to one of Mount Hood's prettiest waterfalls.

Cascading 100 feet in broad, misty sheets over mossy rocks, Ramona splashes past green ferns into clear, cold **Ramona Creek.**

*Lunch:* Picnic at Ramona Falls.

## Afternoon

Return to Route 26 and continue east, ascending the mountain toward the 6-mile spur road to **Timberline Lodge.** The grand old lodge, built as a Works Progress Administration (WPA) project in 1937, is a **National Historic Landmark**. Its wood carvings, wrought iron, massive beams, and Indian-motif fabrics make it an extraordinary work of art, as well as a significant piece of Northwest history.

Don't miss the fine display of craftsmanship in the **Rachael Griffin Historic Exhibition Center** on the main floor. It's accompanied by a recording of President Franklin D. Roosevelt's speech of dedication at the lodge.

Timberline is the second-oldest developed ski area in the United States and the only one offering summer skiing. In mid-July you can ride the lift up **Palmer Glacier** and ski down.

After (or instead of) glacier skiing, stroll the trails that extend in several directions from the lodge. You are literally at the timberline, so if you head down the mountain you'll be among the trees; walk up its slopes and you're in open, rocky terrain. The trail to **Zigzag Canyon** and **Paradise Park** offers both, as well as rushing streams and wild-flower meadows in summer. You may have time to walk part of the trail to a scenic viewpoint above the canyon.

Return to the lodge for a shower and well-deserved evening relax-ation in the **Ram's Head Bar,** a perfect spot for enjoying an aperitif while you watch the sunset's glow on the mountaintop.

*Dinner:* **Cascades Dining Room,** Timberline Lodge. American and Continental dinners served by candlelight.

*Lodging:* **Timberline Lodge,** Timberline, OR 97028. (503) 272-3311. For reservations from Portland, phone 231-5400; in Oregon, (800) 452-1335; in western states, (800) 547-1406. Classic mountain lodge and ski resort on Mount Hood's south flank.

# Day 2

## Morning

*Breakfast:* Cascades Dining Room.

Drive back to U.S. Route 26, and head east to State Route 35, which winds northeast around the mountain toward the **Columbia River Gorge.** Near the spot where **Pacific Crest National Scenic Trail** crosses the highway, you'll come to **Barlow Pass.** The pass was named for pioneer Sam Barlow, who developed a toll road around the south side of Mount Hood in 1846. Until then, wagon trains on the Oregon Trail took the precarious Columbia River passage to reach the western side of the Cascades.

Crossing the **White River** (the canyon here is a favorite among cross-country skiers), continue on Route 35 to **Bennett Pass** (eleva-tion 4,670 feet) and the road to **Mount Hood Meadows Ski Area.** This is the largest ski development on the mountain, with numerous lifts and runs. It's also a focus of controversy, as developers seek to expand the facilities.

The East Fork of the Hood River runs by the ski area, beginning in a glacier high on the mountain and coursing down the slopes to create **Umbrella Falls** and, closer to the main road, **Sahalie Falls.** Easy walks take you through the forest to either falls; a longer hike of 1.7 miles connects them.

If you take the detour loop road to Sahalie Falls, you'll come to **Hood River Meadows,** the biggest meadow on Mount Hood, spangled with the colors of wildflowers in late spring.

As the East Fork turns due north, so does the road, crossing brooks that rush down ravines into the river. Shortly after passing Sherwood Campground, you'll come to a parking area for East Fork Trail 650, the **Tamanawus Falls Trail.** The 2-mile trail is a classic for Northwest scenery as it follows bouncy Cold Spring Creek, shaded by tall evergreens, through a narrow canyon to a waterfall that cascades 100 feet.

After your two-hour, round-trip hike, take Route 35 to the turnoff to **Cooper Spur,** a high ridge between Eliot and Newton Clark glaciers. It's about 2¼ miles in from the road.

Drive 6 miles beyond it to **Inspiration Point,** where you'll have a stunning view of the upper **Hood River Valley** and the mountain's north side, with **Wallalute Falls** cascading down from Eliot Glacier.

Still farther—about 11 miles from the Inn at Cooper Spur—is **Cloud Cap Inn,** a starting point for climbers just below Eliot Glacier. The rustic log hotel, constructed in 1889 and now a National Historic Site, is anchored by cables to resist winter storms. The crisp air and incomparable scenery have drawn visitors for a century. Early travelers to the inn rode the train to Hood River, then paid $12.50 for a six-hour ride in an open coach, with two changes of horses on the way. The first automobile to reach Cloud Cap Inn was a 1907 Cadillac. Now maintained by the Crag Rats, a mountain-climbing and rescue organization, Cloud Cap Inn is not open to the public.

The entire Cloud Cap/Tilly Jane area is a National Historic District. Other points of interest include the Tilly Jane Forest Camp, the American Legion Camp, and the massive public shelter built by the Civilian Conservation Corps in 1939. China Fill memorializes the Chinese laborers who toiled with picks to dig and grade the old wagon road in 1889.

*Lunch:* **The Inn at Cooper Spur,** Mount Hood. (503) 352–6692. Homey mountainside restaurant, part of a small resort. Open for lunch Saturday and Sunday. Try Evelyn Cochrane's homemade soups and award-winning pie.

A lunch alternative is a picnic on the trail.

## Afternoon

Now Route 35, still edging the East Fork, begins its descent into the lush, fertile Hood River Valley, winding through fragrant apple, pear, and cherry orchards. In spring the fields in blossom are as snow-white as the mountain slopes behind them; in autumn the air carries the heady scent of cider.

Stop at **Mount Hood General Store,** in the small community of Mount Hood, to browse through an old-fashioned country market. Fresh produce, gourmet foods, Northwest wines, and gifts are sold in a nostalgic setting. It's a good place for ice cream on a hot day.

Farther north, drive 1½ miles off the highway to **Panorama Point** for a wide valley vista, with lofty Mount Hood in the background. It's a froth of white in spring, but equally beautiful in autumn, when orchard foliage glows yellow-gold and the maples and tamaracks turn rust and orange, with the occasional scarlet-tinged sumac sparking the fall tones. At harvesttime, roadside stands are full of produce.

It's a short drive from Panorama Point into **Hood River.**

Turn west on I-84, and you're in the heart of the **Columbia River Gorge.** In this geological wonder, much of it a designated **National Scenic Area**, the wide Columbia flows on your right. On the left, dancing waterfalls spray from steep cliffs and great basaltic masses exposed by ancient floods. On the ridges around them, thick forests shield a network of hiking trails.

For more activities and attractions in Hood River and for more detail on waterfalls and exploring the gorge, see Portland Escape Seven.

Continuing west, you'll pass **Oxbow Salmon Hatchery,** which is open to the public. When you reach **Cascade Locks,** drive to the riverside **Marine Park.** The grassy, tree-shaded park has play equipment, remnants of the old boat locks (used before dam construction made them unnecessary), a museum, and the Oregon Pony, the first steam locomotive built on the Pacific Coast. In the visitors' information center there are a gift shop, historic photographs of early stern-wheeler days, and 50-cent showers—a boon to hikers fresh off the numerous trails in the gorge.

The Pacific Crest Trail passes through Cascade Locks in **Bridge of the Gods Park.** The Bridge of the Gods, spanning the Columbia, was built in 1926 and raised in 1938 to provide clearance when Bonneville Dam was built. Indian legend says that long ago a natural bridge of stone stretched across the gorge near here.

From the wharf at Marine Park, the ***Columbia Gorge*** stern-wheeler leaves three times a day in summer for two-hour cruises on the river. A hundred years ago stern-wheelers carried passengers and cargo between Portland and The Dalles. Today a 330-ton, three-deck replica of a river paddleboat provides a chance to step into that colorful bygone era. Dinner, dance, and sunset cruises are available.

*Dinner:* Aboard the *Columbia Gorge* stern-wheeler. Dine on an old-fashioned riverboat as it churns past the gorge's magnificent forests and towering basaltic cliffs. Dinner cruises, available June–October, range from ninety minutes to three hours. For information: 1200 Southwest Front, Suite 110, Portland, OR 97209. (503) 374–8427; in Portland, 223–3928.

From Cascade Locks, it's a thirty-minute drive west on I–84 to Portland.

## There's More

**Mushroom collecting,** spring and fall. Mushrooms grow in profusion in Mount Hood's forests. The ranger station has information on the best locations to search. Chanterelles, shaggy manes, boletus, morels, and other exotic species are easy to find; but several poisonous varieties grow here as well. Do not eat mushrooms unless you're certain they are safe.

**Fishing.** Rainbow trout fishing farm, open daily. Fishing rods and bait available. Near the Oregon Candy Farm on Route 26.

Lost Lake, Mount Hood. Picture-perfect mountain lake with rainbow and German brown trout. One of the most photographed lakes in the nation.

Mouth of Hood River. Steelhead run in spring, October, and January. Hood River Marina. Smallmouth bass.

**Mount Hood Railroad.** Scenic train excursions through the Hood River Valley, mid-April through October. (503) 386–3556.

## Special Events

**Mid-April.** Blossom Festival, Hood River Valley. Orchard tours, arts-and-crafts sales, train rides on the Fruit Blossom Special.

**Mid-July.** Sandy Mountain Festival, Sandy. Celebration of Sandy's pioneer heritage. Folk music, food booths, arts and crafts.

**August.** Mount Hood Festival of Jazz, Gresham. Nationally acclaimed jazz series with top musicians playing outdoors at Mount Hood Community College.

**October.** October Harvest Festival, Hood River. Crafts booths, foods, wines.

# Other Recommended
# Restaurants and Lodgings

## Government Camp

Falcon's Crest, P.O. Box 185. (503) 272–3403; in Portland, 227–1155. Chalet-style mountain home and lodge with five suites. Full breakfast. Walking distance to Ski Bowl, largest nighttime skiing area in the United States.

## Hood River

The Coffee Spot, 12 Oak Street. (503) 386–1772. Deli, house specialties, espresso. Afternoon Java Hour, coffees half-price. Delicious chocolate croissants.

## Rhododendron

Log Lodge, 73330 East Highway 26. (503) 622–4865. Good berry pies.
The Barlow Trail, 69580 East Highway 26. (503) 622–3877. Old-time rustic log restaurant, near Zigzag. Tasty omelets, biscuits and gravy, huge burgers. Popular with local folk.

## Sandy

The Elusive Trout, 39333 Proctor Boulevard. (503) 668–7884. Pub selling microbrewed ales, lagers on tap, and foods prepared with care.
Wasson Brothers Winery, 41901 Highway 26. (503) 668–3124. Open for tastings and tours.

## Welches

Chalet Swiss, Highway 26 at Welches Road. (206) 622–3600. Continental dinners, Swiss specialties (raclette, fondue, schnitzel), and seafood—mountain trout amandine, Pacific oysters, and broiled salmon are a few examples.
The Resort at the Mountain, 68010 East Fairway Avenue. (503) 622–3101; within Oregon, (800) 452–4612; outside Oregon, (800) 547–8054. Luxury resort with 27-hole golf course on Salmon River.
Mountain Shadows Bed and Breakfast, Box 147. (503) 622–4746. Log home on fifty-acre forested slope of Mount Hood. Casual, cozy, secluded.

# For More Information

Sandy Area Chamber of Commerce, P.O. Box 536, Sandy, OR 97055. (503) 668–4006.

Mount Hood Recreation Association, P.O. Box 342, Welches, OR 97067. (503) 224–7158.

Mount Hood Area Chamber of Commerce, P.O. Box 158, Welches, OR 97067. (503) 622–3017.

Hood River County Chamber of Commerce, Port Marina Park, Hood River, OR 97031. (503) 386–2000.

# Around Mount St. Helens

Mount St. Helens National Volcanic Monument

## Exploring the Volcano

_____ 1 NIGHT _____

Mount St. Helens National Volcanic Monument • Volcano museum
Devastation area • Hiking trails • Views of Spirit Lake and crater
Longest lava tube in the United States • Scenic lake • Scenic river

Before May 18, 1980, Mount St. Helens was a pristine, symmetrical white peak, the queen of the Cascade range. But mighty forces were brewing beneath that serene exterior. After two months of minor explosions and earthquakes, the mountain erupted in a blast of rock, ash, gas, and steam.

Within ten minutes an immense plume of pumice and ash leapt 13.6 miles into the atmosphere and continued roaring upward for nine hours. The volume of ash fall could have buried a football field to a depth of 150 miles. Mount St. Helens's height dropped from 9,677 feet to 8,363 feet, with a crater more than 2,000 feet deep.

Water, ice, and rock debris formed vast mudflows that uprooted 150 square miles of trees and tore out bridges and houses as they raced through river valleys in the biggest landslide in recorded history. The devastation left a landscape bleak and gray.

Today wisps of gas and ash still rise from the crater, and a lava dome is building. But the mountain remains quiet. Wildlife and plants are returning, along with a million visitors a year. The devastated area is a National Monument now, with 120 miles of trails and 50 miles of roads.

The loop trip described here is intended for summer touring, as some roads are closed in winter. It touches the highlights and will give you a sense of the awesome power that changed the structure of a mountain. As you walk, be careful of the fragile vegetation that is beginning to establish new life.

Bring sturdy walking shoes and water; there are few resources. At Mount St. Helens a concession between Meta Lake and Independence Pass sells emergency supplies, film, and food.

# Day 1

## Morning

Pack a picnic in the cooler and head north on I–5 to **Castle Rock, Washington** (Exit 49). Drive 5 miles east on State Route 504 to **Mount St. Helens Visitor Center,** a well-designed complex set in a wooded grove near the shore of **Silver Lake.** The center is open daily from 9:00 A.M. to 6:00 P.M. in summer (9:00 A.M. to 5:00 P.M. in other months). Trails (some paved and wheelchair accessible) extend from the center through the forest.

In the center you can obtain maps, information, and sight-seeing suggestions from the helpful staff. Don't miss the nine-minute, multi-image slide program that introduces the Mount St. Helens story and the twenty-one-minute film *This Place in Time.* Both are shown hourly, all day.

Exhibits explain the mountain's history of eruptions and graphically illustrate the 1980 devastation. You can even walk into the heart of the volcano—a replica that gives a simulated version of the mountain's interior.

Continue on Route 504 along the **North Fork of the Toutle River.** On the way you'll see an A-frame home that was half-buried in the mudflow; you can walk through the dug-out rooms to see the effects of the disaster. At the end of the road is the new Coldwater Ridge Visitor Center, where there are spectacular views of Coldwater Lake.

Take State Route 505 northwest to Toledo, where you'll turn north toward **Mary's Corner,** at U.S. Route 12. One of the state's first home-steads, **Jackson House,** is in this little community and is occasionally open to the public.

*Lunch:* Picnic in **Lewis and Clark State Park,** Mary's Corner. In this 500-acre park you can walk in one of the last stands of **old-growth forest** along the Portland-Seattle corridor. Many of the Dou-glas fir, hemlock, and cedar trees are 500 years old.

## Afternoon

Follow Route 12 east to **Mossyrock,** a small town set in a beguil-ing valley of farms and rolling green hills. Wild blackberry vines arch over sagging wood fences along this road, and Queen Anne's lace grows tall against red barns. There are acres of Christmas trees, tulip fields, and blueberries. This is logging country, too, and you'll see hills shorn of trees.

East of town there's a view of **Mossyrock Dam;** at 606 feet it's the highest dam in Washington. The dam created **Riffe Lake,** a 23-mile lake stocked with coho and brown trout. Fishing, boating, and sail-boarding are popular here.

**Morton,** a longtime logging town 31 miles east of Mary's Corner, is famous for its annual rough-and-tumble logging show.

The **Old Settlers Museum,** in **Gus Backstrom Park** on the Tilton River, is filled with pioneer relics and is open occasionally. The park caretaker may open the museum, if you ask.

**Marti's Mount St. Helen's Ash Creations,** 630 Westlake Avenue (206–496–5469), sells ceramic items made with volcanic ash, and the shop's friendly owners have lots of information about hiking trails and roads to the volcano.

It's 17 miles from Morton to **Randle.** Along the route you may spot hang gliders riding the wind currents on Dog Mountain. At Randle, turn south on Forest Road 25.

In 9 miles you'll come to Forest Road 26. Pass this road by, remain-ing on Forest Road 25 for 11 miles until you reach Road 99. Turn west on the two-lane, paved road. Starting in deep green forest, it leads into the blast area that appears to be one of total destruction, but look closely and you'll see evidence of life's beginnings in the small plants.

Your first stop is at **Bear Meadow,** famous as the site where pho-tographs were taken of the 1980 eruption as it occurred. Trails, picnic areas, and restrooms are in this area.

Nine miles in, at the junction of Forest Roads 99 and 26, you'll see the **Miner's Car.** The 1973 Grand Prix, resting atop downed trees, was hurled 50 feet by the lateral blast to its present location.

**Meta Lake Trail 210** begins 100 yards west of Miner's Car, off Road 99. This is the only trail offering barrier-free access into the blast zone. Twice a day, at noon and 3:00 P.M., a naturalist leads a walk and explains the changing environment. On the ⅛-mile, level paved path you'll see small trees that survived the eruption, just 8½ miles away, because they were protected by snow and ice. Birds and insects have returned, and in **Meta Lake,** at the end of the trail, trout, salamanders, and frogs now live.

Three miles from Meta Lake Trail, at **Independence Pass,** Trail 227 leads to striking views of the mountain, the crater with its growing lava dome, and **Spirit Lake.** Ascend to walk the ridge for ¼ mile, and you'll have views in all directions of the blown-down trees and acres of ash-covered slopes.

If you hike 1½ miles to a Spirit Lake overlook, you'll find interpretive signs pointing out the locations of buried campgrounds, Harry Truman's lodge, and cabins on the shores of the lake.

Spirit Lake, once a crystal-clear alpine gem, is regaining its blue clarity. When the eruption sent an avalanche of rock debris into the lake, a great wave of water swept up the slopes around it and ripped out thousands of trees. The trees washed back into the basin, with huge amounts of sediment. Many of those trees still float in the lake; others have sunk and caught on the bottom, perhaps to become a future petrified forest.

Farther on, the trail narrows and passes rock pinnacles, eventually joining **Norway Pass Trail.**

Walk Trail 227 back to Forest Road 99, and drive deeper into the National Monument; in 4 miles you'll reach the end of the road at **Windy Ridge Viewpoint,** which is as close as you can drive to the crater. A parking area is on the edge of the restricted zone, which can be entered only with a permit.

On one side you'll notice a sand-ladder trail against a slope. Climb the stair-step path to the top of the hill, and you'll have a good vantage point into the great, often-steaming crater and devastated area.

Retrace your route back to Forest Road 25, and turn south. Drive 25 miles to join Forest Road 90 at **Swift Reservoir,** a long lake south of Mount St. Helens. The lake has a boat launch, picnic and camping grounds, and some tourist facilities. Take Road 90 to Road 83, turning north to drive 2 miles to the **Trail of Two Forests.** One forest is an echo of the past; the other is of living, growing lodgepole pines.

An easy, ¼-mile loop boardwalk (protecting the fragile mosses and plants growing on the lava) passes 2,000-year-old tree molds, formed when a lava flow consumed the forest that once stood here. Interpretive signs tell the tale of the two forests.

Next, take Road 8303 to **Ape Cave,** so called because it was discovered in 1951 by members of a club nicknamed the Mount St. Helens Apes. The cave, formed by an eruption 2,000 years ago, is 12,810 feet long—the longest lava tube in the continental United States. Lanterns and guided trips are available. Wear a jacket; it's 42 degrees Fahrenheit year-round.

Ape Cave has two routes to explore. The lower cave, ¾ mile long and fairly level, is easiest and has unique features such as a "lava ball" wedged in the ceiling. Allow one and one-quarter hours round-trip. The more challenging upper cave has large rock piles to climb and an 8-foot lava fall.

Back on Road 83, turn northeast and travel 9 miles to **Lahar Viewpoint,** which provides a look at the southeast side of the mountain. A short trail leads to an interpretive sign that portrays the path of the lahar (mudflow).

Drive another ¾ mile past the parking lot to the **Muddy River,** and you'll notice the bright colors of stratigraphy bands on the stream bank. With the hill sliced away by debris racing down the channel of Shoestring Glacier, deposits from previous eruptions were revealed. The lower, bright yellow layer was deposited 8,000 to 13,000 years ago.

Return on Road 83 to Road 90 at the western shore of Swift Reservoir. This is one of three reservoirs created by dams on the **Lewis River.**

Drive 8 miles to the town of **Cougar,** on **Yale Reservoir,** a lake known for its outstanding Dolly Varden trout fishing. Stop in at **Cougar Ceramics,** 16834 Lewis River Road (206–238–5371), where Lynn and Dave Birch create smooth, marbled works of Mount St. Helens ash. They were among the first to use local volcanic ash in ceramics. Many of their pieces have become collectors' items.

Travel 5 miles south on State Route 503 to **Jack's Sporting Goods and Restaurant,** 13411 Lewis River Road, Ariel (206–231–4276). This is the place to purchase supplies for camping, fishing, and hunting, and it's where climbers sign in before beginning their trek up Mount St. Helens.

*Dinner:* Jack's. This is logger country; omelets and hamburgers are the size of platters.

*Lodging:* **Lone Fir Resort,** 16806 Lewis River Road, Cougar, WA 98616. (206) 238–5210. Nothing fancy, but fifteen motel units, five with kitchens, are clean and well kept. Swimming pool, laundry facilities, RV sites with hookups.

# Day 2

## Morning

*Breakfast:* Eat at Jack's, or prepare your own breakfast if you have housekeeping lodgings.

Drive Route 503 west, along **Lake Merwin**'s northern shore, 23 miles to **Woodland.** The visitors' center here sells souvenirs and such gifts as emerald obsidianite, a gemlike stone made from heat-fused volcanic rock; the center also provides maps and helpful information. From Woodland, it's a 30-mile drive south on I-5 to Portland.

# There's More

**Coldwater Ridge Visitors' Center,** Highway 504. (206) 247-5473. New interpretive center facing volcano crater. Videos, hands-on displays, trails, picnic tables, gift shop. About 40 miles from I-5, at Exit 49.

**Hopkins Hill.** Four miles west of Morton, the hill provides a commanding view of the Mount St. Helens crater and, often, a column of steam.

**Camping.** Lewis River RV Park, 3125 Lewis River Road, Woodland, WA 98674. On North Fork Lewis River. Swimming pool, picnic supplies, boat rentals. Near golf course.

Cougar Park and Campground (tents only). Swimming, boat launch, fishing.

Beaver Bay Park, east of Cougar on Lewis River Road. Boat launch, fishing, RV sites.

Swift Park, east end of Swift Reservoir.

**Climbing.** Permits not required in winter; 110 permits a day issued in summer. Self-register at Yale Park information station May 15 to October 31. For information, call Climbing Hotline at (206) 247-5800 or write Mount St. Helens National Volcanic Monument, Route 1, Box 369, Amboy, WA 98601.

**Field seminars.** In-depth educational seminars at Mount St. Helens. Examples: Geology of Mount St. Helens, Ecological Recovery, Cave Ecology, Landscape Photography, and Backpacking in Volcanic Terrains. For a free catalog, write Pacific Northwest National Parks and Forests Association, 83 South King Street, Suite 212, Seattle, WA 98104.

**Guided walks,** with forest interpreters.

**Sight-seeing flights.** Blue Bird Helicopters, at Toutle, Randle, and Cougar. (206) 238-5326.

**Chief Lelooska Living History Presentation,** 5618 Lewis River Road, Ariel, WA 98603. (206) 225-9522. Colorful, evocative, educational programs on Northwest Coastal Indian culture. Ceremonial dances, masks, songs, stories. Afternoon performances for school groups; occasional evening performances. Indian art and artifacts displayed in Exhibit Hall.

# Special Events

**Mid-May.** Toutle Volcano Daze Festival, Toutle. Parade, helicopter rides to the volcano, spaghetti or taco feed, Firefighters' Waterball Fight, poetry readings, music, crafts, and food sales. All with a Mount St. Helens 1980 eruption theme.

**Mid-August.** Loggers' Jubilee, Morton. Parades, carnival, arts and crafts, bed races, quilting exhibition, logging skills competition: tree fallers, logrollers, woodchoppers.

# Other Recommended Restaurants and Lodgings

## Morton

St. Helens Manorhouse, 7476 U.S. Highway 12. (206) 498–5243. Bed-and-breakfast with four rooms in 1910-era home. Wooded grounds at west end of Riffe Lake. Full breakfast.

The Seasons Motel, 200 Westlake. (206) 496–6835. New, modern motel with forty-nine spacious rooms.

# For More Information

Mount St. Helens Visitors' Center, 3029 Spirit Lake Highway, Castle Rock, WA 98611. (206) 274–2100. Call for road conditions before attempting to drive into the National Monument area.

Morton Chamber of Commerce, P.O. Box 10, Morton, WA 98356. (206) 496–6086.

# Covered Bridges of Oregon

Larwood Bridge, over Crabtree Creek.

## A Ride Through Yesteryear

——————————— 1 NIGHT ———————————

Historic covered bridges • Country byways • Waterwheel • Pastoral scenery

The country roads that wind through the green Willamette Valley are dotted with covered bridges, picturesque reminders of the past. Once there were 450; only about 50 are left, making Oregon the covered bridge capital of the West. The wooden bridges, which were covered so they would last longer in the damp climate, seem quaint and quiet now, but they've seen some lively action. Political rallies, weddings, funerals, and dances were held on covered bridges. They hid robbers and moonshine, and youngsters dove from them into swimming holes. And they are sometimes called "kissing bridges" because they sheltered many a romantic rendezvous.

This driving tour travels through three of the main clusters of bridges in the state (look for more in other areas, especially Douglas County in southern Oregon). It makes a pleasant outing for those who are chair-bound or elderly, as little effort is necessary. Alternatively, much of the route is good for bicycling, especially in the Linn County section east of Albany.

# Day 1

## Morning

Pack a picnic and drive south from Portland on I–5 to Albany. At the **Albany Visitors Association,** 300 Second Avenue Southwest, pick up a free pamphlet, Covered Bridge Country. (You may also request the pamphlet by mail or phone: write P.O. Box 965, Albany, OR 97321; or phone 800–526–2256.) This pamphlet has a map with excellent, clear directions to Linn County covered bridges. These bridges are lovingly cared for and in good condition—among the best in the state.

First you'll head east on U.S. 20, driving through a rural area where small farms and old red barns mingle with mobile homes and sheds almost swallowed in blackberry vines. Gnarled apple trees grow over roadside ditches, and in spring, white lilacs bloom in fields.

Turn left at State Route 226, crossing the **South Santiam River,** and go to the village of Crabtree, where you'll turn on Hungry Hill Road and travel to **Hoffman Bridge.** Built in 1936, the graceful bridge with Gothic-style windows spans Crabtree Creek and is kept in good condition. When it was constructed, trees were cut on nearby Hungry Hill and hauled by horses to the site.

Drive through the bridge and follow the map's directions to **Gilkey Bridge,** above Thomas Creek. Like most covered bridges, it was built with a Howe truss construction. William Howe, an architect from Massachusetts, designed the trusses as a series of timbers sloping toward the center of the bridge, where they form X-shapes with vertical tie rods.

Travel through Gilkey Bridge, go to Robinson Drive (about a mile) and turn right. You're entering Scio, a good place to stop for coffee at a local favorite, D&J Restaurant on Main Street. In this friendly place you can get a cup of tea and a warm, homemade muffin, served with a smile, for 80 cents. You may wish to have lunch here, depending on the time and your hunger.

For nostalgia's sake you might stop in Northeast Village on Main Street to see the vintage clothing. You'll find more antiques next door in Denny's Collectibles. The **Scio Depot Museum,** at First and Ash, is in a century-old railroad station and contains memorabilia from an earlier day in the Willamette Valley (open Saturday afternoons April through December).

Leaving Scio, the map directs you to turn left on Highway 226. In town it is also First Avenue; watch carefully for the sign, as it's poorly marked. The next stop is **Shimanek Bridge,** on Thomas Creek. This pretty creek twists through hilly woodlands and farms to join the San-tiam River and, eventually, the Willamette. Shimanek, built in 1966 and painted red, is the only bridge in Linn County that has a portal design and louvered windows.

Following the rushing creek, you'll come to **Hannah Bridge,** which has open sides with exposed trusses. Drive through, turn around, and take Highway 226 back to Scio. Follow the map's directions to **Larwood County Park.** There's a small parking lot here and a wooden footbridge that leads to a pretty picnic area where maple trees shade the daisy-dotted grass. Crabtree Creek flows by it, spanned by **Larwood Bridge,** and meets Roaring River. Downstream is an old water wheel, now restored.

*Lunch:* **Picnic** in Larwood County Park. Picnic tables, restrooms, shade trees, creek, quiet country landscape. (Or lunch in Scio restaurant.)

## Afternoon

Drive through Larwood Bridge and continue to Highway 226 for a left turn; take 226 to U.S. 20 and turn south toward Sweet Home. After you travel through the growing town of Lebanon, it's about 14 miles, most of the road a four-lane highway, to **Sweet Home.** Signs are abundant to **Sankey Park** and the **Weddle Bridge.**

This 120-foot bridge once stood over Thomas Creek. To save it, volunteers sold bricks, mugs, and T-shirts to raise the money for its reconstruction. Now it's a walking bridge above Ames Creek, next to another, miniature bridge. Sankey Park has a playground, wading pool, ball diamond, and picnic grounds in a Northwest setting of tall trees and weathered, mossy buildings constructed in the 1930s.

To see what life was like during the early days of the covered bridges, stop in at the **East Linn Museum,** where highways 20 and 228 intersect at Long Street. The museum, housed in a former church, has all kinds of implements, furniture, and clothing, as well as artifacts from the Kalapuya and Santiam Indian tribes.

From Sweet Home, take Route 228 west to the **Crawfordsville Bridge,** which crosses the Calapooia River beside the main road. No longer in use, the 1932 bridge was bypassed by the highway in 1963. You can continue on 228 for 7 miles to the historic village of **Brownsville** (see Portland Escape Twelve for more on Brownsville), and then head to I–5 for the drive south to Eugene. Or you can drive a byway, turning south at Crawfordsville toward Marcola.

This route takes you to Ernest and Wendling bridges in the Mohawk Valley northeast of Springfield. This is in Lane County, the county with the most covered bridges in Oregon. Continue on into Eugene. If you have time, drive up Skinner Butte, off Lincoln Street, for a panoramic view of the city and its environs.

Another interesting place in Eugene is the Lane County Historical Museum, 740 West Thirteenth Avenue, adjacent to the Lane County Fairgrounds. Its collections provide more in-depth views of the region's history and growth (open daily except Monday).

*Dinner:* **Excelsior Cafe,** 754 East Thirteenth Avenue. (503) 342–6963. Excellent cuisine in a former colonial-style home with an atmosphere of charm. Innovative, seasonal dishes and delicately prepared seafood. Special desserts, including a rich hazelnut cheesecake. Light bistro dinners available.

*Lodging:* **Valley River Inn,** 1000 Valley River Way. (503) 687–0123. Well-landscaped, full-service motel by the Willamette River. Outdoor dining overlooking the river. Wheelchair access.

# Day 2

## Morning

*Breakfast:* Fall Creek Bakery, 881 East Thirteenth Avenue. (503) 484–1662. A bakery noted for its coffee and delectable cinnamon rolls.

Take Highway 126 east to Forty-second Avenue; turn south and follow the signs toward Jasper. You're on the Jasper-Lowell Road, which runs beside the Middle Fork of the Willamette River, passing woodlands, farms, and forested areas. At the turnoff to Fall Creek, turn left and make the first right. This is **Pengra Bridge,** closed to both car and foot traffic.

Continue for 4.5 miles to the **Unity Bridge.** (If you want to snack, the I & M Falls Creek Market is on the way.) The covered bridge, near the town of Lowell, is still used. Travel through the bridge and continue straight for 3 miles to Highway 58 and **Lowell Bridge.**

When it was built in 1945, Lowell was the widest bridge in the nation, with a 24-foot roadway. Turn right on Highway 58 toward Dexter and **Parvin Bridge,** now bypassed with a new road beside it. You can walk on this rather dilapidated remnant of times past, in an area where clearcut hills are also silent reminders of human influence.

On Highway 58 it's 21 miles back to Eugene and I-5. You'll pass several parks along the way, including the large and well-kept **Elijah Bristow State Park.** With wide, grassy fields, paths through the trees, and picnic areas, it's a popular gathering place for groups (permits required for groups; phone 503–686–7592).

Turn south on I–5 and drive about 15 miles to Cottage Grove (exit 174). Take Row River Road east through farmlands and hills, some logged off, some mantled in green. At Layng Road, 4 miles from Cottage Grove, turn right to see **Currin Bridge.** The colorful, barn-red bridge was built in 1925 over the Row River and is no longer in use.

Continue on Row River Road to **Dorena Lake,** a reservoir popular for boating, fishing, water skiing, and windsurfing. This loop drive circles the 5-mile-long lake. On the lakeshore side of the road, you'll see **Harms Park,** a county park with a boat launch.

At the far end of the lake is **Dorena Bridge.** This 105-foot bridge was built in 1949 to replace a steel span that was worn down by logging trucks. No longer in use, it stands quietly, white paint peeling, in the midst of mixed forest and hills shorn of their trees. Plans are now underway to develop the site as a rest stop.

Now turn right to travel along the south side of Dorena Lake, turning left at Garoutte Road. After 2.5 miles, driving through mossy oak and maple groves, old orchards, and hills cloaked with blackberry vines, you'll come to **Stewart Bridge,** where Garoutte Road meets Mosby Creek Road. The white bridge, no longer used by vehicles, was built of Douglas fir in 1930. It has curved cornice brackets where the front walls meet the roof and inside railings designed to protect the trusses from being scraped by trucks.

Make a right turn on Mosby Creek Road and travel beside the creek to Layng Road. A few yards to the right is **Mosby Creek Bridge.** Constructed in 1920, it's the oldest standing covered bridge in Lane County and is still in use today. Drive over the wooden planks, through the narrow bridge. There's a small turnaround spot on the other side.

Return to Mosby Creek Road and drive the remaining 2 miles to **Cottage Grove.** This pleasant little town at the southern end of the Willamette Valley has a river running through the downtown core area, a **pioneer museum,** and several **parks** and historic landmarks. There's one more bridge to visit on this tour.

*Lunch:* **Covered Bridge Restaurant,**  401 Main Street, Cottage Grove. (503) 942–1255. Downtown restaurant serving salads and sandwiches for lunch, continental cuisine after 5:00 P.M.

## Afternoon

Stroll from the restaurant to **Centennial Bridge,** unique among covered bridges. Walkways to the bridge are of bricks marked with the names of the Cottage Grove citizens who contributed to the cost of building the bridge in 1987, in honor of the town's centennial year. Centennial Bridge preserves parts of three older bridges that spanned Mosby Creek, the North Fork Siuslaw River, and Row River. When you walk across the bridge, stop at the windows to view the river and the town from an unusual perspective.

The **Cottage Grove Historical Museum,** housed in a historic Catholic church, displays items of pioneer home and farm life, along with mining tools from the Bohemia Mining District. The church itself is interesting to visit; its outstanding features are the Italian stained glass windows and the building's shape. It is said to be the only octagonal public building in the Pacific Northwest.

Stop in at **Studio Caffe** on South Sixth for a good cup of espresso and a look around the art gallery on the premises. The friendly cafe also serves sandwiches, soups, and salads.

Next door is Past 45 Arts & Crafts, a shop selling items handcrafted by local senior citizens. This is the place to pick up a birdhouse or crocheted baby clothes.

Return to I–5 and head north to Portland.

# There's More

**Bridges.** (a sampling; there are many more)

Chambers Bridge, South River Road, Cottage Grove. High and angular, with a metal roof, this railroad bridge was built for log trains and last used in the late 1950s.

Gallon House, Highway 214, Silverton. An 84-foot bridge built in 1917 and still in active use. Supposedly named during Prohibition years for a nearby house where bootleg whiskey was sold by the gallon.

Goodpasture Bridge, Highway 126, McKenzie River. Probably the most photographed bridge in Oregon, this handsome white structure, built in 1938, stands over the McKenzie River, surrounded by cedar and spruce forests.

Jordan Bridge, Stayton. This 1937 bridge, which formerly spanned Thomas Creek, was disassembled, moved, and rebuilt by private citizens between Pioneer and Wilderness parks. It was dedicated at the new site in 1988.

Short Bridge, Cascadia State Park on Santiam River, U.S. Highway 20. The first bridge on the site was built in 1845 and was rebuilt several times. This one dates from 1945.

Swinging Bridge, a footbridge between South River Road and Madison Street in Cottage Grove. Workers in the late 1920s used the bridge to get between west and east Cottage Grove. It was rebuilt after high water damage in 1965.

**Champoeg State Park.** Historic, 615-acre park bordering the Willamette River, about 20 miles south of Portland off I–5. Once a Kalapooya Indian village, then the site where settlers met in 1843 to create the first organized government in the Pacific Northwest. Interpretive center, restored pioneer home, log cabin museum.

**Golf.** Emerald Valley Golf Course, Creswell. (503) 895–2174. Eighteenhole course, pro shop, restaurant.

Hidden Valley Golf Course, Cottage Grove. (503) 942–3046. Ninehole course, pro shop, restaurant.

**Georgia-Pacific Forestry Research Center.** 76928 Mosby Creek Road, Cottage Grove. (503) 942–5516. Five acres of greenhouses where trees are grown, fostered, and shipped—ten million a year. Tours available.

**Parks.** Baker Bay State Park, Dorena Lake. Campsites, boat rentals. (503) 942–7669.

McKercher Park, 1 mile downstream from Crawfordsville Bridge, is a good picnic spot.

Roaring River Park, ½ mile past Larwood County Park. County park with walking paths to the river, open lawns, group picnic areas. Fish hatchery nearby.

**Ponderosa Vineyards,** 39538 Griggs Drive, Lebanon. (503) 259–3845. Tasting room open on Sunday afternoons in summer.

# Special Events

**Mid-May.** Linn County Lamb and Wool Fair, Scio. 4-H sheep competition, sheepdog trials, crafts booths.

**Early June.** Lebanon Strawberry Festival, Lebanon. Carnival, parade with Strawberry Queen, strawberry shortcake.

**Mid-July.** Bohemia Mining Days, Cottage Grove. Grand Miners parade, Prospectors Breakfast, 5-kilometer walk/run.

**September.** State Covered Bridge Festival, Roaring River Park. Country fair in park near Scio and Larwood Bridge.

# Other Recommended Restaurants and Lodgings

## Scio

The Wesely House Bed-and-Breakfast, 38791 Highway 226. (503) 394–3210. Restored historic home in the Willamette Valley countryside, with two rooms and full breakfast.

## Cottage Grove

The Cottage, 2915 Row River Road. (503) 942–3091. Lunch and dinner served in an open, light atmosphere with natural woods and vine-covered patio. Extensive menu.

Lily of the Field Bed-and-Breakfast, P.O. Box 831, 35722 Ross Lane, Cerro Gordo. (503) 942–2049. Two-room B&B on a wooded hill over looking Dorena Lake. Fresh country-style furnishings, natural woods, big windows. Full breakfast.

The Village Green, 725 Row River Road. (503) 942–2491 or (800) 343–ROOM. Best Western motel with swimming pool, restaurants, tennis courts, lovely gardens. Wheelchair access.

Eugene (For more information on Eugene, see Portland Escape Three.)

Campus Cottage 1136 East Nineteenth Street. (503) 342–5346. Bed-and-breakfast in a 1920s home. Three rooms furnished with country-sophisticate flair. Full breakfast.

Eugene Hilton, 66 East Sixth Avenue. (503) 342–2000 or (800) 937–6660. Bustling downtown hotel with all the amenities: modern rooms, indoor pool, sauna, Jacuzzi, restaurants. Convenient to Hult Center and convention center.

Best Western New Oregon Motel, 1655 Franklin Boulevard. (503) 683–3669. Ground-level rooms recently remodeled. Indoor pool, racquet ball, Jacuzzi.

Pookie's Bed 'n Breakfast, 2013 Charnelton Street. (503) 343–0383. Well-landscaped 1918 home in residential area. Period furnishings, tranquil atmosphere, two upstairs rooms. Full breakfast.

# For More Information

Covered Bridge Society of Oregon, 3940 Courtney Lane SE, Salem, OR 97302.

The Linn County Covered Bridge Association, P.O. Box 402, Scio, OR 97374. (503) 394–2052 or 394–2684.

Eugene-Springfield Convention and Visitors' Bureau, 305 West Seventh Avenue, Eugene, OR 97401. (503) 484–5307 or (800) 547–5445.

Cottage Grove Chamber of Commerce, 710 Row River Road, Cottage Grove, OR 97424. (503) 942–2411.

# Columbia River Gorge: Oregon

Multnomah Falls drops 620 feet from a sheer cliff in the Columbia River Gorge.

## A National Scenic Treasure

_____ 1 NIGHT _____

National Scenic Area • Waterfalls • Wildflowers
Woodland trails • River and mountain views • Bonneville Dam
Orchards • Sailboarding • Wineries

Nature was more than generous in lavishing scenic beauty on the Pacific Northwest. The Columbia River Gorge, with its thick green forests, rocky bluffs, rushing streams, and misty waterfalls, is a spectacular example. Much of the gorge is a federally designated National Scenic Area.

The broad Columbia divides northern Oregon from southern Washington as it slices through the Cascade Mountains on its way to the sea. Streams rush into the river from the foothills of Mount Hood, on their journey from melting snow to waterfalls to tumbling creeks to the river and the sea.

On either side, sheer basaltic cliffs reveal a geologic history of earthshaking violence: rock that twisted like taffy under the onslaught of ancient floods, lava casts where trees fell before streams of molten lava, gaping holes where hillsides slid into the river.

This getaway immerses you in natural splendor. You'll walk forested trails to overlooks and waterfalls, watch boaters and sail-boarders (or join them), taste Northwest cuisine, and tour the largest dam on the river.

# Day 1

## Morning

Pack a picnic lunch (or plan to eat at Multnomah Falls Lodge), drive east from Portland on I–84 to Troutdale (about thirty minutes), and take the **Scenic Highway** exit. The historic road, much of it edged with moss-covered stone walls, cuts into riverside cliffs for 24 miles. Built in 1915, the road rises from river level to **Crown Point,** a basalt ledge jutting 720 feet above the Columbia. Stop here for one of the most romantic views in the world—a panoply of forest, moun-tains, and sky, with the mighty river glistening far below. **Vista House,** perched atop Crown Point, is a circular stone structure built in 1918 as a monument to pioneers. It contains information about the gorge and has a gift shop selling local handicrafts.

Continue 2.4 miles on the Scenic Highway to **Latourell Falls,** where a 2-mile trail curves up through ferns and mossy undergrowth to the 100-foot cascade. Lichens grow a brilliant yellow-green against rock walls. Hawks, crows, songbirds, and sometimes eagles soar over-head, while scolding squirrels scamper underfoot.

East from Latourell on the Scenic Highway, make a brief stop at **Shepherd's Dell.** Here a ¼-mile paved path, edged with a curving, mossy rock wall, descends to expose the spraying tiers of a stream not visible from the road.

The next stop is **Bridal Veil Falls State Park,** fifteen acres of foot-paths and camas meadows on an open bluff above the river. Interpre-tive signs explain how Indians and pioneers dug the bulbs of the sky blue camas flowers and dried and baked them for winter food.

The park has picnic tables and rest rooms and a fenced, paved trail, accessible to wheelchairs, that loops along the bluff. The views of the river and across it to the immense basalt columns called the **Pillars of Hercules** are stunning.

An easy ⅔-mile walk takes you to an observation platform under a canopy of alder and maple trees, where you can see **Bridal Veil Falls,** a double cascade of dancing white water.

*Lunch:* Picnic in Bridal Veil Falls State Park.

## Afternoon

Continue east on the Scenic Highway, passing lovely **Wahkeena Falls** as you proceed to **Multnomah Falls,** a shimmering, 620-foot ribbon of spray that is the second highest waterfall in the United States.

Indian legend says that long ago a chief's daughter plunged over the cliff above the falls as a human sacrifice to save her tribe from a devastating plague. Sometimes, people say, when the wind blows through the waterfall, you can see the shape of a maiden in the mist.

For an eagle's-eye view of the Columbia, hike up the paved trail to the fenced platform perched at the top of the falls (about 1 mile). The dizzying, over-the-edge view is what the legendary Indian princess saw.

Rather than heading back down on the paved route, take the main trail into the woods along **Multnomah Falls Creek.** Then follow well-marked **Perdition Trail;** it will give you a two-hour walk through the ferny forest, over streams, and across a ridge to the top of Wahkeena Falls.

Along the trail are picturesque staircases, quaint bridges, and breathtaking glimpses of the river. To the north, on the Washington side, you'll see the snowy slopes of **Mount Adams** and **Mount St. Helens.** At Wahkeena, take the path downward toward the road, and connect with the final ¼-mile segment of the walk, which will lead you back to your car at Multnomah Falls.

(If you did not bring a picnic, order lunch in **Multnomah Falls Lodge.** This may be the only place in the world where you can sip a huckleberry daiquiri as you relax in a glass-enclosed lounge and gaze up at a waterfall as high as a sixty-story building.)

Your next stop is **Oneonta Gorge Botanical Area.** In summer, you can walk upstream in a cool, narrow canyon, which ends at a waterfall. Fifty species of wildflowers, shrubs, and trees grow in this fragile habitat; six grow nowhere else.

Just beyond Oneonta is **Horsetail Falls,** and then **Ainsworth State Park,** where the Scenic Highway ends.

If this is a day trip, you may decide at this point to head back to Portland on I–84.

To continue exploring the gorge, travel eastward on I–84 and stop at **Bonneville Dam,** the oldest and largest hydroelectric project on the Columbia. Open daily for tours, the dam has a visitors' center with exhibits that explain the structure's operation. Underwater windows view fish ladders, so you can watch migrating salmon on their way back to native spawning grounds.

A mile east of the huge dam is **Eagle Creek Trail,** probably the most scenic in the gorge. As the fir needle–strewn path climbs and twists along steep cliffs, Eagle Creek tumbles beside and then below it, bouncing over boulders on its way to the river. Next to the trail are high cliffs, where thick, spongy moss drips showers of silver.

Two miles in from the trailhead you'll come to **Punchbowl Falls.** There's a viewing point above this lovely deep pool, and a short spur path leads down to its pebbled shore. From a rocky cleft, the falls plummet into the pool, while ferns clinging to the cliffs around it tremble in the mist. The stream plunges northward in a broad cascade at Punchbowl's wider end.

You can either make this your turnaround point, thereby retracing your route back down the Eagle Creek Trail, or continue another 4 miles to **Tunnel Falls.** Such a hike (12 miles round trip) would obviously take much of the day and mean excluding some of the other suggested walks.

At Tunnel Falls, another impressive waterfall, you'll pass through a 25-foot-long tunnel cut into the cliff. Eagle Creek Trail continues to **Wahtum Lake,** 14 miles in from the highway; it's an all-day hike.

When you return to your car and are back on I–84, drive east another 22 miles to the **Hood River Valley.** On the dry side of the Cascade Range, the valley's orchards produce fruit for world markets. In spring, Hood River's apple, pear, and cherry trees provide a glorious display of bloom. Mount Hood, mantled in glaciers, rises steeply behind them on the southwest, while northward across the river Mount Adams and Mount St. Helens are snowy sentinels against the sky.

Dozens of roadside stands sell fresh fruit and cider in the fall, and all year the area's wineries are open for tours and tastings.

Take Exit 62 from I–84, and curve around toward the imposing yellow stucco inn that stands on a precipice high above the river. The **Columbia Gorge Hotel** is a fine place to relax with a drink in the **Valentino Lounge.** The historic hotel, built in 1921, hearkens back to the Jazz Age in its furnishings and decor. Adjoining the hotel is **Hood River Vineyards'** tasting room and art gallery, where you can sample local wines.

Continue on I–84 to the next exit, which will take you into downtown Hood River and your hotel.

*Dinner:* **Stonehedge Inn,** 3405 Cascade Drive, Hood River. (503) 386–3940. Once a summer home with lovely gardens; now a fine restaurant with a classic Continental menu.

*Lodging:* **Hood River Hotel,** 102 Oak Street, Hood River, OR 97031. (503) 386–1900. Recently restored 1910 hotel in the heart of town. European ambience, warm hospitality, charming period decor in thirty-two rooms and nine spacious suites.

# Day 2

## Morning

*Breakfast:* Hood River Hotel restaurant.

After the preceding day's vigorous activity, this is a slower-paced morning for exploring Hood River and its peaceful valley. Start with the visitors' center in **Port Marina Park,** which has information on area attractions.

The **Hood River County Historical Museum** (open Wednesday–Sunday, April through October) is also in Port Marina Park and holds intriguing displays of Native American artifacts and relics from early settlement days.

The park has swimming and boating facilities and is a good place to watch **sailboarders** skim over the waves. On a clear, windy day hundreds of the brilliantly colored sails dot the river. Hood River, widely considered the "sailboarding capital of the world," draws fans of the sport from around the country. The best spot for close-up views of sailboarders is Hood River Event Site, at the north end of Second Street. The site, under development for sailboarding events, has a rigging area and bleachers. Other good viewing sites are the West Jetty and Rushton Park, west of the Columbia Gorge Hotel.

If you want to try sailboarding, several shops in Hood River rent equipment and provide a variety of lesson packages.

Drive up to **Panorama Point** (the turnoff is just south of town on Route 35) for a memorable view of the valley and Mount Hood. The view is most striking in spring, when the orchards are frothy with pink and white blossoms. Five miles south of Hood River, at the Odell turnoff on Route 35, is **River Bend Farm and Country Store**, 2363 Tucker Road (800–755–7568). Country gifts and gourmet foods are sold in a quaint setting.

*Lunch:* **Tugboat Annie's,** 1100 East Marine Way. (503) 386–7999. Seafood, hamburgers, tasty fries. At water's edge, with river views.

## Afternoon

Check the shops of Hood River, watch the sailboarders, fish, golf, or just relax on the beach.

You might take a self-guided tour of the **Hood River Brewing Company,** 506 Columbia Street (503–386–2281), and watch traditional brewing techniques. Taste locally brewed, hand-crafted Full Sail Ale in the adjacent **White Cap Pub,** which overlooks the Columbia River.

Head westward on I–84, perhaps stopping at **Three Rivers Winery,** 275 Country Club Road (503–386–5453). (If you've chosen to play golf this afternoon, just follow Country Club Road north from the golf course.) The winery's tasting room, in a turn-of-the-century home, is open daily. There's a deli, too.

If you're feeling ambitious and the cool forests and waterfalls of the gorge look inviting, hike one of the dozens of trails that wind from the road up to Mount Hood's lower slopes. Or continue on into Portland.

## There's More

**Cascade Salmon Hatchery,** near Eagle Creek campground.

**Swimming and picnicking,** at pools of Eagle Creek.

**Mount Hood Railroad,** 110 Railroad Avenue, Hood River, OR 97031. (503) 386–3556. Old-fashioned train excursions (summer only) through Hood River Valley on the Fruit Blossom Special. Dining car, restored historic depot, children's photos with the engineer—and free rides on your birthday.

**Hood River Golf Course.** Scenic, 9-hole public course 5 miles southwest of Hood River.

**Cascade Locks.** A park and museum are located on the site of the river locks that were used for river navigation before Bonneville Dam inundated the rapids. (See Portland Escape Four for more information.)

## Special Events

**Mid-April.** Blossom Festival, Hood River Valley. Arts-and-crafts fairs, dinners, orchard tours, train rides.

**Mid-July.** Gorge Blowout, Hood River. Open water, 20-mile sailboard race. International competition.

**Late August.** Apple Jam, Hood River. Music festival in Port Marina Park by the Columbia River.

**Late October.** Harvest Fest, Hood River Valley. Two days of entertainment, crafts sales, freshly baked goods, fresh produce.

**Day after Thanksgiving.** Light Up the Gorge!, Columbia Gorge Hotel. Historic hotel illuminates grounds for the holidays with more than 65,000 lights.

## Other Recommended Restaurants and Lodgings

### Bridal Veil

Bridal Veil Lodge, Scenic Highway. (503) 695–2333; in Portland,

284–8901. Bed-and-breakfast home, built in the 1920s, across the road from Bridal Veil Falls State Park. Two cozy rooms in knotty pine, shared bath. Full breakfast.

### Hood River

Lakecliff Estate, 3820 Westcliff Drive. (503) 386–7000. Former grand summer home, now on National Register of Historic Places, has four rooms with forest or river views. Full breakfast included.

State Street Inn, 1005 State Street. (503) 386–1899. Classic English home on a hillside in residential Hood River. Clean, bright, stylish, friendly. Full breakfast.

Columbia Gorge Hotel, 4000 Westcliff Drive. (503) 386–5566; outside Oregon, (800) 345–1921; within Oregon, (800) 826–4027. Classic country inn with forty-two rooms, 1920s motif, and river view. Full farm breakfast included. Dining room open to public.

### Troutdale

Tad's Chicken 'n Dumplings, on Crown Point Highway, a mile east of Troutdale, overlooking the Sandy River. Popular for its country cooking and fried chicken. (503) 666–5337.

## For More Information

To learn more about the attractions of the Columbia River Gorge, see Portland Escape Four and Portland Escape Eight.

Hiking trail maps available ($2.00) from U.S. Forest Service, 319 Southwest Pine Street, Portland, OR 97204.

Hood River Valley Visitors Council, Port Marina Park, Hood River, OR 97031. (503) 386–2000 or (800) 366–3530.

# Columbia River Gorge: Washington

The three-story bastion at Fort Vancouver National Historic Site.

## Riverside Discoveries

### 2 NIGHTS

Fort Vancouver replica • Scenic wilderness • Waterfalls • Columbia River
Bonneville Dam • Hot Springs • Historical museum
Art museum • White-water river rafting

Here's a three-day getaway that's filled with variety: It provides glimpses of Northwest history, spectacular views of the Columbia River Gorge, two intriguing museums, hot mineral baths, a brisk hike, a ride on a river raft, and a fish's-eye view of the world.

## Day 1

### Morning

Cross the Interstate Bridge into Washington and take I–5 to exit 1C

(Mill Plain); follow the signs to **Fort Vancouver National Historic Site.**

The huge fort, headquarters for Hudson's Bay Company in the mid-1800s, has been partially reconstructed. Pass through the gates of the log stockade and you're on the spot where a major settlement bustled 150 years ago. Trappers and traders, blacksmiths and bakers worked at this British outpost above the river, overseen by the indomitable Dr. John McLoughlin. You can still hear the ring of the blacksmith's anvil and smell the freshly baked bread, for volunteers often demonstrate the old skills. In one corner stands the three-story bastion. The original was built in 1845 to protect the stockade—not from Indian threats, but from hostile Americans. Up the hill from the fort is a **visitors' center** and excellent **museum.** The fort and museum are open from 9:30 A.M. to 4:00 P.M. daily except holidays (206–696–7618).

Drive east on State Route 14 into the prehistoric past, where ancient basaltic cliffs rise above the shores of the **Columbia River.** On the Oregon side of the wide river, streaming waterfalls cascade from rocky ledges and hanging valleys. Driving the Washington route gives you a different perspective on the beauty of the National Scenic Area.

At **Beacon Rock,** a 900-foot lava monolith, climb the winding trail to the top for a glorious view of fields, forests, cliffs, and river. The trail is fenced much of the way.

Descend Beacon Rock, and continue east to **Bonneville Dam.** Just west of the Second Powerhouse is **Fort Cascades National Historic Landmark,** where a kiosk bears information about the site. One of the largest Native American villages on the river once thrived here, and the old Oregon Trail and the Lewis and Clark Trail converged at this point. There are some good walking paths in the area.

At the dam, see working models of the awesome energy producer, learn about the river's formation, and, in the underwater fish-viewing room, watch salmon swim the ladders as they work their way upstream.

From Bonneville drive on to **Stevenson.** This hillside town above the river has been the seat of Skamania County government since 1893. In an earlier day, riverboats docked in Stevenson for cordwood, used to power the steamships.

*Lunch*: **Skamania Lodge**, Route 14 west of Stevenson. (509) 427–7700. Outstanding regional cuisine in a beautiful setting with views of the Columbia River Gorge. Reservations suggested.

## Afternoon

Down the slope from Skamania Lodge, the **Columbia Gorge Interpretive Center** is scheduled to open in 1994 and will feature a showcase of materials on the natural and cultural history of the gorge. After touring the center, drive into Stevenson and see the **Skamania County Historical Museum,** located in the basement of the Courthouse Annex (509–427–5141). Open every day except holidays, the museum is filled with intriguing pioneer and Indian relics, plus a few unexpected treasures, such as the world's largest collection of rosaries.

Donald A. Brown spent decades collecting the rosaries. There are now 4,000, including the rosary used by John F. Kennedy in World War II, housed in a room that glitters like a jewel box. No matter what your religious beliefs, the display is enthralling.

Continue east to **Carson Hot Mineral Springs Resort.** This hotel on the Wind River dates back to the turn of the century. Rooms are spartan-simple, with lavatories (one for men, one for women) down the hall. There are also a few housekeeping cabins.

There's a golf course on the property, but the resort's major appeal, and all its luxury, lies in the bathhouses. After a blissful soak in steaming-hot mineral water, and perhaps a soothing massage, you understand why this out-of-the-way spot has so many devotees.

It's about 20 miles from Carson east to **Bingen** and, on the hills above it, **White Salmon,** a small town with a pseudo-Bavarian theme. Drive north on State Route 141 for 6 miles, and check in at your lodgings on Oak Ridge Road. Then continue 8 more miles to a well-deserved, relaxing evening meal in the shadow of 12,276-foot **Mount Adams.**

Mount Adams, a broad, snowcapped peak that is part of the Cascade chain, is a recreational wonderland, with miles of hiking and biking trails; fields of huckleberries, blueberries, and wildflowers; and cross-country ski trails. Lesser-known than its sisters, Mount St. Helens and Mount Hood, Mount Adams is an ideal getaway for wilderness seclusion, mountain climbing, and photography.

*Dinner:* **Serenity's Restaurant,** Route 141 (1 mile south of Trout Lake). (509) 395–2500. Dinners nightly, featuring homemade breads, salad bar, seafood, prime rib, chicken. Outstanding food, attractive setting, views of Mount Adams.

*Lodging:* **Orchard Hill Inn,** Route 2, Box 130, White Salmon, WA 98672. (509) 493–3024. A secluded homestead on wooded acreage above the White Salmon River. Three guest rooms plus a bunkhouse that sleeps six.

# Day 2

## Morning

*Breakfast:* At Orchard Hill Inn, Pam and James Tindall serve a plentiful continental breakfast: muffins, yogurt, pâté, cheeses, cinnamon rolls.

Drive north on Route 141 through farming and wooded country to B.Z. Corner, the headquarters of **Phil's Guide Service,** Route 1, Box 552, White Salmon, WA 98672 (509–493–2641). Experienced guides will take you for a three-hour rafting trip on the **White Salmon River.** The White Salmon, which flows south from Mount Adams to the Columbia, is one of the best white-water rivers in the Northwest, with numerous riffles and cascades, and it's surrounded with scenic beauty. You'll encounter Class 2, 3, and 4 rapids all the way on this exciting ride.

*Lunch:* **Fidel's,** 120 East Steuben Street, Bingen. (509) 493–1017. Good, reliable Mexican fare served in large portions.

## Afternoon

Drive east again on Route 14, traveling through the spare, dry hills above the river, on the eastern side of the Cascade Range. In about 30 miles you'll see against an isolated hillside a replica of England's **Stonehenge.** The monument was built by railroad magnate Sam Hill as a memorial to those who lost their lives in World War I. It's open to the public.

Three miles farther is **Maryhill Museum of Art,** a palatial building perched in lonely splendor on a high, open bluff. A tour of Sam Hill's "Castle on the Columbia" is a must. It has fine displays of Indian baskets, antique chess sets, art glass, artifacts given by Queen Marie of Romania, and much more. Concerts are held here periodically.

Tasty box lunches are sold at Maryhill Museum, if you decide on a picnic.

From Maryhill, turn north on Route 97 to **Goldendale,** passing through valleys, irrigated farmlands, and rolling hills of wheat, with snowcapped mountains rising in the distance. In Goldendale, look for the **Presby Mansion,** 127 West Broadway. The twenty-room home, built in 1902, is now the **Klickitat County Historical Museum,** with fine examples of furnishings used during one hundred years of settlement in the area (open daily except Monday).

Nine miles north of Goldendale, deep in the pine-forested Simcoe Mountains, is **Three Creeks Lodge.**

*Dinner:* Three Creeks Lodge. A glass-walled dining room surrounded by trees overlooks wild, rushing creeks.

*Lodging:* Three Creeks Lodge, 2120 Highway 97 Satus Pass, Goldendale, WA 98620. (509) 773–4026. Cedar chalets among the trees are equipped with elaborately carved furniture, fireplaces, and kitchens. Several have outside hot tubs.

# Day 3

## Morning

*Breakfast:* Midweek, a complimentary continental breakfast is served. On weekends, order from the restaurant menu.

Return to Goldendale and buy lunch-to-go at **Neva's** on East Main (509–773–6488). Homemade soups, sandwiches, and salads are available. You can also purchase picnic goods at the Sentry Market on Columbus or the Sub Shop on Main Street.

Drive northeast through the dry, rolling **Horse Heaven Hills** to Bickleton, a tiny hamlet with fewer than one hundred people and the title of Bluebird Capital of the World. Townsfolk have placed trim white-and-blue birdhouses on almost every fence post in the area, attracting flocks of rare mountain bluebirds. You're likely to see other wildlife, too, in this thinly populated, hilly country. Hawks, eagles, pheasant, quail, chukar, partridges, deer, bobcat, and even cougar live here.

Drive south from Bickleton to Roosevelt, on the banks of the Columbia River. The county park here has a playground, swimming area, and overnight camping facilities.

*Lunch:* Picnic in county park.

You're back at the Columbia River Gorge again, where you'll turn west on Route 14 for the return trip along the river to Portland—125 miles.

# There's More

**Goldendale Observatory State Park.** Stargaze at an observatory that has the nation's largest telescope available for public viewing. The best viewing time is around the new moon or when the moon sets early or rises late. Open April–September, Wednesday through Sunday. Call for hours: (509) 773–3141.

**Horseback riding.** At Three Creeks Lodge, Goldendale, you have two choices:

Frank Hill keeps horses on the lodge property and offers guided, 2-mile trips on nearby trails.

Ray Mitchell, White Eagle Expeditions, 401 Ekone Ranch Road, Goldendale, WA 98620. (509) 773–4277 or 773–3891 (or make arrangements through Three Creeks Lodge). Ray takes riders on day rides or pack trips in the Horse Heaven Hills and provides all equipment except sleeping bags. Family and group rates available.

**Klickitat Canyon.** High, scenic canyon road between Trout Lake and Goldendale. Waterfall, views of Mount Adams.

**Whoop-n-Holler Ranch,** south of Bickleton. This private museum holds an impressive collection of antique cars, horsedrawn vehicles, and two buildings full of pioneer tools. There are picnic tables and swings. The museum is open May through fall, by appointment. (509) 896–2344.

# Special Events

**July.** Columbia Gorge Bluegrass Festival, Stevenson.
**August.** Skamania County Fair and Timber Carnival, Stevenson.
**Late September.** Huckleberry Festival, White Salmon and Bingen. Celebrates the wild huckleberries on nearby Mount Adams. Berry feasts, barbecued salmon dinners, square dancing, Indian dance performances, country-and-western music.

# Other Recommended Restaurants and Lodgings

## Carson

Carson Mineral Springs Resort, P.O. Box 370. (509) 427–8292. Simple lodge rooms share baths. Some housekeeping cabins available.

## Glenwood

The Flying L Ranch, Route 2, Box 28. (509) 364–3488. Country resort and lodge on 160 acres near Mount Adams. Eleven rooms plus two cottages. Nature trails, cross-country skiing, art workshops. Full breakfast included.

## Stevenson

Skamania Lodge, P.O. Box 189. (509) 427–7700 or (800) 221–7117. Handsome new inn designed in keeping with the natural environment. Suites, ballrooms, fitness center, swimming pool, tennis courts, 18-hole golf course. Exceptional restaurant.

## Trout Lake

Mio Amore Pensione, P.O. Box 208. (509) 395–2264. Three well-furnished rooms in Victorian bed-and-breakfast home; separate Ice House cabin. Full breakfast included; gourmet dinners available.

# For More Information

Skamania County Chamber of Commerce, P.O. Box 759, Stevenson, WA 98648. (509) 427–8911.

Mount Adams Chamber of Commerce, P.O. Box 449, White Salmon, WA 98672. (509) 493–3630.

Goldendale Chamber of Commerce, P.O. Box 524, Goldendale, WA 98620. (509) 773–3400.

# Oregon Wine Country

Vineyards in the Tualatin Valley, one of Oregon's wine-producing regions.

## Willamette Valley and Tualatin Valley

———————————— 1 NIGHT ————————————

Vineyards · Pastoral countryside · Wine tastings
Museum · Orchards · Fine dining · Antiques

Oregon's Willamette and Tualatin valleys, with a climate similar to the great European wine-growing regions of Burgundy, Champagne, and the Rhine Valley, continue to produce outstanding, award-winning wines. The numerous wineries are usually open for tours and tastings.

This two-day journey takes you through rolling farmlands, fruit- and nut-laden orchards, and acres of vineyards. You'll stop along the way to glimpse Oregon history, visit art galleries and antiques shops, purchase fresh produce, enjoy a picnic, and check the new wine releases. If your party plans on wine-tasting, you'll want to select a designated driver for the tour. Make it a leisurely journey, perhaps passing by some of the wineries suggested in order to fully enjoy the experience.

# Day 1

## Morning

Pack a picnic lunch, and drive west from Portland on U.S. Route 26 to the 185th Street exit. Turn right on 185th, then right again on Springville Road, to Portland Community College. On the campus is the **Washington County Museum,** where you can learn about the area's history, from the Atfalati Indians through nineteenth-century settlement to today's high-tech industries.

Back on Route 26, travel west to the Jackson Road exit, turn south on Jackson, and turn right on Old Scotch Church Road. This will take you to a bonny white church that dates from 1878. Set in a grassy pioneer graveyard under tall fir trees, with farmland around it, the **Old Scotch Church** (Tualatin Plains Presbyterian) is a charming example of the appeal of rural Oregon.

Joseph Meek, one of the founders of the first government in the West, is buried in the graveyard. The church is open from 9:00 A.M. to noon Wednesday through Friday, for Sunday morning services, and at other times by arrangement.

After paying obeisance to a pioneer heritage, turn to present-day pleasures: wine tasting at **Tualatin Vineyards,** on Seavy Road (503–357–5005). It's open from noon to 5:00 P.M. on weekends and from 10:00 A.M. to 4:00 P.M. on weekdays. Get there by following Route 26 (also called the Sunset Highway) to State Route 6. There are signs to the winery along the way, and the visitors association can provide you with a map.

The vineyards, spread across eighty-five acres on the slopes above the Tualatin Valley, have at their center a winery with a spacious tasting room and a picnic area overlooking the valley. In the fall, the vines, orchards, and maple groves are brilliant with color.

Follow Route 6 to turn south on Route 8, where signs direct you through the rolling green countryside to **Shafer Vineyard Cellars,** Star Route, Box 269, Forest Grove (503–357–6604). Shafer, open weekend afternoons, serves pinot noir, chardonnay, riesling, gewürztraminer, and sauvignon wines.

Its first wine was produced in 1978. Since then, Shafer has received several awards, including the gold medal for its 1982 chardonnay at the American Wine Competition in New York.

*Lunch:* Picnic at Shafer Vineyard.

## Afternoon

Continue now on Route 8 to David Hill Road and turn right to **Laurel Ridge Winery** (503–359–5436). It's open daily except major holidays, from noon to 5:00 P.M. Set on one of the oldest vineyard sites in Oregon, Laurel Ridge overlooks the farms of Tualatin Valley, backed by the green Tualatin Mountains. It produces sparkling wines in the *champenoise* method.

After your wine tasting, head south toward **Forest Grove,** a pleasant college town with tree-shaded sidewalks. **Pacific University,** 2043 College Way, was founded in 1850 by Congregational settlers from New England. The centerpiece of its attractive campus is stately **Old College Hall,** which is listed on the National Register of Historic Places. A museum in part, it can be toured weekday afternoons during the school year and on weekends in summer by appointment (503–357–6151, extension 2455). The hall holds Indian and pioneer artifacts and, in the Oriental Room, items reflecting the missionary spirit that founded Pacific University. Intriguing memorabilia from China, Japan, Turkey, India, and Africa are on display.

Leaving Forest Grove, drive south on Route 47 for 2½ miles to Dilley, where you'll turn right and ascend a hill to **Montinore Vineyards.** Tastings and tours are offered in one of Oregon's newest and largest wineries. Most production is devoted to pinot noir, pinot gris, and chardonnay wines.

Return to Route 47 and the hamlet of Gaston. South of Gaston, take Olson Road, off Route 47, to visit **Elk Cove** and **Kramer,** neighboring vineyards. Elk Cove holds a riesling festival each Memorial Day weekend and a Labor Day pinot noir picnic. Visitors are welcome.

Continue south on 47 through Carlton and on to join U.S. 99W. Turn right to head south into McMinnville and your lodgings.

*Dinner:* **Nick's Italian Cafe,** 521 East Third Street, McMinnville. (503) 434–4471. Outstanding Italian dinners. Brick walls, informal atmosphere. One of the region's best restaurants.

*Lodging:* **Steiger Haus,** 360 Wilson Street. (503) 472–0821. Lovely bed-and-breakfast with five rooms in country pine and wicker. Near downtown and college campus. Full breakfast served.

# Day 2

## Morning

*Breakfast:* Steiger House provides a full breakfast that often includes local fruits and berries.

Return to downtown McMinnville for a tour of the historic district, where the tallest building is four stories high. The chamber of commerce provides maps for self-guided walking tours. The little town, once you've left the commercial highway sprawl, has the nostalgic atmosphere of small-town America. There are pleasant parks, tree-shaded sidewalks, shops, and cafes. It's the county seat and the home of **Linfield College**, founded in 1855. See **Pioneer Hall** on the green and leafy campus; it's a local landmark.

In a local shop you may see packages of gourmet candies. They're made locally by the monks in the Brigittine Monastery in Amity. You owe yourself a taste of the chocolate fudge.

**Arterberry Winery Cellars,** 905 Southeast Tenth Avenue, produces wines from grapes grown in the red hills of Dundee. They include pinot noir, pinot blanc, and sparkling chardonnay and riesling. Phone (503) 472–1587; open Saturday and Sunday, noon to 5:00 P.M., May to Thanksgiving. **Eyrie** and **Panther Creek,** also in McMinnville, are open only by appointment.

Return to 99W (labeled 99-Wine in these parts) and head north to **Lafayette.** At this village, formerly named Yam Hill Falls, fur traders and Indians crossed the Willamette River as they traversed the Overland Trail. In a park west of town you can see the remains of the **Yamhill Locks,** where riverboats of a century ago were assisted up the river.

Tour the **Yamhill County Historical Society Museum,** which is housed in an 1893 church, the oldest in the county. The museum contains cases full of items used by early settlers. Similar relics, and many more, are sold in the **Lafayette Schoolhouse Antique Mall** on Highway 99W (503–864–2720).

Near Lafayette, on Mineral Springs Road, is **Chateau Benoit Winery.** This winery began in 1979 and is best known for its sauvignon blancs and sparkling wines and has won awards for its Müller Thurgau. Open daily.

Continue on 99W to Blanchard Lane and **Sokol Blosser Winery,** open daily. This winery's grapes produce pinot noir, chardonnay, white riesling, and Müller Thurgau wines. The tasting room has a sweeping view of the Willamette Valley and Mount Hood.

Your next stop is Dundee.

*Lunch:* **Alfie's Wayside Country Inn,** 1111 Highway 99W, Dundee. (503) 538–9407. Soups, sandwiches, salads, and pasta served in a Dutch barn–style shingled inn.

## Afternoon

Several wineries are located in the red hills of Dundee. They include **Lange, Cameron, Knudsen Erath, Red Hills Vineyard,** and **Dundee Wine Cellar.** Map in hand, track down those you have time to visit as you head northeast on Highway 99W.

In Newberg, stop at **Coffee Cottage**, 808 East Hancock (503–538–5126) for rich espresso and cheesecake or a scone. (Closed Sundays.)

East of Newburg, on the green slopes of the **Tualatin Mountains,** is **Rex Hill Vineyards,** 30835 North Highway 99W (503–538–0666.) This showplace winery, furnished with antiques, emphasizes vintage-dated, vineyard-designated bottlings of pinot noir and chardonnay and has produced a fine pinot gris. Recently expanded, Rex Hill has a large tasting room and cellar and a sizable picnic area with a view of the valley.

Across the highway is **Veritas Vineyard,** 31190 Northeast Veritas Lane (503–538–1470), in a picturesque setting of vineyards above the northern Willamette Valley. Using traditional methods and French oak-barrel aging, Veritas produces pinot noir, chardonnay, riesling, and Müller Thurgau wines. The winery has received regional and national awards. (Open daily in summer.)

It's about 20 miles from the wineries back to Portland on Highway 99W. On the way, stop in Sherwood at **Sleighbells,** a fifty-acre Christmas-tree farm and holiday shop where peacocks roam the land-scaped grounds. It's open June through December. (503) 625–7966.

# There's More

The **Hoover-Minthorn House,** Newberg. (503) 538–6629. Herbert Hoover's boyhood home from 1885 to 1888, now a museum with orig-inal furnishings. Open Wednesday through Sunday, 1:00 to 4:00 P.M.

**Historic walking tours,** Newberg. Tours pointing out turn-of-the-century homes in several architectural styles.

**Dr. John C. Brougher Museum,** George Fox College campus, Newberg. Contains memorabilia of Quakers who founded Newberg and the college. Open by appointment (503–538–8383).

**Fort Yamhill blockhouse.** Used by General Phil Sheridan in Grand Ronde, the structure is now a city park in Dayton, a small town west of Lafayette.

**Gallery Players of Oregon,** Second and Ford streets, McMinnville. (503) 472–2227. Community theater with year-round weekend perfor-mances.

**Golf.** Bayou Golf Course, McMinnville. Nine-hole course. (5030 472–2651.

Riverwood Golf Course, Dundee. Nine-hole course. (503) 864–2667.

**Boating.** Canoe or kayak in the Yamhill and Willamette Rivers. There are boat launches at various points along the riverfront.

**Valley Art Association,** 2022 Main Street, Forest Grove. (503) 357–3703. Regional artists show their works on consignment in this gallery, open Monday through Saturday.

**Spirit of Oregon Dinner Train,** Forest Grove. (503) 324–1919.

Weekend dinner rides on restored vintage railroad cars. Four-hour ride into the Coast Range. Club car with music and dancing. Sunday brunch rides.

# Special Events

**March.** Barbershop Ballad Contest and Gay Nineties Contest, Forest Grove. Barbershop quartet competition.

**July.** Concours d'Elegance, Forest Grove. Vintage auto show, entertainment, food.

**July.** Turkey-rama, McMinnville. Three days of street sales, carnival, music, turkey barbecue, 1950s dance, 8-kilometer run, and biggest-turkey contest. Celebrates local turkey business.

**July.** Tualatin Valley Fourth of July Barrel Tasting Tour. Open House and tastings at six valley wineries.

**Midsummer.** International Pinot Noir Celebration, McMinnville. Meet the winemakers and taste pinot noirs from Oregon, France, and California.

**Thanksgiving weekend.** Holiday Open House, Washington County. Tours, tastings, food, and entertainment at most wineries.

**Weekend after Thanksgiving.** Wine Country Thanksgiving, Yamhill County. Music, tastings, foods at most wineries.

# Other Recommended Restaurants and Lodgings

## Aloha

Yankee Tinker Bed-and-Breakfast, 5480 Southwest 183rd. (503) 649–0932. Ranch-style home with two guest rooms, shared bath. Colonial decor, antiques, tinware collection. Full breakfast.

## Dayton

Wine Country Farm, 6855 Breyman Orchards Road. (503) 864–3446. Historic home on a hilltop with panoramic views of surrounding vineyards, Willamette Valley. Four rooms, wide deck, gardens, Arabian horses. Full farm breakfast.

## Dundee

Tina's, 760 Highway 99W. (503) 538–8880. Small, spare restaurant serving exceptional Northwest cuisine with French country zest. Worth a special trip. Lunches on weekdays only; dinners Tuesday–Sunday. Reservations recommended.

## Forest Grove

El Rodeo, 3331 Pacific Avenue. (503) 357–9410. Local favorite for Mexican food.

Ford's, 1923 Pacific Avenue. (503) 357–0317. Well-prepared hamburgers and sandwiches, 1950s decor.

Jan's Food Mill, 1819 Nineteenth Avenue. (503) 357–6623. Steaks and seafood, Sunday brunch in historic granary with homespun family atmosphere.

## McMinnville

Augustine's, 19706 Southwest Highway 18. (503) 843–3225. Well-prepared, innovative dishes served for lunch and dinner in a glassed-in loft above Lawrence Gallery.

Orchard View Inn, 16540 Northwest Orchard View Road. (503) 472–0165. Secluded, hillside setting among the oak trees. Five guest rooms in octagon-shaped home with wraparound deck. Full breakfast included.

Roger's Seafood Restaurant and Lounge, 2121 East Twenty-seventh Street. (503) 473–0917. Dinners overlooking a tranquil stream. Specializes in fresh seafood, charbroiled steaks, and Oregon wines.

The Sage Restaurant, 406 East Third Street. (503) 472–4445. Lunches on the mezzanine of 1893 Shops. Casual and cozy, with wooden booths and hanging plants. Sandwiches, soups, desserts at low prices.

Third Street Brasserie, 705 East Third Street. (503) 434–6501. European-style lunches and dinners in a bistro setting.

Umberto's, 828 North Adams Street. (503) 472–1717. Italian dinners, veal specialties. Compares well with better-known Nick's Italian Cafe.

Zupan's, 1595 South Baker. (503) 472–7406. Grocery store, cafe, deli, and bakery. A good place to purchase picnic supplies and Oregon wines. Open daily.

## Newberg

Springbook Farm Carriage House, 30295 North Highway 99W. (503) 538–4606. Hideaway cottage in hazelnut orchard near Rex Hill. Kitchen, pond, swimming pool, tennis. Refrigerator stocked with breakfast.

## Yamhill

Flying M Ranch, 23029 Northwest Flying M Road. (503) 662–3222. Rustic log lodge and restaurant 10 miles west of Yamhill, on the old stagecoach route. Horseback riding, swimming, tennis, barbecues.

# For More Information

Forest Grove Chamber of Commerce, 2417 Pacific Avenue, Forest Grove, OR 97116. (503) 357–3006.

McMinnville Chamber of Commerce, 417 North Adams Street, McMinnville, OR 97128. (503) 472–6196.

Newberg Area Chamber of Commerce, 115 North Washington Street, Newberg, OR 97132. (503) 538–2014.

Yamhill County Wineries Association, P.O. Box 871, McMinnville, OR 97128. (503) 434–5814.

Washington County Visitors Association, 5075 Griffith Drive SW, Suite 120, Beaverton, OR 97005. (503) 644–5555.

Oregon Wine Center, 1200 Front Avenue NW, Suite 400, Portland, OR 97209. (503) 228–8403.

# John Day Fossil Beds to Shaniko

A visit to Shaniko will allow you to experience life in the Old West.

## Fossils and Falls

_____ 1 NIGHT _____

Waterfalls · Fossils · Ghost town · Antique shops
Cattle ranches · River rafting · Historic hotel

If you appreciate nature's artistry, history on the grand scale, and a bit of adventure, you'll enjoy this tour. In two days you'll travel through millions of years of geological change, visit a frontier town, raft on a river, and ride through cowboy country. It's all a comparatively short distance from the city, but a long way from urban living.

## Day 1

**Morning**

From Portland, drive east on I–84 to the Bridal Veil exit. Leave the freeway here, and at the top of the hill turn left on the **Scenic High-**

**way.** This was the first federally designated scenic highway in the United States; only a short section remains, but the views are spectacular. In spring, colorful wildflowers bloom beside the winding old road; in all seasons it's surrounded by greenery. Below, on the north, lies the freeway and beyond it the broad **Columbia River** and the hills of Washington.

After passing through the quiet Bridal Veil community, you'll come to **Wahkeenah Falls,** a 242-foot series of falls pouring down the boulder-strewn basaltic cliff. It's a short distance from here along the Scenic Highway to the famous **Multnomah Falls.** Stop for a close look at the long, double cascade and perhaps have coffee and breakfast in the old stone **Multnomah Lodge.**

Next is **Oneonta Gorge Botanical Area**, a narrow canyon with rare plants and dense greenery, and then comes picturesque **Horsetail Falls,** twisting 176 feet into a pool behind a low stone wall. **Ainsworth State Park** is the last stop on the Scenic Highway, a pleasant place for camping and picnics.

Rejoin I–84 at this point and continue east along the Columbia River toward the town of Hood River, another 28 miles (for more on Hood River, see Portland Escape Seven). You're driving through the great cleft in the Cascade Range, with Mount Hood rising immediately on the south and brawny Mount Adams and chopped-off St. Helens across the river on the north. On a clear day you'll see the peaks of Rainier in the distance. East of the Cascades, the scenery changes. The fir forests, waterfalls, and rugged cliffs are left behind, with rounded hills, sere and brown in summer, lying ahead.

After Hood River, take the Mosier/Rowena exit to travel a scenic byway, where cherry orchards grow on the hillsides and balsamroot and lupine carpet the fields with yellow and blue in April and May. As you climb the hill you'll have sweeping, panoramic views of the river and mountains.

Six miles after you leave I–84, you'll come to **Rowena Dell.** Stop to admire the view from **Rowena Crest View Point** and walk the paths of the **Governor Tom McCall Preserve at Rowena Plateau.** Owned by the Nature Conservancy since 1982, this scenic area offers stunning displays of wildflowers on a plateau above the river. You might also walk the 1.5-mile footpath that leads to **McCall Point,** a high overlook.

The cliffs here, composed of dark Columbia basalt, were formed in a series of massive lava flows about fifteen million years ago. Ten million years ago, as the great basalt plain crumbled, erosion carved out Rowena Dell. Later floods and ash from volcanic eruptions created the steep cliffs and landscape visible today.

You can rejoin I–84 after descending from Rowena Dell, or continue on the country byway to Rowena and Mayer State Park, joining

I–84 at **The Dalles.** In spring, the countryside around The Dalles is a pastel sea of cherry blossoms, as this is a prime fruit-growing area.

If time allows, take a look around the history-steeped town. For centuries it was a Native American trading center and then the end of the overland Oregon Trail. A walking tour map points out the original **Wasco County Courthouse,** now an interpretive center. The courthouse was built in 1859 when Wasco was the largest county in the United States, extending into present-day Idaho, Montana, and Wyoming.

**Old St. Peter's Church** dates from 1898. In it, you'll see brilliant stained-glass windows, Italian marble, rich woodwork, and the church's original organ. The former **Surgeon's Quarters** is all that remains of Fort Dalles. In the mid-1800s, it was part of the only military post between Fort Vancouver and Fort Laramie; today the quaint structure is a museum with displays on pioneer life.

Leaving The Dalles, the rocky hills are dotted with fragrant blue-gray sagebrush, while willows and wildflowers grow by the water. From I–84, take exit 97 to State Route 206. **Celilo Park,** between the river and railroad tracks, is a green oasis here, with lawns, trees, and restrooms.

Traveling on Route 206, you'll cross the Deschutes River and come to **Deschutes River Recreation Area.** This large, attractive riverside park is a popular gathering spot. It has boat launches, grassy slopes under locust trees, and campsites. An **Oregon Trail Historic Marker** tells of pioneers crossing the Deschutes on their way west.

At the Fulton Canyon/Wasco sign, Route 206 heads inland, away from the river. You're driving up a winding road into a steep canyon, where sheep paths crisscross the treeless hills. Then you're up and out of the canyon, surrounded by vast grain fields, with cottonwood trees where there is water. By the roadside, in a grove of locust trees, you'll see Locust Grove Church, with its high steeple and arched windows. Now deserted, gray, and weathered, the quaint little church was built in 1895 and last used for a funeral in 1914.

Crossing U.S. 97, you'll arrive in **Wasco,** a small, intensely quiet town dominated by big grain elevators. There are brick buildings and lilacs, a small city park with play equipment, a city hall, a post office, and the Wasco Market, where the community goes to learn the latest happenings. Recent signs in the window advertise garage sales, a junior rodeo, the high school sports schedule, a gun show, and an annual rummage and plastic flower show.

Continue through ranch country, where grain and cattle are the mainstays, to the sagebrush of Cottonwood Canyon, and on to the **John Day River.** At J. S. Burres State Park, a simple wayside with a couple of picnic tables and toilets, boaters often put in to the river.

From the John Day, ascend out of the canyon to a hilltop with a "Mountain Identifier," which names the visible mountains: Jefferson, Hood, St. Helens, Adams, and Rainier.

Forty miles after leaving the Columbia River, arrive in **Condon,** another quiet town where grain elevators loom. The home of the "Blue Devils" and the "gateway to John Day recreation area" has one main street with barber and beauty shops, a few cafes, and numerous empty storefronts. Condon's school neighbors a pretty green park with play equipment and has a pool and tennis courts.

The most interesting place in town for the traveler is **Country Flowers**, which boasts a surprisingly large variety of crafts and gift items—wind chimes, dolls, copper pans, birdhouses, soaps, teddy bears, and many others, all of excellent quality. Fresh flowers and plants are displayed indoors and on the front sidewalk.

*Lunch:* **Country Flowers Soda Fountain,** 201 South Main, Condon. (503) 384–4120. Soups, thick sandwiches, taco salad, Italian sodas, frozen yogurt, ice cream, espresso.

## Afternoon

Leave Condon on Route 19 headed south, driving through old lava flows covered with a thin layer of topsoil that supports sagebrush and a few juniper trees. The town of **Fossil** (population 430) is 20 miles south of Condon. Fossil has several points of interest, including a **museum** with well-displayed nineteenth-century artifacts, a **car museum** where you can see a collection of vintage autos, and the red brick **Wheeler County Courthouse.** The courthouse has fish-scale shingles, two towers (one with four stories, making this the tallest building around), and a curved brick entrance.

Arthur Glover Park has a playground and picnic tables. Fossil Mercantile sells groceries and sundries. Chica's Country Cafe is the place to eat.

Turning southwest on Route 218, you'll drive 20 miles to reach **John Day Fossil Beds National Monument,** a journey that reaches far into the past. The National Monument, established in 1975, encompasses 14,000 acres in three separate units: Sheep Rock, Painted Hills, and Clarno. This visit to the northernmost site, the **Clarno Formation**, explores the oldest fossil beds, some of the best preserved on Earth. Beds spanning more than five million years are rare, yet these show more than forty million years of diverse plant and animal life.

Evidence of ancient subtropical forests abounds, as well as fossils of mammals that roamed the region thirty-four million years ago.

Visitors usually pick up a trail map and hike the short walk to the cliffs, or palisades. The **Clarno Palisades** are high rocks exposed by erosion after volcanic mudflows over millions of years inundated the forests again and again. One trail is fairly steep and leads to a high arch in the rocks; the other is an easier nature trail, with fossils identified. These give you a small sampling; there are many significant sites, deeper in the National Monument, that are not yet open to the public.

Nearby is the **Hancock Field Station,** operated by the Oregon Museum of Science and Industry. It offers field trips and study courses on the geology, paleontology, and ecology of the area.

Leaving the palm trees of the past for the sagebrush of the present, continue on 218 to the John Day River. At the rust-red bridge crossing the John Day, a federally designated Scenic Waterway, you may see rafters and boaters putting in for a ride down the rapids. Then you'll ascend again through mounds where cattle graze near juniper trees and cloud shadows glide over buttes and valleys. In spring, if there has been rain, the landscape is a delicate green sprinkled with yellow flowers.

Tucked into a quiet hollow shaded by poplar trees is **Antelope,** a farm town with a store, a school, and a church. From here, the road turns north for 8 miles to Highway 97, at the crest of a hill, and the ghost town of **Shaniko.** With twenty-five people, it's not quite a ghost town, but that's what it is labeled, as the residents strive to attract tourists to this slice of the Old West.

You can ride a stagecoach, peek into the worn jail, see a collection of well-used buggies and a covered wagon, photograph the picturesque schoolhouse, and shop for antiques. You can even have a western-style wedding at the little **Shaniko Wedding Chapel,** on the boardwalk of the 2-block main street.

Shaniko was once a busy place, the wool shipping capital of the world. Millions of pounds of wool from regional sheep ranches were stored in the big warehouse and shipped out on the rails at the turn of the century. But eventually the train bypassed the town, the economy dropped away, and Shaniko was nearly deserted. In recent years, though, new owners took over the old **Shaniko Hotel** and brought it to life again.

The mood in Shaniko is disturbed only by the rumble of trucks on busy Highway 97, which runs by the edge of town.

*Dinner:* **Shaniko Cafe.** Shaniko Hotel's bright and cheerful restaurant features steak, meatloaf, stew, and hamburgers. Try the crispy-tender fried chicken with home fried potatoes—hearty and delicious.

*Lodging:* **Shaniko Hotel,** Shaniko, OR. (503) 489–3441. Brick hotel with twenty-one simple but clean and comfortable second-floor rooms. Lace curtains hang at high windows; the atmosphere is updated frontier. On the National Historic Register.

# Day 2

## Morning

*Breakfast:* Three breakfast choices are included in the room rate at the Shaniko Hotel—bacon and eggs, French toast, or continental. Or you can order from the menu at additional cost. Portions are generous.

After you've poked around the ghost town, head north on U.S. 97 and take the first right, Bakeoven Road. At this 3,500-foot elevation you can look back toward John Day country, while ahead of you lies the **Deschutes River Canyon.** Mount Hood and Mount Jefferson tower on the horizon, and you can see Mount Adams and Olallie Butte. The near landscape is festooned with power lines, carrying hydroelectric power from The Dalles Dam on the Columbia River.

From the plateau, twist down into the valley where **Maupin** nestles against the Deschutes River. Here you'll meet your **river rafting guides** and board the van that will take you to a put-in point on the river. (Ewing's, P.O. Box 427, Maupin, OR 97037; phone 503–395–2697.)

The Deschutes is a popular rafting river, with weekends, especially in July and August, very busy. It's carefully regulated, but you'll find that off-season weekdays are considerably less crowded. In the 14-foot raft you'll float the Scenic Waterway back to Maupin, encountering several rapids on the way, and have lunch in the park.

*Lunch:* Provided by the **Ewings,** it's set out in the riverside city park at Maupin. Deli sandwiches, chips, fruit, and apple cake are the usual menu. (Executive lunches, at additional cost, include steak or chicken.)

## Afternoon

Climb into the raft again and continue down the river to **Sherar Falls,** a series of cascades that pour over rocky ledges. This is a traditional fishing ground, where the Indians still stand on wooden platforms built out over the falls and dip long-handled nets into the water. Other fishers cast their lines from the shore.

You'll be shuttled back to Maupin when the four-hour ride is over.

From Maupin, travel north on Deschutes River Road, a National Scenic Byway, and parallel your river ride. There are camping and fishing areas all along the road here. Blue Hole Recreation Site has a fishing ramp with handicap access.

On your left, the river rushes by and above it rise steep, rocky cliffs topped by a flat plateau. Past Sherar Falls, where you have a good view of the fishing activity, cross Sherar Bridge. It's often crowded near here, with RV campers parked by the bridge and along the shore. Now you're on Route 216, headed for Tygh Valley.

Three miles from the bridge, watch for the state park sign and turn left at **Tygh Valley Wayside,** where there's an attractive, well-tended day park with lilacs and maple trees, grass and picnic tables. As soon as you arrive you'll hear the roar of the water—**White River Falls,** the most spectacular sight for miles around.

In a series of three cataracts, the falls drops 90 feet through a steep basalt canyon. The White River begins in a glacier on Mount Hood and flows to join the Deschutes. In spring, when there's abundant snowmelt, the falls is at its most powerful, plunging into pools that roil with action. You can see the falls from a fenced viewpoint or walk down a fairly steep dirt trail in order to view all three sections at once. On the site are also the concrete remains of an abandoned hydro plant.

From the wayside, drive on to **Tygh Valley,** home of the All-Indian Rodeo (see **Special Events**) and head west on the road to Wamic. This becomes Route 48, the White River Road. The pioneers who chose to travel overland, rather than float their covered wagons down the Columbia from The Dalles, came this way and often traded with the Tygh Indians. Sam Barlow forged a trail around Mount Hood and set up a tollgate to charge travelers coming through on his road.

You can drive part of the Old Barlow Road, which parallels White River Road and goes all the way to Barlow Pass and Highway 35. There are several turnoffs and signs pointing the way from Route 48.

Now you've left the sagebrush and ponderosa pines of central and eastern Oregon and entered the thick fir forests of the western Cascades and **Mount Hood National Forest.** Continue into the foothills of Mount Hood, crossing several creeks, with the great mountain looming directly before you.

When you reach Highway 35, you have two choices: turn west toward Route 26 and head for Portland around the mountain's south side, or go north on 35 to Hood River and take the freeway, I–84, west to Portland. If you choose the latter course and have time, stop at East Fork 650, just north of Sherwood Campground, for a two-hour walk up to **Tamanawus Falls,** another cascade of breathtaking beauty (see Portland Escape Four for details).

# There's More

**John Day River.** The John Day, much less used than the lower Deschutes, offers solitude and quiet within its dramatic canyon walls. It's also good for rafting, especially in spring. The 47-mile run from Service Creek to Clarno is a two-day trip with some rapids.

**Fishing.** The John Day is noted for its smallmouth bass, salmon, and steelhead. The Deschutes is famous for its summer steelhead and trout.

# Other Recommended
# Restaurants and Lodgings

## Fossil

Chica's Country Cafe. (503) 763–4328. Inviting, cheery cafe, a popular eatery in the area.

## Maupin

The Oasis Resort, P.O. Box 365. (503) 395–2611. Small vintage cabins, most with kitchens, on a grassy, tree-shaded slope near the Deschutes River. Reasonable rates. Also has a restaurant known for good food.

# Special Events

**Mid-April.** Northwest Cherry Festival, The Dalles. Orchard tours, cherry cook-off, street fairs, parade, runs.

**Mid-April.** Celilo Salmon Feed, The Dalles. Indian dancing, feast of salmon, venison, root potatoes. Celebrates long Indian fishing tradition in the Columbia.

**May.** All-Indian Rodeo, Tygh Valley. Bronc riding, wild-horse race, team roping, bulls, Buckaroo breakfast, Native American crafts, fun runs, kids carnival, dances, beer garden.

**Early June.** Pioneer Days, Shaniko. Three-day event with parade, Old West shoot-outs, dances, pie social, stagecoach rides, mountain man camp.

**Early August.** Shaniko Festival, Shaniko. Parade, beef barbecue, beer garden, street dance, music, cloggers, flea market, old-time fiddlers.

# For More Information

The Dalles Convention and Visitors Bureau, 901 East Second Street, The Dalles, OR 97058. (503) 296–6616 or (800) 255–3385.

Hancock Field Station, Fossil, OR 97830.

Superintendent, John Day Fossil Beds National Monument, 420 West Main Street, John Day, OR 97845.

# Oregon City/Salem Loop Trip

Built in 1867, this Oregon City home is now the Fellows House Restaurant and Inn of the Oregon Trail.

## End of the Oregon Trail

———————————— 1 NIGHT ————————————

Oregon Trail historic sites · Rural countryside · Spectacular waterfalls
Bird sanctuary · State capitol · National Historic District
Nineteenth-century religious commune · Antiques shops

This two-day excursion into the Willamette Valley will take you back 150 years. There's a wealth of pioneer history in Oregon City, Salem, and points between. On the way, you'll explore pastoral countryside, rushing streams, and forests with sensational waterfalls—the wonders that lured early settlers westward and beckon tourists today.

## Day 1

### Morning

Drive south from Portland 13 miles to **Oregon City.** Known as the end of the Oregon Trail, the little town on the eastern bank of the

Willamette River was the only seat of American government in the Oregon Territory until 1852. It was the first incorporated city in the West and established the first western newspaper and first mint.

Tour the **End of the Trail Interpretive Center,** 500 Washington Street (closed Mondays), to learn about the challenges the pioneers faced as they journeyed westward; 30,000 died in their 2,200-mile quest to reach Oregon in the mid-1800s. Videotapes provide a brief history, telling of the Native Americans who lived on the site for 3,000 years and of the coming of the missionaries, trappers, and settlers.

With a walkers' guide from the interpretive center, stroll the historic heart of town, set on a high basaltic cliff above the riverside commercial district.

Even on the frontier, life had its comforts. You'll see some of them in **McLoughlin House,** at 713 Center Street. This National Historic Site is furnished as it was when Dr. John McLoughlin, the chief factor of the Hudson's Bay Company, lived there with his family in 1848. Almost every schoolchild in northern Oregon makes a field trip to the impressive white frame house. It's open daily except Mondays, 11:00 A.M. to 5:00 P.M.

The **Barclay House,** a pioneer home, is a gift shop open Tuesday through Sunday. The **Mertie Stevens House,** a 1908 Georgian Revival at Sixth and Washington streets, is now a museum housing Indian artifacts and a rare collection of exquisitely dressed French and German dolls.

Ride the unique ten-story **elevator** that travels between the upper, mostly residential part of town to the lower downtown area. The oldest commercial building in Oregon is here, at 423 Main Street, but don't expect a quaint log cabin; the only traces left of the original store are the hand-hewn beams in its basement.

**Trail's End Heritage Center,** the Clackamas County Historical Society's museum, opened in 1990 with myriad artifacts on display. The center is perched on a rocky bluff above **Willamette Falls** at the south end of town. The 40-foot falls spill over a horseshoe-shaped basaltic reef; in 1889 it was the site of the first long-line power transmission in the United States.

*Lunch:* **Fellows House,** 416 South McLoughlin Boulevard. (503) 650-9322. Restored historic home; excellent meals are served in the parlor (closed Sunday).

## Afternoon

Head south on Route 213, through a rural landscape of farms, orchards, and fields of Christmas trees, to **Silverton,** a friendly hamlet where people always have time to stop for a chat and where the downtown parking meters still have penny slots.

The **Silverton Country Museum,** with displays of local history, is open Thursday and Sunday afternoons or by appointment (call 503–873-2394). The old train depot next door is adjacent to a wooded, grassy park that slopes down to **Silver Creek.** A number of artists and craftspeople live and work in Silverton. One makes fine wooden boxes; another designs award-winning note cards. There are several antiques and gift shops and art galleries.

Drive 15 miles southeast, and you come to one of the natural wonders of Oregon, beautiful in any season: **Silver Falls State Park.** The "Trail of Ten Falls," a 7-mile loop trail, winds past the park's most spectacular waterfalls. The trail even curves behind one of them. A cavernlike ledge, created by the erosion of volcanic ash, lies behind the 136-foot cascade of water at **North Falls.** From the trail you look through the misty veil to the gurgling creek below and at the cliffs, maple and fir trees, moss, and ferns that border its banks.

Silver Falls is the largest concentration of waterfalls in the United States. The spacious park has picnic facilities, an interpretive lodge, a swimming pond with a sandy beach, and fifty-two camping sites with fireplaces and water.

From Silver Falls drive west on State Route 214 and follow the signs to **Stayton.** A small town on the north bank of the **Santiam River,** Stayton has charm and vitality. There are pretty parks, public tennis courts, an 18-hole golf course, bike paths, fishing streams, and a bird sanctuary.

Stayton's historic roots date from the sawmills and woolen mills of the 1860s.

History-conscious volunteers have restored and preserved an architectural landmark, the **Jordan Covered Bridge,** which now stands above a gentle stream in **Pioneer Park,** at Marion and Seventh streets.

Between March and July, thousands of birds flock to **Bird Haven,** a private sanctuary on Kingston-Lyons Drive. With advance appointments (call 503–769–5597), Tony and Betty Koch welcome visitors to their 230-acre farm overlooking the river. A visit to this extraordinary refuge, with its 800 birdhouses and small museum, is well worth the nominal fee charged. There are picnic facilities, a demonstration area showing Tony's ingenious birdhouse designs, and bird feed and houses for sale.

By now it's late afternoon and time to take Route 22 west into **Salem,** leaving the bucolic countryside for Oregon's capital.

*Dinner:* **Alessandro's Park Plaza,** 325 High Street SE. (503) 370–9951. Fine Italian fare in a stylish restaurant by Mill Creek park. Fairly dressy.

*Lodging:* **State House Bed and Breakfast,** 2146 State Street, Salem, OR 97301. (503) 588–1340 or (800) 800–6712. A casual, comfortable inn on Mill Creek, 10 blocks from the capitol. Four guest rooms and cottage, gazebo, and hot tub.

# Day 2

## Morning

*Breakfast:* State House Bed and Breakfast serves a full, generous morning repast—virtually anything you request.

A tour of the gleaming white **state capitol,** topped with a bronze-and-gold figure of a pioneer, is not to be missed when you're exploring Salem. Inside, the walls are painted with murals depicting scenes from Oregon history. A polished travertine rotunda rises 106 feet to a painted ceiling. Guided tours of the building are offered daily.

Historic **Deepwood Estate,** 1116 Mission Street SE, is a short drive from the capitol and a step into a Victorian past. In this mansion and its well-kept gardens, you're surrounded by the quiet gentility of a previous century. The beautifully crafted home, with its oak woodwork and stained glass, was built in 1893. The property is now owned by the city of Salem.

The "garden rooms," divided by hedges and lattice fencing, are open six days a week from dawn to dusk; for information on house tours, call (503) 363–1825.

Deepwood is at one end of eighty-nine-acre **Bush Pasture Park,** a lovely stretch of green with a playground and walking paths under tall trees. At the other end of the park, on a grassy hilltop, are an art gallery and **Bush House,** a Victorian Italianate home. Built in 1877 by Asahel Bush II, a prominent figure in Oregon history, the restored home is open for afternoon tours Tuesday through Sunday. Its richly furnished rooms contain unique marble fireplaces, French wallpapers, and fine mahogany and walnut woodwork.

Three blocks from the state capitol, and across the street from **Willamette University,** is a four-and-a-half-acre village that represents a significant piece of Oregon's history: **Mission Mill Village,** 1313 Mill Street SE (503-585-7012). The museum complex on Mill Creek comprises nineteenth-century homes, a sizable woolen mill, shops, the Marion Museum of History, and landscaped grounds with picnic tables and old-fashioned gardens.

In the mill, elaborate displays show how wool was made in the 1890s, from fleece to fabric. The historic homes include the 1841 residence of pioneer missionary Jason Lee, the oldest remaining frame house in the Pacific Northwest.

*Lunch:* **Karma's Cafe.** (503) 370–8855. Salads, soups, hot and cold sandwiches, and pastas; all homemade, fresh, and top quality. Eat indoors or at outside tables. Open 10:00 A.M. to 4:00 P.M.; closed Sundays.

## Afternoon

Stop at **Honeywood Winery,** 1350 Hines Street (503–362–4111) for a tour and a taste of grape, fruit, and specialty wines from the state's oldest winery. The shop and tasting room are a few blocks from the visitors' center and Mission Mill Village.

From Salem take Highway 99E north through the countryside 20 miles to the quaint village of **Aurora.** Begun as a religious commune in 1856, Aurora has preserved its architectural heritage and is a National Historic District. A former ox barn has been turned into a museum complex filled with artifacts from the colony.

Displays in the **Old Aurora Colony Museum,** Second and Liberty streets, are extraordinary. They include brass-band instruments (the early colonists were well known for their music) and such ingeniously designed tools as a foot-treadle lathe for woodworking, a boot crimper, and a unique spinning wheel. On the grounds are two pioneer homes, both furnished with items your grandmother might recognize—tin candle molds, a chain-mail pot scraper, a cabbage cutter, and a butter press.

Aurora is one of the best places in Oregon for **antiques shopping.** Four Seasons specializes in oak; Union Mills has Country Primitives. Impressions, located in a turn-of-the-century home, and Aurora Antique Mall each house numerous dealers selling everything from heavy oak cabinets to delicate perfume bottles.

Behind the shops in Antique Colony is the only structure left of the original colony's hotel complex (the hotel, known among stagecoach and railroad passengers for its excellent German meals, was torn down in 1934). The oddly shaped **Octagon Building** may have been a storage or smokehouse; no one knows. It now contains historical photographs and information about Aurora Colony.

**For You Only** is a tiny cafe where Mitzi Bauer sells soup, pastries, and antiques. This is the place for a coffee break accompanied by a wonderfully flaky slice of fresh apple pie.

Continue on Highway 99E 4 miles through the undulating, fertile hills to **Canby,** a small, pleasant town with an agricultural base. Along with vegetables, berries, poultry, grains, and Christmas trees, ornamental shrubs and flowers are important products. Just north of town is the largest dahlia farm in the United States, **Swan Island Dahlias,** 995 Northwest Twenty-second, where fifty acres of flowers bloom with color in summer. (Open 9:00 A.M. to 4:30 P.M.) The growers present a dahlia show in September, but you can purchase flowers, bulbs, and plants anytime they're available.

Farther down the road is the **Flower Farmer,** a delightful place to stop for flowers, produce, and a ride on a miniature train. On weekends, Leo Garre gives rides all day, circling the fields of corn, delphinium, and asters on a ½-mile, narrow-gauge track. Fun for kids and train buffs is guaranteed, at no charge (a donation box stands at the entrance).

You can buy hamburgers and hot dogs at a red-and-yellow food wagon on the grounds and eat at the picnic tables the Garres have set up on the lawn.

Near Canby, where the Molalla River enters the Willamette, there's a day-use park with broad lawns, picnic tables, a path leading to grassy riverside beaches, and boat-launching areas. Walk the Marsh Bridge Loop Trail in **Molalla River State Park,** and you'll see red-winged blackbirds, wild iris, and dark ponds covered with creamy white water lilies.

Just past the park is the quaint **Canby ferry,** which crosses the Willamette from early spring to late fall, carrying four cars per trip. It runs from 6:00 A.M. to 10:00 P.M.

Take the ferry ride, and head back through the hills quilted with crops and dotted with red barns, to the suburbs and on to Portland.

## There's More

**Marquam Hill Vineyards,** just north of Marquam on Route 213. (503) 829–6677. Open for tastings noon to 6:00 P.M. daily from June to November. Picnic area near an eight-acre lake.

**Mount Angel,** 5 miles west of Route 213. The squeaky-clean, peaceful village set among hop fields and maple groves holds an annual Oktoberfest that draws thousands. St. Mary's Church here is noted for its extraordinary stained-glass windows.

**Mount Angel Abbey,** St. Benedict. (503) 845–3066. The abbey's buff brick buildings stand in peaceful seclusion on a hilltop above the village of Mount Angel. The library is one of only two buildings in the United States designed by the famed Finnish architect Alvar Aalto. In its rare book room are manuscripts hand copied by Benedictine monks centuries ago.

The abbey's museum, tucked away in a basement, is decidedly quirky. It has everything from an immense, shaggy bison to the key to an English castle. (Admission free, open upon request.)

**Cooley's Gardens,** 11553 Silverton Road NE, Silverton. (503) 873–5463. The world's largest iris farm, near Salem. Flowers are sold in May and June. Bulbs available.

**St. Josef's Weinkeller Winery,** Canby. Grape picking and wine tastings. Open daily, noon to 5:00 P.M. (503) 651–3190.

**Fisher's Old Fashioned Meats,** Canby. (503) 266–5678. Top-quality meats and sausages (you'll be offered sample tastes).

**Grand Kid Acres,** 8243 Golf Club Road, Stayton. (503) 749–2154. Exotic animal farm.

**Santiam Historical Museum,** 260 North Second Avenue, Stayton. (503) 767–1406. Exhibits of local history.

# Special Events

**Mid-July to early August.** Oregon Trail Pageant. Outdoor play, "Oregon Fever," dramatizes wagon train days of mid-1800s.

**Mid-July.** Aurora Colony Days, Aurora. Demonstrations of pioneer crafts (spinning, weaving, woodworking, butter churning), music, tour of historic homes.

**First weekend in September.** Oregon State Fair, Salem. Livestock and produce exhibitions, carnival rides, food booths, baking contests.

**First weekend in October.** Oktoberfest, Mount Angel. Largest festival of its kind in the West. Sausage, beer, music, costumed folk dancers.

# Other Recommended Restaurants and Lodgings

## Oregon City

Hing's, 517 Main Street. (503) 655–6688. Chinese menu, popular with local folk. Short on atmosphere, but good food.

Inn of the Oregon Trail. Hospitable bed-and-breakfast in the historic Fellows House, 416 South McLoughlin. (503) 650–9322. Three rooms share two baths. Full breakfast served in the former parlor.

Jagger House, 512 Sixth Street. (503) 657–7820. Bed-and-breakfast in the upper-level historic district. Pine furniture and patchwork quilts in three rooms, one with private bath. Full breakfast served.

## Silverton

Ducky Deli, 209A North Water Street. (503) 873–8685. Highly rated cheeseburgers and generous sandwiches in a light and cozy country atmosphere. Owner Patty Geddes, originally from Scotland, serves warm scones with butter and jam at teatime. Luscious berry and pumpkin pies, made by a local baker.

Silverton Bed and Breakfast, 421 Water Street. (503) 873–5858. Restaurant and bed-and-breakfast in 1890 hotel. Two upstairs rooms share a bath in a country Victorian atmosphere. Full breakfast.

The Town House, 203 East Main. (503) 873–2841. Coffee shop, bar, and small dining room in a former stagecoach stop. Sunday prime rib dinners are reasonably priced, good quality, and served in hefty portions. Highly popular.

## Stayton

Gardner House, 635 North Third. (503) 769–6331. Victorian bed-and-breakfast and flower shop. Two rooms, one a large suite with kitchen. Full breakfast.

Horncroft B&B, 42156 Kingston-Lyons Drive. (503) 769–6287. Large colonial home on a hillside above town. Three guest rooms, one with private bath. Swimming pool. Full breakfast served.

## Salem

Geppetto's, 616 Lancaster Drive NE. (503) 378–1271. Pizza and other Italian foods.

Thompson's Microbrewery, 3275 Liberty Road. (503) 370–7800.

Inn at Orchard Heights, 695 Orchard Heights Road NW. (503) 378–1780. Where locals go for fine continental cuisine, spiced with unique touches. Contemporary atmosphere in an old-fashioned home.

Chumaree Comfortel, 3301 Market Street NE. (503) 370–7888 or (800) 248–6273. Comfortable motel with sunken whirlpool, sauna, swimming pool, restaurant.

Executive Inn, 200 Commercial Street NE. (503) 363–4123. Similar amenities to Chumaree. Black Angus Restaurant on premises.

## Aurora

Chez Moustache, 21527 Highway 99E. (503) 678–1866. Gourmet dinners, intimate French country atmosphere.

## Canby

Filbertreats, 356 First Avenue NW. (503) 266–8172. Oregon-grown hazelnuts, candies, gift packs. See candy-making process on weekdays.

Elm Street Inn, 101 North Elm. (503) 263–6955. Colonial-style restaurant and lounge. Steak and seafood.

Jarboe's Grill, 1190 First Avenue SW. (503) 266–3805. Casual lunches, dinners, microbrewery.

# For More Information

Oregon City Chamber of Commerce, 500 Abernethy Road, Oregon City, OR 97045. (503) 656–1619.

Silverton Chamber of Commerce, 424 South Water Street, Silverton, OR 97381. (503) 873–5615.

Stayton Chamber of Commerce, 1203 First Street, Stayton, OR 97383. (503) 769–3464.

Salem Visitors Association, 1313 Mill Street SE, Salem, OR 97301. (503) 581–4325.

Aurora Colony Historical Society, P.O. Box 202, Aurora, OR 97002. (503) 678–5754.

Canby Chamber of Commerce, 266 First Street NW, Canby, OR 97013. (503) 266–4600.

# McKenzie River Highway

White-water rafting draws thousands of thrill-seekers to the McKenzie River.

## A Classic Northwest Adventure

### 1 NIGHT

Festive markets · Covered bridge · Scenic wild river · Hot springs
Old-growth forest · Stagecoach stop · Waterfalls · Historic village

Oregon's McKenzie River, which flows from hidden springs in Clear Lake, in the central Cascade Range, through lava fields, forests, and farmlands to join the Willamette, is internationally known for its great fishing and white-water rafting. Dozens of river guides and outfitters are eager to take you out in a raft or McKenzie River drift boat and introduce you to the joys of the river and the gorgeous scenery that surrounds it.

A ribbon of green in a green forest, with high, snow-topped mountains rising against the eastern sky, the McKenzie is one of the state's outstanding scenic attractions, and the road that runs beside it offers a chance to sample its pleasures in a brief getaway. You can always come back for more.

# Day 1

## Morning

Drive from Portland on I–5 to **Eugene,** 100 miles to the south. There's a lot to do in this university town, where counterculture meets high culture. You can tour art galleries and attend world-class concerts, or buy beads from street vendors at **Saturday Market.**

Eugene has shaken off the economic doldrums and is full of lively activity. To start your holiday on a vibrant note, head for the **Fifth Street Public Market,** in the historical downtown area. Under one roof, ninety shops and restaurants on three levels are bursting with wares. Browse through the market, relax in the brick courtyard, listen to the musicians, and watch the fountain play and people go by.

*Lunch:* **Mekala's,** 296 East Fifth Street, Eugene. (503) 342-4872. Extensive menu of perfectly spiced Thai food, to eat indoors or on the terrace. Located in Fifth Street Public Market.

## Afternoon

Leave Eugene, driving east on State Route 126; within a few miles you'll be edging the **McKenzie River** shore. (Alternatively, to allow more time by the river, you might skip the Eugene visit and turn directly off I–5 to east Springfield and Route 126.)

Long before white settlers arrived, Indians from eastern Oregon were traveling this route. They came to fish during salmon runs, pick berries, hunt game, and gather herbs in the valley. Then came the explorers, pioneers, and loggers. Today, it's sport fishers and tourists.

As you leave the city, homes become more widely spaced and fields and farms predominate. Soon you're passing groves of dark fir trees and the occasional clear-cut area, and you may see a deer standing by the roadside before it leaps into the shrubbery.

When you reach **Leaburg Dam,** 24 miles from I–5, stop to watch the salmon and steelhead as they climb a fish ladder during migration periods. The **trout hatchery** here, open for public observation, annually releases thousands of trout, summer steelhead smolt, and cutthroat trout fingerlings. The ponds also contain albino trout and Columbia River sturgeon.

Twenty-six miles upriver you'll come to **Goodpasture Covered Bridge.** The well-maintained, picturesque bridge, built in 1938 to replace a ferry that crossed the river here, is 165 feet long.

At the 30-mile point is Ben and Kay Dorris State Park. This is the place to watch the tumbling water of **Marten Rapids,** most famous of the McKenzie's white water.

**The Village Cafe** (also called Mom's Pies) is a small cafe with an old-fashioned soda fountain, outdoor tables on a terrace, and a cook who bakes superb pies. Ten or more varieties are served daily; try the Black-and-Blue, a flavorful combination of black- and blueberries.

Continue east to **Blue River.** The river, a tributary of the McKenzie, was named for the blue hues in the riverbed rocks. In the late 1800s, this was active mining country, after the discovery of gold in Blue River and in Lucky Boy mines. Most mining was abandoned in the 1920s, when the richest ore was gone.

Forest Road 15, which curves around the east end of Blue River Reservoir, leads to **Wolf Rock,** a massive hunk of basalt rising 4,500 feet. From gentle slopes covered with Douglas fir, you suddenly reach the base of the towering, solid black stone that erupted as molten lava thousands of years ago. It's an imposing sight, about 15 miles from the highway.

The next point of interest along the McKenzie is **Cougar Dam and Reservoir,** off Forest Road 19, which is paved and a federally designated Scenic Byway. Here, in Delta Campground, you'll find a trail that loops for ½ mile through an old-growth grove of Douglas fir and western red cedar. Some of the giant conifers are 200 to 500 years old.

A mile past the dam is a large parking area, and beyond it a lovely, ¾-mile trail to **Terwilliger Hot Springs.** Three pools of naturally heated water lie among the rocks and trees. This very popular destination is frequented by counterculture folk; avoid it if you're uncomfortable around nudity.

Tokatee Golf Course, located off Route 126, is an 18-hole golfer's paradise. It's considered one of the top courses in the Northwest and is surrounded by magnificent scenery.

Drive 5 miles east of Cougar Reservoir and you'll reach **McKenzie Bridge,** once called Strawberry Flat because of the abundant wild strawberries in the region. The present bridge spanning the river at this point is the fourth since 1869.

*Dinner:* **Log Cabin Restaurant,** McKenzie Bridge. Open for lunch on weekdays and for breakfast, lunch, and dinner on weekends. Varied menu with noted specialties: beer cheese soup, prime rib, buffalo, venison, and marionberry cobbler.

*Lodging:* **Log Cabin Inn,** 56483 McKenzie Highway, McKenzie Bridge, OR 97413. (503) 822-3432. Eight log cabins, one with a kitchen, on a meadow by the river. Rustic but modernized. Occupies the site of a former stagecoach stop and hotel, built in 1885 and rebuilt in 1907, when the first structure was destroyed by fire.

# Day 2

## Morning

*Breakfast:* Log Cabin Inn. Full breakfast menu with specials.

Route 126 and the river turn north after McKenzie Bridge and run past **Belknap Springs.** The hot mineral springs, discovered in 1859, have long been favored by those seeking the benefits of a hot springs soak. A hotel first opened here in 1972; now there's a resort with an RV park. Nonguests can use the hot mineral pool (102 degrees Fahrenheit) that has been constructed on the riverbank.

To see **Belknap Crater** close up, you have to take the Clear Lake cutoff. From this volcano came the lava flows that over the past 3,000 years formed the ravines and ledges where waterfalls now drop in spectacular cascades. One, at Milepost 70.5 on Route 126, is **Koosah Falls,** which plunges 70 feet into a deep bowl. Another—probably the most impressive of the entire McKenzie water network—is **Sahalie Falls,** just ¼ mile north of Koosah. Sahalie drops 100 feet to a lava ledge, then falls another 40 feet. Easy paths lead from the parking area to the falls.

At **Clear Lake,** ½ mile off the road, rent a rowboat (no motors are allowed on the lake) and row about fifteen minutes to the east shore. There you'll see a submerged forest lying deep within the lake's cold, crystal-clear waters. The trees are nearly 3,000 years old.

Several mountain peaks are visible: Jefferson, Three Fingered Jack, the Sand Mountain cones, Mount Washington, and the Three Sisters.

*Lunch:* Sandwiches or hamburgers from the concession at **Clear Lake Resort.**

You've reached the end of Route 126; turn west here on U.S. Route 20, and drive 43 miles to the small town of **Sweet Home.** In **Sankey Park,** a couple of blocks from the main street, stroll **Weddle Bridge,** a 120-foot covered bridge over Ames Creek. The reconstruction of the historic bridge was made possible by local volunteer support. The park also has a playground, picnic area, and log shelters in groves of fir trees. The sturdy shelters were built as a WPA project in the late 1930s.

The **Santiam River** edges the road here, swinging north. Take the short detour to **Brownsville,** a village with a strong sense of history. Established in 1846 on the Calapooia River, it's the third-oldest continuing settlement in Oregon. Those who took land claims in this lush valley said that the grass was so tall you could tie it over your saddle, and the cattle would become lost in the fields.

Brownsville began with a ferry service over the Calapooia, and in the early 1850s the town was laid out. It was a bustling trade center by 1884. In 1919 a fire destroyed much of the town, but some buildings escaped the blaze and are still standing. The **Linn County Museum** provides a free walking-tour map of the historic structures.

The historical museum is outstanding. Its carefully designed exhibits include an old-fashioned Main Street complete with general store, bank, and blacksmith shop, and barbershop. Kalapooya Indian artifacts, a miniature wagon collection, and much more are on display. A sign beside the covered wagon lists the costs of crossing the plains (one hundred pounds of coffee, $8.00; a thirty-pound tent, $2.50).

An outstanding example of Brownsville's historic buildings is the **Moyer House,** an elegant Italianate home with fine detailing, built in 1881. It now contains period furnishings and can be seen by appointment or on special occasions.

*Lunch:* **The General Store,** North Main and Stanard streets, Brownsville. (503) 466–5334. Simple, casual restaurant serving soups, thick sandwiches, pie, and oversize cookies. Closed Sundays.

## Afternoon

Browse among the small antiques and handcrafts in the gift shop that is part of The General Store; then head west from Brownsville on State Route 228.

Watch for **The Living Rock Studios** (503–466–5814), a unique gallery that is a must when exploring the area. The hand-built stone structure and its contents are the results of one man's dream to construct a memorial to the pioneering spirit.

Howard Taylor, his wife, Faye, and their family created an exhibition of petrified wood, family heirlooms, mineral specimens, wood carvings, and paintings depicting Oregon's history. The chief exhibit is a series of "Living Rock" biblical pictures made from translucent stone and backlighted to show their vivid colors. The studio is closed Mondays.

Rejoin Route 20; at Lebanon, take Route 34 west to join I–5 for the one-and-a-half-hour drive back to Portland.

An alternative would be to continue on Route 20, crossing the freeway into Albany and touring that historic town.

# There's More

**Water Board Park,** east of the state trout hatchery at Leaburg Dam. This well-kept, fifty-five-acre park has hiking trails, a softball field, horseshoe pits, a boat landing, a playground, and cooking grills.

**Fishing.** Cutthroat and German brown trout, Dolly Varden trout, summer-run steelhead, salmon, and rainbow trout are caught in the McKenzie. There are more than fifty licensed members in the local guides' association. For information, contact Bob Spencer, McKenzie

River Guides Association, 656 North Seventy-first Street, Springfield, OR 97478. (503) 747–8153.

**Hiking.** Pick up trail maps at the ranger station in Blue River or McKenzie Bridge. Notable hikes include:

McKenzie River National Recreation Trail, a 27-mile path, passes through some of the most historic and dramatic countryside on the McKenzie. It still bears evidence of the Old Santiam Wagon Road. The trail crosses side canyons on log bridges, winds among old-growth Douglas fir, passes by streaming waterfalls, and edges lakes with lava bottoms so porous they dry up and become meadows in summer.

Clear Lake. A gentle, 5-mile trail encircles the lake. On the way you see lava fields, dense forest, and hand-built log bridges.

**Hot Springs.** There are fifty-six hot springs near McKenzie Bridge. For a map and descriptions, send $8.00 to Oregon Department of Geology and Mineral Industries, 910 State Office Building, 1400 Southwest Fifth Avenue, Portland, OR 97201.

**River Rafting.** The McKenzie is famous for its white-water rafting thrills and float trips. One of the best guides and outfitters is McKenzie River Rafting Company, 7715 Thurston Road, Springfield, OR 97479. (503) 747–9231.

## Special Events

**Mid-June.** Linn County Pioneer Picnic, Brownsville. Oldest continuing celebration in Oregon, begun 1887. Picnic in Pioneer Park, parades, fiddlers' jamboree, arts-and-crafts fair, races, carnival.

**June–July.** Oregon Bach Festival, Eugene. Top-quality musical performances by internationally renowned artists.

## Other Recommended Restaurants and Lodgings

### Eugene

The House in the Woods, 814 Lorane Highway. (503) 343–3234. Bed-and-breakfast in turn-of-the-century home on wooded country road near the city. Full breakfast.

### Leaburg

Marjon Bed-and-Breakfast Inn, 44975 Leaburg Dam Road. (503) 896–3145. Two rooms in a chalet in the woods by the river, 24 miles from Eugene. Wondrous garden of rhododendrons, ferns, and azaleas. Full breakfast.

## Vida

The Wayfarer Resort, Star Route. (503) 896–3613. Cozy, well-equipped cabins with fireplaces and decks on the McKenzie and Marten Creek.

# For More Information

Eugene/Springfield Convention and Visitors Bureau, P.O. Box 10286, Eugene, OR 97440. (503) 484–5307; within Oregon, (800) 452–3670; outside Oregon, (800) 547–5445.

McKenzie River Chamber of Commerce, P.O. Box 1117, Leaburg, OR 97489. (503) 896–3330.

# Central Oregon

Skiers flock to Mount Bachelor for its slopes of powder snow and excellent facilities.

## High Desert Country

——————————— 2 NIGHTS ———————————

Mountain wilderness · Lava fields · Caves · Panoramic views · Wildlife
Frontier-style town · Indian museum · Boutique shopping
Fine dining · Hiking · Bird-watching · Fishing · Golf

Sunny central Oregon is a popular weekend getaway for rain-weary Portlanders. On the dry side of the Cascade Range, its weather is predictably pleasant in summer and clear, crisp, and cold in winter. In this land of rugged mountains with powder-snow ski slopes, 235 miles of streams, and more than a hundred lakes, outdoor recreation is a way of life. You can grab a good bite of it in three days and taste a bit of luxury on the way.

This itinerary emphasizes summer activities. In winter, if you're a skier, you know how you'll spend the weekend: on the lifts and runs of Mount Bachelor or Hoodoo, or slicing through the silent forest on cross-country trails. Other winter recreation includes ice skating, sleigh rides, and relaxing by a cozy fire.

# Day 1

## Morning

Drive U.S. Route 26 east from Portland to the **Warm Springs Indian Reservation.** As you cross the pass at Mount Hood, you'll leave the cool green rain forests behind and enter a dry landscape of sagebrush and ponderosa pine, steep cliffs and rocky canyons, backdrops to many Western movies.

A must on this route is a tour of the new **Museum at Warm Springs.** The innovative museum, constructed of native stone and timbers and designed to resemble an encampment among the cottonwoods along Shitike Creek, shows the heritage of the Confederated Tribes of the Warm Springs Reservation. Using petroglyph replicas, song, photographs, family heirlooms, and trade items, it tells of Indian traditions and how they were affected by the settlers. Open daily 10:00 A.M. to 5:00 P.M.

Just past the reservation border, take the **Pelton Dam** exit south for the 25-mile scenic route along the **Deschutes River Canyon.** Overlooks along **Rim Road** present panoramic views across the canyon to cliffs of gray columnar basalt and a wide, sage-covered plain that reaches to the snow-cloaked Cascades. **Mount Jefferson, Three Fingered Jack,** and the **Three Sisters** seem to float on the horizon, white against a deep blue sky.

You'll notice a plaque at one overlook, placed by Fuji Television Network to commemorate the 1984 filming of a popular Japanese TV program, "To Oregon with Love." You are likely to find solitude here, with the only sounds the cries of birds and the occasional roar of a motorboat far below. The air is pungent with the scent of juniper and sage.

South of **Round Butte Dam** and the overlooks, a winding road leads down to a bridge that crosses the Crooked River arm of **Lake Billy Chinook.** The lake, formed by dams holding back the waters of the Deschutes, Squaw Creek, and Crooked River, lies at the heart of 7,000-acre **Cove Palisades State Park.**

Walls of rock, carved by volcanic eruptions ten million years ago, tower above the deep green Billy Chinook and line its 72-mile shore. The lake and its watery arms are favorites with boaters and fishers.

Back on Rim Road, head for Culver and Highway 97, and turn south to Bend.

*Lunch:* **Deschutes Brewery and Public House,** 1044 Northwest Bond Street, Bend. (503) 382-9242. Dark woodwork, light menu, locally brewed beers. A microbrewery with style.

## Afternoon

Take Greenwood Avenue east to **Pilot Butte,** and drive—or, if the gate is closed, walk—to the top. A twenty-minute walk to the cinder cone's summit will present you with a 360-degree view of Bend, the valley, and the mountains that surround it. Under clear skies you can see virtually all the Oregon Cascades.

Next pay a visit to **Deschutes Historical Center,** housed in a former stone school building on Idaho Street, between Wall and Bond. Displays include pioneer memorabilia, arrowheads, thunder eggs, and a book of biographical sketches of early settlers. (Phone 503–389–1813; open Wednesday through Saturday afternoons.)

Spend the rest of the afternoon browsing through the inviting shops and galleries in **downtown Bend.** Buy note cards from Papers Perfect, select a piece of fine jewelry at Marty's, look for collectibles in Trivia Antiques.

Buy wines and pastas at La Strada and step into the new age of global- and self-awareness in The Curiosity Shoppe.

These shops and dozens more line Wall and its side streets.

*Dinner:* **Pescatore!,** 119 Northwest Minnesota Avenue, Bend. (503) 389-6276. Northern Italian menu with seafood, beef, and homemade pastas. Piano bar.

*Lodging:* **Lara House,** 640 Northwest Congress Avenue. (503) 388-4064. Bed-and-breakfast home near Drake Park. Well-furnished, comfortable guest rooms, cozy sunroom.

# Day 2

## Morning

*Breakfast:* Lara House serves a full breakfast.

Drive 6 miles south on Route 97 for a tour of the **High Desert Museum,** 59800 South Highway 97 (503–382–4754). This outstanding center of natural and cultural history shows wildlife (beavers, otters, owls) in natural settings, re-creations of historic events, and interpretive programs that help to increase your knowledge of the high desert country. Open daily.

Continue south on Route 97 for 5 more miles to **Lava Lands Visitor Center.** Watch an introductory slide presentation; then follow interpretive trails through the rough black lava and adjoining pine forest. From here, shuttles carry visitors to the summit of **Lava Butte,** a cinder cone formed 6,160 years ago, for stunning views of the lava flows and Cascade Mountains. You can see Newberry Volcano and the Blue Mountains of eastern Oregon.

Drive a few more miles to **Sunriver,** a self-contained resort community with a lodge, tennis courts, two 18-hole golf courses, an airport, and shopping malls. This is one of the Northwest's major planned recreational and retirement developments.

*Lunch:* **Trout House,** Sunriver. (503) 593–8880. Waterside restaurant at the river marina. Hot sandwiches, hamburgers, salads, specials (grilled trout, poached salmon).

## Afternoon

Rent a bicycle at the Sunriver shop, and ride the numerous paved, winding paths; or stroll to **Sunriver Nature Center,** where injured birds and animals are sheltered. If you'd prefer a game of golf on a sprawling green course traversed by streams and surrounded by high mountain peaks, club rentals are available at **Sunriver Lodge.**

An alternative to the Sunriver trip is to bring a picnic with you to Lava Lands Visitor Center. After your tour, drive 4 miles past the center to a picnic area for lunch. Then take the mile-long path that leads downstream, across a footbridge, and on to beautiful **Benham Falls.**

For other short hikes through the spectacular central Cascades, take Highway 97 south 22 miles from Bend and turn east at the signs to Paulina and East lakes. From here, walk the **Peter Skeen Ogden Trail** to cascading waterfalls, or take the **Newberry Crater Obsidian Trail** (a fifteen-minute walk) to see one of the world's largest obsidian flows.

Drive back to Bend and relax before dinner.

*Dinner:* **Pine Tavern Restaurant,** 967 Northwest Brooks Street, Bend. (503) 382–5581. Bend's oldest eatery. Prime rib, lamb, barbecued ribs in a warm, natural wood setting. Windows view tree-shaded lawn and the Deschutes River.

*Lodging:* **Lara House,** Bend.

# Day 3

## Morning

*Breakfast:* Lara House.

Feed bread crumbs to the ducks and Canada geese that claim ownership of **Drake Park;** then head north on U.S. Route 20 toward **Sisters.** You're likely to see llamas behind ranch fences along the way; this is the llama capital of North America. The exotic animals are used for show competition, pack trips, and pets, and their wool is prized by spinners and knitters.

The town of Sisters looks like a scene from the Old West, with its wooden boardwalks and false storefronts. Behind them, boutiques and art galleries sell gifts, trendy clothing, Indian and wildlife art, carved burl furniture, frozen yogurt, and whimsies of all kinds.

Because the frontier town churns with activity in summer, chances are strong that you will find yourself in the midst of one of the many festivals.

Fill your water canteen and buy picnic foods at a deli—there are several—and then drive north of Sisters toward **Camp Sherman** and **Black Butte,** a symmetrical cinder cone 6,436 feet high.

The two- to three-hour hike up the butte will present you with splendid views of the pine-covered foothills and jagged white mountains. The trail is an easy grade through the woods and up to open clearings. It culminates in a flat summit with a lookout station. From here, the western views of the Three Sisters, Mount Jefferson, and Mount Hood are breathtaking. To the east you can see the steep, sheer **Smith Rocks** rising from the desert.

For a longer hike (about four hours) and an even higher perspective, drive 11 miles west of Sisters on Route 242 to **Black Crater Trail.** It's open from July through mid-October. Steep in spots, the hike is challenging but not unreasonable. And the vista is worth the effort.

After climbing wooded slopes and ridges to a 7,251-foot summit of rough lava, you'll see Mount Washington, Three Fingered Jack, the Three Sisters, Mount Jefferson, Olallie Butte, and Mount Hood's snowy cap rising 11,235 feet on the north—all the major peaks of the Oregon Cascades. Clearly evident is the Belknap Crater flow of black lava, spreading below.

*Lunch:* Picnic along the trail.

## Afternoon

Return to your vehicle, and travel north on Route 20 over **Santiam Pass,** which lies between the Mount Jefferson and Mount Washington wilderness areas. When you reach State Route 22, angle northward to follow the curving, cascading **Santiam River**. On either side of the mountainous road are evergreen and deciduous forests dotted white with dogwood blooms in spring.

The Santiam flows into the deep green, dammed reservoir of **Detroit Lake.** Past the dam, rocky cliffs rise sharply on your right. Waterfalls bounce over them, occasionally splashing the road.

Descending from the mountains, passing small timber towns, you'll eventually reach the lush farmlands of the **Willamette Valley.** Continue on to Salem and the juncture with I–5 for the forty-five-minute drive north on the freeway to Portland.

# There's More

**Crooked River Dinner Train,** 115 Northwest Oregon, Bend. (503) 388–1966 or (800) 872–8542. Weekend evenings and Sunday brunch. Entertainment (murder mysteries, western hoedowns) and two-and-a-half-hour scenic rides.

**Horseback riding.** Blue Lake Corrals, Blue Lake. (503) 595–6681 or 595–6671. All-day, breakfast, steak, and pony rides.

High Cascade Stables, Sisters. (503) 549–4972. Hourly, moonlight, cookout, hay wagon, and wilderness pack trips.

**Whitewater rafting.** Hunter Expeditions, Bend. (503) 389–8370. Float and white-water guided rafting trips on the Deschutes.

Inn of the Seventh Mountain, Bend. (503) 382–8711.

**Rock climbing.** Smith Rock State Park, north of Redmond in Crooked River Canyon, has massive, colorful rock formations that present a steep challenge to climbers and a fascinating spectator sport for watchers. There's a climbing school and guide service in Terrebonne. Call (503) 548–1888.

**Spelunking.** For information on exploring lava tube caves, call (503) 382–3221.

**Cascade Lakes Highway.** This 89-mile scenic loop road provides glorious views of lakes, meadows, Mount Bachelor, the Three Sisters, and Broken Top. At Crane Prairie Reservoir, stop to walk a ¼-mile nature trail to see one of the few osprey nesting sites in the United States. (Cascade Lakes Highway is closed to autos in winter.)

**Pine Mountain Observatory,** 25 miles east of Bend. Observe the skies on Friday and Saturday evenings in spring and summer; reservations required (503–382–8331).

**Petersen Rock Garden,** 10 miles north of Bend off Route 97. Four-acre park of miniature bridges, towers, and buildings, all made with various types of rocks. Picnic area, lily ponds, peacocks. Open daily.

**Operation Santa Claus,** 2 miles west of Redmond on State Route 126. World's largest commercial reindeer ranch, with one hundred reindeer. Visitors welcome; open daily.

**Lava River Cave,** 12 miles south of Bend on Route 97. In summer months, lanterns are rented for tours of the mile-long lava cave. Bring walking shoes and a warm jacket.

**Lava Cast Forest,** 14 miles south of Bend. From Route 97, turn east on Forest Road 9720, opposite the Sunriver turnoff. This is the world's largest grouping of lava tree molds. A paved, self-guided nature trail leads through the lava flow.

# Special Events

**January.** Sled Dog Race, Sisters. Mushers and spectators gather for "The Old Oregon Championship" dogsled race.

**Mid-February.** Art-Hopping Tour, downtown Bend. Evening walking tour to get acquainted with the arts. Showings, demonstrations.

**May.** Pole, Pedal, Paddle Race, Bend. Downhill and cross-country ski, run, bicycle, and canoe on the Deschutes River.

**Mid-June.** Sisters Rodeo, Sisters. Rodeo extravaganza with top competitors from around the nation.

**Late June.** Cascade Festival of Music, Bend. Eight-day series of concerts in Drake Park. Jazz, classical, chamber music, Broadway favorites. Concession stands, strolling minstrels, open rehearsals, student workshops.

**Fourth of July.** Gem and Rock Show, Sisters. Gem dealers gather to buy, sell, and trade.

**Mid-July.** Quilt Show, Sisters. Hundreds of handmade quilts on outdoor display.

**December.** Christmas Festival, Sisters. Santa parade, camels, wise men, llamas, music, and a peppermint bear.

# Other Recommended Restaurants and Lodgings

## Bend

Inn of the Seventh Mountain, P.O. Box 1207. (503) 382–8711. Family resort on Century Drive, between Bend and Mount Bachelor. Lodge and condo units with kitchens, three swimming pools, ice rink, good restaurants.

Le Bistro, 1203 Northeast Third Street. (503) 389–7274. Light French provincial cuisine in former church. Open kitchen, European chef, downstairs lounge.

Goody's, 957 Northwest Wall. (503) 389–5185. Old-fashioned soda fountain, candy, toys.

Pastries by Hans, 915 Northwest Wall Street. (503) 389–9700. Toothsome pastries, sandwiches, coffees in European shop. Closed weekends.

Rosette, 150 Northwest Oregon. (503) 383–2780. Casual restaurant, lunch and dinner daily. Pacific Northwest cuisine with Oriental touch.

Stuft Pizza, 125 Northwest Oregon Avenue. (503) 382–4022. Zesty Sicilian-style pizza. *Calzone,* sandwiches, salads, beer and wine. In historic building.

Westside Cafe, 1005½ Northwest Galveston Avenue. (503) 382–3426. Highly popular for breakfast and lunch. Natural foods, great muffins and sandwiches, reasonable prices.

## Black Butte Ranch

Black Butte Ranch, P.O. Box 8000. (503) 595–6211 or (800) 452–7455. Quiet retreat and top-quality contemporary resort in spectacular setting of wide meadows surrounded by mountains. Golf, tennis, restaurant.

## Sisters

Conklin's Guest House, 69013 Camp Polk Road. (503) 549–0123. Homey, friendly bed-and-breakfast on four and a half acres with mountain views. Four guest rooms, full breakfast, swimming pool.

The Fourth Sister Lodge, P.O. Box 591. (503) 549–6441. Bedroom units and one- and two-bedroom suites with kitchens and fireplaces.

Hotel Sisters, 101 Cascade Street. (503) 549–RIBS. Good food, Sunday specials (chicken and dumplings) in an 1880s-style restaurant. Cowboy boots and spurs hang above the swinging doors to Bronco Billy's Saloon.

## Sunriver

Sunriver Lodge and Resort. (503) 593–1221 or (800) 547–3922. Major resort community, with lodge rooms and rental homes. Many amenities and recreational facilities.

## Warm Springs

Kah-Nee-Ta, P.O. Box K. (503) 553–1112 or (800) 831–0100. Resort and convention center on a hilltop in Warm Springs Indian Reservation. Tribal culture and heritage displayed throughout lodge. Swimming, golf, fishing, mineral baths. Comfortable accommodations, good restaurant.

# For More Information

Bend Chamber of Commerce, 63085 North Highway 97, Bend, OR 97701. (503) 382–3221.

Sisters Chamber of Commerce, P.O. Box 476, Sisters, OR 97759. (503) 549–0251.

Wilderness maps and trail information available from Deschutes National Forest, 1230 Northeast Third Street, Bend, OR 97701. (503) 388–5664.

# Long Beach Peninsula

Victorian home in Oysterville, a history-steeped village on the Long Beach Peninsula.

## Vacation by the Sea

_____ 2 NIGHTS _____

Lighthouses · 28-mile beach · Ocean views · Historic village
Oyster beds · Cranberry bogs · Seaside resort town · Fine dining

Long Beach Peninsula, a slim stretch of land in Washington's far-southwestern corner, is a getaway with something for almost everyone. It offers wide beaches and sand dunes, gourmet dining, good fishing, raucous fun for the kids, and a quiet village steeped in history.

## Day 1

### Morning

Drive west on U.S. Route 30, along the Columbia River, for 96 miles to Astoria, and cross the bridge that spans the wide, choppy mouth of the river.

Turn west on Washington State Route 401 to **Chinook.** This was once a rich fishing town; back in the early 1900s, one man with five traps caught 12,000 pounds of salmon in a single day. It's still a fishing community, with a packing company its main industry.

Continue around the curving bay to **Ilwaco.** The small community, named after a local Indian chief, had a rough reputation at the turn of the century, when gill-netters and trappers fought ferociously over fishing grounds. Today it's a peaceful village with a busy waterfront, noted for its charter fishing and boating.

Tour the **Ilwaco Heritage Museum** on Lake Street (206–642–3466; open daily) and learn about the Northwest heritage, from Chinook Indian life to the logging and fishing industries. There are a restored depot and a model train (a replica of the 1920 peninsula railroad), as well as artifacts from early-day explorations. You'll notice **outdoor murals** on the walls in Ilwaco and elsewhere on the peninsula. They're part of a plan to attract visitors, who enjoy watching the artists at work and observing colorful scenes from the area's history. At the museum, pick up a scenic loop map, which will guide you on a 3-mile trip around the southwestern tip of the peninsula. Your first stop will be at **North Head Lighthouse,** which was built in 1899 to warn boats approaching from the north. From this bluff above the Pacific you have a panoramic ocean view.

The road then curves toward **Fort Canby State Park** and the **Lewis and Clark Interpretive Center** (open daily in summer, weekends in winter). The center traces the intrepid explorers' adventures through pictorial displays and original journal entries. Walking ramps take you from the planning of the expedition in 1804, through the team's travels, to its final destination—the Pacific Ocean as you see it here. If the weather is stormy, you'll have the thrill of watching surf action at its wildest, as monster breakers slam against steep cliffs.

Near here is **Waikiki Beach,** a local picnic favorite. It's the only relatively safe swimming beach in the area.

South of the Lewis and Clark Interpretive Center is the **Coast Guard station** (lifeboat skills are taught here) where you can park and then walk the ¼-mile path to the **Cape Disappointment Lighthouse.** Built in 1856, it's one of the oldest lighthouses on the West Coast. Far below you lie the churning river mouth and the white-capped sea.

This location, **Cape Disappointment,** was named by Captain John Meares in 1788, when he was unable to cross the rough Columbia bar. More than 200 ships have wrecked or sunk in these treacherous waters.

The loop drive will take you back to Ilwaco, one of several Northwest towns claiming the title of Salmon Capital of the World. Drive down to the harbor to see the busy tangle of boats and crab pots, charter fishing companies, canneries, and cafes, all mingling on the waterfront. The harbor has moorage for 1,000 boats.

**Dockside Cannery and Gift Shop,** on the waterfront, sells fresh seafood and gift packs.

*Lunch:* **Smalley's Galley,** Ilwaco harbor. (206) 642–8700. Hamburgers, fish-and-chips, homemade chowder, wharfside atmosphere.

## Afternoon

Head north 2 miles into **Seaview,** once a fashionable resort town. Turn-of-the-century Portlanders went by steamer down the Columbia and then on a narrow-gauge train to the village that still retains a pleasantly drowsy, old-fashioned atmosphere in its byways.

This is a place for quiet walks on the sand and musing in art galleries. **The Sea Chest,** showing the works of watercolorist Charles Mulvey, is probably the best known.

**Long Beach,** just north of Seaview, is a lot livelier and more commercial. Youngsters love its go-cart track, irresistible candy shop (Milton York's), moped rentals, horseback riding, and Marsh's Museum, which is crammed with oddities and kitschy souvenirs. Several mini-parks have whimsical wooden sculptures to climb on.

The wide, windy beach, said to be the longest (28 miles) in the world, is perfect for kite flying. Buy a kite at **Long Beach Kites,** and spend an exhilarating hour holding a bright dragon, box, or bird against the sky.

Peruse the vintage clothing, glassware, china, and dolls at **Ancient Crest Antiques,** next to Marsh's Museum. At **Pastimes,** on South Fifth Street and Pacific Highway, choose among clocks, china, and linens and sip espresso while browsing through the collection of magazines and newspapers. Pastimes serves Italian sodas, teas, cookies, a cheese plate, and muffins. You can purchase sweets made from the local product at **Cranberry House** and pick up a book at **The Bookvendor,** 101 Pacific Highway, to take to a sheltered dune on the beach.

Check in at **The Shelburne Inn,** and enjoy a Northwest wine or beer at the inn's **Heron and Beaver Pub.**

*Dinner:* **Shoalwater Restaurant** in Shelburne Inn, Seaview. (206) 642–4142. Gourmet dining emphasizing regional foods and fine wines. Candlelight, linens, stained glass, quiet atmosphere.

*Lodging:* The Shelburne Inn, P.O. Box 250, Seaview, WA 98644. (206) 642–2422. Antiques-furnished inn, on National Register of Historic Places. Calico quilts and plenty of charm.

# Day 2

## Morning

*Breakfast:* Full country breakfast served family style in the Shoalwater Restaurant, included in the hotel's room rate.

Drive north from the Shelburne, stopping at **My Mom's Pie Kitchen** for a picnic lunch-to-go. The pies are messy to take out, but order a slice anyway; My Mom's world-class pies are worth it.

As you travel up the peninsula, with sand dunes on one side and forests on the other, you'll pass **cranberry bogs.** In this major cranberry-growing center, the roads are bordered with acres of brilliant red berries in the fall. If you call ahead, you're welcome to visit Washington State University's cranberry research and extension center on weekdays (206–642–2031).

Stop at **Briscoe Lake,** north of Long Beach, to watch the trumpeter swans. The rare, majestic birds, which weigh up to thirty pounds, migrate to peninsula lakes and Willapa Bay in December and January.

Passing **Klipsan Beach** and **Ocean Park,** seaside communities with good beach access, turn east and cross the peninsula to **Oysterville,** the town that time passed by. Here great sailing ships loaded with oysters sailed to San Francisco during gold-rush days, in the mid-1800s, when oysters sold for a dollar apiece. The industry collapsed, the village faded, and now all the gracious old homes and the pretty church are on the National Register of Historic Places. Pick up a walking-tour map of the town at the **Oysterville Church,** and amble into a previous century.

Drive north on Stackpole Road to **Leadbetter Point State Park,** at the northern tip of the peninsula. Honeycombed with hiking trails, it's a quiet world of sand dunes, beach grasses, forest, and low shrubs.

The park is a part of **Willapa National Wildlife Refuge,** home to thousands of shorebirds that feed and rest on the tidal flats and salt marshes during their migrations. In the nesting season (April–August), the dunes portion of Leadbetter Point is closed to the public to protect the snowy plover. The rest of the park is open year-round.

*Lunch:* Picnic in Leadbetter Park.

Walk **Eliot Hiking Trail** into the state park, watching for birds, or surf fish or dig for clams. Spend a couple of hours relaxing on the beach with the book you bought the preceding day.

Travel south on Sandridge Road to **Nahcotta.** This was the northern terminus of the railroad that used to carry vacationers up and down the peninsula. Once a booming community, it's still active in the oyster business. You can see white mountains of shells near the docks at the Port of Peninsula.

At **Wiegardt Brothers' Jolly Roger Oysters**, Nahcotta Boat Basin, buy oysters shucked or in the shell. Oysters and other seafood can also be purchased at **East Point Seafood Company** (closed Sundays); you can select crab, lobster, clams, oysters, and mussels from a live tank.

*Dinner:* **The Ark,** Nahcotta. (206) 665–4133. Nationally acclaimed restaurant featuring regional seafood specialties, homemade breads, and fabulous desserts. Picturesque setting overlooking Willapa Bay.

*Lodging:* **The Shelburne Inn**.

# Day 3

## Morning

*Breakfast:* Another Shoalwater breakfast, perhaps with homemade sausage omelet and buttery pastries.

Walk to the beach for a last stroll on the sand, and head south to Route 401. Turn east to Route 4 and I–5 for the drive back to Portland; or cross the toll bridge and return via U.S. Highway 30.

# There's More

**Golf.** Peninsula Golf, North Long Beach. Nine-hole course. (206) 642–2828.

Surfside Golf Course, 2 miles north of Ocean Park. Nine-hole course, snack bar, pro shop. (206) 665–4148.

**Fishing** (salmon, tuna, sturgeon, flounder, sole). Ilwaco Charter Service, Inc., Box 323, Ilwaco, WA 98624. (206) 642–3232.

Ocean Adventures, P.O. Box 803, Ilwaco, WA 98624. (206) 642–8338.

**Art galleries.** Maxwell-Muir Pottery, Northwest corner of Portland and Main streets, Chinook. Open every day but Tuesday.

Gallery on the Hill, 608 Hemlock Street, Ilwaco. Open weekends.

Wiegardt's Studio, between Highway 103 and Sandridge on Bay, Ocean Park. Open weekends.

**Cranberries.** Coastal Washington Research and Extension Service, Pioneer Road. (206) 642–2031.

**Clamming.** The peninsula has several excellent clamming locations. Locals like digging the Surfside beach for razor clams.

**Boating.** Bring your own boat to Long Beach Peninsula. Suggestions:

Canoe Loomis Lake, in Loomis Lake State Park, where you may come upon a stand of wild rice.

Boat from Nahcotta to Long Island, in Willapa Bay, and hike up to the last known groves of old-growth cedar in the United States. In this wilderness, home to deer, elk, grouse, bear, and 1,000-year-old trees, you can experience a bit of what the Northwest was like when Lewis and Clark arrived. Note: The bay is subject to tidal action; consult a tide table and use caution.

**Seaview Antiques and Collectibles Mall,** 4705 Pacific Highway South. (206) 642–2851. Several dealers sell wares in colorful old Seaview house.

# Special Events

**April.** Ragtime Rhodie Festival, Long Beach. Weekend performances of Dixieland jazz.

**First Saturday in May.** Blessing of the Fleet, Ilwaco. Children's parade to the harbor, Indian salmon barbecue, flowers cast on waters at the mouth of the river.

**June.** Garlic Festival, Ocean Park. Garlic peeling contest, music, dancing, food booths.

**Mid-June.** World's Longest Beach Run, Long Beach. 10-kilometer and 3-mile courses.

**July.** Sand Sculpture Contest, Long Beach. Cash prizes for winning sand sculptures.

**Mid-August.** International Kite Festival, Long Beach. Annual kite-flying competition on the beach; one of the world's largest kite events.

**Late October.** Cranberry Festival, Ilwaco. Honors cranberry farming with exhibits ranging from cranberry candy to cranberry quilts.

# Other Recommended Restaurants and Lodgings

## Chinook

Sanctuary Restaurant, Highway 101 and Hazel Street. (206) 777–8380. Local seafood, superbly prepared, and friendly service in a restored former church.

## Ilwaco

The Inn at Ilwaco, 120 Williams Street NE. (206) 642–8686. Former church converted to bed-and-breakfast hotel and performing arts center. Cozily furnished rooms, friendly ambience. Full breakfast.

## Seaview

42nd Street Cafe, Forty-second and Highway 103. Lunch and dinner in cozy, quiet, nostalgic atmopshere. (206) 642–2323.

Sou'Wester Lodge, Beach Access Road. (206) 642–2542. Historic home of former U.S. senator, very casual, on the beach. Three rooms in lodge plus several cabins and mobile homes.

## For More Information

Willapa Bay National Wildlife Refuge, Highway 101, Ilwaco, WA 98624. (206) 484–3482.

Peninsula Visitors Bureau, P.O. Box 562, Long Beach, WA 98631. (206) 642–2400 or (800) 451–2542.

# Seattle Escapes

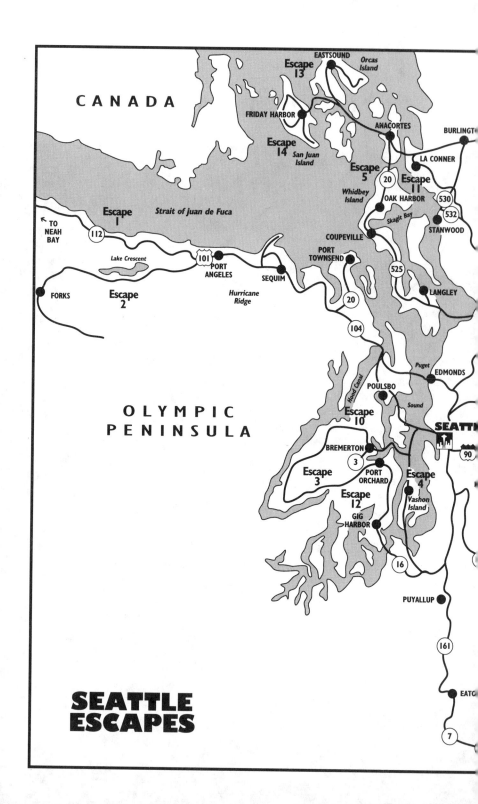

SEATTLE
ESCAPES

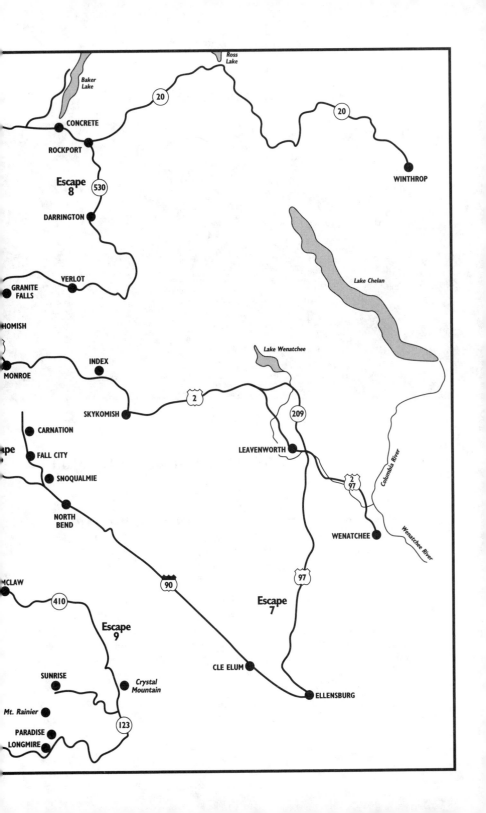

# Strait of Juan de Fuca

Lake Crescent Lodge, a classic hotel on the Olympic Peninsula.

## Touring the Northern Olympic Peninsula

_____ 2 NIGHTS _____

Ferry rides • Views of Puget Sound and Strait of Juan de Fuca
Historical museums • National Wildlife Refuge • Herb farm
Native American museum • Northwest corner of United States
Makah Indian reservation • Hiking trails • Rugged coastline

Between the Olympic Peninsula's verdant wilderness and the southern
rim of Vancouver Island lies the Strait of Juan de Fuca, dividing the
United States from Canada. The sometimes-treacherous, always-
fascinating waterway separates Puget Sound and the San Juan and
Gulf islands from the wild Pacific.

The 110-mile road edging the strait takes you through a microcosm
of the variety found on the peninsula. From its eastern tip, where a
quaint town clings to its Victorian heyday, to the Indian fishing village

and fog-shrouded coast on the far western corner, the peninsula provides glimpses of great diversity.

# Day 1

## Morning

Take the Winslow ferry from Elliott Bay, Seattle, to Bainbridge Island, and head for the Hood Canal Bridge. Cross the bridge to the **Olympic Peninsula,** and turn north on Paradise Bay Road, which follows the coastline (passing Port Ludlow Resort and housing development) and curves inland toward U.S. Route 20. Through the trees you'll catch glimpses of pleasure boats on **Admiralty Inlet** as you continue north to **Port Townsend.**

Much of this attractive town, which is divided between a downtown waterfront district and a residential area on a bluff above it, is a designated **National Historic District.** Victorian homes and commercial buildings, built in the late nineteenth century when Port Townsend was expected to become a great seaport, have been restored with pride.

The town was named in 1792 by Captain George Vancouver in honor of an English marquis, but it wasn't officially established until 1851, when the first settlers built a log cabin at the corner of Water and Tyler streets. The community grew, and its prospects as a center of commerce seemed limitless until the transcontinental railroad was laid—and stopped at Seattle.

Out on the peninsula, Port Townsend was left to languish until its charm as a little-changed Victorian seaport was recognized in the 1970s. Now it booms with tourism and as an arts center.

At the chamber of commerce office, pick up brochures and a tour map that points out seventy-two historic homes and sites. Then continue into town to the end of Water Street and the city hall and museum. Park your car in this area; most of the tour is easy walking from here.

Start at City Hall, which houses the **Jefferson County Historical Museum.** Built in 1891, this was once the county courthouse. Now it houses an eclectic assortment of memorabilia: early photos, Victorian and Indian artifacts, a rifle and sword collection, Chinese fans and tea canisters. In one corner there stands a chair made of buffalo horn and bearskin; in another lies a mastodon tusk.

Those who advocate no frills for prisoners will approve of the dungeonlike jail cells in the basement. Rumor says that author Jack London once spent a night here.

*Lunch:* **The·Landfall,** 412 Water Street. (206) 385–5814. Casual, friendly spot serving hamburgers, alder-barbecued seafood, Mexican dishes. Overlooks marina at Point Hudson.

## Afternoon

Highlights you'll see as you explore this history-steeped town include the following:

**The Haller Fountain,** Taylor and Washington streets. The bronze figure, variously named Galatea, Venus, and Innocence, was shown at the Chicago Exhibition of 1893. It was donated to Port Townsend by Theodore Haller in honor of the early pioneers.

**Chinese Tree of Heaven,** a spreading, one-hundred-year-old tree said to be a gift from the emperor of China. It was intended for San Francisco, but the ship carrying it was blown off course near Port Townsend. In thanks for his happy stay here, the ship's captain left the tree.

**Jefferson County Courthouse,** Jefferson Street. Built in 1892, the castlelike building is one of the two oldest courthouses still in use in the state. Its one-hundred-foot clock tower is a beacon to sailors.

**Old Bell Tower,** on a bluff at Tyler and Jefferson streets, overlooking the downtown district, dates from 1890. It's the only one of its kind in the United States.

**Rothschild House,** Taylor and Washington streets. This 1868 home of an early Port Townsend merchant is open for tours daily in summer, weekends in winter.

**Ann Starrett Mansion,** Clay and Adams streets. The most elaborate Victorian mansion in Port Townsend was built in 1899 in classic stick style. Its circular staircase, ceiling frescoes, and elaborate furnishings make afternoon tours popular with visitors. The house is now in use as a bed-and-breakfast inn.

After your walking tour of this waterfront town, check the myriad **shops of Water Street and "Uptown,"** a business district on Lawrence Street that was originally begun so that respectable ladies would not have to venture to the rougher waterfront area to shop.

Sooner or later everyone stops for ice cream or a delectable espresso-chip brownie at **Elevated Ice Cream,** 627 Water Street. The bright little shop is reputed to have the best ice cream in the state.

A drive out to **Fort Worden State Park** will take you to the location where *An Officer and a Gentleman* was filmed. Built at the turn of the century as a base to defend Puget Sound, Fort Worden is a 330-acre estate with an army cemetery, officers' quarters, theater, parade grounds, gun emplacements, bronze foundry, and Point Wilson Light Station.

The Centrum Foundation, a nonprofit arts organization, is based here. Numerous workshops, classes, and programs are presented regularly.

At the **Port Townsend Marine Science Center,** in a historic building on the public fishing pier at Fort Worden, visitors can touch and handle sea creatures at open "wet tables." Starfish, sea cucumbers, tube worms, and other marine life live in the touch tanks. The center holds classes in marine ecology, shows informative slide shows, and runs workshops. It's open afternoons in summer, Tuesday through Sunday, and weekends in fall and spring (other times by request; call 206–385–5582 or 385–4730).

On the return trip into town, stop at **Chetzemoka Park** to stroll the grassy grounds and enjoy the fragrant rose garden. The park is named for a Clallam Indian chief who assisted the community in its earliest days. Chetzemoka Park has a bandstand, picnic tables, playground equipment, and access to the beach.

*Dinner:* **Fountain Cafe,** 920 Washington Street. (206) 385–1364. Small, unpretentious restaurant on a hillside above the downtown area. Sublime chowder, pastas, dinners, and desserts.

*Lodging:* **James House,** 1238 Washington Street, Port Townsend, WA 98368. (206) 385–1238. Grand Victorian home built in 1891. Three floors of antiques-furnished rooms, some with private baths.

# Day 2

## Morning

*Breakfast:* Fruit, yogurt, and granola, plus a basket of hot scones and muffins, served in the kitchen at James House.

Drive 13 miles south on Route 20 to U.S. Highway 101; turn right to curve around Discovery Bay and Sequim Bay. Continue 17 miles west to **Port Angeles.** On your right is the **Strait of Juan de Fuca,** a wide channel that defines the border between Washington and Vancouver Island, Canada. On the left the Olympic Range rises 7,000 feet, snow clad and craggy, in Olympic National Park.

Drive to **Port Angeles Fine Art Center,** 1203 East Eighth Street. This gallery is in an award-winning home on five parklike acres overlooking the city, with views of the mountains and water. Visual arts exhibitions are shown year-round. The center is open from 11:00 A.M. to 5:00 P.M. Thursday through Sunday.

If it's a weekday, tour the **Clallam County Historical Museum,** Fourth and Lincoln streets (206–452–7831; open 10:00 A.M. to 4:00 P.M. Monday through Friday). On the second floor of the brick, Georgian-style courthouse are photographs of early Port Angeles, maritime exhibits, and a replica of an old-fashioned country store complete with a checkers game set up on a barrel.

The courthouse itself is interesting. Built in 1914 and now on the state and national historic registers, it has a stained-glass skylight, a clock tower, and a view of **Port Angeles harbor** 4 blocks down the hill. On a clear day you can see across the strait to downtown Victoria. *Lunch*: **The Greenery**, 117B East First Street. (206) 457–4112. Continental menu, homemade pasta, local seafood.

### Afternoon

Drive west on 101 for 5 miles, and branch onto Route 112, which skirts the rim of the peninsula. Far less traveled than the main highway, the route has a greater sense of wilderness. On your left is **Olympic National Park;** on your right the rolling surf of Juan de Fuca and beyond it Vancouver Island, its hills looming hazily green and peaked with frost. Eagles perch in the trees and soar above the water; smoke from wood stoves drifts through the air.

At **Salt Creek Recreation Area,** stop to explore the tide pools among the rocks. Now a county park, Salt Creek was once a World War II defense site. You can still see bunkers and gun emplacements. The park has hiking trails, a kitchen shelter and picnic area, showers, a playground, a softball field, and horseshoe pits.

Farther west, **Clallam Bay** and **Sekiu,** neighboring communities divided by a harbor, host thousands of visitors yearly who come in search of salmon and immense halibut. Resorts and charter companies offer boat rentals and ocean trips. Scuba divers seek abalone and octopus off the coast.

The tide pools at **Slip Point** are particularly interesting for their teeming sea life. You may encounter scuba divers in search of abalone and octopus.

Continue to the **Makah Indian Reservation** and the village of **Neah Bay** (67 miles west of Port Angeles). This is the home of the **Makah Cultural and Research Center,** a highlight of the trip.

The $2 million museum, built in 1979, contains a superb collection of Northwest Indian artifacts—more than 55,000. Most were found in the Makah archaeological dig at **Lake Ozette.** There are canoes, intricate weavings of cedar and bird feathers, whale and seal harpoons, baskets, and a replica of an Indian longhouse. One striking exhibit is a cedar carving of a whale's fin inlaid with more than 700 otter teeth.

The museum, which has a gift shop selling the works of Makah artists, is open daily in summer from 10:00 A.M. to 5:00 P.M. Mid-September through May it's closed Monday and Tuesday (206–645–2711).

From Neah Bay, it's an 8½-mile drive to **Cape Flattery.** Walk the wooded (often muddy) trail to the tip of the cape (a thirty-minute walk) and you are standing at the northwesternmost point in the contiguous United States. The tree-clad cliff, 150 feet high, faces **Tatoosh**

**Island.** Far below, ocean waves crash against jagged rocks, sending plumes of spray skyward. Whales and elephant seals swim these waters, and seabirds nest in rock hollows.

Retrace your drive on Route 112 east to the Sappho turnoff and turn south. At Sappho head east on Highway 101, along the **Soleduck River** toward Olympic National Park and **Lake Crescent.** The deep blue, glacier-formed lake has some 4,700 surface acres and varies in width from ½ mile to 2 miles. The lake is completely surrounded by national parklands.

*Dinner:* **Lake Crescent Lodge restaurant,** on the south shore of the lake. Good, hearty fare, featuring Northwest seafood and homemade breads, soups, and pies.

After dinner, enjoy a stroll by the lake or relax before the big stone fireplace in the antiques-furnished lobby.

*Lodging:* Lake Crescent Lodge, HC 62, Box 11, Port Angeles, WA 98362. (206) 928–3211. Historic, peaceful hotel facing the lake and forested mountains. Old-fashioned lodge rooms, modern motel units, and separate cottages available. Some fireplaces, no kitchens. Open May through October.

# Day 3

## Morning

*Breakfast:* Substantial, tasty breakfasts are served in Lake Crescent Lodge restaurant, which overlooks the lake.

The restaurant kitchen will prepare a box lunch if you request.

There are many ways to enjoy a morning at Lake Crescent. You can rent a rowboat, fish for Beardslee trout, sit in a lawn chair and read, or go hiking. Don't miss a walk up to lovely **Marymere Falls.** The ¾-mile trail can be reached from the lodge or from the nearby Storm King Ranger Station. The path winds through ancient fir and hemlock trees, over a stream on rustic wooden bridges, past mushrooms and flowering plants, and finally ascends sharply to an observation point with a full view of the 90-foot cascade of water. The first ½ mile of the trail is wheelchair accessible.

From the Marymere Falls Trail, you can continue on **Mount Storm King Trail** for a 2¾-mile climb that offers high views of Lake Crescent.

*Lunch:* Picnic by the lake or in the forest, or return to Lake Crescent and eat in the restaurant.

## Afternoon

For a different perspective on the lake, drive to the northeast shore and take East Beach Road. Park at the end of the road; from here you can hike all or part of **Spruce Railroad Trail,** which travels for 4 miles through the only roadless wilderness area around Lake Crescent.

Then retrace your route back to Seattle, 144 miles from Lake Crescent.

# There's More

**First Friday Gallery Walk,** Port Townsend. On the first Friday evening of the month, galleries and studios are open late.

**City Pier, Port Angeles.** This shoreline park has an observation tower, lawns, picnic area, boat moorage, and promenade decks.

**Arthur D. Feiro Marine Laboratory,** City Pier, Port Angeles. Displays of local marine specimens, including a large octopus. Seas stars and other creatures in the touch tank. Open daily.

**Bicycling.** The city of Port Townsend lends bicycles; find them at various downtown locations such as the corner of Quincy and Water streets.

**Boating.** Boat rentals at Lake Crescent, Port Angeles, and Sequim.

Strait and Narrow Kayak Tours, 1306 East Third Street, Port Angeles. (206) 452–3487. Guided sea kayak day trips.

**Fishing.** Salmon season starts in late spring, closes September. Bottom fishing from February to November. Fish for the famous Beardslee trout in Lake Crescent.

Port Angeles Charters represents three charter fishing companies in the area. (206) 457–7629.

**Golf.** Dungeness Golf Course, Dungeness. (206) 683–6344. Eighteen-hole course, driving range, clubhouse, restaurant.

Peninsula Golf Course, Port Angeles (206) 457–7348. An eighteen-hole, combination public and private course east of town.

Port Ludlow Golf Course, Port Ludlow. (206) 437–2222. Eighteen holes on hillside above Admiralty Inlet, east Olympic Peninsula.

**Hiking.** Olympic National Park has 600 miles of hiking trails. Before hiking on beaches, consult a tide table. Headland crossings can be dangerous. The *Strip of Wilderness* pamphlet, available at visitors' centers, is helpful.

**Hurricane Ridge,** 17 miles inland from Port Angeles. Mountain ridge with forest and meadow trails, breathtaking views.

**Dungeness Spit,** near Sequim. Longest sand jetty in the United States, 7 miles of sand, agates, and driftwood. National Wildlife Refuge with waterfowl, shorebirds, seals.

# Special Events

**Early May and late September.** Historic Homes Tours, Port Townsend. Self-guided tours of the city's Victorian architecture: mansions, cottages, country inns, public buildings.

**Mid-May.** Rhododendron Festival, Port Townsend. Parade, bed race, flower show, arts-amd-crafts fair, dancing, fireworks.

**Mid-July.** Clallam–Sekiu Fun Days, Clallam Bay. Parade, fun run, logging show, arts-and-crafts booths, salmon bake, fireworks, salmon derby.

**Late July.** Port Townsend Jazz Festival. Musicians from around the country perform on the Fort Worden main stage in daytime and in the evenings in downtown pubs.

**Last weekend in August.** Makah Days, Neah Bay. Traditional Makah Indian salmon bakes, costumes, dances, canoe races, parades.

**Early September.** Wooden Boat Festival, Port Townsend. Hand-crafted wooden boats on display. Films, demonstrations.

# Other Recommended Restaurants and Lodgings

## Port Angeles

The Bavarian Inn, 1126 East Seventh Street. (206) 457–4098. European-style home with flower boxes and Bavarian decor. Three guest rooms, two with private bath. Full breakfast served.

## Port Ludlow

The Resort at Port Ludlow, 9483 Oak Bay Road. (206) 437–2222 or (800) 732–1239. Resort on Admiralty Inlet with 188 condominium rentals. Tennis, golf, pools, bicycles, croquet, restaurant, lounge.

## Port Townsend

Ann Starrett Mansion, 744 Clay Street. (206) 385–3205. The most opulent bed-and-breakfast in town. Historic home with Victorian gingerbread, nine guest rooms. Full breakfast.

Bread and Roses Bakery, 230 Quincy Street. (206) 385–1044. Home-baked pastries, soups, sandwiches, espresso.

Lizzie's, 731 Pierce Street. (206) 385–4168. Victorian bed-and-breakfast home with eight guest rooms. Full breakfast.

Ravenscroft Inn, 533 Quincy Street. (206) 385–2784. Nine spacious rooms in a hillside inn with a classic look. Antiques, peaceful atmosphere, full breakfast.

Salal Cafe, 634 Water Street. (206) 385–6532. Healthy, home-style foods, mostly vegetarian. Plant-filled solarium.

## For More Information

Washington State Ferries, 801 Alaskan Way, Pier 52 Colman Dock, Seattle, WA 98104. (206) 464–6400; within Washington, (800) 84–FERRY.

Olympic National Park, 600 East Park Avenue, Port Angeles, WA 98362. (206) 452–4501.

Port Townsend Visitors' Information Center, 2437 Sims Way, Port Townsend, WA 98368. (206) 385–2722.

Port Angeles Visitors' Information Center, 121 East Railroad Avenue, Port Angeles, WA 98362. (206) 452–2363.

# The Hoh River Valley, Olympic Peninsula

The rain forest grows dense and thick in the Hoh River Valley.

## Exploring the Rain Forest

_____ 1 NIGHT _____

Rain forest · Wilderness trails · Isolated beaches
Scenic ocean and mountain views · Hot springs · Trout fishing

A temperate rain forest is so intensely green it's almost eerie. Even the sunlight has a green cast as it filters through the treetops, ferns, and hanging moss. The air, hushed and humid, smells of decay and fresh new growth.

There are only three such forests on Earth. One is in southern Chile, another in New Zealand, and a third on the western side of the Olympic Peninsula in Washington. Here the crumpled, snow-topped Olympic Range intercepts air masses that flow in from the Pacific and wrings from them 140 inches of rain a year, creating a lush, verdant jungle.

This two-day venture into that jungle will give you a satisfying glimpse of a primeval world, inspiring you to return and further explore its wild depths.

# Day 1

## Morning

*Breakfast:* In Edmonds (north of Seattle), at **brusseau's,** 117 Fifth Avenue South (206–774–4166). The cafe, which has an outdoor patio, is known for its freshly baked muffins and pastries.

Take the ferry west from Edmonds to Kingston, on the Kitsap Peninsula, a thirty-minute ride across Puget Sound. From the ferry, you can see, on a clear day, the majestic, snow-clad Olympic Mountains rising above forested slopes.

Follow State Route 104 to cross the bridge over **Hood Canal.** This is the longest bridge over an inland waterway in the United States; it stretches to the eastern coast of the Olympic Peninsula.

When you arrive on the peninsula, continue 15 miles on 104 to join Highway 101. Turn north on 101, which skirts the **Strait of Juan de Fuca** on the northern shore of the peninsula (see Seattle Escape One for a detailed itinerary of this region).

Five miles beyond Port Angeles, Highway 101 branches south and curves around the south rim of **Lake Crescent.** The lake's cobalt blue waters, 600 feet deep, are surrounded by deep green forests of fir, hemlock, spruce, and cedar.

Stop at **Storm King Information Station** on the lake's eastern edge for maps, brochures, and hiking suggestions; then continue on 101 to Soleduck River Road. Turn left and drive 12 miles beside the river to Sol Duc Hot Springs Resort.

*Lunch:* **Sol Duc Hot Springs Resort.** At the informal resort's poolside deli window, purchase a sandwich or hamburger and beverage (beer is available) to eat at an outside table. (206) 327–3583. The main restaurant here is open only for breakfast and dinner.

Alternatively, you can bring a picnic lunch from home or one purchased in Port Angeles.

## Afternoon

Drive to the end of Soleduck River Road for a 1-mile hike through the dense, mossy rain forest, ending at lovely **Soleduck Falls. Lover's Lane** continues past the falls to make a 5-mile loop that takes you back to the resort. **Mink Lake Trail,** which begins at the hot springs, is another 5-mile round-trip hike. It climbs 1,100 feet through thickly forested country to the lake, where you can fish for trout.

At Sol Duc Hot Springs Resort you can, for a nominal fee, swim in an Olympic-size pool and soak in three pools of hot (102 to 109 degrees Fahrenheit) mineral water. There are few more satisfying ways to ease tired muscles after a hike. The resort is open from May to October.

Retrace your route along the Soleduck River to Highway 101, and head west through the river-webbed woodland to **Forks.** Forks is the only community of size on the northwestern peninsula and is arguably one of the rainiest in the United States. It's been a farming and timber settlement since the late 1880s.

*Dinner:* **North South Garden.** (206) 374–9779. Good Chinese food, mostly spicy Szechuan.

*Lodging:* **Miller Tree Inn,** Sixth and Division streets, P.O. Box 953, Forks, WA 98331. (206) 374–6806. Bed-and-breakfast in a 1917 homestead on three parklike acres. Six rooms share three baths.

# Day 2

## Morning

*Breakfast:* Prue and Ted Miller serve an ample breakfast at Miller Tree Inn—pancakes, fruit, cereal, eggs cooked to order, and plenty of hot coffee will prepare you for an active day.

Purchase picnic foods at the **Shop-Rite** supermarket deli in the middle of Forks on Highway 101 and travel 12 miles to Hoh Valley Road. The **Hoh Rain Forest Visitor Center** is another 19 miles into the park, along the Hoh River. Tour the attractive, well-designed center to learn about the botany, wildlife, and natural history of the rain forest. The staff is knowledgeable and helpful.

There are three trails in the **Hoh River Valley,** plus a paved mini-trail accessible to wheelchairs. Each begins at the visitors' center.

The **Hall of Mosses,** a ¾-mile loop, is a striking sample of life in this damp, iridescent world. The path is silent and spongy beneath immense big-leaf maples, Sitka spruce, western hemlock, and Douglas fir. The ground is carpeted with lettuce lichens, ferns, and sorrel. Tree branches are shaggy with club moss and licorice fern, and a green canopy curtains the sky. When a breeze ripples leaves and fronds, you feel that you've stepped into an aquarium, with undersea plants swaying above you.

The **Hoh River Trail** extends deeper into the wilderness, following the river path for 12 miles, then angling up the shoulder of Mount Olympus to the edge of Blue Glacier. The long, broad finger of oozing ice marks the starting place for climbers ascending the 8,000-foot peak.

The **Spruce Nature Trail,** a 1¼-mile loop walk, leads to a sandy bank of the Hoh River, a good resting and picnicking stop. You may see elk and deer.

*Lunch:* Picnic along the trail.

### Afternoon

Continue your exploration of the Hoh River Valley, or turn back to Highway 101 and drive northward. Two miles north of Forks, turn west and drive 13 miles to **Rialto Beach.** A ⅛-mile paved trail takes you to a beach overlook with a view of James Island and Cake Rock.

Rialto is a favorite among those who know the peninsula's beaches. The scenery is spectacular, with offshore sea stacks and thundering surf. At low tide you can stroll the sand, and when the tide's in, search among the pebbles for agates and pick your way through piles of drift logs, "the bones of the forest." One mile north of Rialto is the sea-carved rock arch called Hole-in-the-Wall.

Return to Highway 101, and drive north and east toward Port Angeles, rejoining Route 104 for the return to Seattle. You can either take the ferry from Kingston to Edmonds or head south to Route 305 and Bainbridge Island. Have dinner in **Winslow;** then ferry across Puget Sound to the Seattle waterfront.

*Dinner:* **Little Italy West,** 104 Madison Avenue North, Winslow. (206) 842–0517. Not much to look at from the outside, but the pizza and pastas in this tiny cafe are outstanding.

## There's More

**Forks Timber Museum,** on Highway 101 across from the city park. Displays show local logging industry history. (206) 374–9663. (Open daily.)

**Tillicum Park,** Forks. Large city park with tennis courts, ball fields, and playground equipment. Look for the train engine on Highway 101 and Forks Avenue North.

**Camping.** Several campgrounds along the Hoh River. Reserve space early. Obtain information through Olympic National Park Headquarters (address below).

## Special Events

**June 30–July 4.** Old-fashioned Fourth of July, Forks. Grand parade, kiddies' parade, frog-jumping contest, talent show, logging show, dog show, Moonlight Madness sales, teen dance, Firecracker Fun Run.

# Other Recommended
# Restaurants and Lodgings

## Forks

Manitou Lodge, P.O. Box 600. (206) 374–6295. Secluded log lodge on the Soleduck River, 3½ miles from Rialto Beach. Five rooms, one with fireplace. Full breakfast included.

# For More Information

Washington State Ferries, 801 Alaskan Way, Pier 52 Colman Dock, Seattle, WA 98104. (206) 464–6400; within Washington, (800) 84–FERRY.

Olympic National Park, 600 East Park Avenue, Port Angeles, WA 98362. (206) 452–4501.

Forks Chamber of Commerce, P.O. Box 1249, Forks, WA 98331. (206) 374–2531.

# Central Kitsap and Hood Canal

Murals on the walls of Port Orchard buildings illustrate scenes from the town's past.

## Waterside Relaxation

_____ 2 NIGHTS _____

Ferry ride · Historic ship tour · Art gallery · Marina
Museums · Antiques · Waterfront estate · Specialty shops

## Day 1

### Morning

In Seattle board the ferry to **Bremerton,** a one-hour ride across Puget Sound, passing the southern shore of Bainbridge Island and into Sinclair Inlet and Bremerton.

This longtime Navy town, headquarters of the Puget Sound Naval Shipyard, is home port to numerous ships. On the waterfront you'll see bristling battleships, vessels of the inactive fleet. You can tour one ship, the *USS Turner Joy*, which is linked to the ferry terminal by a boardwalk. The destroyer, built in 1957–1958, served in Vietnam and has been a naval memorial since 1988. Now it's a musuem, open for tours. Wear flat shoes and be prepared to climb steep steps when you come aboard.

Stroll up to Fourth Street and check in at the visitors' center for brochures and maps. Next door is the **Naval Museum,** which preserves and depicts the history of the U.S. Navy and the naval shipyard. It has an array of artifacts and marine displays.

On the corner of Fourth Street and Pacific Avenue is the new **4th Pacific Arts Building,** which houses four art galleries. It's well worth a tour to see the works of regional artists. Another interesting browsing spot is **Yesterday's, Today's, and Tomorrow's**—a soda fountain, deli, toy store, and vintage emporium where you can buy traditional Christmas ornaments, Tiffany-style lamps, and collectible salt and pepper shakers.

*Lunch:* **Boat Shed,** 101 Shore Drive. (206) 377–2600. Flavorful clam chowder and hearty sandwiches, prompt service; views of water, Mannette Bridge, and a rocky beach.

## Afternoon

Drive Highway 3 north, on the west side of Dyes Inlet, and follow the map's directions to Olympic View Road. Your destination is **Seabreez Cottage,** on the western shore of Kitsap Peninsula, facing **Hood Canal.** On the way you'll pass homes and farms and heavily wooded areas of elderberry trees, alders, cedars, and, eventually, miles of the cyclone fencing that marks the edge of Bangor Naval Base.

When you get to Seabreez, you'll never want to leave. The cozy, secluded cottage at the base of a steep hill is an ideal retreat for two, though it can accommodate four. Spend the rest of the afternoon here, lounging in the hammock at the water's edge, soaking in the spa, or just enjoying the salt air from the private deck. You might like to walk the rocky beach and collect oysters to eat raw or cooked (Seabreez has a tidy little kitchen).

In the late afternoon, drive into Old Town **Silverdale** and visit **Silverdale Waterfront Park.** The county park has a boat launch, picnic tables, lawns, a gazebo, and playground equipment. Adjacent to the park is the **Kitsap County Historical Museum,** with exhibits from the peninsula's past.

*Dinner:* **Yacht Club Broiler,** 9226 Bayshore Drive. (206) 698–1601. In an office complex at water's edge; a good dinner house serving updated continental cuisine. Sizable wine list.

After dinner, stop at the nearby Safeway or Thriftway market to buy

picnic foods for the next day; they can be stored in your cottage's refrigerator.
*Lodging:* Seabreez Cottage, 16609 Olympic View Road NW, Silverdale. (206) 692–4648. A private little dream house on the shore. Fireplace, washer/dryer, equipped kitchen, two bedrooms in the loft (very steep stairs to the loft).

# Day 2

## Morning

*Breakfast:* The Seabreez host, Dennis Fulton (whose separate home is above, on the hillside) placed breakfast foods in your refrigerator before you arrived. Fix your own juice, cereal, pastries, and fruit. Ample supplies of coffee, tea, and cocoa.

Spend the morning relaxing at your hideaway, reading, playing darts, or watching the seals and seagulls. You may see submarines from the naval base.

Midmorning, pack up and head southwest for **Scenic Beach State Park,** off Seabeck Way. Walk the trails of this woodsy, mossy, green park, which has a saltwater beach, great views of Hood Canal and the Olympic Mountains, and a boat launch. There's good fishing, swimming, oystering, and scuba diving here.

*Lunch:* Picnic in the park.

## Afternoon

From the park drive on to **Seabeck,** a former logging site known mainly for its retreat and conference center, and stop for a latte or espresso and a wedge of homemade pie at **Seabeck Espresso,** a tiny cafe with a lot of character.

Continue on toward Holly Road and your destination for the evening, **Willcox House.** For the rest of the day, wallow in luxury at this waterfront estate. Stroll the landscaped grounds, where azaleas grow in profusion, and admire the saltwater pool (unheated), fish pond, and paths through the woods where bracken fern grows head high. Steps lead down to the pier, where boats and float planes dock, and the oyster-strewn beach. Across the canal lies the Olympic Peninsula, with the jagged, snow-topped Olympics rising against the sky.

Indoors, you might play a game of pool or chess in the game room or browse through the dozens of books and magazines in the library. The mansion was built in 1936 for Colonel Julian Willcox and his wife, Constance. In later years it was used as a school and retreat center. In the late 1980s Cecilia and Philip Hughes restored the home in period style, so that now it reflects its former grandeur, with walnut paneling, several fireplaces, and an art deco motif.

Complimentary wine and cheese are served every afternoon in the library.

*Dinner:* Willcox House. Outstanding cuisine served in a small dining area overlooking lawns and Hood Canal. A typical dinner might include a salad of mixed exotic greens, alder-smoked salmon with lime butter, wild rice, and chocolate gâteau. Wines from California, Europe, and the Northwest are available.

*Lodging:* Willcox House. There are five guest rooms, one with a marble fireplace and 1930s-style bathroom, all mirrors and chrome. The Clark Gable Room (the actor was a guest here) has a king-size bed and private balcony.

# Day 3

## Morning

*Breakfast:* Included in the Willcox House room rate is a full breakfast. Serve yourself juice, coffee or tea, granola, yogurt, and fruit from the sideboard. An entree of waffles or crepes or another breakfast dish follows.

When you (reluctantly) leave Willcox House and return to Holly Road, travel south about a mile to Dewatto Road and turn left. As you climb the hill of fir trees and rhododendrons, you'll catch glimpses of Hood Canal and the Olympic Peninsula. This road, up a slope and down, takes you by tree farms, clear-cuts, the occasional small farm and orchard, and then a creek, tumbling through greenery that glows incandescent when the sun shines.

Following the signs to Belfair and then Tahuya, you'll come to North Shore Road, which borders Hood Canal. Cottages line the shore, where herons fly over mud flats and rocky beaches. Traffic is usually light. This is the most secluded part of Hood Canal, with grand views of the mountains to the west.

North Shore Road becomes Route 300 on the way to Belfair. At Belfair turn north on Route 3 heading toward **Port Orchard,** another 13 miles. Port Orchard, a pleasant waterfront town with a nautical air, is well known among collectors of antiques. At the recently remodeled **Olde Central Antique Mall,** 801 Bay Street, sixty-odd dealers sell antiques, collectibles, and arts and crafts. There are several art galleries and antique shops within a 4-block radius. **Bernier's Booty** is crammed with country gifts of high quality. **Agape Gallery** has Native American and ethnic crafts.

Free parking is available by the waterfront, which has a nice park with a gazebo and sandy beach. Concerts are often held in the park, adjacent to the **Port Orchard Marina** and a block from the center of town. Also by the marina is the local **passenger ferry,** which will take you over the inlet to Bremerton in fifteen minutes.

For a glimpse of life as it was a century ago on the Kitsap Peninsula, tour the **Log Cabin Museum.** Themed exhibits change regularly. The **Sidney Art Gallery** has several rooms of paintings by regional artists; on the second floor of the building are historical displays. On Saturday mornings from May through October, you can buy fresh produce at the **farmer's market** on Frederick Street, between Bay Street and the marina.

*Lunch:* **Tweten's Lighthouse,** 429 Bay Street. (206) 876–8464. Salads and hearty sandwiches in a waterside restaurant with an exterior that resembles a lighthouse. Sunday buffet brunch; lunch and dinner (seafood, steak, pasta, chicken) daily. Eat indoors or on the patio, overlooking the inlet.

### Afternoon

Take Bethel Road from Port Orchard and, if you're interested in collections, stop at **Springhouse Dolls and Gifts,** 1044 Bethel Road SE. The small shop is filled with dolls of every kind, many of them collectors' items.

Continue to **Long Lake Park,** at the north end of a large lake. The park offers fishing, boating, picnic areas, and a playground. After stretching your legs with a walk by the lake, continue east toward the **Southworth ferry landing,** and board the ferry back to Seattle.

# There's More

**Belfair State Park.** Former Native American gathering place, 3 miles south of Belfair. Swimming, fishing, clamming, crabbing, bicycling, camping.

**Twanoh State Park.** On Hood Canal, popular for oystering, clamming, hiking, fishing, boating. Boat launches, campsites, fire pits. Well-maintained park.

**Golf.** McCormick Woods, Port Orchard. Eighteen-hole course with driving range, pro shop, putting and chipping greens. (206) 895–0130.

Gold Mountain, Bremerton. Popular municipal course. (206) 674–2363.

Lakeland Village Golf Course, near Bremerton. Eighteen holes, pro shop, fine restaurant. (206) 275–6100.

**Harbor Tours.** Narrated boat tours of Bremerton waterfront, cruising by ships and shipyard. Hourly departures June to October from *USS Turner Joy* dock. (206) 377–8924.

**Silver Bay Herb Farm,** 9151 Tracyton Boulevard, Bremerton. (206) 692–1340. A working farm on Dyes Inlet near Silverdale. Herb classes, garden tours, tea parties, gift shop, "gourmet herbal picnics."

# Special Events

**Mid-July.** Whaling Days, Silverdale. Three-day festival with parade, street fair, races, volleyball, entertainment, food.

**Late August.** Kitsap County Fair and Rodeo, Silverdale. Carnival, pie-baking contests, local bands, 4-H events, rodeo, destruction derby.

**Early September.** Bremerton Blackberry Festival. Music, outdoor theater, clowns, blackberry baking contest.

# Other Recommended Restaurants and Lodgings

## Seabeck

Summer Song Bed-and-Breakfast, P.O. Box 82. (206) 830–5089. A charming cottage with kitchen, sitting area, deck. Situated on a slope by a rose garden; some water views, beach access.

Tide's End Cottage, 10195 Manley Road NW. (206) 692–8109.

## Silverdale

Silverdale on the Bay Resort Hotel, 3073 Bucklin Hill Road. (206) 698–1000 or (800) 528–1234. Beachside resort with restaurant, indoor pool, comfortable rooms.

Waterfront Park Bakery and Cafe, 3472 Byron Street. (206) 698–2991. Sandwiches, coffee, rich and chewy cookies, and brownies.

# For More Information

Bremerton/Kitsap Visitor and Convention Bureau, 120 Washington Avenue, Suite 101, Bremerton, WA 98310. (206) 479–3588.

Port Orchard Chamber of Commerce, 727 Bay Street, Port Orchard, WA 98366. (206) 876–3505.

Silverdale Chamber of Commerce, 9729 Silverdale Way, P.O. Box 1218, Silverdale, WA 98383. (206) 692–6800.

# Vashon Island

Fishing and pleasure boating are an important part of life on Vashon Island.

## Life in the Slow Lane

### 1 NIGHT

Rural landscape · Rocky beaches · Fishing · Boating · Hiking
Arts and crafts · Lighthouse · Peaceful country lanes

Vashon Island is a secluded getaway in southern Puget Sound, a fifteen-minute ferry ride from West Seattle. The 12-mile-long island is woodsy, rural, and unpretentious—quintessential Northwest. Tidy farms are bordered by acres of unruly blackberry vines heavy with clusters of sweet, juicy berries in late summer. Battered cabins face pebbly beaches strewn with driftwood. There are thick green forests, grassy meadows dotted with Queen Anne's lace, boating marinas, and hiking trails. The air smells of brine and fir needles.

Maury Island, on Vashon's southeast corner, was once a separate island but was connected to Vashon years ago. It has boating marinas, parks, a golf course, and a lighthouse.

# Day 1

## Morning

Take Fauntleroy Way southwest to the ferry landing. There are crossings almost every half-hour. Avoid commuters' hours when the ferries are invariably crowded.

From the ferry dock, drive Vashon Island Highway 5 miles into **Vashon,** the island's major community. You'll find that the people are friendly and visitors are welcome. On Saturdays, April through October, it seems that everyone on the island is in Vashon, checking the produce and crafts for sale at Saturday Market.

Stop at **Stewart Brothers Coffee,** on the corner of Vashon Highway and Cemetery Road. Fragrant coffee beans are roasted, bagged, and sold in this old-fashioned white frame building, where pots filled with flowers brighten the long veranda. On weekdays and some weekends, you can watch green coffee beans roast to black nuggets of flavor in the big red roaster.

The company has based its headquarters on Vashon for twelve years. Jim Stewart takes pride in producing top-quality, chaff-free coffees from beans shipped from far corners of the world. He sells more than twenty varieties here and in Seattle outlets.

Cross the street to **Owens Antiques** (closed Tuesdays) to browse through eleven rooms of American antiques, jewelry, Orientalia, and country primitives. The building began as a single tiny room, the first store on the island. A home was added in 1884.

Don't overlook **McFeed's,** on another corner of the same intersection. This store has more than animal supplies. There are tropical fish, cages of small animals (hamsters, gerbils, mice, rabbits, lizards), and exotic birds.

A few yards down the road from McFeed's is the best art gallery on the island, **Blue Heron Center for the Arts.** Recently expanded, the gallery sells silk scarves, glazed tiles, raku pieces, and batik earrings. Under the same roof is a performing arts center where concerts, dances, and dramas are often presented.

*Lunch:* **Sound Food Restaurant and Bakery,** Vashon Island Highway (206–463–3565; closed Tuesday). Casual, cheerful atmosphere. Delectable quiche, homemade soups and pastries. Eat indoors or on the patio next to a pretty garden.

## Afternoon

Buy island-made crafts at **Minglement,** in the same building as Sound Food Restaurant. The cozy, rustic shop also sells natural foods, herbs, and vitamins.

Step across the road to **Maury Island Farm Retail Shop,** where you can buy island-made berry preserves, smoked salmon, scone mixes, and other Northwest treats. Vashon Island is home base for several other sizable companies, including K-2 Skis, Island Spring, Inc. (a tofu producer), and Wax Orchards, which makes low-sugar preserves and syrups (the rich-tasting fudge sauce has only fifteen calories per teaspoon).

Midisland is **The Country Store and Farm.** Vy Biel's general store carries numerous products made on Vashon (herb vinegars, seeds, preserves, coffees), as well as clothing and garden supplies.

Drive southeast to **Portage** and the **Portage Store.** One of the oldest buildings on the island, this is where local folk gather to visit on the porch, play chess, or read a paperback from the store's book exchange. It's a good place for discussing the weather, getting acquainted, and admiring the fine view of **East Passage.**

Continue down Portage-Dockton Road to **Dockton Park,** on the western side of Maury. The park is mainly used as a boating and picnicking facility; a million-dollar improvement project a few years ago gave it moorage for sixty boats. Dockton has harbor views and free showers for swimmers. Walk the rocky beach and you'll see driftwood, shells, and fishing boats by the wharves.

*Dinner:* **Casa del Sol,** next to the northern ferry terminal. Well-prepared Mexican food in a prime location facing the Sound and Seattle skyline. (206) 567–5249.

*Lodging:* **Goosie's,** 18017 Thorsen Road SW, Vashon Island, WA 98070. (206) 463–2059. Romantic charm in a private country cottage set among flower gardens. Television, sitting room, kitchenette.

# Day 2

## Morning

*Breakfast:* A full breakfast, perhaps with waffles, is provided in your cottage at Goosie's.

Take a brisk morning walk on a nearby nature trail (ask your innkeeper, Carol Applegate, for directions). Then borrow bicycles from Carol, and ride to **Point Robinson Park,** on Maury's far-eastern corner. Bring a piece of fruit from the orchard at Goosie's, and buy picnic makings along the way at The Portage Store (or make a picnic from the preceding day's purchases). At Point Robinson, walk the trails, pick blackberries, stroll the narrow beaches, gaze across the passage at the Seattle skyline, and tour Point Robinson lighthouse grounds. The lighthouse dates from 1855.

Return the bicycles to Goosie's, and head back to Vashon Island

Highway. In Vashon, stop at **Antiques and Interiors,** which sells fine pieces of country pine and oak. This is the place to buy superbly crafted rosewood boxes made by William Franklin, who's known as the Wood Poet.

Follow the cinnamon and coffee scents to **Bob's Bakery,** in central Vashon. Take your coffee and pastry to the bakery's sidewalk bench, and watch the people go by.

At the north end of town, check the offerings at **Old Dreams.** In this former home, every room, even the bathroom and kitchen, is filled with antiques and collectibles: pincushions, baskets, utensils, glassware, china, Oriental vases—a dazzling hodgepodge of treasures.

**Puget Garden Resources,** open Thursday–Saturday, is a nursery at the edge of the woods, where you can amble among the native plants, unusual shrubs, and hardy eucalyptus.

Continue north to the ferry terminal for the ride back to Seattle. Alternatively, you can take the ferry from **Tahlequah,** at the southern tip of Vashon Island, to Rushton. From there it's easy to connect with Tacoma and I–5 and continue on to Seattle. If you leave the island early in the day, this route provides a prime opportunity to tour **Point Defiance Park,** just past the Rushton ferry terminal. The park's zoo, set against rolling green, wooded slopes, is world renowned. There are also aquariums, a rose garden, and a Japanese garden. The water's-edge scenery is unsurpassed.

## There's More

**Inspiration Point.** Scenic overlook on Vashon Island Highway, halfway between Burton and Tahlequah.

**Jensen Point Park.** Boat launching, picnicking, hiking trails. On the tip of the peninsula between Inner Harbor and Quartermaster Harbor.

**Quartermaster Marina.** Marina on Quartermaster Harbor at southern end of Vashon. (206) 463–3624. Small rental boats available.

**Tramp Harbor Fishing Pier,** on the coast north of Maury Island. Renovated pier open to the public for fishing.

**Vashon Country Club Golf Course,** 18-hole course on Maury Island. (206) 463–2005.

## Special Events

**Mid-July.** Strawberry Festival, Vashon. Street booths, parade, carnival rides, pancake breakfast, baby-photo contest, music, dancing, races. Strawberries and homemade ice cream at the Methodist church.

**Mid-September.** Harvest Fair, Vashon. Lively, folksy event with food and crafts booths, farmers' market, pony rides, petting zoo.

# Other Recommended Restaurants and Lodgings

The Crown and Sceptre, 20611 Eighty-seventh Avenue SW, Vashon. (206) 463–2697 or (206) 463–3556. Immaculate upstairs apartment in big red former barn. Secluded area. Four-poster bed, kitchen with breakfast provided in refrigerator.

Dog Day Cafe, Vashon Highway, Vashon. (206) 463–6404. Vegetarian cafe.

Happy Garden Restaurant and Lounge, Vashon Highway, Vashon. (206) 463–9109. Chinese dinners and a lounge where locals gather for open-mike performances on Wednesday nights. Open every day, all day.

The Malt Shop and Charburger, Vashon Plaza, Vashon. (206) 463–3740. Soda fountain and twenty-nine varieties of hamburgers and sandwiches. Outdoor service in summer.

The Old Tjomsland House B & B, 17011 Vashon Highway SW, Vashon. (206) 463–5275. Upper floor of Victorian farmhouse. A good choice for a family with children: informal atmosphere, crib and high chair provided, no charge for child under twelve. Bountiful breakfast.

Peabody's B&B, 23007 Sixty-fourth Avenue SW, Vashon. (206) 463–3506. Victorian farmhouse, shared with family, above the shore. Open May to October.

The Swallow's Nest, 6030 Southwest 248th Street, Vashon/Maury Island. (206) 463–2646. Romantic country cottages with kitchens or kitchenettes. Also a village harborside home accomodating eight.

Cafe Tosca, 9924 Southwest Bank Road. (206) 463–2125. Italian restaurant serving pasta, pesto, calamari, cheescake. Opera poster decor.

Tramp Harbor Inn, P.O. Box 741, Vashon. (206) 463–6794. Restored historic home, antiques, trout pond, view of harbor. Three rooms.

Vashon Island Hostel, Route 5, Box 349. (206) 463–2529. Several teepees and large log home with bunk beds on ten acres of pasture and woodland.

*Note:* Vera LeLouche (206–463–3556) will make reservations at most bed-and-breakfast inns. There's no charge for her service. Some places have a minimum stay of two nights. Or call the Vashon B&B Association (206–463–9186).

# For More Information

Vashon Business Association, P.O. Box 1035, Vashon, WA 98070. (206) 463–3591.

Washington State Ferries, 801 Alaskan Way, Pier 52 Colman Dock, Seattle, WA 98104. (206) 464–6400; within Washington, (800) 84–FERRY.

# Whidbey Island, Fidalgo Island

Paul Luvera's carved totem poles line the walk by his home on Whidbey Island.

## Island Getaway

_____ 2 NIGHTS _____

Pastoral countryside · Evergreen forests · Ocean views · Quaint villages
Boutique shopping · Historic sites · Hiking · Beachcombing
Fishing · Fine dining · Wine tasting

Whidbey Island, northwest of Seattle, is the longest island in the contiguous United States—60 miles from tip to tip. It has forested hills, farmlands, rocky beaches, and a rich history. Salish Indians, English explorers and traders, and American sea captains and settlers all played important roles in Whidbey's development.

North of Whidbey, across a bridge above a narrow, precipitous pass, is Fidalgo Island. Both islands are easily toured in this two-night getaway that provides both a relaxing change of pace and a stimulating change of scene.

# Day 1

## Morning

Drive I–5 north from Seattle to State Route 525 and on to Mukilteo, a forty-five-minute drive. The hourly ferry will take you on a fifteen-minute ride across the channel to Clinton, on the southeastern shore of **Whidbey Island.** From the terminal, follow the main road to **Langley** (watch for the turnoff; the sign is small).

Langley, the most charming and picturesque town on the island, is set on a cliff above **Saratoga Passage.** Facing the waterfront, it's backed by stands of Douglas fir and western red cedar, acres of rolling green pasture, and gnarled vestiges of pioneer orchards.

The town was formed in 1880 when Jacob Anthes stepped ashore and set about establishing a cordwood cutting business for the steamers that plied Puget Sound. Today it's one of those special places that visitors (and residents) love for its expansive water views, stylish shops with turn-of-the-century facades, and sense of community.

There's not a lot of active recreation; you come to Langley to relax. Stroll the streets, gaze at the mesmerizing sound and distant mountains, pose for a photo beside Georgia Gerber's captivating sculpture of a boy with his dog, looking out to sea.

Shop for candy and jewelry at The Wayward Sun and for country collectibles at The Blue Heart. Buy boat-related items at Virginia's Nauticals, old linens and laces in The Cottage, and snazzy women's clothing and jewelry at Sister.

Admire the totem poles in tiny **Seawall Park,** and taste a smoothie at JB's Juice Bar; browse among the French country and Audubon prints at Lowry James Antiques and the two floors of books at Moonraker.

*Lunch:* **Star Bistro,** 201½ First Street, Langley. (206) 221–2627. Ask for a table on the terrace roof and lunch on pasta, seafood, chicken pot pie, or Caesar salad.

## Afternoon

Langley boasts several **art galleries** that carry the works of regional artists. An example is Childers Proctor Gallery, which displays yellow cedar sculptures, raku pottery, unique earrings, and watercolors, among other items.

Tour **South Whidbey Historical Museum,** on the corner of Edge Cliff Drive and Camano Avenue, to see an array of items from the past: Logging equipment, Indian tools and arrowheads, dolls, vintage clothing, maps and photos, and an early-day mercantile store are part of the collection. Open Sundays and by appointment.

Explore the woodlands and country roads around Langley by horse or bicycle. Call Virginia Knapp (206–221–7106) to arrange a horseback ride; rent a bicycle at The Pedaler, 5603½ South Bayview Road (206–321–5040).

Return to quench your thirst while you listen to a 1923 nickelodeon player piano at The Dog House. This is a waterfront tavern with character. Its bar dates from 1881.

*Dinner:* **Cafe Langley,** 113 First Street. (206) 221–3090. Mediterranean foods served in a light setting of white walls, washed pine beams, and Mexican tile floors. Excellent soups, pasta, souvlakia, and crab cakes.

After dinner, attend a stage performance by the **Island Theater Community** at the **Clyde Theater.**

*Lodging:* **Eagle's Nest Inn,** 3236 East Saratoga Road, Langley, WA 98260. (206) 321–5331. A bed-and-breakfast that has four guest rooms and is situated high on a hill outside of town. Spacious, contemporary, expansive views.

# Day 2

## Morning

*Breakfast:* At Eagles Nest, the morning starts with a wake-up tray of juice and coffee in your room. Later, breakfast in the dining room may include baked apples and Belgian waffles.

Drive Route 525 west and north, passing Freeland, where Holmes Harbor cuts sharply into the island, and on to the rural countryside around **Greenbank.** Stop at **Whidbey's Greenbank Farm,** the largest loganberry farm in the world, where a brief, self-guided tour is offered. Then taste and purchase the farm's velvety loganberry liqueur and fruity, ruby-red wine. Fresh loganberries are available in season.

Continue north on Routes 525 and 20 to historic **Coupeville,** on **Penn Cove.** In a quick tour of the village you'll see the **John Alexander Blockhouse** (built in 1855 to repel hostile Indians), Victorian homes, and the quaint waterfront. Shops include Tartans and Tweeds, with an array of imported goods, and Coupeville Spinning Shop, which sells its yarns and weaving supplies all over the United States.

Buy sandwiches-to-go at the County Deli (206–678–3239) drive north on Route 20 to Libbey Road, then turn west and follow the signs to **Fort Ebey State Park.** Fort Ebey was built on a forested bluff in 1942 to protect Puget Sound from attack. Now part of **Ebey's Landing National Historical Reserve,** the park has gun batteries and bunkers to explore, a plank boardwalk to the beach, and superb views of the Olympic Peninsula and mountains and Canada in the distance. The

National Historical Reserve covers 22 square miles of beaches, parks, and historic buildings. It's named for the pioneer homesteader and legislator Colonel Isaac Neff Ebey.

*Lunch:* Picnic on the beach at Fort Ebey State Park while you watch the gulls and boats go by.

## Afternoon

Explore the park, swim, or fish for bass in **Lake Pondilla** (there's a trail to the lake from the picnic site). Later, take Route 20 north to **Deception Pass.** A high bridge crosses the steep pass between Whidbey and Fidalgo islands. **Deception Pass State Park** extends on both sides; the scenery is spectacular.

Part of the 2,400-acre park is preserved untouched for ecological study. The rest is dense forest and sandy shores, with boat launches, campsites, and wooded picnic grounds overlooking the water. This is one of the most-used parks in Washington.

Drive north along Rosario Road to Marine Drive, which overlooks **Burrows Bay** on Fidalgo's western shore, to Sunset Avenue. Turn left toward **Fidalgo Head** and **Washington Park.**

As you drive the 2½-mile loop through the large, forested park, you'll glimpse the waters of **Rosario Strait** through the trees. There are overlooks, grassy picnic sites, beaches, and a public boat ramp. At the playground, notice the thunderbird totem pole facing north. The colorful 30-foot totem was carved by artist Paul Luvera.

If you prefer to hike in the park, walk **Fidalgo Head Loop Trail,** which winds for 2.3 miles through forests of fern, cedar, and madrona, or take the stairs down to **Sunset Beach** on the north edge of the park.

Late in the afternoon, return to Sunset Avenue and take Skyline Way to **Flounder Bay** (a five-minute drive). Watch the pleasure boats, many with exotic destinations, from the wide windows of **Breezes** as you enjoy a drink and a snack. Breezes, a cheerful restaurant with a nautical motif, overlooks the busy marina.

Back on Sunset Avenue, drive east into downtown **Anacortes.** The largest city on the two islands is known to tourists mainly as the place to catch the ferry to the San Juan Islands and Canada, but it has much more to offer.

Still a rugged lumber and fishing town, with boatyards and lumber mills edging the water, Anacortes is sprucing up for the tourist trade. It has historic brick buildings, some nice shops, and a great setting for outdoor recreation.

Parks and greenery abound. There are 2,200 acres of forest, lakes, and mountaintops in and around the city. Five marinas provide more than 2,300 moorage slips for boats of all sizes. Many boaters begin their San Juan Island cruises from Anacortes.

*Dinner:* **La Petite,** 3401 Commercial Avenue, Anacortes. (206) 293–4644. A delightful surprise. Exceptional French and Dutch cuisine served in the restaurant of a plain motel on a busy street.

For a pleasant after-dinner stroll by the water, go to Rotary Park. It has a paved path, beach access, and marina views. The walkways are wheelchair accessible.

*Lodging:* **The Majestic European Country Inn,** 419 Commercial Avenue, Anacortes, WA 98221. (206) 293–3355. Beautifully restored downtown historic building, now a European-style luxury inn.

# Day 3

## Morning

*Breakfast:* Enjoy coffee and croissants in The Majestic's library (complimentary to guests) or a full breakfast in the light and airy restaurant.

As you tour downtown Anacortes (not a time-consuming experience), note the life-size outdoor murals that depict scenes from the city's past.

A stop at **Marine Supply and Hardware,** which occupies a city block on Second and Commercial streets, will give you a glimpse of the region's nautical history. This is the largest contiguous set of buildings on the National Register of Historic Places and the oldest operating marine supply store on the North American coast. Within the store's brick walls you'll find boat fittings, buoys, hardware, hip boots, maps, and kitchenware intermingled with all kinds of antiques. There's even a telephone pole running through one section; the friendly owners will tell you that story.

Among the interesting shops along Commercial Avenue are Burton's, with a sizable jewelry selection (the best outside Seattle, some claim), and Potlatch Gifts, offering fine Native American handicrafts. Sweet-n-Sassy is the place to buy luscious chocolate truffles and other candies, as well as specialty travel items.

If this is a summer weekend or holiday, take a ride in the elegant parlor cars of a narrow-gauge steam train. You'll find the train at the refurbished **Anacortes Depot,** 611 R Avenue. Next to the depot is a 163-foot stern-wheeler, the *W.T. Preston,* open for tours in summer.

Drive west on Ninth Street to E Avenue and watch for the totem poles. You won't miss them—a row of brilliantly painted, tall totems next to a house overlooking Guemes Channel. This is the home of Paul Luvera, a totem-pole carver whose works are displayed in Sweden, Japan, the Netherlands—and here, against the Anacortes seascape.

*Lunch:* **Gere-a-Deli,** 502 Commercial Avenue, Anacortes. (206) 293–7383. Casual cafe and deli with good soups and sandwiches. A local hangout, popular with both businessfolk and mothers with babies in strollers.

## Afternoon

Head for Fidalgo Bay, where Specialty Seafoods, at T Avenue and Thirtieth Street, sells fresh-from-the-sea products. Buy hand-shucked oysters or smoked salmon; then turn east on Route 20 and cross to the mainland and Interstate 5 for the 70-mile trip back to Seattle.

# There's More

**South Whidbey State Park,** off Smugglers Cove Road, Freeland. Probably the favorite park of islanders, with its campsites, picnic areas, outdoor amphitheater, 5 miles of beach trails, and sweeping views of the Olympics and shipping lanes. Trail access from the main parking lot is handicapped accessible.

**Island County Museum,** Coupeville. Pioneer memorabilia, walking-tour maps of historic area. Open afternoons, May–October.

**Fort Casey State Park,** south of Coupeville. Attractions in this former U.S. Defense Post include campsites, hiking trails, salmon and steelhead fishing, scuba diving in an underwater marine park, boat launch sites, and old gun batteries. Admiralty Point Lighthouse dates from 1860 and is now an interpretive center.

**Maiden of Deception Pass,** Rosario Beach. Hand-carved figure from single piece of cedar. A nearby plaque tells the Ko-kwal-al-wood Indian legend the carving represents.

**Guemes Island Ferry.** Seven-minute cruise from Anacortes to little Guemes Island. A ride aboard the 124-foot ferry is a hassle-free, inexpensive way to see the water, forests, and mountains.

**Mt. Erie,** off Heart Lake Road, south of Anacortes. A winding road to the summit (1,270 feet) and wide views of the Cascades, green islands spread across a blue sea, and, in spring, masses of tulip fields.

**Lake Campbell,** 3 miles south of Anacortes. Offers waterskiing, fishing, and a boat launch. An island in the middle of the 410-acre lake makes this the world's only island on an island.

**Cranberry Lake,** off Oakes Avenue, Anacortes. This twenty-seven-acre lake has good fishing and swimming, plus nine loop trails for hiking, biking, and horseback riding.

**Cap Sante,** Anacortes. Enjoy excellent views from a bluff at the eastern edge of the city.

# Special Events

**Mid-February.** Langley Mystery Weekend. Clues are placed in shops around town; a prize is awarded to the person who deciphers the mystery.

**Early July.** Choochookam, Langley. Arts-and-crafts fair, street fair, juried art show, street dance, food booths.

**Mid-August.** Island County Fair, Langley. 4-H shows, canning and baking displays, log show, flowers, photography.

**Early August.** Anacortes Arts-and-Crafts Festival. Two days of non-stop entertainment and art displays.

# Other Recommended Restaurants and Lodgings

## Anacortes

The Admiral's Hideaway, 1318 Thirtieth Street. (206) 293–0106. A four-room bed-and-breakfast with indoor swimming pool and hot tub. Located in a quiet, residential area. Full breakfast.

Channel House, 2902 Oakes Avenue. (206) 293–9382. Victorian home turned bed-and-breakfast. Rooms with antiques, plus cottage with two fireplace suites. On the way to the ferry landing. Full breakfast.

## Coupeville

Captain Whidbey Inn, 2072 Whidbey Island Inn Road. (206) 678–4097. Madrona log lodge, built in 1907 on a wooded shore of Penn Cove. An old favorite. Rooms and restaurant.

## Langley

Blue House Inn, 513 Anthes. (206) 221–8392. Cozy, charming bed-and-breakfast with friendly hosts; in residential area. Full breakfast served.

Galittoire, 5444 South Coles Road. (206) 221–0548. Luxurious contemporary country home on ten acres. Two suites, full breakfast.

The Inn at Langley, P.O. Box 835. (206) 221–3033. Top-quality accommodations and service. All twenty-four rooms have fireplaces, Jacuzzi tubs, and views of Saratoga Passage. Restaurant serves notable Northwest cuisine.

# For More Information

Langley Chamber of Commerce, P.O. Box 403, Langley, WA 98260. (206) 221–6765.

Central Whidbey Chamber of Commerce, P.O. Box 152, Coupeville, WA 98239. (206) 678–5434.

Anacortes Chamber of Commerce, 1319 Commercial Avenue, Anacortes, WA 98221. (206) 293–3832.

Washington State Ferries, 801 Alaskan Way, Pier 52 Colman Dock, Seattle, WA 98104. (206) 464–6400; within Washington, (800) 84–FERRY.

# Snoqualmie Falls and Fall City

Salish Lodge, a luxury inn, perches on the cliff above thundering Snoqualmie Falls.

## Waterfall of the Moon People

_____ 1 NIGHT _____

Dramatic waterfall · Steam train ride · Luxury resort · Golf courses
Herb farm · Winery · Bicycling · Hiking · Antique shopping

Long before the explorers and hop growers reached Snoqualmie Valley, Native American tribes met for trade and council beside the thundering torrent now called Snoqualmie Falls. Early settlers referred to the Indians who lived along the riverbanks as the "moon people," for their name was said to be derived from _Snoqualm,_ meaning "moon."

The first white settlers arrived in 1855. By the early twentieth century, hops, timber, and electrical power that harnessed the falls' tremendous energy were important segments of the local economy. Today it's tourism.

The scenic valley, just 30 miles east of Seattle, is webbed with quiet backroads that pass farmlands, forests, mountains, and gurgling streams on their way to the Snoqualmie River. This getaway offers both a chance to refresh the spirit and a variety of recreation.

# Day 1

## Morning

Travel on I–90 east from Seattle to exit 27, a thirty-minute drive. Follow the signs to **Snoqualmie.** Plan to arrive about 10:00 A.M. so that you'll have an hour to explore the little town and its quaint, restored **train depot** before your train ride. The depot, built in 1890, is on the National Register of Historic Places. Its displays include a sizable collection of rolling stock from steam, electric, and logging railroads.

At 11:00 A.M., board the old-fashioned steam- or diesel-powered train for a 10-mile trip through the scenic valley. The vintage coaches pass by the base of rugged **Mount Si,** the top of **Snoqualmie Falls,** and through dense forests. They clickety clack over bridges and through lush green fields to a scenic viewing point before making the return trip to the Snoqualmie depot.

Trains run on summer weekends and on Memorial Day, Independence Day, and Labor Day. Fares are $6.00 for adults, $5.00 for seniors over sixty-two, and $4.00 for children three to twelve. The ride takes seventy minutes. For information, phone (206) 746–4025.

*Lunch:* Isadora's, 132 Railroad Avenue. (206) 888–1345. Cafe serving quiche, sandwiches, tea, espresso, scones. Also a gift and antiques shop. Alternatively, purchase picnic goods to take to Snoqualmie Winery, 1000 Winery Road. (206) 888–4000.

## Afternoon

After lunch, or carrying your picnic, continue on 384th Avenue to the freeway on-ramp and Winery Road (watch for the sign to Snoqualmie Winery; the road goes under the freeway). At the winery you can sample local wines while enjoying your picnic and a panoramic view of the Cascades and Snoqualmie Valley.

Turn back toward Snoqualmie and follow the signs to Snoqualmie Falls, which are 1 mile from town. Fenced, paved paths along the cliff offer viewing points for watching the great cascade—100 feet higher than Niagara—as it roars to a misty pool at the bottom.

To get closer to the falls, walk the ½-mile trail that descends to a rocky beach at the falls' base. Behind the powerhouse that stands above the beach you'll find a plank walk leading to an elevated platform, which provides a satisfying overlook.

The trails and landscaped park on the cliff near the lodge were developed by Puget Power, which has received awards of recognition for park design and environmental contributions.

Check in at **Salish Lodge,** a hotel perched at the brink of the falls. Borrow a bicycle—Salish lends mountain bikes—and wheel along the area's country roads. The lodge also lends fishing gear, if you'd rather try your luck at casting for steelhead in the river.

Golfers can head for one of the four nearby courses (for details, see "There's More" at the end of the chapter). If your top priority is simply relaxation, you'll enjoy lounging on the hotel terrace while the Snoqualmie torrent thunders below.

*Dinner:* Salish Lodge. Northwest cuisine emphasizing regional produce, game, and fish. Special touches include Indian-style potlatch salmon and farm-raised game meats smoked with apple and cherry woods. Superb service, a fine view.

*Lodging:* Salish Lodge, P.O. Box 1109, Snoqualmie, WA 98065. (206) 888–2556; within Washington, (800) 826–6124. Outstanding, luxury accommodations in an informal country atmosphere. Down comforters, stone fireplaces, two-person whirlpool tubs, balconies viewing the river and falls (some views much better than others).

# Day 2

## Morning

*Breakfast:* Salish Lodge. The highly popular breakfast is a five-course extravaganza that includes fresh fruit, hot oatmeal, sourdough biscuits with honey, pancakes, and a main course such as trout with game sausage, eggs Florentine, or smoked salmon in scrambled eggs.

Drive south to **North Bend,** turn left at the traffic signal (the only one in the valley), continue to Mount Si Road, and turn north. Follow this road across the **Snoqualmie River** to 432nd Avenue SE, and park at a gravel area near the bridge. Walk a few yards on 432nd Avenue to the trailhead for **Little Mount Si.**

The 2-mile trail, forested to the top of the mountain, leads to a 1,000-foot summit with sweeping views of the valley, Mount Si, and the Cascade Range in the distance. The hike up Mount Si itself is more time consuming and a greater challenge. The trail zigzags to the top of the great monolith, 4,190 feet high. A panoramic summit view makes the 4-mile trip worthwhile and popular; Mount Si is the second-most-hiked mountain in the state.

If you (or someone in your party) are not interested in hiking, you might visit the **Snoqualmie Valley Historical Museum** at 320 North Bend Boulevard. In this former private home, volunteers maintain exhibits of pioneer memorabilia.

A few blocks from the museum is a large, village-style complex of factory discount outlets. The recently opened stores represent numerous brand name manufacturers.

After your hike and/or museum and shopping tour, drive north on State Route 202 to **Fall City** and **The Herbfarm,** 32804 Issaquah–Fall City Road (800–866–HERB). Here you'll find a peaceful world where caged doves coo and the air carries the fragrance of more than 450 herbs.

Growing herbs is only part of Lola and Bill Zimmerman's operation. The Herbfarm holds classes in herb uses and basketry, sells gifts and books, and has a superb small restaurant serving unique six-course luncheons on weekends ($32.50 per person). Chefs Bill Kraut and Ron Zimmerman say their goal is "to give you one of the ten best meals of your life."

*Lunch:* The Herbfarm. A typical luncheon: rosemary biscuits with lemon thyme and calendula butter, king salmon in basil-zucchini sauce, scented geranium sorbet, local lamb medallions with wild morel mushrooms and farm vegetables, a salad of herbs and flowers, and lavender ice cream with wild ginger root sauce. *Reservations essential:* Call the number above or (206) 784–2222 as far in advance as possible.

Alternatively, if you're not able to have lunch at The Herbfarm, bring a picnic with you and take it to your next destination, **Carnation Research Farm.**

## Afternoon

Driving from Fall City to **Carnation** on State Route 203 takes about fifteen minutes and leads you to the Carnation Research Farm (206–788–1511). At the 1,200-acre farm you can take self-guided tours through the contented cows' milking parlor, through maternity and calf barns, and through Friskies Acres. Picnic facilities are provided in the well-kept rose and fuchsia gardens.

After your tour, return to Fall City on Route 203 and turn southwest on Preston Road to I–90. Travel west to exit 17 and leave the freeway for **Issaquah,** a pretty village with a tree-shaded creek running through it. Signs direct you to the **state fish hatchery,** where you can see thousands of salmon fingerlings being reared with loving care.

Also treated with great care are the hand-dipped chocolates at **Boehm's Candies.** The Edelweiss Chalet on Gilman Boulevard is the headquarters for the renowned candy company.

Drive north on Gilman and you'll find **Gilman Village,** a complex of fifty-odd shops, restaurants, and tearooms, many of them in old homes that were moved to the site. They're connected by boardwalks.

A short distance past Gilman Village is **Gilman Antique Gallery,** a must for antiques lovers. Here 170 exhibitors display thousands of antiques of all kinds.

If you'd like a stroll on a sandy beach to finish the journey, stop at **Lake Sammamish,** northwest of Issaquah off I–90. By then you'll probably be ready to head the last few miles into Seattle.

## There's More

**Snoqualmie Falls Forest Theatre and Family Park,** Fall City. Outdoor dinner theater; summer weekends only. (206) 222–7044.

**Golfing.** There are four 18-hole courses in the valley:

Mount Si Golf Course, 9010 Meadowbrook–North Bend Road SE, Snoqualmie. (206) 888–1541.

Snoqualmie Falls Golf Course, 35109 Southeast Fish Hatchery Road, Fall City. (206) 222–5244.

Carnation Golf Course, 1810 West Snoqualmie River Road NE, Carnation. (206) 454–7543.

Tall Chief Golf Course, 1313 West Snoqualmie River Road SE, Carnation. (206) 222–5106.

## Special Events

**Early August.** Snoqualmie Days, Snoqualmie. Arts-and-crafts booths, parade, music, food concessions, children's games, helicopter rides.

## Other Recommended Restaurants and Lodgings

### Carnation

Idyl Inn on the River, 4548 Tolt River Road. (206) 333–4262. Luxurious solar villa on seven riverside acres. Indoor pool, sauna. Continental breakfast included.

### Issaquah

The Wildflower, 25237 Southeast Issaquah–Fall City Road. (206) 392–1196. Two-story log home in the woods, offering four guest rooms, antique furnishings and quilts, and a gazebo in back. Full breakfast served.

## North Bend

George's Bakery, 127 West North Bend Way. (206) 888–0632. Noted for delicious pastries, baked fresh daily.

## Snoqualmie

The Old Honey Farm Country Inn, 8910 384th Avenue SE. (206) 888–9399. Bed-and-breakfast hotel offering country comfort in ten rooms, five with views of Mount Si and the Cascades.

# For More Information

Puget Sound Railway Historical Association, P.O. Box 459, Snoqualmie, WA 98065. (206) 746–4025.

Snoqualmie Falls Chamber of Commerce, 108 Railroad Avenue, P.O. Box 356, Snoqualmie, WA 98065. (206) 888–4440.

North Bend Chamber of Commerce, P.O. Box 357, North Bend, WA 98045. (206) 888–4440.

Issaquah Chamber of Commerce, 155 Northwest Gilman Boulevard, Issaquah, WA 98027. (206) 392–7024.

# Leavenworth to Ellensburg

Leavenworth is a quaint, Bavarian-style village in the foothills of the Cascade Mountains.

## Apple Orchards and Ranch Country

——————————————— 2 NIGHTS ———————————————

Mountain scenery · Waterfalls · Pioneer village · Wild rivers
Apple orchards · Bavarian town · Historical museums
Hiking · Boating · Horseback riding · Columbia River

One of Seattle's great attractions is its proximity to magnificent mountainous wilderness. You can breakfast in a cosmopolitan restaurant and be deep in a silent forest by lunchtime. This three-day getaway will take you east through the rugged North Cascades, into the softer valleys where 60 percent of the nation's apples are grown, and on to dry ranching country. On the way you'll encounter breathtaking scenery, rivers that invite white-water adventure, beckoning trails, and a few surprises.

# Day 1

## Morning

Drive north from Seattle to State Route 202, headed toward Wood-inville, and stop for a tour of the famed **Chateau Ste. Michelle Winery.** The state's leading winery is based in a turreted château that resembles a French country manor.

Tours and tastings are available every day, and the eighty-seven acres of landscaped grounds are a pleasure to stroll. There are trout ponds, manicured lawns, formal gardens, experimental vineyards, and picnic tables.

North of the winery, join State Route 522 headed northeast toward U.S. Route 2. Traveling east on the scenic highway, you'll follow the **Skykomish River,** a ribbon of clear blue water that flows west from the high lakes of the Alpine Wilderness. Popular with rafters for both its rapids and its serene stretches, the Skykomish offers steelhead fishing, riverside trails, and gold panning, as well as float trips. Eagles soar above all the activity, indifferent and majestic.

Amid the new-growth forests found on either side of the river are the stumps of virgin old growth, long since logged. The stumps indicate the size of these giants; some are 6 feet in diameter.

Two miles east of Gold Bar, at **Wallace Falls State Park,** stop to hike the trail, which climbs to 1,200 feet and affords grand views of **Wallace Falls,** a 365-foot cascade. South of the Skykomish you'll see imposing **Mount Index,** nearly 6,000 feet high.

The next stop on the highway is the village of **Index.**

*Lunch:* **Bush House Country Inn,** 300 Fifth Street, Index. (206) 793–2312. Rustic dining room with river-rock fireplace. Soups, sandwiches, salads, light entrees, homemade desserts. Open daily.

## Afternoon

Near **Skykomish,** a timber town that fills with hikers and backpackers in summer and with skiers in winter, you can take a short walk to **Deception Falls,** a tumbling waterfall that splashes down the mountainside and under the highway bridge.

Continuing on Route 2, you'll leave the Skykomish River and drive through coniferous forest, passing Alpine Falls and rising into the Cascade Mountains to **Stevens Pass,** at an elevation of 4,061 feet. One thousand feet below runs a 7-mile tunnel, the longest railroad tunnel in North America. If you walk from the summit to **Stevens Pass Ski Area,** you'll have a peerless view of the snowy peaks of the Cascade Range.

Descending now on the east side of the Cascades, drive 20 more miles to **Coles Corner.** From here, State Route 207 leads 4 miles to

**Lake Wenatchee State Park.** This busy recreation area on the edge of **Lake Wenatchee** offers skiing, fishing, boating, and beaches.

Take Route 2 through the **Tumwater Canyon,** along the bouncing, cascading **Wenatchee River** as it rushes toward the Columbia. In any season the landscape is lovely, but in autumn, when the woodlands blaze with color, it's particularly glorious.

Sixteen miles south of Coles Corner, in **Icicle Valley,** you'll enter **Leavenworth.** Almost the entire town is designed to resemble a quaint Bavarian village, with chalets, carved railings, peaked gables, and hundreds of hanging flower baskets.

In the 1960s, when the local economy was rapidly fading, the townsfolk began the Bavarian village project as a way to stimulate tourism. It's succeeded beyond imagining, drawing visitors by the thousands every year to shop, gawk, eat, and participate in the lively festivals (see **Special Events**).

The alpine setting is an even-greater draw. Leavenworth is a gateway to wilderness adventure, white-water rivers, mountain lakes, fishing, rock climbing, and skiing.

For the rest of the afternoon you might choose to hike or birdwatch, play golf, or linger in the dozens of quaint shops. Browse through the hand-painted country pine items in **Pie In The Sky,** the many cuckoo clocks at **Smallwood's Clock Shop,** and the woodcarvings in **The Woodworks.** The U.S. Forest Service Information Center in downtown Leavenworth has maps that direct you to mountain trails and wildflower displays.

Don't miss a walk along the Wenatchee River in tranquil **Waterfront Park,** off Commerical Street. Just a block and a half from the busy shopping area, the park is a quiet spot with benches, trees, and views of the river and the steep peaks around Icicle Canyon.

*Dinner:* **Terrace Bistro,** 200 Eighth Street, Leavenworth. (509) 548–4193. Upper-level restaurant, romantic setting, out-of-the-ordinary food.

*Lodging:* **Run of the River,** 9308 East Leavenworth Road, P.O. Box 285, Leavenworth, WA 98826. (509) 548–7171. Bed-and-breakfast in a log lodge on the river a mile from downtown. Six comfortable rooms, warm hospitality, deck with hot tub.

# Day 2

## Morning

*Breakfast:* A bountiful country breakfast is served in the open dining room at Run of the River.

Continue on Route 2 to **Cashmere,** passing miles of apple orchards that bloom white and pink in spring and are laden with fruit in fall. Apples are big business in Washington; seven billion are grown annually, 60 percent of the nation's apple production.

In Cashmere, at the **Aplets and Cotlets** manufacturing plant, 117 Mission Street (509–782–2191), take the brief tour and watch the making of the famous fruit-and-nut confections. Sample a few, make your purchases, and then stop in **Rosemary's Kitchen** for locally made apple and pear jams and strudel.

**Bob's Apple Barrel,** on Route 2, sells cider, apple butter and jam, and has a large selection of Washington wines.

Not to be missed is **Chelan County Historical Museum,** 500 Cottage Avenue (509–782–3230), where you step from the highway into the past. On the museum grounds, a typical pioneer village, complete with blacksmith shop, mission, assay office, saloon, dentist's office, hotel, millinery shop, and jail house, is open to the public.

From Cashmere, drive on to **Wenatchee,** the apple capital, where the Wenatchee and Columbia rivers meet. The **North Central Washington Museum,** in downtown Wenatchee, features out-of-the-ordinary displays. A coin-operated 1892 railroad diorama, aviation exhibits showing the historic 1931 trans-Pacific crossing, a nine-rank Wurlitzer theater organ, and Native American artifacts are part of the disparate collection.

A side trip north on U.S. Route 97, on the west bank of the river, leads you to the **Washington Apple Commission Visitor Center,** 2900 Euclid Street (509–663–9600). It's open daily from May through October and on weekdays from November through April. You'll get an in-depth look at the apple industry at the center, which offers souvenirs, an eighteen-minute video, pies, and free samples of Washington's famous apples.

*Lunch:* **Steven's at Mission Square,** 218 North Mission Street, Wenatchee. (509) 663–6573. Sophisticated Northwest cuisine in an open, split-level room overlooking gardens. Seafood, pasta, good desserts.

## Afternoon

Drive south on U.S. 97, leaving the orchards to head into the forests of the Wenatchee Mountains and descend from there into cowboy country. The climate here is hot and dry in summer, while winters are harsh, with far more snowfall than occurs west of the Cascade Range.

The scenic route, over Blewett Pass, is narrow and winding and closed in winter. It is a shortcut that leaves, then rejoins Route 97.

When you reach **Ellensburg,** stop at the Chamber of Commerce on Sprague Street for a walking tour map of the historic downtown. It's full of interesting architecture, with red brick buildings dating from the late 1800s, an Art Deco theater, and modern structures on the Central Washington University campus. Antique shops abound, along with stores selling the famous Ellensburg Blue agate (found only in this region).

In the **Clymer Gallery** view the paintings of John Clymer, a noted western artist; in the **Kittitas County Historic Museum** see what frontier life was like. Tour the **Thorp Grist Mill,** built back in 1883 when Ellensburg (having changed its name from Robbers' Roost) was booming.

Southeast of town, off I–90, is **Olmstead Place State Park,** where you can step into one of the first farms in Kittitas Valley. There's a log cabin, built in 1875, and several buildings, including a barn and schoolhouse, open for tours in summer.

*Dinner:* In summer, **Circle H Holiday Ranch.** Meals are included in the room rate, with western-style dinners cooked on the grill— T-bone steak or spareribs, salad, and strawberry shortcake are examples. In other seasons **Valley Cafe,** 105 West Third, Ellensburg. (509) 925–3050. Art Deco surroundings, good Mexican and Italian dishes.

*Lodging:* Circle H Holiday Ranch, Route 1, Box 175, Thorp, WA 98946. (509) 964–2000. Betsy Ogden runs a fifty-eight-acre ranch with five cabins in a western theme. Riding trails, horses and other animals, pond, play equipment.

# Day 3

## Morning

*Breakfast:* The Circle H serves a full breakfast.

Take a **horseback ride** through the hills behind the ranch, in the **L. T. Murray Wildlife Recreation Area.** It offers 100,000 acres of wilderness, honeycombed with walking and riding trails. If you're not enthused about horses, go hiking, relax at the ranch, or go to Ellensburg to see what you missed the day before.

You might choose a **rafting trip** on the Yakima River instead (Betsy Ogden will make the arrangements for you), or travel 25 miles east to Vantage, on the Columbia River. This section of the river is a dam-created lake, **Wanapum Lake.** The views are spectacular, overlooking the river and surrounding dry, brushy hills. Nearby is **Ginkgo Petrified Forest State Park,** where you can see prehistoric petrified woods of many species. In the park there are Indian petroglyphs, an interpretive center, walking trails, wildlife, and picnic areas.

*Lunch:* The Circle H provides a saddle-bag lunch; eat at the ranch or take it with you for a picnic in Ginkgo Petrified Forest State Park.

## Afternoon

Leaving your peaceful ranch retreat, take I–90 northwest (or a byway, State Route 10) to Cle Elum. Once a coal-mining and railroad town, it's now a gateway to mountain and lake outdoor recreation. Stop at the **Cle Elum Bakery** for caramel-nut rolls and coffee (509–674–2233; closed Sunday). Almost every town has its special museum; Cle Elum preserves phone history in the **Cle Elum Historical Telephone Museum.** Another interesting spot is the **Carpenter House**, a stately mansion that now houses exhibits from life in an earlier day in the region.

Continue west to **Roslyn** and have a quick look at the town that is gaining fame—some of it not welcomed by local folk—as the setting for the television show "Northern Exposure." The television presence has created a stir and some change, but for the most part Roslyn remains a quiet, pleasant little community with a couple of good cafes and what is said to be the oldest operating saloon in Washington state, **The Brick.**

Proceeding northwest on I–90, you'll come to **Kachess Lake,** a recreation area with beautiful old trees, walking paths, and a pretty lake where you can swim, boat and fish.

Continue on I–90 through thick forests and mountain terrain over Snoqualmie Pass and on to **Snoqualmie Falls** (for more information on the Snoqualmie Falls area, see Seattle Escape Six).

On your way back to Seattle, if there's time, stop in **Issaquah** for coffee or tea and a look around the shops of Gilman Village. While you're so close, you might as well pick up a sample from **Boehm's Candies**—a sweet touch to end your trip.

# There's More

**Bicycling.** Bicycle routes for all abilities surround the Leavenworth area. Rent bicycles at Der Sportsman (509–548–5623) or Leavenworth Sports Center (509–548–7864). Run of the River B&B (509–548–7171) offers the "Tour de Pomme," a bicycling route from inn to inn.

**Golf.** Leavenworth Golf Course, 18 holes. (509) 548–7914.

Rock Island Golf Course, east of Wenatchee, 18 holes. (509) 884–2806.

**Rafting.** Raft the white water of the Wenatchee River with Leavenworth Outfitters. (509) 763–3733. Scenic float trips also available.

**Skiing.** Leavenworth: Cross-country ski trails are numerous in the Leavenworth/Wenatchee area. Icicle River Trail and Lake Wenatchee are popular and so are the golf course and city park in Leavenworth.

Stevens Pass: Open November to mid-April. Downhill: Six double chair lifts, two triples, longest run 6,047 feet. (206) 634–1645. For cross-country ski information, (206) 754–1253.

Wenatchee: Mission Ridge has four chair lifts and runs up to 5 miles long. (509) 663–7631.

# Special Events

**Late April/early May.** Apple Blossom Festival, Wenatchee. Parades, carnival, arts-and-crafts fair.

**Mid-May.** Maifest, Leavenworth. Maypole dance, bandstand entertainment, hand-bell ringers, outdoor breakfast, flea market, antiques bazaar, fun run, street dancing, flowers.

**Early September** (Labor Day weekend). Ellensburg Rodeo. One of the major U.S. rodeos. Four-day event, with cowhands competing for high cash prizes. Also carnival rides, produce and craft displays, homemade pies, and music.

**Early October.** Autumn Leaf Festival, Leavenworth. Grand parade, accordion and oompah music in bandstand, art displays, street dance, food booths, pancake breakfast.

**Mid-October.** Cashmere Apple Days, Cashmere. Pie-baking contest, races, music, dancing, pioneer entertainment. Fund-raiser for Chelan County Museum.

**Early December.** Christmas Lighting, Leavenworth. Snowman contest, sledding, food booths, concerts, lighting of village.

# Other Recommended Restaurants and Lodgings

## Cashmere

Cashmere Country Inn, 5801 Pioneer Avenue. (509) 782–4212. Remodeled farmhouse with four guest rooms, each furnished with charm and taste. Outstanding breakfast, often with the main local product, apples, included.

The Pewter Pot, 124½ Cottage Avenue. (509) 782–2036. Good old-fashioned American food—roast turkey with the trimmings, pot roast, chicken with cider sauce.

## Cle Elum

The Moore House, 526 Marie Street, P.O. Box 2861, South Cle Elum. (509) 674–5939 or (800) 22–TWAIN. A former bunkhouse for railroad workers, restored as an attractive bed-and-breakfast with a railroad theme. Full breakfast.

Hidden Valley Guest Ranch, Hidden Valley Road, HC 61, Box 2060.

(509) 857–2322. Wildreness ranch with cabins, horses, swimming pool, hiking trails, cross-country skiing. All meals included.

## Ellensburg

Best Western Ellensburg Inn, 1700 Canyon Road. (509) 925–9801. Clean and comfortable rooms, restaurant, lounge, pool, putting green.

Giovanni's on Pearl, 402 North Pearl. (509) 962–2260. Lamb and seafood, pasta, light meals at tables with linens and candlelight.

## Leavenworth

All Seasons River Inn, 8751 Icicle Road. (509) 548–1425. Bed-and-breakfast with three spacious rooms. Private decks, river views, antiques, hearty breakfast.

Enzian Motor Inn, 590 Highway 2. (509) 548–5269 or (800) 223–8511. Hotel combining Old World atmosphere with contemporary comfort. Heated pool, hot tub, fifty-seven rooms, some fireplaces. Continental breakfast included.

Homefires Bakery, 13013 Bayne Road. (509) 548–7362. Freshly made whole grain breads, European and specialty breads, pies, cinnamon rolls, and cookies, baked in a wood-fired masonry oven.

Mountain Home Lodge, P.O. Box 687. (509) 548–7077. Intimate getaway in roomy stone-and-wood lodge with pool. In the hills, 3 miles from town. Full breakfast included.

Walter's Other Place, 820 Commercial Street. (509) 548–6125. Greek and Italian specialties; the cannelloni's good.

## Monroe

Ixtapa, 19303 Highway 2. (206) 794–8484. Moved, expanded, better-than-ever cafe serving spicy, well-prepared Mexican food. Lunch and dinner.

# For More Information

Cle Elum/Uppper Kittitas County Chamber of Commerce, 221 East First Street, Cle Elum, WA 98922. (509) 674–5958.

Ellensburg Chamber of Commerce, 436 North Sprague, Ellensburg, WA 98925. (509) 925–3137.

Monroe/Sultan Chamber of Commerce, P.O. Box 38, 211 East Main Street, Monroe, WA 98272. (509) 794–5488.

Leavenworth Chamber of Commerce, P.O. Box 327, Leavenworth, WA 98826. (509) 548–5807.

Wenatchee Area Visitor and Convention Bureau, 2 South Chelam Avenue, P.O. Box 850, Wenatchee, WA 98807. (509) 662–4774.

# North Cascades

Glaciers and snowfields abound on the slopes of the rugged North Cascades.

## Untamed Wilderness

_____ 2 NIGHTS _____

Alpine peaks · Wildflowers · Forests · Waterfalls
Glaciers · Hiking trails · Bald eagle refuge · Old West town

Because of their jagged peaks, immense glaciers, and high meadows splashed with summer wildflowers, the North Cascades are often called the American Alps. The wilderness around them, a 505,000-acre national park bisected by only one road, provides a remarkable retreat from crowded streets into natural beauty.

Along the route through North Cascades National Park, and on the occasional side roads that extend from it, you'll encounter numerous opportunities for outdoor adventure. This three-day trip suggests a few. It's a summer excursion, as much of the road is closed in winter. To reach the skiing areas mentioned during the ski season, you have to take a different route, approaching from the south.

# Day 1

## Morning

Travel north from Seattle on State Route 9 to **Snohomish,** about 30 miles. The river town, founded in 1859 on the banks of the Snohomish and Pilchuck rivers, is one of Washington's oldest communities. It's thus fitting that Snohomish not only has examples of Victorian architecture but is known as the antiques capital of the Northwest. Dozens of shops, many within a 4-block radius, sell antiques of all kinds.

The three-level **Star Center Mall,** 829 Second Street, houses 150 dealers who sell everything from Indian artifacts to art nouveau. It's open every day (phone 206–568–2131). **First Bank Antiques,** 1019 First Street (206–588–7609), carries oak and mahogany furniture and country primitives; **The Antique Market Place Mall** represents twenty dealers offering Hummel figures, glassware, furniture, china, and collectibles.

At the **Pioneer Village Museum,** on Second and Pine streets, and at **Blackman House Museum,** 118 Avenue B, you can see how many of these antiques were once used in daily life. Both museums are open daily for tours in summer.

At **Townsend's Deli and Espresso,** 102 Avenue D, buy sandwiches-to-go. Then head north toward **Lake Stevens,** curving to State Route 92 toward Granite Falls.

On this scenic route, known as the **Mount Loop Highway** (part of it is closed in winter), you'll follow the **South Fork of the Stillaguamish River** and pass through the evergreen forests of **Boulder River Wilderness,** eventually turning north toward Darrington and the North Cascades Highway.

From **Granite Falls,** follow Route 92 11 miles east to Verlot. The ranger station, across the road from 5,324-foot Mount Pilchuck, will provide maps and suggestions. The 7-mile road leading to the trail up the mountain is east of Verlot. From the trailhead, the hike up Mount Pilchuck is 2½ miles, leading to **Mount Pilchuck Lookout.** From here you gain one of the finest viewing points in the state for scenic splendor.

The forest fire observation tower was built in 1918 on the western edge of the Cascade Range, near Boulder River Wilderness. From the lookout you can see for miles, a view encompassing White Horse and Three Fingers mountains.

As you enter the **Mount Baker–Snoqualmie National Forest,** edging the Stillaguamish shore, you'll drive for 14 miles, through Silverton to the turnoff for the **Big Four Mountain.** At the base of the immense escarpment, which soars 6,120 feet, a popular inn once stood. It was destroyed by fire, long ago, but the site is a good picnic spot.

*Lunch:* Picnic at **Mount Pilchuck** or Big Four Mountain.

## Afternoon

Follow the trail to the **Big Four Ice Caves,** which some say is the lowest-lying glacier in the contiguous United States. The ¼-mile-long ice field is fed from a snow cone on Big Four.

Continue now over **Barlow Pass** (elevation 2,600 feet), turning north to travel beside the tumultuous **South Fork of the Sauk River** for 19 miles to Darrington. The road is unpaved, but it's well graded.

The slate blue Sauk is a favorite with white-water rafters and kayakers because of its swift rapids. Through the trees on this narrow, winding road you'll glimpse mountain peaks—Sloan, Pugh, and White Chuck—and the Monte Cristo Range in **Henry M. Jackson Wilderness.** The Monte Cristo area was once the site of gold, copper, and silver mines.

When you reach **Rockport,** you'll see **Rockport State Park** on the bank of the **Skagit River.** The attractive park has campsites and a network of trails, partially accessible to wheelchairs.

On the western border of the park, a 7-mile road winds up Sauk Mountain, leading to **Sauk Mountain Trail.** This trail, a one-and-a-half-hour walk, is considered by many hikers to be one of the most beautiful walks in the North Cascades, with wildflowers and panoramic views from the mountain. You may see hang gliders here.

After your hike, drive west on State Route 20 12 miles to your night's lodging.

*Dinner:* **North Cascades Inn,** 4286 Highway 20, Concrete. (206) 853–8771. Standard, dependable American fare.

*Lodging:* **Cascade Mountain Inn,** 3840 Pioneer Lane, Concrete, WA 98237. (206) 826–4333. European-style inn with six rooms on ten acres of grounds. Down comforters, friendly hosts. View of Sauk Mountain.

# Day 2

## Morning

*Breakfast:* Enjoy expansive views and a full breakfast in the dining room or on the patio of Cascade Mountain Inn.

Take the picnic lunch the innkeepers have packed for you (request this in advance), and drive east on Route 20, the North Cascades Highway. Considered the most scenic mountain drive in Washington, this route is closed in winter.

Again keep an eye out for eagles, especially between **Rockport State Park** and **Marblemount.** In Marblemount you can pick up maps and backcountry permits (and gasoline—this is the last gas stop for 75 miles).

There's a good lunch stop in Marblemount, if you didn't bring a picnic: **Mountain Song Restaurant,** on Route 20 (206–873–2461). Sandwiches, soups, and salads are available in a casual atmosphere.

Route 20 and the Skagit River flowing beside it divide the northern portion of North Cascades National Park from its southern part. There are almost no other roads in the national park, a wonderland of high mountains, jagged ridges, countless waterfalls, and glacially sculpted valleys. There are 318 glaciers, more than half of all the glaciers in the contiguous United States. On off-road trails, you'll hear crashing ice-falls and see broad snowfields and flower-dotted slopes.

Two short walks are located near the manicured village of **Newhalem. Trail of the Cedars** is a nature walk, handicapped accessible, with interpretive signs that explain the forest's growth. The **Ladder Creek Rock Garden** walk winds up a hillside, passing fountains and landscaped plantings to reach Ladder Creek Falls.

*Lunch:* Picnic in Newhalem or along the trail, or eat at Mountain Song Restaurant in Marblemount.

### Afternoon

Continue in leisurely fashion on Route 20, stopping at the numerous turnouts to admire particularly striking views of ridges and green valleys. At **Diablo Lake Overlook,** enjoy a panoramic vista of the smooth blue lake, Sourdough Mountain, Davis Peak, Colonial Peak, Pyramid Peak, and the Skagit River.

Beyond Diablo is **Ross Lake,** its blue-green glacial waters extending far north into the wilderness, across the Canadian border. The only access to the lake is by boat or trail.

Ross Lake is named after James Ross, the engineer who designed dams on the Skagit River. Another Ross, Alexander, explored the southern section of the present park in 1814. After him came more explorers, then miners (mining efforts were abandoned because of the arduous terrain) and a few homesteaders.

The dams were built by Seattle City Light to generate electricity; today, the power company runs railway and boat tours to Diablo and Ross dams (see **There's More** for additional information).

Fall is especially beautiful in the North Cascades. An example of the leaf color you can see, flaming red and orange against the hillsides, is at **Ruby Creek,** 20 miles past Newhalem.

**Rainy Pass** has an elevation of 4,860 feet. It's crossed by the Pacific Crest National Scenic Trail. Near the Rainy Lake rest stop is the **Rainy Lake National Recreation Trail,** a 1-mile paved path, wheelchair accessible, that leads to **Rainy Lake.** There's a memorable view here of the subalpine lake and waterfall streaming in from snowfields.

**Whistler Basin Viewpoint** provides an opportunity for a close look at the wildflowers that grow in alpine meadows. In July and August, these fragile, open spaces are full of color.

For the most splendid close-up view of the Cascades, don't miss the **Washington Pass Overlook** (elevation 5,400 feet). **Liberty Bell Mountain** soars 7,808 feet above the valley; next to it, almost as high, are the **Early Winter Spires;** and **Silver Star Mountain** rises a steep 8,875 feet on the east. Against the dark ridges and snow-filled ravines, the leaves of Lyall larch glow a brilliant yellow.

Now, as the road descends east of the Cascades into Washington's dry side, the scenery changes. There are no dense rain forests, thick with ferns and mosses; the vegetation thins, and firs give way to widely spaced pines. To the north lie the mountains and forests of the rugged, roadless **Pasayten Wilderness.** In recent years, wolves have been found living deep in the wild—a welcome comeback, since they were thought to have disappeared.

Twelve miles from Washington Pass you'll come to **Mazama,** a popular ski resort.

*Dinner:* **Mazama Country Inn.** Pasta, chicken, and barbecued ribs are favorites here. Light suppers of soup, salad, and bread available.

*Lodging:* Mazama Country Inn, P.O. Box 275, Mazama, WA 98833. (509) 996–2681; within Washington, (800) 843–7951. Spacious cedar lodge, simple but immaculate rooms. Stone fireplace in living/dining area, windows on three sides offering views of forest. Two separate cabins and ranch house available. Bicycle rentals and horseback rides.

# Day 3

## Morning

*Breakfast:* Mazama Country Inn. The lodge serves three meals a day (included in the American Plan rates in winter only).

Drive eastward on Route 20 into the lovely **Methow Valley,** carved by glaciers 11,000 years ago. Farmers' fields, punctuated with rocky outcroppings, extend from the meandering **Methow River,** while its banks are outlined by poplar and ponderosa pines.

Drive 13 miles from Mazama, and you'll arrive in **Winthrop,** a town nestled in the upper Methow Valley, almost surrounded by national forestland. Here migrant Indians once camped along the river, digging for camas root and fishing for salmon. White settlers and miners arrived after 1883.

When you visit Winthrop, you might think the townsfolk never left the late 1800s. The entire town has a frontier motif, with boardwalks, Old West storefronts, and saloon replicas.

Guy Waring and his wife and two children were among the early settlers. They came from Massachusetts and named the town after the governor of that state, John Winthrop. The Warings' home, built in 1897 after most of the town was destroyed by fire, is now the **Shafer Museum.** It contains historical artifacts, wagons, and a stagecoach.

With 300 days of sunshine a year and an abundance of lakes, forests, mountainous terrain, and clean country air, the Methow Valley offers virtually limitless outdoor recreation. Fishing, photography, boating, river rafting, and skiing are among the most popular activities.

*Lunch:* **Duck Brand Cantina,** 248 Riverside Avenue, Winthrop. (509) 996–2192. Tasty Mexican dishes, as well as sandwiches, steaks, delicious pies, and chocolate cake.

### Afternoon

Turn west on Route 20 for the return trip, stopping at the overlooks and trails you missed on the way out, continuing this abundant feast for the senses.

In Marblemount, stop at Mountain Song Restaurant for a coffee break; then continue westward toward Sedro Woolley. At Burlington, join I–5 for the forty-five-minute drive south to Seattle.

## There's More

**Boating.** Ross Lake provides superb high-country canoeing in the wilderness. From Ross Dam parking lot, portage your canoe down a ¾-mile trail. You can choose to paddle to Ross Dam from Diablo Lake; for a fee, Ross Lake Resort will haul you up to the lake. Call Ross Lake Resort, Radiotelephone Newhalem 7735.

**Dam and river tours.** Seattle City Light offers a four-hour tour (summers only) that includes a ride on the historic Incline Railway, which rises 560 feet up Sourdough Mountain, and a cruise on Diablo Lake to Ross Dam Powerhouse. The tour ends with an all-you-can-eat, bunkhouse-style dinner. A ninety-minute tour gives you the railway ride, slide show, and tour of the art deco Diablo Powerhouse. Phone (206) 684–3030.

**Fishing.** In streams and lakes, fish for brook, Dolly Varden, golden, and rainbow trout.

**Horseback riding.** Horse Country, 8507 Highway 92, P.O. Box 2, Granite Falls, WA 98252. (206) 691–7509. Trail rides in the Cascade foothills, along the Pilchuck River. Ponies, lessons, family trail rides available.

**Skiing.** Methow Valley Ski Touring Association, Box 147, Winthrop, WA 98862. Provides information and maps on Nordic ski trails in Sun Mountain, Rendezvous, and Mazama areas. Methow Valley Sport Trails Association gives recorded updates on trail conditions. (800) 682–5787. The Methow Valley, with 100-odd miles of cross-country ski trails, is known as one of the best Nordic skiing centers in the world.

# Special Events

**July.** Bluegrass Festival, Darrington.
**Late September.** Norba Mountain Bike Races, Glacier.
**Late September.** Historic Home Tour, Snohomish.
**Early October.** Granite Falls Railroad Days, Granite Falls.

# Other Recommended Restaurants and Lodgings

## Methow

Cafe Bienville, P.O. Box 745, Highway 153. (509) 923–2228. Small, casual cafe serving Northwest foods spiced with Cajun flair.

## Winthrop

Sun Mountain Lodge, P.O. Box 1000. (509) 996–2211; within Washington, (800) 572–0493. Rustic, log-beamed lodge in the Methow Valley. Rock fireplace, swimming pool, tennis, beautiful mountain setting.

# For More Information

Snohomish Chamber of Commerce, 116 Avenue B, Snohomish, WA 98290. (206) 568–2526.

North Cascades National Park and Ross Lake National Recreation Area, Skagit District Office, Marblemount, WA 98267. (206) 873–4590.

Concrete Chamber of Commerce, P.O. Box 739, Concrete, WA 98237. (206) 853–8400.

Winthrop Visitors' Center, P.O. Box 39, Winthrop, WA 98862. (509) 996–2125; within Washington, (800) 551–0111.

National Park Service, 800 State Street, Sedro Woolley, WA 98284. (206) 873–4500.

# Mount Rainier Loop

Mount Rainier is the highest mountain in the Cascades.

## Cascades Grandeur

_____ 1 NIGHT _____

Mount Rainier National Park · Historic lodge · Backcountry hiking
Steam-train ride · Wildlife park · Daffodil fields

The highest mountain in the Cascade Range can be seen for 200 miles when the weather is clear. Mount Rainier's snowy bulk rises 14,410 feet, enticing climbers, hikers, and other lovers of the wilderness. Twenty-six massive glaciers hold an icy grip on the tallest volcanic mountain in the contiguous United States.

Old-growth forests encircle the mountain. Douglas fir, red cedar, and western hemlock soar 200 feet above the moss-covered valley floors. Through those trees, more than 300 miles of trails meander, leading to wildflower-spangled meadows and clear ponds. Glacier-fed streams rush through every valley, tumbling in rapids and waterfalls.

Rainier is moody, and its weather unpredictable. Rain and snow may suddenly appear on a mild day and retreat as quickly. Glimpsed through the clouds, the mountain is beautiful. Under sunny skies, when Rainier appears in all its dazzling glory, it is magnificent.

Much of the route outlined here is open only in summer; check with the visitors' information centers for road conditions.

# Day 1

## Morning

Drive south from Seattle to State Route 164, and turn east. At Enumclaw, stop at **Baumgartner's,** 1008 Roosevelt East (206–825–1067). This deli has everything: cheese, sausage, beer, sandwiches, luscious pastries. Purchase your picnic makings here, tuck them into your cooler, and take Route 410 east into the wilderness.

At Greenwater, the road turns south and within a few miles enters **Mount Rainier National Park.** You're on the Mather Memorial Parkway, paralleling the White River in the shadow of Sunrise Ridge. At the Sunrise/White River road, turn right and drive 17 miles to the 6,400-foot ridge top. Trails lead from the visitors' center through the fragile, subalpine vegetation to ever-higher and more breathtaking views of glaciers and rocky crags.

From **Sunrise Point,** the summit's crater rim and **Emmons Glacier,** 4½ miles long, are clearly visible. Mount Adams lies to the south, and Mount Baker rests on the northern horizon.

*Lunch:* Picnic at Sunrise.

## Afternoon

Return to Highway 410, continue south to **Cayuse Pass** (4,694 feet), and veer left toward **Chinook Pass.** Drive 3 miles for a striking view of Mount Rainier's east side.

Return to Cayuse Pass and take Route 123 south. Near the **Stevens Canyon** entrance, at the southeastern end of the national park, watch for signs to the **Grove of the Patriarchs.** Walk the 1-mile trail, crossing the Ohanapecosh River on a footbridge, to an island where you'll be in the midst of an ancient forest. The princely trees that grow on the island—Douglas fir, western red cedar, and western hemlock—are 1,000 years old.

Drive the Stevens Canyon road west to **Paradise.** The road angles through thick forest, across rivers and creeks, rounding the bend at **Backbone Ridge** and heading north to **Box Canyon.** Through this narrow canyon, scoured by glaciers and carved by water, runs the Muddy Fork of the Cowlitz River.

Traveling west from Box Canyon, you'll see Stevens Ridge looming high on the right, with Stevens Creek below. In the fall, the vine maples on the slopes of the ridge in this U-shaped valley blaze with color.

As the road twists toward the southern shores of Louise and Reflection lakes, at the base of the **Tatoosh Peaks** you'll see Stevens, Unicorn, and Pinnacle peaks thrusting sharply skyward, dramatically punctuating the rugged landscape.

When you reach the Paradise Valley Road, turn right and climb upward until you arrive at last in Paradise. **Nisqually Glacier** and **Wilson Glacier** hang above, with Rainier's peak capping the view. At **Jackson Visitors' Center,** pick up maps and trail information. The center offers slide and film programs on Rainier and the park's history, as well as 360-degree views of the awe-inspiring surroundings.

During July and August, the slopes of **Paradise Park** become tapestries of color and beauty, as delicate subalpine flowers bloom by the thousands. Trails wind through the meadows and over trickling brooks, luring you to explore.

Head out on your own, or join one of the **naturalist-led walks** that begin at the visitors' center. An easy one-hour walk exploring the flower fields starts at 2:00 P.M. Another undemanding hike leaves the center at 2:30 P.M. and concentrates on the geology, glaciers, and fine views of the dirty snout and pristine, almost-blue interior of Nisqually Glacier.

Take **Skyline Trail** to **Panorama Point** for a comfortable, half-day hike replete with grand vistas. Marmots whistle and streams sing in the crisp, clear mountain air. A side trail crosses snowfields to end at Ice Caves, remnants of the once-immense caves carved by water flowing under glaciers.

*Dinner:* **Paradise Inn**. Grilled salmon, steak, and chicken, served in the dining room of a grand old lodge.

At 7:30 P.M., meet a park naturalist in the lobby for a one-hour **evening stroll** in the valley. It's an excellent opportunity for taking photographs and for observing wildlife.

At 9:00 P.M., interpreters give **slide-illustrated talks** in the lodge lobby. Topics vary: Meadow ecology, volcanic geology, human effects on the mountain, and Native American views are a few.

*Lodging:* Paradise Inn. Imposing, 126-room lodge of Alaskan cedar. Simple rooms; some share baths. The views are incomparable. For reservations (a must), contact Mount Rainier Guest Services, P.O. Box 108, Ashford, WA 98304. (206–569–2275).

# Day 2

## Morning

Rise at dawn for an early hike, if the weather is clear. There are few sights more exhilarating than Rainier's rosy-hued glaciers under the first rays of the morning sun.

*Breakfast:* Paradise Inn. Standard breakfast menu, lavish Sunday brunch.

Head south from Paradise Park to the small community of **Longmire,** and stop for a tour of the second-oldest national park museum in the country. Open daily, the small museum offers exhibits that cover Rainier's geology, wildlife, and history.

As you drive west toward the Nisqually entrance, 6.2 miles from Longmire, you're surrounded by trees 600 to 800 years old. Their high branches create a green canopy above the road.

From the park's entrance, continue west on Route 706, along the banks of the **Nisqually River.** At Elbe, follow the signs to **Mount Rainier Scenic Railroad** (Box 921, Elbe, WA 98330; 206–569–2588). The old-fashioned train takes visitors three times daily in summer on a 14-mile ride. Behind a vintage steam engine, open cars chug, steam, and whistle across high bridges and through deep forest to Mineral Lake. The train ride takes ninety minutes. The dinner train ride on Sundays lasts four hours.

At Elbe, turn north on Route 7 to Eatonville (Route 161) and **Northwest Trek,** a 600-acre wildlife park (phone 206–832–6116). Here the visitors are enclosed in a bus for a forty-five-minute tour, and the animals roam freely in their natural habitat. Bison, moose, bighorn sheep, and caribou move undisturbed through the woodlands and open meadows. Cougar, wolves, eagles, and owls are kept in spacious, caged areas. Spring is a good time to see the newborns.

Northwest Trek has 5 miles of nature trails; one is accessible to wheelchairs.

*Lunch:* **Northwest Trek snack bar.** Sandwiches, soups, and hamburgers. Eat indoors or take your lunch to the picnic meadow, where tame deer may wish to share your meal.

## Afternoon

Continue on Route 161 north to **Puyallup,** home of the daffodil and once the bulb basket of the world. Valley farmers shipped worldwide a generation ago, and tourists flocked in to admire the acres of fragrant flowers and watch the street parade held in spring in their honor.

That was before urban development covered many fields and before fresh-cut flowers became a lucrative business; now most of the daffodils are cut and shipped while they're unopened buds. But you can still see a few fields in bloom—glorious yellow carpets, with Mount Rainier an immense white backdrop. The April festival and parade remain a major annual event.

In Puyallup, tour **Meeker Mansion,** a seventeen-room home of the 1890s. Among its ornate splendors are six fireplaces with carved ceramic tiles, Victorian furnishings, and floral painted ceilings. Well worth a visit, the mansion is open afternoons, Wednesday through Sunday.

Another restored home, this one in neighboring Sumner, is **Ryan House,** built in 1875 by the town's first mayor. He was a hops farmer and lumberman.

To return to Seattle, drive north on State Route 167 or take Route 161 to I–5 for the final 15 miles.

# There's More

**Hiking.** Naches Loop Trail, near Chinook Pass and Tipsoo Lake (off Route 410, on the eastern border of the national park), is enchant- ･ ing, with its subalpine firs and mountain hemlock trees, wooden bridge, and summer wildflowers. The trail connects with the Pacific Crest Trail, which extends from Mexico to Canada.

Silver Falls Trail, above Laughingwater Creek on the Ohanapecosh River, is a 3-mile loop trip from Ohanapecosh Campground, 2 miles south of the Stevens Canyon junction on Route 123. The trail leads to an 80-foot cascade of water so clear it has a silver cast. The vibrant green of the ferns and mosses in the Silver Falls gorge is stunning on a cloudy day.

Trail of the Shadows is a ½-mile trail through a meadow with bubbling mineral springs; you may see a beaver family. The trail begins across the road from Longmire Museum.

**Mountain Climbing.** Climbing Rainier demands skill and experience. One-day seminars and equipment rentals are available from Rainier Mountaineering, Inc., Paradise, WA 98398 (206–569–2227). Winter address: 201 St. Helens Avenue, Tacoma, WA 98402 (206–627–6242).

**Skiing.** Crystal Mountain, one of the state's major ski areas.

Camp Muir snowfield. Gentle slope, snow covered all year, on Rainier's south side.

Reflection Lakes. Safe cross-country trail skiing, easy access, and scenic grandeur. Camping allowed when snowpack is 3 feet deep. Park at Narada Falls, near Paradise.

**Van Lierop Bulb Farm,** 13407 Eightieth Street East, Puyallup, WA 98372. (206) 848–7272. Stroll brick walkways in a small garden with flowering trees and a gazebo. Buy bulbs and plants in the gift shop. Put your name on the mailing list for a lovely catalog.

**Farmers' Market** at Pioneer Park, Puyallup. Fresh fruit and produce from local farms on summer Saturdays.

# Special Events

**Mid-April.** Daffodil Festival, Puyallup and Tacoma. Elaborate parade, flower show, bake sale, dog show, barbecues, auction, dances.

**Late June and early July.** Ezra Meeker Community Festival, Puyallup. Honors an early Puyallup pioneer. Arts-and-crafts fair, fun run, pancake breakfast, family track meet, chicken barbecue, and ice-cream social.

**September.** Western Washington State Fair, Puyallup. One of the state's major fairs, with livestock exhibitions, races, carnival rides, food booths, and handicrafts.

# Other Recommended Restaurants and Lodgings

## Crystal Mountain

Crystal Mountain Resort, P.O. Box 1. (206) 663–2265. Some of Washington's best ski slopes and cross-country trails. Condominium rentals, a sports shop, restaurants. Open mid-November to mid-April.

## Longmire

National Park Inn. Historic cedar lodge, remodeled 1989–1990. Rustic and woodsy, with twenty-six rooms (two handicapped accessible) and a view across Longmire Meadow to mountain's peak. The only lodge in the park open all year. Reservations: Mount Rainier Guest Services, P.O. Box 108, Ashford, WA 98304. (206–569–2275).

## Ashford

Alexander's Country Inn, Route 706. (206) 569–2300; within Washington, (800) 654–7615. Landmark country restaurant and inn with twelve rooms. Fresh fish entrees and memorable blackberry pie.

Wild Berry Restaurant and Cabin at the Berry, Route 706 East. (206) 569–2628. Good sandwiches, great pie. Rustic but comfortable log cabin across the road sleeps eight.

Moore's Mountain Village, Route 706 East. (206) 569–2251. Restaurant, motel, and gallery of arts and crafts, with historic, hand-carved carousel in front.

## Packwood

Hotel Packwood, 102 Main Street. (206) 494–5431. Renovated Victorian inn 10 miles from Mount Rainier National Park. Nine comfortable, antiques-furnished rooms, two with private baths. Theodore Roosevelt stayed here.

## Puyallup

Balsano's, 127 Fifteenth SE. (206) 845–4222. Well-prepared Italian food that's out of the ordinary.

Earthquake Burgers, 11526 Meridien South. (206) 848–9850. Small cafe serving platter-sized hamburgers. For those with large appetites.

Paw Paw's, 9708 East 112th. (206) 848–0331. Gift shop and cafe serving light, savory lunches in a cozy, country-calico setting.

## Sumner

Manfred Vierthaler Winery and Restaurant, 17136 Highway 410 East. (206) 863–1633. Unusual dining room on a hill, offering view of valley and vineyards. German-style wines in the tasting room, steak and Bavarian dishes on the menu.

# For More Information

Enumclaw Chamber of Commerce, 1421 Cole Street, Enumclaw, WA 98022. (206) 825–7666.

Mount Rainier National Park, Tahoma Woods, Star Route, Ashford, WA 98304. (206) 569–2211.

Puyallup Chamber of Commerce, 322 Second Street SW. (206) 845–6755.

# North Kitsap Peninsula

Chief Seattle's grave lies under a frame of dugout canoes.

## A Northwest Heritage

_____ 1 NIGHT _____

Ferry rides • Chief Seattle's grave • Native American museum • "Little Norway"
Secluded country resort • Oldest operating sawmill in America
Historic Victorian village

There's a lot of diversity within a comparatively small area on the northern Kitsap Peninsula. You can drive from a Scandinavian-style village to a New England mill town in less than a half-hour, with time out for sight-seeing, or you can watch Suquamish Indians carve a dugout canoe a few miles from fine dining opportunities on a country estate.

## Day 1

### Morning

**Kitsap Peninsula** lies west of Seattle, across Puget Sound. Board the Winslow ferry at Elliott Bay for the thirty-five-minute crossing to **Winslow,** on **Bainbridge Island.** Have breakfast here at the **Streamliner Diner,** 397 Winslow Way (206–842–8595), or drive Route 305 north toward Agate Passage and the bridge to the peninsula.

Take an immediate right on Suquamish Way, and follow the signs to the grave of **Chief Seattle** (or Sealth). The grave of the famous Salish Indian leader, who died in 1866 and for whom Seattle is named, lies in a hilltop cemetery beside a small church. Marked by a cross and framed with traditional dugout canoes, the great chief's resting place overlooks the waters of the sound. On the horizon rise the tall buildings of Seattle's skyline.

After paying homage to the man who sought peace between his people and the white settlers, the man who said that "the very dust under your feet . . . is the ashes of our ancestors," visit nearby **Old Man House State Park** (signs clearly mark the way). This shady, hillside park above the bay was the site of an Indian communal home, the "Old Man House," built of cedar and 900 feet long.

Learn more about the culture of these Native Americans at the **Suquamish Museum.** Follow Route 305 west; the museum is just off the highway on the **Port Madison Indian Reservation.** Near the entrance, under a shelter, you may see carvers patiently forming a long, dugout canoe from a huge log of cedar. The excellent, sometimes poignant museum artifacts and photographs depict Indian life as it was for thousands of years before white settlement and the results after it.

Continue west on Route 305 as it curves up toward Liberty Bay and **Poulsbo.** Turn left on Lincoln Road, which ends at the waterfront. When you see painted murals on downtown buildings and signs reading VELKOMMEN TIL POULSBO, you know you're deep into Scandinavian country.

The little town was settled in the late 1880s by fishers, loggers, and farmers, many of them from Norway; *Poulsbo* means "Paul's Place" in Norwegian. Liberty Bay, then called Dogfish Bay, and its inlets reminded the settlers of the fjords of their native land. The town's tie to the water remains strong today, with three marinas on the bay's waterfront.

The people of Poulsbo take pride in their rich heritage. They hold several traditional festivals to honor their roots, and numerous shops sell Scandinavian handicrafts, jewelry, and foods.

*Lunch:* **Judith's Tea Room,** Olympic Square on Front Street in Poulsbo. (509) 697–3449. Home-baked goods, sandwiches, special salads of mixed greens and edible flowers. Another good lunch choice is **New Day Seafood,** on Front Street overlooking the water (206–697–3183); with both a restaurant and a fishing boat in the family, you know the seafood is fresh.

## Afternoon

Upstairs from Judith's Tea Room is Verksted, an artists' co-op. Wood carvings, leather work, hand-painted shirts, chocolate sculpture, and cribbage boards made from elk horn are some of the unusual items in the gallery.

Stroll **Liberty Bay Park,** which is connected by a wooden causeway over the water to American Legion Park, to soak up the maritime flavor of this engaging town. Pennants snap in the wind on fishing and pleasure boats as they come and go in the busy harbor. Liberty Bay has a picnic area and a covered pavilion used during the summer for dancing, concerts, and arts festivals. At the new $1.4 million Poulsbo Marine Science Center on Liberty Bay, you can examine sea life under microscopes, touch anemones, see ghost shrimp, and watch videos and documentaries.

**Raab Park,** at Caldart Avenue off Hostmark Street, is Poulsbo's largest park. On its fourteen acres are grassy slopes, covered picnic facilities, barbecue grills, a playground, horseshoe pits, a sand volleyball court, and an outdoor stage.

Browse the shops along **Front Street** for unusual souvenirs, such as the brass and nautical items in Cargo Hold and merchandise imported from Norway at Five Swans. The fragrance wafting from Sluy's Bakery will draw you to this famous shop, where fresh-baked breads and toothsome pastries are sold.

Leaving Poulsbo, take Bond Road west to Big Valley Road and turn left. Drive 4 miles through idyllic countryside, where forested hills back green fields, to **The Manor Farm Inn.** Arrive by 3:30 P.M. and you'll be in time for tea, a regular ritual at this country estate.

After tea, stroll around the farm and reacquaint yourself with tranquility. In this setting, right from *All Creatures Great and Small,* Manor Farm Inn offers an opportunity to experience a slower pace. Horses and dairy cows graze in the pastures, and lambs gambol in the fields. Walk to the trout-stocked pond in back, or sit on the veranda and admire the flower-filled courtyard.

Eventually you'll repair to the drawing room for hot canapés and a glass of sherry before dinner.

*Dinner:* The Manor Farm Inn dining hall. Five-course dinners change nightly. French cuisine with Northwest flair. Choice of three entrees (menu changes monthly).

*Lodging:* The Manor Farm Inn, 26069 Big Valley Road NE, Poulsbo, WA 98370. (206) 779-4628. French country–style farmhouse with seven rooms in two wings, plus cottage. Masses of flowers, luxurious rooms, outdoor spa, enthusiastic hospitality.

# Day 2

## Morning

Hot scones, juice, and coffee or tea in your room begin the day. Then comes breakfast in the dining hall or on the lawn.

*Breakfast:* The Manor Farm Inn. Full country breakfast at 9:00 A.M. is included in your room cost. On Sundays a lavish "new country breakfast" is served (juice, fruit, porridge, pastries and scones, omelets, crepes, waffles, sausage). Open to nonguests at additional cost.

Spend the morning at the farm petting the animals or reading on the veranda, or borrow a bicycle and explore the winding country roads.

**Kitsap State Memorial Park** is less than 2 miles from the inn.

*Lunch:* After the morning's bountiful meal, most guests prefer to skip lunch.

## Afternoon

Follow Big Valley Road to State Route 3, and turn north toward **Port Gamble.** This historic, picturesque village, which lies across an inlet from the eastern, and northernmost, tip of Kitsap Peninsula, is one of the last company towns still in existence. Port Gamble is owned by Pope and Talbot, one of the world's major timber companies. The **oldest sawmill** in North America is still in full operation at water's edge, at the foot of the bluff below town. From afar you can smell the sawdust as you watch logs tumble through the noisy machinery.

The founders of Port Gamble came from New England in the mid-nineteenth century and built the new town to resemble the one they'd left—East Machias, Maine. Today Port Gamble has been restored to its turn-of-the-century appearance, with neat Victorian homes, a steepled church, and a general store. The store, which was begun as a trading post by Julian Pringle in 1853, has recently been renovated to include a delicatessen, a museum, and a replica of the lobby of the elegant hotel that once graced the town.

**Main Street** is lined with elm trees brought around Cape Horn from Maine in 1872. The entire town is on the National Register of Historic Places. The **Port Gamble Historical Museum** explains the area's history. **Of Sea and Shore Museum** holds a collection of more than 14,000 species of shells and marine life. For information on the town, call (206) 297-3341.

From Port Gamble turn south on State Route 104, along the wooded bluff above Port Gamble inlet to Port Gamble–Suqaumish Road. You're headed back to the village of Suquamish.

*Dinner:* **Karsten's,** 18490 Suquamish Way NE, Suquamish. (206) 598–3080. Sumptuous meals in Suquamish Village Square. Seafood and prime rib buffet on Friday; Sunday brunch. Live music Wednesday, Friday, and Sunday. Open daily.

Take Suquamish Way to Route 305 and recross Agate Passage. Drive again through the woodlands and pastoral countryside of Bainbridge Island, and at Winslow catch the ferry back to Seattle.

## There's More

**Old Schoolhouse.** Brick two-story school at Kola-Kola Park, Kingston.

**Point No Point Lighthouse.** White, square tower in Hansville, at the tip of Kitsap Peninsula. Lighthouse established in 1879; present structure built in 1900.

**Thomas Kemper Brewery,** 22381 Foss Road NE, Poulsbo. (206) 697–1446. Microbrewery with Old World–style specialty lagers. Taproom and beer garden in the countryside north of Poulsbo. Open daily, tours on weekends.

## Special Events

**Mid-May.** Viking Fest, Poulsbo. In honor of Norway's Independence Day, a Sons of Norway luncheon, pancake breakfast, arts-and-crafts show, fun run, carnival, food booth, parade.

**Mid-June.** Skandia Midsommarfest, Poulsbo. Skandia Folk Dance Society performs in costume. Midsummer pole raising and dance.

**Mid-August.** Chief Seattle Days, Suquamish. Indian dancing, canoe races, food stands, softball games.

**December.** Yule Fest, Poulsbo. Scandinavian legends and story-telling, lighting of the Yule Log, Sons of Norway bazaar, Lucia Bride, strolling musicians.

## Other Recommended Restaurants and Lodgings

### Bremerton

Willcox House, 2390 Tekiu Road. (206) 830–4492. Luxurious retreat in former private waterside mansion. Five rooms, marble fireplaces, pool, view of Hood Canal, Olympic Mountains. Full breakfast served; dinner available by reservation.

# For More Information

Suquamish Tribal Center, Route 305, Suquamish, WA 98392. (206) 598–3311.

Greater Poulsbo Chamber of Commerce, 19131 Eighth Avenue, P.O. Box 1063, Poulsbo, WA 98370. (206) 779–4848.

Washington State Ferries, 801 Alaskan Way, Pier 52 Colman Dock, Seattle, WA 98104. (206) 464–6400; within Washington, (800) 84–FERRY.

# Skagit County

The charming waterfront town of La Conner.

## Spring Flowers By the Sea

_____ 1 NIGHT _____

Fields of spring flowers · Quaint waterfront · Boutiques
Art galleries · Historical museum · Wildlife refuge
Antiques shops · Jetboat ride

Here's a two-day sojourn into the country, a brief escape that's full of
color and activity. Have fun with this one—maybe do your gift shopping for the year in La Conner's myriad shops, where you may find
unexpected treasures.

The route suggested allows time to stroll La Conner's busy downtown area (packed with tourists on summer weekends and during the
tulip festival), but it takes you to quiet byways, too, where you can
observe wildlife, smell the flowers, and revel in rural serenity.

# Day 1

## Morning

Drive north on I–5, past Mount Vernon and over the **Skagit River** to State Route 20 (about 60 miles), and turn west. When you reach Best Road, turn right; at Bayview Road, turn left, and then veer right on Bayview-Edison.

This road edges the shore of **Padilla Bay,** a body of water well protected by a circling group of islands: Fidalgo, Guemes, and Samish. You're headed for the **Breazeale-Padilla Bay National Estuarine Research Reserve and Interpretive Center,** which offers hands-on learning about the estuary and local plant and animal life.

The reserve is one in a nationwide system that teaches visitors about estuaries—mixes of salt- and freshwater—that teem with life. Walk the uplands nature trail, view aquatic displays and Padilla Bay, and, if you're still curious, learn more in the center's research library. (206) 428–1558. Hours vary seasonally.

From Bayview-Edison Road, turn east on Sullivan to rejoin Best Road (Route 237). Follow Best Road south. You're in the heart of the tulip, iris, and daffodil fields of the **Skagit Valley,** where great swaths of springtime color draw hordes of admirers. The world's greatest volume of tulips comes from the fertile farmlands of Skagit County.

In other seasons the valley is equally beautiful, if not as brightly colored, with its tawny summer fields and autumn mists and leaf and harvest fragrances. **Mount Baker** stands on the far horizon, a high, snow-mantled cone.

When you come to **La Conner Flats,** 1598 Best Road (206–466–3821), stop for a tour of this English country garden. Eleven acres bloom with color March through October, from the daffodils and rhododendrons of March to June's roses, August's dahlias, and the brilliant foliage of fall. In addition to the array of flowers are savory-scented herb gardens and vegetable and berry gardens.

*Lunch:* **The Granary,** La Conner Flats. Homemade soup, salads, sandwiches, desserts, served in a rustic former granary near the entrance to the gardens. (High tea served 2:00 to 5:00 P.M. Open March to October; closed Mondays).

## Afternoon

Continue on Best Road to Chilberg Road, and turn west toward **La Conner** proper. The historic, picturesque little town had its beginnings in 1867 as a trading post. A few years later, John Conner, from Olympia, bought the store and town and seventy additional acres for the sum of $500. In 1872 he named the settlement after his wife, Louisa Ann Conner, using her initials.

La Conner, perched on the edge of **Swinomish Channel,** which lies between the mainland and Fidalgo Island, grew into an active port and fishing community. But when the Great Depression brought business to a standstill, La Conner began to fade.

In the 1970s energetic townsfolk decided to make some changes to encourage tourism. Their efforts succeeded beyond all expectation. La Conner has not only been discovered; it's gained fame for its charming waterfront and turn-of-the-century architecture, its numerous shops and art galleries.

On your way to the downtown district, stop at **Tillinghast Seed Company,** 623 Morris Street (206–466–3329). The wooden porch overflows with flowers at this old-fashioned store, the oldest mail-order seed company in the Northwest. Inside you'll find seeds, plants, kitchen tools, country gifts, and spicy scents; upstairs there's a Christmas shop, and out in back a nursery in the shade of a one hundred-year-old tree—the largest European beech on the West Coast.

First and Second streets, above the harbor, are lined with **antiques shops, boutiques, and art galleries.** A sampling: Earthenworks, showing top-quality Northwest ceramics, fabrics, watercolors, and photographs; La Conner Gallery, a channel-side showroom with crystal and jewelry; The Wood Merchant, for finely carved sculptures and tools; Homespun Market, where European laces, handwoven throws, and homespun fabrics are sold; and The Scott Collection, with Northwest pottery and porcelains, jewelry, bronze and brass sculpture, and soapstone carvings.

As you explore the town you'll see, just off Second Street, one of La Conner's oldest landmarks—a bank built in 1886, now City Hall, a triangular-shaped building. Near it is the **Magnus Anderson Cabin,** a pioneer home constructed in 1869 by a Swedish immigrant.

**The Gaches Mansion,** also on Second Street, is a twenty-two-room structure that dates from 1891. Once used as a hospital, the mansion has been restored and is open for tours on weekend afternoons. The Gaches Mansion also houses the **Valley Museum of Northwest Art.**

**Skagit County Museum** is on Fourth Street. Its exhibits show life as it was in a previous century, and its windows frame views of the valley's fields with Mount Baker behind them.

*Dinner:* **Palmers,** 205 East Washington Street in La Conner. (206) 466–4261. The town's consistently best restaurant, serving Northwest and French cuisine. Fresh local seafoods, pastas, wines. Tables upstairs, cozy booths in the downstairs pub.

*Lodging:* **The Channel Lodge,** P.O. Box 573, La Conner, WA 98257. (206) 466–1500. Stylish inn with country-contemporary decor. Forty rooms, all with fireplaces, most with harbor views.

# Day 2

## Morning

*Breakfast:* The Channel Lodge.

You might rent a bicycle and take a ride in the country, passing fields green or ablaze with color; perhaps you'll see swans gliding through the marshes in the morning mist.

Alternatively, check the shops you missed yesterday. If you're interested in **antiques,** La Conner has plenty to offer. Cameo Antiques showcases Victorian and American primitives in oak and pine, Creighton's Quilts is known for its Amish quilts, and Morris Street Antique Mall carries a wide range of furniture, glassware, toys, and books. Nasty Jack's has a large selection of oak furniture.

For a different view and an invigorating experience, book space with **Viking Star** (509–466–2639) for a jetboat ride. Ken McDonald will cruise through Skagit Bay and the scenic splendor of Deception Pass on a two-hour trip. Longer cruises are available on a forty-nine-passenger vessel.

*Lunch:* **Legends,** 708 South First Street. (206) 466–5240. Indian barbecued salmon and fry bread, prepared and eaten outdoors on a deck overlooking the water.

## Afternoon

Leaving La Conner, take Chilberg Road south to Fir Island. Less than a mile after you cross the bridge, the toasty scent of freshly baked waffles will draw you to **Snow Goose Produce.** The open market sells produce, flowers, fresh seafood, and, most important, huge and delicious ice cream cones. The hot waffle cones are baked as you watch.

The Fir Island coast, along Skagit Bay, is ragged with islands and waterways, as the Skagit flows into the bay in a dozen places. Take Fir Island Road to Game Range Road, about 1½ miles west of Conway, and you'll come to **Skagit Wildlife Recreation Area.** In this 12,000-acre preserve you'll see hundreds of waterfowl and, in winter, Siberian snow geese.

Back on Fir Island Road, head east across the Skagit to Route 530 and turn south. It's a few miles down the road to **Stanwood,** a small farming community. **Scandia Bakery,** on 3-block-long Main Street, is a good place to stop for a coffee break and pastry. Lace curtains and Norwegian rosemaling decorative trim emphasize the Scandinavian theme of the bakery (along with the sign by the coffeepot that reads NORWEGIAN GASOLINE).

From Stanwood, drive to Silvana on State Route 531. The pastoral valley is far more picturesque and relaxing than the freeway ride, and it doesn't add much time. You'll pass sprawling green fields and tidy plots, a red barn half-submerged in ivy and a gray one with a moss-covered roof. A flag flies from the porch of an old-fashioned farm-house, behind the lilacs.

About 7 miles from Stanwood, you'll see a small white church on a hill. **Peace Lutheran Church,** built in 1884, is now a historic site, still in use and a favored location for weddings.

Blink as you enter the village of Silvana, on your way to join I–5, and you may miss it. You left the Fir Island turnoff just 23 miles ago.

Drive south on I–5 for the return to Seattle.

## There's More

**RoozenGaarde,** 1587 Beaver Marsh Road, Mount Vernon. (206) 424–8531. Display garden and gift shop, open daily.

**Skagit Gardens,** 1695 Johnson Road, Mount Vernon. One of the oldest public display gardens in Skagit County. Year-round botanical garden: thousands of tulips, crocuses, daffodils in spring; brilliant annuals in August; poinsettias in November. Visitors welcome; bring a lunch to the gazebo and picnic table.

**Skagit Valley Bulb Farms,** Memorial Highway and Young Road. (206) 424–8152. Picnic facilities; walk in fields of flowers.

**Westshore Acres Bulb Farm and Display Garden,** 956 Downey Road, Mount Vernon. (206) 466–3158.

## Special Events

**April.** Skagit Valley Tulip Festival. Major Northwest festival, with parades, flower shows, street fair, pancake breakfast, salmon barbecues, dances, pick-your-own and display flower fields, food fair, sports events (gymnastics, Slug Run).

## Other Recommended Restaurants and Lodgings

### La Conner

Calico Cupboard, 720 South First Street. (206) 466–4451. Cafe that's famous for cinnamon rolls, muffins, breads, biscuits. Eat here, or take pastry to go and eat by the water. Coffee drinks, too. (Crowded in the busy season.)

Downey House Bed-and-Breakfast Inn, 1880 Chilberg Road. (206) 466–3207. Charm and comfort in the country, in a home with five guest rooms. Hot tub, antiques, homemade blackberry pie. Hearty breakfast served.

Heather House, 505 Maple Avenue. (206) 466–4675. Replica of an 1890 Cape Cod home. View of Skagit Valley, three bedrooms. Full breakfast served.

La Conner Country Inn, 107 Second Street. (206) 466–3101. Attractive, twenty-eight-room inn with theme of a country guest house. In the heart of town. Continental breakfast.

Ridgeway Bed-and-Breakfast, 1292 McLean Road, P.O. Box 475. (206) 428–8068 or (800) 428–8068. Yellow brick Dutch Colonial farm home on two acres. Tulip fields, five guest rooms, homemade desserts, full breakfast.

White Swan Guest House, 1388 Moore Road, Mount Vernon. Storybook Victorian farmhouse 6 miles from La Comner. Three guest rooms, cottage. Lovely gardens. (206) 445–6805.

## For More Information

La Conner Chamber of Commerce, P.O. Box 1610, La Conner, WA 98257. (206) 466–4778.

Mount Vernon Chamber of Commerce, 325 East College Way, P.O. Box 1007, Mount Vernon, WA 98273. (206) 428–8547.

# Gig Harbor

From Jerisich Park, visitors enjoy the picturesque view of Gig Harbor.

## In and Around the Water

_____ 1 NIGHT _____

Ferry ride on Puget Sound · Views of Seattle skyline · Antiques shops
Quiet country roads · Waterfront village · Fishing boats
Pleasure boats · Intriguing shops · Hiking · Boating

All these attractions in one overnight getaway? Yes, a quick trip to Gig Harbor can seem like a full vacation, with its variety of things to see and do. You can simply stroll the shop-lined streets and watch the sailboats, if you prefer total relaxation, or you can fill the time with action.

The sleepy fishing village that was Gig Harbor is rapidly disappearing, with new housing developments and even a sizable shopping center, complete with McDonald's, going in. But residents are struggling to retain the small-town atmosphere and slower pace that give the town its charm. And despite its discovery by tourists, Gig Harbor remains a boat-centered community with a focus on commercial fishing.

# Day 1

## Morning

Ride the ferry from Fauntleroy Cove across Puget Sound to **Southworth.** Head west across Kitsap Peninsula to the waterside town of **Port Orchard,** where you can search for treasures in the many antiques shops, browse through the art galleries, and shop for handicrafts. Stroll by the busy marina, tour the **Log Cabin Museum,** and, on summer Saturdays, buy fresh produce at the farmers market. (For more details on Port Orchard, see Seattle Escape Three.)

*Lunch:* **Bay Coffee Company and Espresso,** 807-B Bay Street. (206) 895–2115. The name describes it: coffee, espresso, sandwiches, and pastries in a small, casual cafe near the water.

## Afternoon

Take Bethel Road from Port Orchard, and head east on Sedgwick to Banner Road; then turn south. This country road passes through the woodlands, fields, and homes along **Colvos Passage,** with green **Vashon Island** lying on the east.

Passing Olalla, you'll see the Carl Nelson home, a Victorian estate still owned by descendants of the sea captain who built it. Continue south on Crescent Valley Drive, driving by Canterwood, a security-conscious, planned country-club community with luxurious residences, townhouses, a golf course, a swimming pool, tennis courts, and stables.

Turn right on Vernhardson and left on Peacock Hill, and you will reach the heart of **Gig Harbor:** Harborview Drive. The road edging the little bay is lined with specialty shops, some offering souvenirs of the T-shirt-and-coffee-mug variety, others with original art, stylish clothing, and antiques. Intermingled with the boutiques are marina offices, a yacht sales broker, and a wholesaler of smoked herring. Wharves and boats dot the protected inlet.

Nisqually Indians were the only human inhabitants of Gig Harbor until 1841, when the Wilkes expedition stumbled upon it. One of the party's small boats, a captain's gig, took shelter in the bay during a storm; hence the name Gig Harbor. After that discovery, settlers and fishers, many from Yugoslavia, immigrated and began a still-active fishing fleet.

Stop at the chamber of commerce office on Judson Street for maps and brochures; then amble back to the waterfront and stroll the new walkway that edges the harbor. Life loses its sometimes-hectic quality here, as you watch the gulls swoop and shriek above the pilings and the boats bob gently on the waves. Dream over the luxurious vessels pictured at the yacht sales office or afloat in the bay.

Check in at your lodgings.

*Dinner:* **Neville's Shoreline,** 8827 North Harborview Drive, Gig Harbor. (206) 851–9822. Great location above the inner harbor, with high, angled windows overlooking the water. Northwest wines, Continental cuisine, variety of appetizers. Crab feed on Sunday, lobster special on Monday. Dine outdoors and ducks will come begging.

*Lodging:* **The Pillars Bed and Breakfast,** 6606 Soundview Drive, Gig Harbor, WA 98335. (206) 851–6644. Gracious home on a hillside, offering views of Colvos Passage, Vashon Island, and Mount Rainier. Three large, comfortable rooms, two with water and mountain views.

# Day 2

## Morning

*Breakfast:* Juice, fresh fruit, cereals, and freshly baked sticky buns are served every day at The Pillars. If you want an omelet or other egg dish, the agreeable hosts, Alma and Bill Boge, are happy to prepare it.

Work your way along Harborview Drive, browsing through the dozens of shops and boutiques as you go. At **Mariners Museum,** 3311 Harborview Drive, you can see nautical artifacts displayed.

Next buy picnic makings and drive Rosedale Street west about 5 miles to **Kopachuck State Park**. On the way, you might like to stop at **Rosedale Gardens** to see the greenhouse and nursery under the cedar trees.

Kopachuck is a popular park for its location and amenities. Roads are paved, and campsites are numerous, wooded, and well maintained. Pass the camping section and head for the parking lot in the picnic area. From here you can walk the sloping path to the rocky beach or take one of the side trails that lead to nooks with picnic tables and grills under the trees. On sunny days, dappled light filters through the maple and cedar branches. The view across Carr Inlet to the snow-mantled Olympic Mountains is outstanding.

*Lunch:* Picnic in Kopachuck State Park.

## Afternoon

Enjoy the woodlands and beaches at Kopachuck; then return to Gig Harbor, and drive to the dock at Neville's Shoreline Restaurant for your **boat ride.** You can rent a runabout boat, a paddleboat, or a 27-foot sailboat from Jack Bujacich, who will also provide instruction if it's needed. (Rentals available daily in summer and on weekends in spring and fall; phone 206–858–7341.) Boat around the harbor for an hour, or, if you're feeling ambitious, sail east to **Point Defiance,** near **Tacoma.** You'll find good fishing in these waters.

Back at the Gig Harbor dock, turn in your boat and head for **The**

**Tides Tavern** for a late-afternoon drink on the deck overlooking the water. You can't say you've truly seen Gig Harbor if you haven't stopped at least once at the local gathering place. The convivial tavern on Harborview Drive serves pizza, beer, good chowder, and desserts made at a local bakery.

*Dinner:* **W. B. Scott's,** 3108 Harborview Drive, Gig Harbor. (206) 851–6644. Quiet, expensive, no views, but superb food. Specializes in blackened salmon and planter's-style halibut. Fresh seafood, entree-size salads.

Drive Route 16 toward Tacoma and connect with I–5 north for the one-hour trip to Seattle.

## There's More

**Golf.** Gig Harbor Golf Club, 6909 Artondale Drive NW, Gig Harbor. (206) 858–2376. Nine-hole course.

Madrona Links, 3604 Twenty-second Avenue NW, Gig Harbor. (206) 851–5193. Eighteen-hole course.

**Peninsula Historical Society Museum.** 3510 Rosedale Street, Gig Harbor. (206) 858–6722. Artifacts and photos show the history of the region in Old St. Nicholas Catholic Church, a quaint white structure with a bell steeple.

**Performance Circle Theater.** Evening theatrical events, outdoors in summer at 9916 Peacock Hill Avenue, Gig Harbor. (206) 851–PLAY.

## Special Events

**Early June.** Salmon Bake, Jerisich Park, Gig Harbor. Theme parade, bike rodeo, baked salmon dinner in waterside park.

**Mid-July.** Gig Harbor Art Festival, Judson Street. Display of regional artworks: oils, pottery, stained glass, watercolors.

**Mid-August.** Gig Harbor Jazz Festival. Nationally acclaimed jazz performers entertain all weekend.

**Early December.** Tide Fest. Tree lighting, boat parade, arts-and-crafts sale.

## Other Recommended Restaurants and Lodgings

### Gig Harbor

Cimarron, 3211 Fifty-sixth Street NW. (206) 851–6665. Friendly, western-style saloon and steakhouse with old-time wagons on display. Country dancing lessons on Tuesday and Thursday nights.

Harbor Inn Restaurant, 3111 Harborview Drive. (206) 851–5454. Waterfront dining overlooking the bay.

Ketch Krestine, 3311 Harborview Drive. (206) 858–9395. Bed-and-breakfast aboard a 100-foot sailing trader. A nautical, salty adventure. Full breakfast.

The Parsonage, 4107 Burnham Drive. (206) 851–8554. Homey bed-and-breakfast in former parsonage 1 block from harbor. Full breakfast.

## For More Information

South Kitsap Chamber of Commerce, 727 Bay Street, Port Orchard, WA 98366. (206) 876–3505.

Gig Harbor Chamber of Commerce, 3125 Judson Street, Gig Harbor, WA 98335. (206) 851–6865.

Washington State Ferries, 801 Alaskan Way, Pier 52 Colman Dock, Seattle, WA 98104. (206) 464–6400; within Washington (800) 84–FERRY.

# Orcas Island

Turtleback Farm Inn is one of Orcas Island's unforgettable bed-and-breakfast inns.

## Gem of the San Juans

_____ 2 NIGHTS _____

Ferry rides • Rocky beaches • Scenic ocean views • Bicycling
Highest point in San Juan Islands • Sea kayaking • Hiking
Wildlife • Bird-watching • Whale watching

Orcas Island, a green jewel set in an azure sea, has been considered a prime vacation spot since ferry runs to the San Juans began, back in the 1890s.

Orcas was named not for the orca whales that frequent the surrounding waters but for the viceroy of Mexico in 1792, the year in which the Spanish explorer Francisco Eliza found the island. What he saw was a 54-square-mile, U-shaped island, hilly and thickly forested, with fjordlike inlets and 125 miles of pebbled shoreline. That's what visitors see today, though the land is now marked with farms, resorts, campgrounds, and small communities.

Generally you'll find Orcas a peaceful retreat, but if you seek to avoid tourist crowds, better come off-season. The busy summer months can be hectic, and long lines waiting for the ferries are standard.

Ferry traffic to the San Juans rises from about 50,000 in February to 250,000 in August. If you leave your car at the landing and travel by foot or bicycle, you'll have no problem getting aboard. This itinerary is designed for an auto tour; however, it can be adjusted to accommodate other transportation.

# Day 1

## Morning

From Anacortes, 80 miles north of Seattle, catch the ferry west to **Orcas Island.** The 1¼-hour ride through island-dotted waters stops first at **Lopez Island.** The level country roads on Lopez make it popular with bicyclists; you may wish to stop here and explore for a couple of hours. You can take the next ferry to Orcas.

During your journey across Rosario Strait, you'll see surf-washed, rocky cliffs and secluded coves, frolicking harbor seals, and rookeries of pigeon guillemots. Gulls swoop and cry, and the sea breeze carries a briny fragrance in this exhilarating seascape.

When you land at Orcas, take Horseshoe Highway 13 miles to **East-sound,** passing farmlands and forests of fir, hemlock, and madrona. The only town of size on the island, Eastsound is a snug community set against the inner curve of the bay, facing a shallow tide flat.

Turn north on North Beach Road from Main Street, proceeding 2 blocks to the **historical museum.** Created from four log cabins, the museum displays pioneer and Indian artifacts. Much of the valuable Indian collection was saved by Ethan Allen, the San Juan Islands' superintendent of schools around the turn of the century. His hand-built boat, used to row among the islands when he visited the schools, is in the exhibition.

*Lunch:* **Rose's Bakery Cafe,** Eastsound Square, Eastsound. (206) 376–4220. Sandwiches, salads, quiche, herbal teas.

## Afternoon

Browse through Eastsound's numerous shops. The most interesting is **Darvill's,** a combination bookstore–rare print shop. It's the oldest art gallery in the San Juan Islands and has an extensive collection of antique and contemporary prints.

Rent a bicycle from **Wildlife Cycles** (phone 206–376–4708), and ride the backroads or the mountain-bike paths that have recently been constructed in Moran State Park. Here's one scenic, two-hour cycling route: Take Horseshoe Highway west toward the ferry terminal, and turn left on Dolphin Bay Road, about 2½ miles from Eastsound. The gravel road winds to the sound, then turns inland to meet White Beach Road. Take this road to Horseshoe Highway, at the ferry terminal. Head back toward Eastsound via Horseshoe Highway and Crow Valley Road.

On Crow Valley Road you'll see signs to **The Right Place Pottery Shop** and **The Naked Lamb Wool Shop.** Detour to visit these out-of-the-way studios on West Beach; each offers unusual, finely made crafts. Nearby is **Orcas Island Pottery,** a chinked log home that is the island's original pottery studio.

After dropping off your bicycle, return to Crow Valley Road, stopping at **Turtleback Farm Inn.** Check in, relax over tea or a glass of complimentary sherry, and take time to get acquainted with this peaceful country enclave.

*Dinner:* **Bilbo's,** on A Street, Eastsound. (206) 376–4728. Southwestern setting with arching windows and a flower-filled courtyard. Known for its excellent, brightly spiced Mexican fare.

*Lodging:* Turtleback Farm Inn, Route 1, Box 650, Eastsound, WA 98245. (206) 376–4914. A classic farmhouse-turned-country-inn. Seven comfortable rooms with private baths, common room with fireplace, expansive deck overlooking eighty acres of pasture and woodland. Susan and Bill Fletcher operate the best bed-and-breakfast on the island; book a room early.

# Day 2

## Morning

*Breakfast:* A full and fortifying breakfast at Turtleback Farm Inn: fruit juice, homemade granola, plus waffles and bacon or other main dish.

Take an after-breakfast stroll to the pond at the foot of the pasture, keeping an eye out for Oscar, the rambunctious brown ram, and the resident blue herons.

Drive Horseshoe Highway to **Moran State Park** and **Cascade Lake.** The biggest lake on the island has three campgrounds, a playground, picnic tables, rest rooms, and rental boats. Swimming is good, but it's crowded in summer.

Rent a rowboat, and fish for trout in the stocked lake. Or hike the 2½-mile loop trail that starts west of the picnic area. It winds along a bluff above the lake, crosses a log bridge, and curves through forests of Douglas fir before circling back to the starting place. You may spy ducks, muskrat, otter, and great blue herons.

Continue down Horseshoe Highway east 2 miles beyond the state park to **Olga.** The tiny community is centered by a post office and a combined art gallery and cafe.

*Lunch:* **Cafe Olga,** Olga Junction. (206) 376–4408. Cozy, mellow surroundings, adjoining gallery. Good soups and nice sandwich combinations (such as roasted cashew and chicken). The blackberry pie is remarkable.

## Afternoon

**The Orcas Island Artworks,** in the same building as the cafe, is housed in a former strawberry-packing plant. More than fifty island artists display their wares: hand-spun yarns, baskets, decorative tiles, pottery, jewelry, meticulously carved woods, stained glass, wearable art, and more. Choosing which to purchase is pleasant postlunch recreation.

From Olga, turn back to Moran State Park and up **Mount Constitution Road.** The narrow, steep road leads to the highest point in the San Juans, 2,407 feet. A 50-foot **stone lookout tower,** built in 1936 by the Civilian Conservation Corps, stands at the summit. From here there's a see-forever view. At your feet the forested mountain, lakes sparkling on its slopes, drops to a blue ocean and an archipelago of green islands that stretch to the horizon. To the east, on the mainland, you can see the white peaks of **Mount Baker** and **Mount Rainier.**

After drinking in the beauty of this panoramic seascape, drive back to Horseshoe Highway and again turn south, this time passing the Olga turnoff and heading out Doe Bay Road. At **Doe Bay Village Resort,** begin your kayaking adventure.

**Island Kayak Guides** (206–376–2291 or 376–4755) offers several kayak trips, encompassing all skill levels. No experience is necessary. On one ride that's suitable for all ages, you'll paddle to **Doe Island Marine Park** and **Gorilla Rock,** returning via **Rosario Strait.** You're likely to spot dolphins, whales, and bald and golden eagles.

Back in Doe Bay Resort, step into a relaxing outdoor mineral bath (suits optional). The hot sulphur-water baths are tucked against a wooded hillside and overlook a rushing creek and inlet. There's also a three-tiered cedar sauna that holds twenty people.

Drive to Horseshoe Highway, and head north, following the signs to **Rosario Resort,** which faces **Cascade Bay** on the edge of the sound. The centerpiece of the resort is the mansion built by Robert Moran, a shipbuilder and one-time mayor of Seattle. Moran came here in 1905 thinking he had only a short time to live. In his fifty-four-room home he installed a swimming pool, a bowling alley, and a music room containing an enormous pipe organ. Moran then lived on to a ripe old age. In 1920 he donated much of what is now Moran State

Park to the state of Washington. If you arrive at Rosario by 5:00 P.M. on a weekend, you'll be in time for the organ concert and a lively talk on the history of the estate.

*Dinner:* Rosario Resort, Eastsound. (206) 376–2222. Multilevel restaurant overlooking the sheltered waters of Cascade Bay. Serves a variety of American and Continental dishes.

*Lodging:* Turtleback Farm Inn.

# Day 3

## Morning

*Breakfast:* Another generous breakfast at Turtleback Farm Inn.

Take Crow Valley Road south to **Deer Harbor West,** which curves around West Sound to Deer Harbor.

Tom Averna, at **Deer Harbor Charters,** offers numerous sailing options: You can sail bareboat or with a skipper, rent a small boat by the hour or day, take a water taxi to any island destination, go whale watching, charter a guided fishing trip, or take a sunset cruise. Phone (206) 376–5989 or (800) 544–5758.

*Lunch:* **Deer Harbor Lodge** (206–376–4110). This casual restaurant, set in an old apple orchard on grassy slopes above the sea, serves fine seafood.

## Afternoon

Drive Deer Harbor Road to Horseshoe Highway and the ferry landing. You may have time for a cup of coffee in the lounge of the historic **Orcas Hotel,** across the road from the landing, before your ferry ride back to Anacortes.

# There's More

**Sailing.** Miles McCoy, Box 10, Orcas, WA 98280. (206) 376–4305. Picnic and three-hour sunset/moonlight sail in classic wooden boat, the *Sharon L.* Skipper with forty years' experience.

**Fishing.** Moby Max Charters, Inc., Route 1, Box 1065, Eastsound, WA 98245. (206) 376–2970. Twenty-two-foot Seasport, moored at Westsound Marina. Year-round salmon fishing; gear and bait supplied.

Pete Nelsen, King Salmon Charters, P.O. Box 394, Shaw Island, WA 98286. (206) 468–2314. Will pick you up at the ferry landing.

**Hiking, beach walking.** There are 23 miles of trails in Moran State Park; you'll find maps at the park entrance kiosk. Two good public beaches are Madrona Point and Obstruction Pass Park.

**Orcas Aerodrome**. (206) 376–2733. Scenic flights in a vintage red biplane. Leather helmet, goggles, and white scarf provided.

**Orcas Community Center.** Dramatic and musical performances presented regularly in summer (206–376–ACT 1).

## Special Events

**Memorial Day weekend.** "A" Street Festival, Eastsound. Crafts shows, dance and music performances for Waldorf Dolphin Bay School, an alternative school.

**Saturday after the Fourth of July.** Historical Day, Eastsound. Parade, pie-eating contest, games, music, fireworks.

**August.** Orcas Island Library Fair, Eastsound. Book sales and celebrations.

# Other Recommended Restaurants and Lodgings

### Lopez Island

Inn at Swift's Bay, Route 2, Box 3402, Port Stanley Road. (206) 468–3636. Remodeled Tudor home with five handsomely furnished rooms. Luxury, privacy, numerous amenities, excellent breakfast.

### Eastsound

Christina's, North Beach Road and Horseshoe Highway. (206) 376–4904. Famous (and expensive) restaurant serving imaginative, well-prepared Northwest cuisine. Ask for a table on the porch for the best views of East Sound.

Rosario Resort, One Rosario Way. (206) 376–2222; within Washington, (800) 562–8820. Former private estate on gorgeous Cascade Bay. Rooms in outlying buildings have basic motel amenities; the mansion has a restaurant and lounge, indoor and outdoor pools, and spa facilities.

### Orcas

Orcas Hotel, P.O. Box 155. (206) 376–4300. Remodeled historic hotel with Victorian flavor. Overlooks ferry landing.

# For More Information

San Juan Visitors' Information Service, P.O. Box 65, Lopez Island, WA 98261. (206) 468–3663.

Orcas Island Chamber of Commerce, P.O. Box 252, Eastsound, WA 98245. (206) 376–2273.

Washington State Ferries, 801 Alaskan Way, Pier 52 Colman Dock, Seattle, WA 98104. (206) 464–6400; within Washington, (800) 84–FERRY.

# San Juan Island

The ferry landing at Friday Harbor is busy year-round.

## Exploring Sea and Shore

_____ 2 NIGHTS _____

Ferry rides · Scenic water · Island views · Seaside resort
Whale watching · Boating · Rural countryside · Historic sites

The most populated of the 172 islands in the archipelago off Washington's northwestern corner, San Juan Island buzzes with activity in summer. Visitors throng from the ferries to fish, go whale watching, shop, sail, and, mostly, relax in this sunny haven east of Vancouver Island and 60 miles northwest of Seattle.

Some lodgings are booked a year in advance for summer stays. Other seasons are slower paced on the island, and ferries are far less crowded. If you choose to come on foot or bicycle, you'll find that most amenities are within walking distance or available by public transportation from the ferry landing.

This itinerary is designed as an auto tour, but it can easily be adjusted to other transportation.

Friday Harbor is the largest town in the islands and has an ample supply of tourist facilities. The rest of San Juan is open fields and forestland, with several parks and lakes.

# Day 1

## Morning

Drive northwest from Seattle 80 miles to Anacortes, and board the ferry headed toward the San Juans. It will stop at Lopez and Orcas islands before landing at **Friday Harbor,** giving you a pleasant 1½-hour ride. The ferry, which carries some 2,000 passengers, is a part of the Washington State Ferry system, largest in the world.

From the decks of the ferry, you'll watch the blue waters slide away as you pass island after island, the green and rocky remnants of a mountain range that stood here a hundred million years ago.

When you disembark at Friday Harbor, a bustling, wharfside village, you'll be driving up Spring Street. Stop at the visitors' information center at 125 Spring Street (open daily in summer) for maps and brochures. Then continue to First Street, and turn right. On the corner of First and Court is the **Whale Museum,** one of the great attractions on the island. Stop here for a tour; it's open every day.

This is the place to learn about and marvel over the biggest mammals on the planet. Life-size models of orca whales and numerous exhibits provide a quick education on whale life and habits. One room is devoted to children's activities, including drawing materials and puzzles. Marine-related items and T-shirts are sold in the gift shop.

*Lunch:* **Springtree Eating Establishment and Farm,** Spring Street, Friday Harbor. (206) 378–4848. Cheery, light-filled restaurant that claims to serve "Northwest cuisine with an island accent." Organically grown produce, imaginative salads, good desserts. Eat on the terrace if you prefer.

## Afternoon

Start with a tour of the **San Juan Island Historical Museum** on Price Street (open in summer on Wednesday and Saturday, 2:00 to 4:00 P.M., or by appointment). Once a farmhouse, the museum is furnished in turn-of-the-century style and has historical exhibits that explain the island's contentious past.

During the mid-1800s Britain and the United States shared the island in an uneasy truce. When an American farmer shot a British pig that was disturbing his potato patch, the British authorities threatened to arrest him. The farmer appealed for help, and soon both sides were lined up for war (not solely because of the pig; San Juan Island has a most strategic location). The dispute was settled peaceably, however, with the two camps establishing headquarters at opposite ends of the island. Arbitration finally agreed in favor of American rule. Now the incident is remembered as the "Pig War."

After this historical overview, climb aboard a **double-decker bus** at The Inn at Friday Harbor, 410 Spring Street (206–378–4351). The bus, a 1954 model from England, will take you for a two-hour ride around the island, through the town and rolling hills to the surf-splashed shore.

Back in Friday Harbor, spend the rest of the day wandering through the **art galleries and gift shops.** In Churchill Square's Atelier Gallerie, monoprints and finely detailed scrimshaw work are displayed. Calohan Studio exhibits marine art and sculpture. Waterworks Gallery has changing shows, usually themed (flowers, landscapes, and mythology are examples), with works by regional artists.

*Dinner:* **Cafe Bissett,** 170 West Street, Friday Harbor. (206) 378–3109. Considered the best restaurant on the island. Nouvelle cuisine in an intimate setting.

*Lodging:* **Hillside House,** 365 Carter Avenue, Friday Harbor, WA 98250. (206) 378–4730 or (800) 232–4730. Bed-and-breakfast in contemporary home on acre of woodland ½ mile from downtown district. Seven rooms, some with water views.

# Day 2

## Morning

*Breakfast:* Enjoy a full country breakfast with fresh eggs from the henhouse at Hillside House.

Buy the makings for a picnic at a local market and head northwest for 10 miles on Roche Harbor Road to British Camp, at Garrison Bay. This portion of **San Juan Island National Historical Park** is where British troops were stationed during the infamous Pig War. Four restored buildings house interpretive exhibits. From the small, formal garden, a trail rises to an overlook where officers were quartered.

Walk the **Bell Point Trail,** a level, 1-mile hike above Garrison Bay, to reach a beach and a view of neighboring Westcott Bay. Another trail that begins at the barracks exhibit leads to a cemetery where servicemen who died during the British occupation are buried. Climb another ½-mile up 650-foot **Mount Young** for a far-reaching view of the sea, scattered islands, and the Olympic and Cascade mountains.

From British Camp, drive south on West Valley Road to Bay Road, and turn toward the shore. Continue south on Westside Road toward **Lime Kiln Point State Park.** There's a trail here to **Lime Kiln Lighthouse,** a picturesque structure built in 1919 and now on the National Register of Historic Places.

A short distance south on Westside Road is a small parking area and a path, sheltered by tall madrona trees, that leads to a grassy, rocky bluff. This is **Whalewatch Park,** the best location on the island for observing whales. Signs and pictures tell you how to identify porpoises and orca and minke whales. While you wait and watch, binoculars at the ready, spread your lunch on a picnic table. You'll never find a more scenic spot for a picnic than this surf-sprayed cliff, with the blue waters of Haro Strait dancing at its base.

*Lunch:* Picnic at Whalewatch Park.

## Afternoon

Three pods of black and white orcas, about one hundred individual whales, live in the waters around the San Juans. They can be seen any time of year, with a little patience, but most often in summer. To watch these sleek, splendid creatures spout and blow and breach is a memorable experience.

If you sight whales, call the toll-free **Whale Hotline:** (800) 562–8832 in Washington and (800) 334–8832 in British Columbia. Reports of sightings help the Moclips Cetological Society to further its research.

Continue south on the shore-hugging road to Bailer Hill Road, which will take you to Cattle Point Road and, at the southern tip of the island, **American Camp.** This section of the National Historical Park may seem bleak, with its windswept shores and open fields, but it, too, played an important part in island history.

From the **Exhibit Center** an interpretive loop trail leads to the Officers' Quarters and Hudson's Bay Company farm site. Farther down the road you'll find a parking area for several more walking paths.

The hike to Jakle's Lagoon, along the old roadbed, passes through a grove of Douglas firs, while a walk up Mount Finlayson (290 feet high) presents another broad seascape and mountain vista.

On South Beach, the longest public beach on San Juan Island, birdwatchers will spot terns, plovers, greater and lesser yellowlegs, and bald eagles. Tide pools hold an abundance of marine life.

*Dinner:* **Duck Soup Inn,** 3090 Roche Harbor Road, Friday Harbor. (206) 378–4878. Fresh seafood and a varied wine list. Entree choices change regularly. Located north of town, closed in winter.

*Lodging:* Hillside House.

# Day 3

## Morning

*Breakfast:* A full Hillside House breakfast.

Aboard the *Way to Go,* a 30-foot hydrofoil, you'll take off across the water for an exciting whale-watching and bird-watching cruise. Lisa Lamb, the licensed skipper, knows the island waters and wildlife well and designs trips to suit her passengers. You may see orca and minke whales, Dall's porpoises, seals, and other marine life. For reservations, call Fair Weather Water Taxi Tours at (206) 378–2826.

*Lunch:* **Front Street Cafe,** 7 Spring Street West, Friday Harbor. (206) 378–2245. Simple, cafeteria-style eatery serving sandwiches, chili, soups, and ice cream.

## Afternoon

Watch for your ferry while you have lunch. When it arrives, board for the ride back to Anacortes. Expect to pass through U.S. Customs when you disembark; since you haven't been across the border into Canada, it's a momentary procedure.

From Anacortes, return to Seattle via Whidbey Island or east to I–5.

# There's More

**Charter cruises.** Captain Clyde's Charters, P.O. Box 1212, Friday Harbor, WA 98250. (206) 378–5661. Experienced skipper Clyde Rice offers sportfishing charters on *Silver Girl,* a 27-foot Tolley Express cruiser.

Western Prince Cruises, P.O. Box 418, Friday Harbor, WA 98250. (206) 378–5315. Summertime, four-hour wildlife cruises, daily except Tuesday. Narrated by Whale Museum naturalist.

**Biking.** Island Bicycles, 180 West Street, Friday Harbor. (206) 378–4941. Bike rentals, sales, repairs.

Susie's Moped, 2 Spring Street, Friday Harbor. (206) 378–5244 or 378–5074. Moped rentals by the hour or day. Free gas; maps provided.

**Park programs.** See history come to life at British Camp, when rangers and volunteers dress in period costumes and explain events of the past.

**San Juan Kayak Expeditions,** 3090B Roche Harbor Road, Friday Harbor, WA 98250. (206) 378–4436. Two- to five-day sea-kayak expeditions around the San Juans and Canadian Gulf Islands.

**San Juan Boat Rentals,** Box 2281, Friday Harbor, WA 98250. (206) 378–3499. C-Dory 16-foot sportboats, skippered or drive-your-own, available for diving, fishing, and sight-seeing.

# Special Events

**Late July.** San Juan Goodtime Jazz Festival, fairgrounds outside Friday Harbor. Top jazz bands perform all weekend. Free bus service between downtown Friday Harbor and fairgrounds.

# Other Recommended Restaurants and Lodgings

### Friday Harbor

Lonesome Cove, 5810A Lonesome Cove Road. (206) 378–4477. Secluded retreat on Speiden Channel. Six log cabins, all with kitchens and fireplaces.

Olympic Lights, 4531A Cattle Point Road. (206) 378–3186. Bed-and-breakfast in 1895 farmhouse on five acres at south end of island. Five rooms with contemporary furnishings, white carpets. Full breakfast included.

San Juan Chocolate Company, Cannery Landing. (206) 378–4443. Small cafe conveniently located next to ferry landing. Snacks, sandwiches, desserts.

San Juan Inn, 50 Spring Street. (206) 378–2070. Victorian inn ½ block from the ferry landing. View of the harbor. Continental breakfast.

Trumpeter Inn B&B, 420 Trumpeter Way. (206) 378–3884. Quiet country inn of charm and grace.

Wharfside B&B, P.O. Box 1212. (206) 378–5661. Two cozy rooms aboard the *Jacquelyn*, a sloop docked in the harbor. Bountiful breakfast included.

# For More Information

San Juan Island Chamber of Commerce, P.O. Box 98, Friday Harbor, WA 98250. (206) 378–5240.

San Juan Visitors' Information Service, P.O. Box 65, Lopez Island, WA 98261. (206) 468–3663.

Washington State Ferries, 801 Alaskan Way, Pier 52 Colman Dock, Seattle, WA 98104. (206) 464–6400; within Washington, (800) 84–FERRY.

# Vancouver Escapes

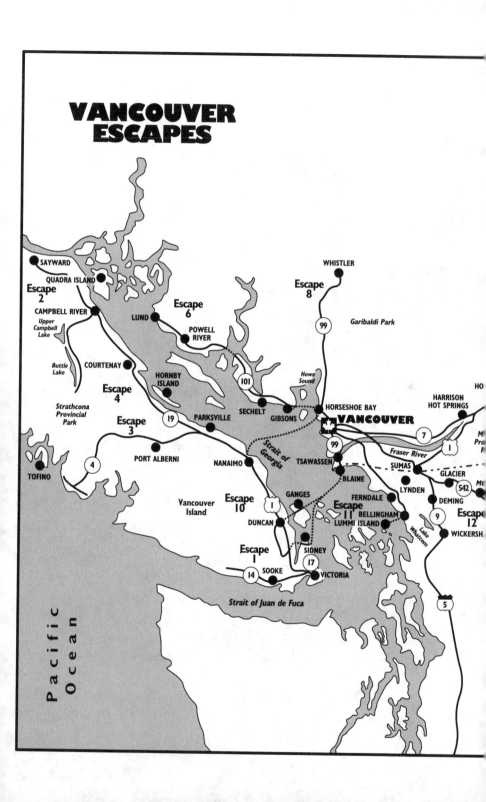

# VANCOUVER ESCAPES

# South Vancouver Island

A totem pole and the Parliament buildings represent Victoria's unique blend of cultures.

## High Tea and High Seas

_____ 1 OR 2 NIGHTS _____

Ferry rides · Scenic water views · World-renowned museums
Provincial capital · Antiques shopping · Indian crafts
Heritage sites · Beaches · Fine cuisine

The southern end of Vancouver Island is rich with contrast and beauty. It has pastoral farmlands and rugged wilderness, clear streams and ocean whitecaps, quiet villages and a city known for its shopping and dining. This itinerary will give you a taste of them all, as you curve from east to west, sampling some of the best a lovely land has to offer.

## Day 1

### Morning

Board the ferry at Tsawassen, crossing the **Strait of Georgia** to

**Swartz Bay,** on Vancouver Island. The scenic ride across the strait's blue waters takes about ninety minutes.

From here it's 13 miles (21 km) south to **Victoria,** the province's capital city, where British traditions and Canadian breeziness meet on the Pacific shore.

If you've never visited Victoria, start with a stroll around the lively **Inner Harbour** to soak in the atmosphere. Sailboats bob on the water, and ferries nose against the wharves; bagpipers play on the corners under hanging baskets of flowers, while tourists climb into double-decker buses. The venerable **Empress Hotel,** the **Parliament Buildings,** the wax museum, the undersea garden, and the **Royal British Columbia Museum** cluster around these harbor streets. The atmosphere is festive.

*Lunch:* Early tea (12:30) at the Empress Hotel, 721 Government Street. (604) 384–8111; reservations recommended. Sandwiches, tea, and scones in a historic landmark. The grand old ivy-covered hotel, facing the harbor, has been renovated with style. If you want a heartier lunch in the Victorian mode, try the curry special in the Empress Bengal Lounge.

### Afternoon

Cross the street to one of the world's great museums, the Royal British Columbia Museum. It traces Vancouver Island's story from the Ice Age to the present day. Indian totems and masks, the lives of early trappers and settlers, explorers' ships, homes of the early twentieth century—all these and more are brilliantly presented to allow visitors a sense of participation.

Outside, totem poles are grouped in **Thunderbird Park,** eloquent reminders of a rich past and a living form of expression.

Poking about in the intriguing shops is a must for visitors to downtown Victoria. You'll find dozens of antiques shops and specialty stores selling woolens, tweeds, china, and chocolates. In **Bastion Square** you'll see how the city began. James Douglas, a British explorer, established a Hudson Bay Company fort on this site in 1843. The complex of nineteenth-century buildings now houses restaurants, shops, art galleries, and the **Maritime Museum,** which has an outstanding collection of marine artifacts.

Check **Eaton's Department Store** for the best finds in inexpensive souvenirs of good quality.

When it's time for tea, head for the mezzanine of the **Bedford Hotel,** 1140 Government Street (604–384–6835) to feast on finger sandwiches, fruits, cakes, and crumpets with marmalade and Devonshire cream.

Drive about ½ mile from downtown to **Craigdorrach Castle** on

Joan Crescent off Fort Street. The baronial stone manor, built by a coal magnate in 1887, is open for tours. Lavishly furnished, the thirty-nine-room home exemplifies Victorian opulence.

Travel east to **Oak Bay,** a bayside district of gracious homes and well-kept gardens, and check in at your hotel.

**Sealand of the Pacific** is nearby, on Marine Drive (604–598–3373). Canada's largest oceanarium, Sealand offers a close look at Pacific Northwest marine life. Watch killer (orca) whales and sea lions perform, and see octopus grottoes and wolf-eel dens in underwater galleries. (Open daily.)

Back at the **Oak Bay Beach Hotel,** enjoy a pint of ale in the Snug. Weather permitting, take a table on the terrace and enjoy the view.

*Dinner:* **The Tudor Room,** Oak Bay Beach Hotel, Victoria. Roast beef and Yorkshire pudding, with a view of the bay.

*Lodging:* Oak Bay Beach Hotel, 1175 Beach Drive, Victoria, B.C. V8S 2N2. (604) 598–4556. Tudor-style, very British in tone, overlooking Oak Bay. Colorful gardens slope to the sea.

# Day 2

## Morning

*Breakfast:* **The Demitasse,** 1320 Blanshard Street, Victoria. (604) 386–4442. This tiny cafe serves commendable croissants and coffee.

Cross the **Johnson Street Bridge** to **Esquimault.** On Lampson Street you'll find a bit of England that predates the Victorian era by 400 years. Sam and Rosina Lane, owners of the **Olde England Inn,** have painstakingly built **Anne Hathaway's Cottage,** a reproduction of William Shakespeare's wife's home and an authentic example of a sixteenth-century residence. The guided tours are well informed and interesting.

From here, join Route 1A (Island Highway) traveling west to Ocean Boulevard. Follow the signs to **Fort Rodd Hill National Historic Park.** On its peaceful, grassy grounds are bunkers and gun batteries erected between 1878 and 1956.

Cross the Causeway to tour **Fisgard Lighthouse,** the first lighthouse on Canada's west coast. It has been restored to its 1859 condition. Looking east from the lighthouse, your view is of the Victoria skyline across Esquimault Harbour.

Continue on Route 1A to **Mill Hill Park** in Langford for a short walk to the summit observation point or a hike in **Galloping Goose Regional Park.** The park, opened in 1988, follows an old railbed for 26 miles (42 km).

Take Route 14 west, and when you reach **Sooke** (46 miles, or 60 km, from Victoria), stop at the historical museum. It's a treasure of a find, with handsome displays of pioneer and Indian artifacts. On the property is a pioneer homestead that shows how life was lived here a century ago.

Sooke, the home of Salish Indians for centuries, has a comparatively mild climate and bountiful supplies of fish, fowl, berries, and produce.

*Lunch:* **Margison House**, 6605 Sooke Road, Sooke. (604) 642–3620. Lunch and tea served in the parlors of a charming home with a sea and garden view. Open May to October.

Browse through Margison House's gift shop and Country Crafters, a working arts-and-crafts shop.

If this is a one-night trip, turn back on Route 14 toward Victoria. Join Route 17 for the drive north to Swarz Bay; from there a ferry will take you back to the Tsawassen terminal near Vancouver.

If you are continuing your travels, drive from Margison House to **Sooke Harbour.** Board a charter boat that will take you out to sea for some of the best salmon fishing on the coast. (Whale-watching cruises are available, too, March through October.) As you sail past the rugged cliffs and green forests of the island and head for deeper waters, you may see bald eagles, whales, and sea lions.

For a fishing cruise, contact **Sooke Charter Boat Association,** 8760 West Coast Road, Sooke, B.C. V0S 1N0. (604) 642–7783. Tackle and bait are supplied. Boats are 17 to 30 feet long.

*Dinner:* **Sooke Harbour House.** One of the finest restaurants in British Columbia, with innovative cuisine featuring local fresh seafood (probably caught that morning by the owner). Herbs, vegetables, and edible flowers are grown in gardens on the premises. Incomparable setting and atmosphere.

*Lodging:* Sooke Harbour House, 1528 Whiffen Spit Road, Sooke, B.C. V0S 1N0. (604) 642–3421. Exquisite inn on two waterfront acres. Beautifully furnished rooms with views of well-tended gardens and the sea.

# Day 3

## Morning

*Breakfast:* Sooke Harbour House. Breakfast included in room rate.

From the inn, drive northwest on Route 14 to surf-washed shores. Waves toss high, and spindrift streams in the wind on blustery days. The coast has seen storms so wild, and has had so many shipwrecks, that sailors call it the graveyard of the Pacific. On mild days, however, the coast is benign, and you may see divers and surfers catching the waves.

A majestic rain forest grows in green splendor on the east. In this forest stand the largest Douglas fir tree, 41 feet (13 m) around, and the tallest Sitka spruce, 310 feet (95 m), in Canada. Environmental controversy rages around the spruce and its tall companions.

Stop at **French Beach Provincial Park** to watch for birds and orca and gray whales.

Ten miles (16 km) past **Point No Point,** a fifteen-minute walk through the forest will lead you to **China Beach,** a lovely, protected cove of white sand. You might see black bears in this park.

Another pretty spot on the coast is **Sandcut Beach.** A short trail provides access to the beach, which has small waterfalls and sandstone formations.

Revel in the expansive ocean views; then head back toward Sooke.

*Lunch:* Included in your room rate at Sooke Harbour House.

## Afternoon

Stroll through the inn's gardens, with their forty varieties of geraniums and 300 types of herbs; then hike out **Whiffen Spit** for a last view of the far southwest corner of Canada and the Strait of Juan de Fuca.

Take Route 14 to Victoria and Route 17 north to Swartz Bay and the Tsawassen ferry.

# There's More

**Afternoon tea.** You'll find Victoria's best afternoon teas at the Empress Hotel, the Bedford Hotel, Blethering Place, Oak Bay Beach Hotel, and the Tudor Rose. Outside Victoria, go to enchanting Fernie Farm, 4987 William Head Road, Metchosin (no reservations taken). (604) 478–1682. It's open Wednesday through Sunday and closed in September.

**Golf.** The Greater Victoria area has numerous 18-hole golf courses, most of them open all year. A sampling:

Cedar Hill Municipal Golf Course, 1400 Derby Road (604) 595–2823.

Victoria Golf Club, 1110 Beach Drive. (604) 598–4321.

Uplands Golf Course, 3300 Cadboro Bay Road. (604) 592–7313.

**Hatley Castle.** The majestic stone mansion, built in 1908, is now a military academy. Its gardens and grounds are open to the public daily. On Route 14 near Colwood, west of Victoria.

**Sooke Potholes Provincial Park,** Sooke. Off Sooke River Road, a forested park with waterfalls, hiking trails, swimming in river.

**West Coast Trail.** This rugged wilderness path, originally constructed to assist shipwrecked sailors, begins at Port Renfrew, 50 miles (80 km) west of Sooke. Hikers take a water taxi across the inlet to the southern end of the trail, which extends 48 miles (78 km) north. It's part of Pacific Rim National Park.

## Special Events

**May.** Swiftsure Yacht Race, Victoria. World-class regatta.
**June.** Oak Bay Tea Party, Victoria.
**Third Saturday of July.** All Sooke Day, Sooke. Indian-style grilled salmon, barbecued beef feast, loggers' sports.

## Other Recommended Restaurants and Lodgings

### Sooke

Malahat Farm, RR 2, Anderson Road. (604) 642–6868. Farmhouse and cottage on forty-five acres. Peaceful and idyllic, charming accommodations, ample breakfast.

Point-No-Point Resort, RR 2, West Coast Road. (604) 646–2020. Cottages in a spectacular cliff-top setting in the woods, above the island's western shore.

### Victoria

Chez Daniel, 2522 Estevan Avenue. (604) 592–7424. Small, expensive French restaurant serving perfectly prepared classic dishes with a few innovations.

Dashwood Manor, 1 Cook Street. (604) 385–5517. Bed-and-breakfast mansion near Beacon Hill Park, overlooking the water. Suites have fireplaces and kitchens.

The Empress Hotel, 721 Government Street. (604) 384–8111. Grand old ivy-covered hotel, renovated, with stylish and comfortable rooms. A major tourist attraction, facing Inner Harbour.

Hotel Grand Pacific, 450 Quebec Street. (604) 586–0450 or (800) 663–7550. Luxury hotel in the center of Victoria. Swimming pool, athletic club, attractive restaurant, 149 rooms and suites.

Metropolitan Diner, 1715 Government Street. (604) 381–1512. Offbeat little restaurant serving foods for the adventurous, prepared with a sure touch.

Olde England Inn, 429 Lampson Street. (604) 388–4353. Antiques-furnished rooms and restaurant in British manor house and village. Colorful gardens.

Swans, 506 Pandora Avenue. (604) 361–3310. Charming hotel and pub in one of Victoria's oldest buildings, beautifully restored.

Prima's on Wharf, 218 Wharf Street. (604) 381–2112. Italian menu, pleasant atmosphere.

The Victoria Regent Hotel, 1234 Wharf Street. (604) 386–2211 or (800) 663–7472. Downtown waterfront hotel with suites, kitchens, fireplaces, balconies.

## For More Information

Tourism Association of Vancouver Island, Suite 302, 45 Bastion Square, Victoria, B.C. V8W 1J1. (604) 382–3551.

Sooke–Jordan River Chamber of Commerce, Box 18, Sooke, B.C. V0S 1N0. (604) 642–6112.

BC Ferries, 1112 Fort Street, Victoria, B.C. V8V 4V2. Vancouver (604) 669–1211, Victoria (604) 386–3431.

# Vancouver Island: Northeast Coast

Quadra Island, in the Strait of Georgia, is a short ferry ride from Campbell River.

## Tracking Sea Life

### 2 NIGHTS

Sandy beaches · Tidal pools · Marine life · Native art · Secluded island
Luxury lodge · Salmon fishing · Whale watching · Fine dining

In the protected waters of Johnstone Strait, between the British Columbia mainland and the northeast coast of Vancouver Island, life is abundant. Bald eagles, seabirds, fish, and seals are commonly seen. But the animal that most fascinates visitors is the orca, or killer whale. This three-day itinerary, best taken from May through October, includes a whale-watching excursion that will take you close to the resident whale population in the strait.

The trip offers a mixture of civilized and rustic pleasures designed to refresh the senses.

# Day 1

## Morning

Take the ferry from Horseshoe Bay to Nanaimo, on Vancouver Island. Drive north on Route 19 to **Parksville.**

Stop at **Pipers Lagoon,** northeast of town, to watch the numerous birds circling and soaring above the cliffs that rise from the sandy spit.

Just south of Parksville you'll see the quaint old **Knox Heritage Church** in **Craig Heritage Park.** Weddings are often held here. Proceeds from the wedding fee go toward maintaining the historic park, which has pioneer buildings, the town's original fire hall, and a museum.

*Lunch:* **Herons,** Bayside Inn, 240 Dogwood Street, Parksville. (604) 248–8333. The outdoor terrace above the bay makes a fine setting for a lunch of fresh seafood, a thick sandwich, or a tangy salad.

## Afternoon

The Parksville/Qualicum area is known for its scenic hiking trails. Most famous is the path up **Mount Arrowsmith,** which stands 6,000 feet (1,830 m) against the eastern sky. Other wooded paths lead to **Little Qualicum Falls** and **Englishman River Falls** (see Vancouver Escape Three for descriptions).

From Parksville, drive north to **Qualicum Beach,** sometimes referred to as Carmel North for its plethora of artists and craftspeople. Painters, sculptors, weavers, and wood-carvers make their homes here and display their works.

In the **Old School House Gallery and Art Centre,** 122 Fern Road West, numerous artists offer classes and items for sale. **Heritage Pottery and Gallery** carries the creations of more than one hundred Vancouver Island artists. **The Handcrafter** is a cooperative craft shop selling cards, candles, pottery, jewelry, and paintings.

Pieces done by several island artisans are available in **The Workshop.** Most notable is the finely crafted jewelry of goldsmith John Rhys. At **Hy'emass House,** Indian-made arts and crafts include murals, button blankets, wood carvings, and prints.

**Larry Aguilar Pottery Studio** is situated in a lush garden at Good Earth Farm in Little Qualicum. It has a bonsai collection and the largest display of tuberous begonias on Vancouver Island, as well as porcelain, stoneware, and raku.

The **Comox Valley,** north of Qualicum, calls itself the Recreation Capital of Canada with good reason. Fishing, boating, golfing, hiking, surfing, diving, and cycling are a few of the sports easily available.

There are four towns in the little valley, centering on **Comox Harbour,** the terminal for the ferry from Powell River.

Drive up the highway, with the shore on your right and rolling rural countryside and high wooded ridges and mountains on your left, to arrive at the Visitors InfoCentre. Stop here for maps, brochures, and a close look at the Kwakiutl-carved **Talking Bear Totem** that graces the grounds.

Enter **Courtenay** (Island Highway skirts the downtown area on the east), and go to the **Native Sons Hall,** which houses **Courtenay and District Museum and Archives,** 360 Cliffe Avenue. The "largest log cabin in the world," it's open daily in summer and Tuesday through Saturday in winter. In 7,000 square feet of exhibit space, the general history museum shows the chronology of the Comox Valley. Permanent displays include native history, exportation, agriculture, logging, and pioneer life.

Alternatively, if you're an aviation buff, you might visit the **Comox Air Force Museum,** across the highway in Comox. The museum, open daily May through September and weekends October through April, focuses on flight in Canada, from the early Silver Dart to the jet age and space technology. Various aircraft are on outdoor display.

Near the Comox Air Force Base is **Kin Beach Provincial Park,** which has a good picnic site with cooking shelters, a playground, a tennis court, a small store, campsites, and beach access. A small breakwater creates a gentle tidal pool.

Don't miss **Comox Marina Park,** the little park with the big view. Tucked against the waterfront, it has a boat launch, picnic shelters, a bandstand, and a magnificent view of the ocean and mountains.

Stop in at **Leeward Pub and Brewery** on Anderton Road in Comox for a tour of the facility and a taste of the valley's only cottage beer.

Plan to arrive early at **The Old House Restaurant** so that you'll have time to browse through **Dower Cottage,** a fetching country gift shop on the restaurant's grounds.

*Dinner:* The Old House Restaurant, 1760 Riverside Lane, Courtenay. (604) 338–5406. Lovely old home transformed into a busy two-level restaurant by the river. Lawns, gardens, gazebo, river (and sawmill) view. Formal dining in an inviting lodge atmosphere upstairs, with classic French dishes; casual, less expensive fare on the main level—pastas, salads, sandwiches. Very special.

*Lodging:* **Greystone Manor,** 4014 Haas Road, Courtenay, B.C. V9N 8H9. (604) 338–1422. Gracious gray home on one and a half parklike acres above the sea. Four comfortable rooms share two baths. Antique furnishings, hospitable hosts.

# Day 2

## Morning

*Breakfast:* Full breakfast in Greystone Manor's dining room. French toast, egg dishes, wild blackberries, light scones studded with raisins, and homemade jams may be served.

Turn north on Route 19 to what's been called Vancouver Island's best-kept secret, **Miracle Beach Provincial Park.** The developed park has miles of sandy beach and warm, shallow water on a protected shore. It's a fine swimming spot on a warm day, and there's a large changing house.

The park's **Nature Centre** has saltwater aquariums, forest displays, and history exhibits. Nature programs are led by park interpreters in summer. Tide pools are full of sea urchins, sea stars, crabs, anemones, and other marine life. Nearly 200 campsites are scattered throughout the coastal forest.

*Lunch:* **Salmon Point Marine Pub and Restaurant,** Salmon Point. (604) 923–7272. Open, natural-wood restaurant with hanging greenery, Indian art, and water views. Delectable seafood chowder, good burgers, croissant sandwiches, salads.

## Afternoon

Continue north to **Campbell River.** Drive on the main road to **Tyee Plaza** and the Visitors InfoCentre, which has maps, brochures, and information. In the same building is the **Campbell River Museum.** Exhibits portray the traditional Kwakiutl, Nuu-Chah-Nulth, and Salish cultures; early coastal exploration; settlement of the area; and industrial development. It's worth a tour just to see the display of carved Indian ceremonial masks.

You can purchase Indian-made crafts at **Hill's Indian Crafts,** across from the information center on Shoppers Row. Preserving the West Coast heritage, the Hill's outlet sells Cowichan Indian sweaters, wood carvings, souvenirs, and artworks.

This is fishing country, "the salmon capital of the world." Here is your chance to catch the tyee salmon that give the town its claim to fame. Tyee are the big ones: salmon that weigh more than thirty pounds.

For a dollar a day (free if you're under sixteen or over sixty-five), you can fish from **Discovery Pier,** just south of downtown. Wheelchair accessible, the public pier has won several design awards.

To get out on the water and fish, rent a boat or charter a guide at **Sportfish Centre,** 975 Tyee Plaza (604–287–4911). The center has bait and tackle and boats ranging from 16-footers to 44 feet. Another boat operator is Campbell River Sportfishing Rentals (604–287–7279).

After (or instead of) your fishing trip, board the ferry to **Quadra Island.** It's a ten-minute ride across **Discovery Passage** to the forests of Quadra.

Drive ten minutes to **Quathiaski Cove** and **Cape Mudge,** on the southern tip of the island. The **Kwaguilth Museum and Cultural Centre** in the Indian village here is the heart of the native community, reflecting its revival of a traditional culture. The facility contains historical artifacts and a wealth of carved masks and regalia that were used in potlatches of old.

The potlatch, a ceremony of feasts and gift exchanges, was banned in the late 1800s and the items taken by the government; they were at last returned in the late 1970s and are now on proud display. The museum is open daily in July and August and Tuesday to Saturday afternoons in other months.

In the park across from the museum you can see petroglyphs, a collection of ancient stone carvings. Other petroglyphs are at their original sites along the high-tide line at Wa-Wa-Kie Beach and Francisco Point.

*Dinner:* **April Point Lodge,** Quadra Island. Water-facing restaurant serving perfectly prepared classic standards (prime rib, lamb) and salmon and Dungeness crab. Mrs. Peterson's freshly baked desserts are unbeatable.

*Lodging:* April Point Lodge, P.O. Box 1, Campbell River, B.C. V9W 4Z9. (604) 285-2222. Top-quality resort with lodge rooms and cottages, on 3 miles of waterfront. Some units with fireplaces and kitchens. Stunning views of Discovery Passage, bald eagles, orca whales. Boston whalers available for fishing trips.

# Day 3

## Morning

*Breakfast:* Complimentary coffee and muffins in April Point dining room, or order full breakfast from the menu.

Return to Campbell River on the morning ferry and drive 53 miles north on Route 19 to **Sayward.** Mile-high **Mount H'kusam,** capped with snow and often ringed with fog, guards the east side of the **Salmon River Valley,** where the logging town of Sayward nestles. The Indian name for the mountain was *Hiyatsee Saklekum,* meaning "where the breath of the sea lion gathers at the blowhole."

On the east is **Johnstone Strait,** where jagged islands are scattered like puzzle pieces over cold blue waters.

Stop along the way to buy a picnic lunch.

At the Sayward junction on Route 19, tour **Valley of a Thousand**

**Faces** (604–282–3303). Visitors are welcome in Hetty Fredrickson's parklike forest and indoor gallery. On the grounds are cedar slab paintings of historical figures, cartoon characters, birds, animals, and flowers. Open daily in summer, other times by appointment.

Drive on to the boat launch in **Kelsey Bay,** and join **Robson Bight Charters** for a whale-watching excursion (phone or fax 604–282–3833). You'll board a 56-foot motor yacht, *Le Caique,* for an unforgettable quest to locate and observe the sleek black-and-white orca whales. This is the wilderness habitat of bald eagles, porpoises, harbour seals, Steller sea lions, and other birds and mammals. Be sure to bring a warm jacket.

On an all-day trip, the boat goes to **Robson Bight Ecological Reserve,** a marine sanctuary where the orcas gather to rub against the barnacles on the beach. The resident population of 12 pods has about 135 whales.

*Lunch:* Picnic aboard the boat. Coffee, tea, juice, and a fruit basket are provided.

### Afternoon

You'll return to Sayward in the late afternoon. With the conclusion of your boat trip, head back to Route 19 and turn south to Parksville.

*Dinner:* **Kalzas Restaurant,** 180 North Moilliet, Parksville. (604) 248–6933. Continental cuisine, specializing in fresh seafood.

Drive 21 miles (35 km) south on Route 19 to Nanaimo and board the ferry at Departure Bay, headed for Horseshoe Bay and Vancouver.

# There's More

**Fishing.** Sea Spray Charters, P.O. Box 1632, Qualicum Beach, B.C. V0R 2T0. (604) 248–4280.

Blue Goose Fishing, 2608 Willeman Avenue, Courtenay, B.C. V9N 6L2. (604) 338–5485. Sport fishing, diving, sight-seeing cruises aboard the *M.V. Blue Goose,* a 37-foot yacht.

Campbell River District Fishing Guides Assocation, P.O. Box 66, Campbell River, B.C. V9W 4Z9. Organization of professional fishing guides, with boats from 15 to 28 feet. Will refer you to the charter that suits your needs.

**Flights.** Lake Union Air, Seattle. (800) 826–1890. Flies from Seattle to Campbell River.

Sound Flight, Renton. (206) 255–6500. Offers flights from Seattle to several B.C. destinations.

Vancouver Island Air, Ltd., Campbell River. (604) 287–2433. Daily and charter flights to Vancouver, April Point, Seattle.

**Golf.** Nanaimo Golf Club, Nanaimo. (604) 758–6332. Eighteen challenging holes; views of Georgia Strait.

Eaglecrest Golf Course, Qualicum Beach. (604) 752–6311. A 3,100-yard course, driving range, restaurant, lounge. Open daily.

Qualicum Beach Memorial Golf Club, Qualicum Beach. (604) 752–6312. Nine-hole, par 36.

Fairwinds Golf Course, Nanoose. (604) 468–7666. Eighteen-hole course; part of hotel and marina resort.

Longlands Par Three, Comox. (604) 339–6363. Manicured eighteen-hole course, easy for the novice but with some challenges.

Sunnydale Golf Course, Courtenay. (604) 334–3342. Eighteen holes, driving range, dining and lounge facilities, mountain view.

Storey Creek, Campbell River. (604) 923–3673. Championship eighteen-hole course carved from dense forest. Restaurant, driving range, pro shop.

Sequoia Springs, Campbell River. (604) 287–9414. Hillside course with harbor views, eighteen holes.

**Hiking Trails.** Mount Arrowsmith Trail. This well-marked trail is easy but long. Plan on a six- to nine-hour hike. It starts at Cameron Lake picnic site, 14½ miles (23 km) from Parksville.

Wesley Ridge Trail. Energetic hikers can walk this route in five hours. Starting in Little Qualicum Falls Park, west of Parksville, it leads to broad views of Mount Arrowsmith, the Strait of Georgia, and the coastal mountain range.

Hamilton Swamp. Take thirty minutes to walk around the swamp in a woodland sanctuary filled with waterfowl and flora. It's on Route 4A between Qualicum Beach and Whiskey Creek.

Rathtrevor Park. This park south of Parksville is famous for its long, sandy beach. There's great bird-watching here, with more than 150 species recorded. Nature trails are well marked.

Parksville Flats Wildlife Estuary. The 216-acre estuary lies on Englishman River tidal flats. It has hiking paths, birds, wildlife, and trees.

Forbidden Plateau. Several loop trails wind through forests of red cedar, Douglas fir, and western hemlock in this area, leading to lakes and panoramic views. Paradise Meadows is an easy 1½-mile (2.4 km) walk over carpets of wildflowers. Begin at Mount Washington Nordic ski lodge, 15 miles (24 km) west of Courtenay.

Seal Bay Regional Nature Park. A wooded, 342-acre park on Seal Bay is a fifteen-minute drive north of Courtenay and Comox. It has one-hour loop trail hikes, one adapted to wheelchair use. You'll see wildflowers, seabirds, and seals.

Dalrymple Creek Nature Trail. This self-guided, forest-interpretation trail is in Kelsey Bay Woodlands, 5 miles (8 km) south of the Sayward turnoff on Route 19, 42 miles (68 km) north of Campbell River.

Rebecca Spit Provincial Park, Quadra Island. The park is ideal for picnicking, beachcombing, and swimming.

Mitlenatch Island and Bird Sanctuary. This island has unique plant and marine life, history, and climate. There are beaches and picnic areas. Twelve miles (20 km) east of Campbell River, the sanctuary is accessible by plane or boat.

## Special Events

**Mid-July.** International Sandcastle Competition, Parksville Beach. Popular sand-sculpture contest draws thousands of visitors a year.

**July and early August.** Courtenay Youth Music Centre, Courtenay. Classes, concerts, musical theater productions by students from all over Canada.

**Early August.** Summer Festival, Campbell River. Parade, arts-and-crafts displays, fishing derby, fireworks, dancing, music, children's games, arm-wrestling contests.

**Early August.** Filberg Festival, Comox. Juried crafts show, entertainment, music, children's programs, food stands. On the grounds of Filberg Heritage Lodge and Park.

## Other Recommended Restaurants and Lodgings

### Campbell River

The Dolphins Resort, 4125 Discover Drive. (604) 287–3066. Shoreside cedar cabins and luxury bungalows with wood stoves and stone fireplaces, equipped kitchens. Fishing gear and guided charters supplied. Your catch frozen, canned, or smoked and shipped.

Painter's Lodge, 1625 MacDonald Road, Campbell River. (604) 286–1102. Modern fishing resort overlooking Discovery Passage. Restaurant, lounge, outdoor heated pool. Accommodation rates include eight hours of fishing.

### Courtenay

Homestead Restaurant, 932 Fitzgerald Avenue. (604) 338–6612. Bungalow converted to an intimate eatery, open for lunch, dinner. Fresh ingredients, lots of garlic. Closed Saturday and Sunday.

La Cremaillere Restaurant, 975 Comos Road. (604) 338–8131. Tudor-style dining house with river view. Outstanding French cuisine and wines.

## Parksville

Island Hall Beach Resort, Island Highway. (604) 248–3225. One-hundred-room beachside motel with restaurant, lounge, lawns, flowers. Lovely blue-tiled indoor pool and whirlpool/sauna.

Tigh-na-Mara Resort, RR 1. (604) 248–2072. Beachfront lodge and cabins, some with fireplaces and kitchens. Restaurant, pool, tennis courts.

## Qualicum Beach

Qualicum College Inn, Box 99. (604) 752–9262 or (800) 663–7306. Former boys' school, historic landmark overlooking Georgia Strait. Resort hotel with Old English atmosphere, indoor pool, restaurant.

## Quathiaski Cove

Tsa-Kwa-Luten Lodge, P.O. Box 460. (604) 285–2042 or (800) 665–7745. Resort on Quadra Island based on Pacific coast native traditions. Fir lodge with 33 rooms and restaurant.

# For More Information

Parksville Tourist Centre, 1275 East Island Highway, Parksville, B.C. V9P 2G3. (604) 248–3613.

Campbell River Tourism, P.O. Box 482, 1235 Island Highway, Campbell River, B.C. V9W 5C1. (604) 286–1616.

BC Ferries, 1112 Fort Street, Victoria, B.C. V8V 4V2. Vancouver (604) 669–1211, Victoria (604) 386–3431.

# Vancouver Island: West Shore

Long Beach, on Vancouver Island's west shore, is a part of Pacific Rim National Park.

## The Wild Pacific Coast

### 2 NIGHTS

Spectacular waterfalls · Pristine wilderness · Ancient forests · Native art
Whale watching · Beaches · Boat rides · Scenic hikes

The western coast of Vancouver Island holds some of the world's most dramatic wilderness scenery. In this temperate, wet climate, where rainfall is 160 inches a year, vegetation grows in lush profusion; dense jungles of ferns, mosses, and shrubbery grow under the tall evergreen trees. This is logging country, but some of the wilderness is almost untouched, allowing visitors to gain a sense of the primeval forests that once covered the entire island.

An abundance of water makes for lush, verdant growth, and Vancouver Island has plenty of both. The coast is fringed with fjordlike inlets, bays, and coves, while dozens of lakes and rivers are scattered throughout the inland regions. It's a recreational wonderland, waiting to be explored.

# Day 1

## Morning

Pack a picnic lunch and take the ferry from Horseshoe Bay west across the Georgia Strait to Nanaimo, on **Vancouver Island.** Drive north 21 miles (35 km) on Route 19 to Parksville.

When you reach the Route 4 junction, turn west and travel 3 miles (5 km) to Errington Road. Head south to **Errington,** a small farming community; you'll pass the general store, a log complex with a cafe, post office, laundromat, and video store. Across the street is the **Farmers' Market.** Stop here for fresh fruits and produce in season.

From the highway it's 5 miles (8 km) to **Englishman River Falls Provincial Park.** The road travels through rolling rural countryside dotted with horse ranches and enormous old barns before entering the cool, dense forest of the park.

Tall cedars, firs, and hemlocks form green canopies over fern-filled hollows and mossy boulders in this scenic retreat. Walk the easy trail to **Englishman Falls,** a roaring torrent of water that pours into a narrow chasm between two wide rock ledges. The park contains picnic tables, a shelter, fireplaces, firewood, drinking water, and campsites.

*Lunch:* Picnic at Englishman River Falls.

## Afternoon

Continue west to **MacMillan Provincial Park** and **Cathedral Grove.** In this awe-inspiring ancient forest, giant hemlock trees and Douglas firs stand in silent, shadowed splendor. Some of the oldest trees in British Columbia, they've been living for up to 800 years. Trails wind through the virgin grove, crossing weathered wooden bridges and logs with chinked steps. Interpretive signs explain the trees' long cycle of growth and decay.

Continue to **Port Alberni,** a logging community at the tip of a long fjord. The port is named after a Spanish explorer, Don Pedro Alberni, whose expedition came to the West Coast in 1791. The area's first sawmill was built here in 1860; now the MacMillan-Bloedel Company maintains a large complex that includes two sawmills and a pulp-and-paper mill.

Fishing is another significant industry, with 320 commercial vessels operating from Port Alberni's harbor. Recreational fishers are lured to the area during the peak salmon runs of August and September. The famous *M.V. Lady Rose,* a stout packet freighter and passenger ferry, leaves daily from the Harbour Quay, steaming down the scenic fjord to the **Broken Group Islands** and the coast, 30 miles (48 km) west. From Port Alberni, Highway 4 winds along the Taylor and Kennedy rivers, passing thickly forested ridges and logged-off slopes, on its way to the ocean shore. **Pacific Rim National Park,** established in 1970, borders this untamed coast, stretching along the shoreline from **Tofino** to Port Renfrew. The park has three divisions: the rugged **West Coast Trail** to the south; Broken Group Islands, one hundred picturesque islands dotting Barkley Sound; and **Long Beach,** a 7-mile (12-km) stretch of surf-washed sand and rocky headlands north of Ucluelet.

At Long Beach, 2 miles (3½ km) off Route 4, is **Wickaninnish Centre,** just above the beach. Tour the center to learn about marine life and wave action, enter a replica of the *Explorer 10* submersible, see a native whaling canoe, and watch a presentation on humpback whales. The inn that adjoins the interpretive center serves excellent food and has a panoramic view of the ocean and the long sweep of beach directly below. This is a good spot for a coffee break.

After a brisk walk in the briny air of Long Beach, return to the highway and drive on to the **Shorepine Bog Trail.** A boardwalk trail rests upon the surface of this fascinating, soggy forest of stunted trees and sphagnum moss. Pick up a pamphlet from the box at the trail entrance for an explanation of the delicate, colorful ecosystem.

Continue on Highway 4 to check in at **Pacific Sands Beach Resort.** Drive 4 miles (7 km) more to Tofino for a stroll around town before dinner. Surrounded on three sides by water, this quaint village at the end of the road has unparalleled views of **Clayoquot Sound,** the moody ocean, and the thick forests of fir, pine, cedar, and hemlock that rise from the shore.

Cafes, shops, and galleries line the main street, quiet in the off-season and jammed in summer. The population of 1,000 swells when visitors flock to the cool coast for recreation and natural beauty.

*Dinner:* **The Blue Heron,** at Weigh West Marine Resort, Tofino. (604) 725–3277. Attractive restaurant above a busy marina; views of Clayoquot Sound and Strawberry Island. Steak, chicken, and seafood; the fresh crab is best.

*Lodging:* Pacific Sands Beach Resort, P.O. Box 237, Tofino, B.C. V0R 2Z0. (604) 725–3322. Fifty-eight ocean-facing rooms on lovely Cox Bay. Lodge rooms, housekeeping units, cabins. Spacious and clean, with balconies and some fireplaces.

# Day 2

## Morning

*Breakfast:* If you are lodging in a housekeeping unit, you can prepare your own morning repast; or drive into Tofino and enjoy a healthful breakfast at **Common Loaf Bake Shop** on First Street (604–725–3915). The cozy, offbeat cafe serves good home-baked breads and pastries and will stoke you up for the morning's adventure.

After breakfast, go to **Meare's Landing,** 71 Wharf Street (beside the Coast Guard dock) for your whale-watching trip. Phone (604) 725–3163. (Cost of tour: $35 per adult. Trip available March through October only.) **Zodiac Whalewatching** will supply you with boots, a hat, and a full-length, waterproof flotation outfit. At a nearby wharf, you'll board a 24-foot Zodiac (a 12-person, rigid-hull rubber craft) and ride twenty-five minutes to the feeding grounds of the gray whales.

An experienced skipper will provide commentary on the sights, as well as a safe, exhilarating journey through flying, salty spray. High mountains and glaciers are the backdrop as the zippy Zodiac winds through Clayoquot Sound, passing native villages, sea lion rookeries, and a reserve where tufted puffins reside. Seals, otters, and occasionally orca whales may be seen.

On a two-and-a-half-hour expedition, you'll watch the 50-foot grays spout and dive, and maybe, if you're lucky, see one of these magnificent, gentle mammals breach or "spy-hop."

On the return trip, your skipper may run the boat past **Strawberry Island** for a close view of **Weeping Cedar Woman,** a figure carved in 1984 as a protest against logging the virgin forests of **Meares Island**. This issue is still unresolved; Tofino residents are fighting to preserve some of the last of the old-growth forests.

An interesting feature on little Strawberry is the ferry that perches on dry land like a wide brown ark. The boat was used as transportation in Vancouver before the Lion's Gate Bridge was constructed over Burrard Inlet. Now it's a private home.

On land again, return your borrowed gear and cross the street to **The Loft.**

*Lunch:* The Loft, Campbell and Second streets. (604) 725–4241. Pleasant, low-key restaurant frequented by locals and visitors alike. Praiseworthy sandwiches, salads, fish-and-chips, hamburgers.

## Afternoon

One of Tofino's greatest attractions is its collection of art galleries showing native works. Not to be missed is the **Eagle Aerie Gallery,** where Roy Vickers's paintings and books are strikingly displayed.

**House of Himwitsa,** 346 Campbell Street, sells limited-edition prints, silver jewelry, weavings, carvings, and pottery.

Stop in at **Alley Way Cafe** for a cup of tea or coffee and a rich, sweet pastry.

Buy a batch of fresh crab at **The Crab Bar** and a bottle of white wine and return to Pacific Sands Resort. Spend the rest of the afternoon relaxing on the beach at Cox Bay.

*Dinner:* Picnic on the Cox Bay beach or on your balcony as you watch the sunset.

*Lodging:* Pacific Sands Beach Resort.

# Day 3

## Morning

*Breakfast:* Prepare your own, or breakfast at The Blue Heron, Weigh West Marina.

This is a good day to stroll on the beach, take a hike in the rain forest, or go bird-watching. Some 250 species of birds live in the area. You're likely to see blue herons, bald eagles, osprey, cormorants, tufted puffins, and swans, plue several varieties of gulls. You might ask if a trip to Meares Island is available. The trails on the tribal park have been closed in recent years, but a boardwalk may be installed so that visitors can walk among the majestic old-growth trees.

Meares is a place of legends and ancient tradition. Rootlets from the towering spruce were once used by the Clayoquot Indians to make stout ropes, the yew made harpoon shafts, and cedar was the material of daily goods: clothing, utensils, homes, baskets. Salal berries and herbs were gathered for food and medicinal uses.

*Lunch:* Picnic on the beach or trail.

## Afternoon

Drive south on Route 4. Follow the road as it turns east. You'll pass the steep slopes of the heavily logged MacKenzie Range on your way back toward Port Alberni and the island's east coast. Nearing **Parksville,** stop at **Little Qualicum Falls,** where white cascades foam into the rushing green **Little Qualicum River.** Woodsy trails wind through the park, leading to overlooks.

About a half mile (1 km) west of Coombs is **Butterfly World** (604–752–9319). In this unusual, tropical greenhouse garden a thousand butterflies live and fly freely. It's a unique opportunity to photograph exotic species and see the colorful creatures at close hand. Wheelchair accessible, Butterfly World is open from 10:00 A.M. to 6:00 P.M., April through October.

Coombs is known for its **Old Country Market**. The picturesque landmark has a turf roof; many a visitor has halted in surprise at the sight of goats placidly walking on the roof and nibbling the grass.

At Parksville, turn south on Route 19.

*Dinner:* **Old Mahle House,** Cedar and Heemer roads, Nanaimo. (604) 722–3621. (Closed Monday and Tuesday.) Country-home-turned-restaurant, serving excellent Northwest cuisine. Fresh seafood and produce, pastas, homemade desserts, daily specials.

From Nanaimo, catch the ferry east to Horseshoe Bay and Vancouver.

## There's More

**M.V. Lady Rose.** Passenger and cargo freighter makes daily runs from Port Alberni to Broken Group Islands and Ucluelet. Riders return by boat or bus from Ucluelet. (604) 723–8313.

**Diving.** Barkley Sound's clear, quiet waters make it a popular divers' destination. It has rich marine life, reefs, and 200-year-old shipwrecks to explore.

**Fishing.** Weigh West Marine Resort, Tofino. (604) 725–3277. Boat rentals, guided charters at marina.

Canadian Princess Resort, Ucluelet. (604) 726–7771. Fishing and sight-seeing charters.

**Golf.** Long Beach Golf Course, Tofino. (604) 725–3332. Nine-hole scenic course, narrow and challenging.

**Kayaking.** Tofino Sea Kayaking Company, 320 Main Street, Tofino, B.C. V0R 2Z0. (604) 725–4222. Kayak rentals and guided trips around Clayoquot Sound and Barkley Sound, among the best sea kayaking areas in the Pacific Northwest.

**Hot Springs Cove.** A natural geothermal hot springs lies in a sheltered inlet north of Tofino, inaccessible by road. Its steaming pools, sea caves, and abundant marine life and wildlife make it an appealing side trip. (Bring sneakers; there are sharp rocks).

**Amphitrite Point,** Ucluelet. Rhododendrons, ferns, and coastal pines grow profusely near paved paths leading to the coast guard station and lighthouse. Watch the surf crash against jagged rocks.

**He Tin Kush Park,** Ucluelet. A fifteen-minute hike on the boardwalk takes you to the beach or up to a viewing point above the sea. Secluded coves, tide pools.

**West Coast Trail.** This notoriously rugged wilderness trail, 48 miles

(78 km) long, was originally built as a lifesaving trail for shipwreck survivors. It comprises one of three sections of Pacific Rim National Park and lies between Bamfield and Port Renfrew, south of Barkley Sound.

## Special Events

**March through May.** Pacific Rim Whale Festival, Tofino and Ucluelet. Films, displays, exhibits, whale-watching excursions, and hikes.

**July.** Pacific Rim Summer Festival, Tofino and Ucluelet. Chamber music, multicultural concerts.

**Late July.** Ukee Daze, Ucluelet. Fishing derby, arts-and-crafts displays, music, dances, crab and salmon feeds.

**Early September.** Salmon Derby, Port Alberni. Fishing competition with cash prizes up to $20,000. Derby winner for 1989 was a 50.86-pound chinook salmon. Other events: children's bullhead derby, horse rides, bed race, entertainment, boat raffle, fireworks, salmon barbecue.

## Other Recommended Restaurants and Lodgings

### Ucluelet

Burley's, 1078 Helen Road, Box 550. (604) 725–4444. Bed-and-breakfast home facing the waterfront. Beautiful lawns and rhododendron gardens. Six bedrooms share four baths. Extended continental breakfast.

Canadian Princess Resort, P.O. Box 939. (604) 726–7771 or (800) 663–7090. Moored survey ship with lodgings and nautical restaurant and lounge. Small berths on board, larger units in modern hotel section on shore. Open March through September.

Eagle's Nest Pub, foot of Bay Street on the waterfront. (604) 726–7515. Marine pub and RV site. Good lunches, pub food. Open daily.

Little Beach Resort, Box 68. (604) 726–4202. White, 1930s-style duplex cottages overlooking a small, protected cove where newer accommodations have been built.

Pot-Belly Restaurant, 1566 Peninsula Road. (604) 726–7441. Family restaurant with sandwiches, steaks, seafood. Breakfast, lunch, and dinner. Wheelchair accessible.

Wickaninnish Inn, in Wickaninnish Centre, 9.6 miles north of

Ucluelet. (604) 726–7706. Seaside location, admirable food. Tender, crisply battered fish-and-chips; savory salad with raspberry vinaigrette and lightly smoked salmon.

## Tofino

Chesterman's Beach Bed and Breakfast, Box 72. (604) 725–3726. Three separate, spacious, beachside suites; one in cedar home, one with second-story view, the third a secluded garden cottage. Continental breakfast served.

# For More Information

Port Alberni Travel InfoCentre, Highway 4, RR 2, Site 214, Port Alberni, B.C. V9Y 7L6. (604) 724–6535.

Pacific Rim National Park, Box 280, Ucluelet, B.C. V0R 3A0. (604) 726–4212.

Ucluelet Tourist Information, P.O. Box 428, Ucluelet, B.C. V0R 3A0. (604) 726–4641.

Tofino Chamber of Commerce, 351 Campbell, Box 476, Tofino, B.C. V0R 2Z0. (604) 725–3414.

BC Ferries, 1112 Fort Street, Victoria, B.C. V8V 4V2. Vancouver (604) 669–1211, Victoria (604) 386–3431.

# Strathcona and Hornby

The breathtaking wilderness of Strathcona Provincial Park on Vancouver Island.

## Action Getaway

### 3 NIGHTS

Primeval wilderness · Pristine lakes · Kayaking · Canoeing
Mountain hikes · Forests · Farmlands · Secluded islands · Quiet coves

Here's a warm-weather getaway that will satisfy the most avid outdoors lover. Within a four-day period you'll move from paddling a canoe or kayak on a freshwater lake, surrounded by forests and mountains, to the salty waters of island bays and coves. You'll hike mountain trails, sea bluffs, and an island mountain.

It's an action-packed trip, with interludes of relaxation, good food, and sunset watching.

# Day 1

## Morning

Load the canoe or kayak on your vehicle (or plan to rent one), and ferry from Horseshoe Bay to Nanaimo. Drive north on Route 19 to **Comox.** The trip will take about three hours.

*Lunch:* **Leeward Pub,** 649 Anderton Road, Comox. (604) 339–5400. A casual, inexpensive menu with savory soups and seafood chowder, sandwiches, and Leeward's own beer. You can watch the brewery in action.

## Afternoon

Continue on Route 19 26½ miles (43 km) to **Campbell River,** the shoreside town that's known worldwide for its rich salmon fishing. Purchase picnic supplies and, if you plan to do your own cooking, other groceries. Then turn west on Route 28; you're headed for the rugged mountain wilderness of **Strathcona Provincial Park,** in the heart of central Vancouver Island.

The oldest provincial park in British Columbia, Strathcona is laced with rivers, lakes, and streams and dominated by snow-cloaked peaks with glistening glaciers. **Golden Hinde,** at 7,260 feet (2,200 m), is the highest point on Vancouver Island. **Della Falls,** at the south end of the park and accessible only by walking trail, is the highest waterfall in North America.

Deer, wolves, Roosevelt elk, cougars, and several bird species, including the unique Vancouver Island white-tailed ptarmigan, inhabit the coastal forests. These stands of red cedar, fir, and western hemlock give way to subalpine fir, mountain hemlock, and creeping juniper on the higher slopes. Wildflowers bloom in profusion all through the park during the summer.

From Campbell River, it's 28 miles (45 km) to **Strathcona Park Lodge,** a private resort on the eastern shore of **Upper Campbell Lake.** The unusual resort, a complex of rustic cedar-and-stone buildings, offers accommodations and meals but is also a center for outdoor education. Classes in wilderness survival, leadership, ecology, canoeing, and kayaking are a few of the many topics taught by experts.

The beachfront cabins and log or rough-hewn timber chalets face the lake and its western arm, which points to shadowy foothills and rugged mountains. Kings Peak soars 6,815 feet (2,075 m) in the distance.

When you arrive at the lodge, check in and proceed to the beach, where colorful canoes are lined in a row, waiting to be set afloat.

You can take a class or simply rent a canoe (or kayak, if that's your preference) and launch into the crystal-clear waters of Upper Campbell Lake. Paddle southward to **Sevan Bay** for a close look at islands and a beaver dam, or ride out to **Treasure Island.** There are many good canoeing routes nearby and deeper in the park. The staff at Strathcona Park Lodge is happy to provide suggestions.

When the afternoon wanes, glide back to the lodge and relax with a stroll around the sloping, wooded grounds and perhaps a drink in the dining-room bar before dinner.

*Dinner:* Strathcona Park Lodge. Separate dining area for adult visitors, upstairs in the main lodge. Quiet atmosphere, bar, western view over the lake. Good, hearty meals served buffet-style. (Cabins have kitchens, so you can prepare your own food if you prefer.)

*Lodging:* Strathcona Park Lodge, Box 2160, Campbell River, B.C. V9W 5C9. (604) 286–2008 or 286–3122. Rustic resort in a spectacular wilderness setting. Simple, comfortable rooms in lodge buildings or separate cabins. Open year-round.

# Day 2

## Morning

*Breakfast:* Prepare your own, or join other guests and students in Strathcona's dining hall for fruit, baked goods, toast, and eggs.

Gather picnic foods for your daypack and drive south from the lodge, following long, slim **Buttle Lake** to **Lupin Falls Trail.** The short, pleasant walk to the falls takes you into a forest of cedar and fir, splashed with the colors of columbine, salmonberry, and wild roses. Lupin Falls is a ribbon of white, leaping from a cleft in immense polished boulders. On either side, the fronds of sword fern and maidenhair wave constantly in the misty breeze.

A few miles farther on the lakeside road is **Karst Creek Trail,** a 1.2-mile (2-km) loop path ascending through a forest that shows evidence of former fires. Some trees are now ghostly, burned spires, but many of the Douglas firs, though blackened, are still living, their heartwood protected from fire by thick bark.

Dogwood and the tiny bunchberry bloom white in spring along Karst Creek, with wildflowers, lacy ferns, moss-covered rocks, and cascading water at every bend. Karst was named for the phenomenon of water dissolving limestone, creating sinkholes and disappearing streams.

The next nature walk, a short drive from Karst Creek, is on **Wild Ginger Trail.** Winding through a fantasy forest of moss and ferns, the leaf-softened trail meets **Ralph River,** which tumbles and turns on its way to Buttle Lake. Watch for the glossy, heart-shaped leaves of wild ginger; under the leaf grows a tricornered, deep vermilion flower.

Next on the map is the path up **Shepherd Creek.** The 1.2-mile (2-km) trail, not a loop trip, is fairly level and travels through a virgin watershed.

If you have time, you may wish to continue on Route 28 as far as it goes, rounding the southern tip of Buttle Lake and ending at Westmin Resources' large mining operation. Mining is currently a point of controversy in the park, as several companies claim rights to various sections.

When you hear about **Flower Ridge Trail,** which starts at **Henshaw Creek,** at the south end of Buttle Lake, you may decide to skip the other trails and concentrate on one long hike. Flower Ridge has glorious views and, with a 4,300-foot (1,250-m) elevation gain, climbs through several mountain zones.

You start in a forest of coastal western hemlock, with undergrowth of deer fern, salal, Oregon grape, and huckleberry. The trail ascends to subalpine mountain hemlock and black huckleberry. Farther still, you come to white-flowered rhododendron and alpine tundra, with red and yellow mountain heathers, and finally to alpine azalea and white heather.

Allow five hours for the round-trip, hiking back the way you came.

*Lunch:* Picnic along the trail or eat in the Strathcona Park Lodge dining hall.

## Afternoon

Return to the lodge for another canoe or kayak excursion. Numerous other options for the active tourist are available. Each week during the summer, you can choose from a smorgasbord of workshops and guided trips. You might learn animal-tracking skills from a noted expert on cougars and other wildlife, discover how to find your way in the woods with a map and compass, or gain confidence in a rope-walking class. Boating classes and guided paddle trips are popular choices.

*Dinner:* Strathcona Park Lodge dining room.

*Lodging:* Strathcona Park Lodge.

# Day 3

## Morning

*Breakfast:* In Strathcona's dining hall, or prepare your own.

Leave the provincial park, and drive the 28 miles (45 km) east to Campbell River. Turn south on Route 19 to **Buckley Bay** (about 42 miles or 68 km) and head for the Denman/Hornby islands ferry landing.

It's a ten-minute ride across **Baynes Sound** to **Denman Island;** ferries leave hourly. On Denman you'll pass orchards and roadsides abloom with daisies and buttercups on your way to the Hornby Island ferry. Another ten-minute ride across the water takes you to **Hornby.** Both islands are famous for their artists and craftspeople, who produce exceptional works. Most studios and galleries are open to visitors.

Diminutive Hornby is an idyllic getaway, with its bucolic landscape, lovely beaches, grassy sea bluffs, and quiet coves. Travel about 6 miles (10 km) on Central Road to **Hornby Island Co-op,** and purchase the makings for a picnic. The co-op is the center of community life, selling island essentials: groceries, meats, hardware, video movies, fuel, and fishing tackle.

**Zucchini Ocean Kayak Centre** is here, too, renting bicycles, canoes, sailboards, and kayaks (604–335–2033 mornings and evenings, 335–0045 days and weekends). Zucchini also offers guided day trips and lessons.

Rent a canoe or kayak, and take St. John Point Road to **Tribune Bay Provincial Park.** The park has the finest sandy beach in the region, 3,300 feet (1,006 m) long, and the waters of the protected bay are warm enough for comfortable swimming. Sheltered from ocean swells, they're ideal for sea kayaking or canoeing.

As you paddle around the inlets and small bays of the coast, you'll see abundant marine and plant life, along with views of Hornby's cliffs and forests and, on the west, the mountains and green ridges of Vancouver Island.

*Lunch:* Picnic on the beach in one of Hornby Island's pretty coves.

## Afternoon

When you tire of paddling, go ashore and return the rented canoe or kayak to Zucchini Centre. Then head for **Tralee Point** and your destination, **Sea Breeze Lodge.** Gail and Brian Bishop have created a little Eden-by-the-sea at their family-oriented resort on twelve acres. Summer lodging is American Plan, with all meals included. Off-season, housekeeping cottages are available.

*Dinner:* Sea Breeze Lodge. Gail Bishop is renowned for her home-cooked meals, and Brian grills a delectable salmon. Children eat at 5:30, adults at 7:00 P.M.

*Lodging:* Sea Breeze Lodge, Hornby Island, B.C. V0R 1Z0. (604) 335–2321. Twelve cabins, some separate, some duplex units. All have kitchens and light, modern furnishings. Grass tennis court; hot tub on a cliff above the beach.

# Day 4

## Morning

*Breakfast:* Sea Breeze Lodge.

With one of Gail Bishop's tasty picnic lunches tucked in your knapsack, drive to **Helliwell Provincial Park.** This splendid park on **St. John Point** features a 3.6-mile (6-km) trail that loops through mature Douglas fir forest to a rocky headland, across broad grassy fields and back among the firs, western hemlock, and lodgepole pine to the starting point.

The open meadows lie on cliffs above the sea, good vantage points for viewing birds and wildlife; whales, porpoises, seals, and sea lions often cavort in the waves below the rocks, and you may see pelagic cormorants, pigeon guillemot, harlequin ducks, and black oystercatchers.

If you're feeling energetic, climb the trail to **Mount Geoffrey**'s summit, highest point on the island. It affords an exhilarating view of the islands, the boat-dotted sea, and the mountains on both Vancouver Island and the mainland. The loop trip is a four- to five-hour walk.

An alternative to the above hikes is to further explore the coastal waterways in a kayak or canoe.

*Lunch:* Picnic at Helliwell or Mount Geoffrey.

## Afternoon

Ferry to Denman Island and back to Vancouver Island. Drive south on Route 19 to Nanaimo, about 40 miles (65 km).

*Dinner:* **Gina's Cafe,** 47 Skinner Street, Nanaimo. (604) 753–5411. Informal, inexpensive cafe serving Mexican foods with a Northwest touch. Just right after all that appetite-inducing activity.

Catch the ferry at **Departure Bay,** and cross Georgia Strait back to Horseshoe Bay. You may be in time to watch a glorious sunset over Vancouver Island as you plow the waves.

# There's More

**Elk Falls.** This forested park, west of Campbell River and near the John Hart Dam, has trails, impressive waterfalls, a salmon hatchery, and campgrounds.

**Fillongley Park,** Denman Island. In a wooded, eighty-acre grove facing Lambert Channel, you'll find beaches, clam digging, trails through old-growth fir, and a salmon spawning stream.

**Denman Island General Merchants.** This old-fashioned general store sells a little of everything.

**Boyle Point Provincial Park,** Denman Island. A woodland trail leads to the island's tip, across the channel from Hornby. The park overlooks the Strait of Georgia and Chrome Island lighthouse.

**Bicycling:** Denman Island's level country roads, with little traffic, make the island a popular cycling destination.

## For More Information

Tourism Association of Vancouver Island, Suite 302, 45 Bastion Square, Victoria, B.C. V8W 1J1. (604) 382–3551.

Ministry of Parks, 1610 Mount Seymour Road, North Vancouver, B.C. V7G 1L3. (604) 929–1291.

Denman/Hornby Tourist Services, Denman Island, B.C. V0R 1T0. (604) 335–2293.

BC Ferries, 1112 Fort Street, Victoria, B.C. V8V 4V2. Vancouver (604) 669–1211, Victoria (604) 386–3431.

# The Gulf Islands

Galiano Island has numerous driftwood-strewn, secluded beaches.

## Island Hopping in the Georgia Strait

———————————— 3 NIGHTS ————————————

Picturesque landscapes · Ocean views · Mild climate · Wildlife
Whale watching · Tranquil setting · Evergreen forests
Hiking trails · Secluded beaches · Fine dining

Between British Columbia's mainland and Vancouver Island lies the Strait of Georgia, its waters sprinkled with lumpy green hummocks called the Gulf Islands. Some are tiny and uninhabited, but several are populated year-round and draw tourists for the outdoor recreation, natural beauty, and pebble-strewn beaches.

This itinerary will introduce you to three islands: Galiano, North and South Pender, and Mayne. Each has a distinct character and much to offer the curious traveler.

(The largest and most densely populated island, Salt Spring, is described in Vancouver Escape Seven).

A note about riding the ferries: You can reserve space on Canadian ferries (unlike U.S. vessels), and it will be held for you until thirty minutes before departure. This is a boon to line-weary travelers, especially on busy summer weekends when long waits are common. Fares to Gulf Islands are the same as to Victoria, while traveling interisland costs much less.

There are many routes and schedules you can follow in touring the islands. This itinerary is just one example, designed for a Friday-through-Monday getaway and based on current ferry schedules for those days. Those schedules may change without notice; be sure to consult an up-to-date one.

# Day 1

## Morning

From the Tsawassen docks, south of Vancouver off Route 17, board the ferry to the **Pender Islands.** With a mighty blast of its whistle, the great white behemoth will ease into the channel and plow its way past densely forested islands. Seabirds wheel and call, clouds scud across the sky, and your tensions begin to slip away.

After a stop at **Mayne Island,** the ferry continues to **North Pender,** arriving at **Otter Bay.** North and South Pender are divided by a channel and connected by a narrow bridge. A rock isthmus once joined them, but it was blasted out in 1903 to allow boats through. The little bridge was built in 1950.

While housing development has increased rapidly in recent years, the Penders have retained much of their wild charm. There are several coves, lakes, and parks where you can enjoy the natural surroundings, and country roads that are fine for bicycling.

From Otter Bay, head south on Otter Bay and Bedwell Harbour roads toward **Port Browning.** The sheltered harbor bustles with action in summer, as boats enter and depart the marina. Walk the rocky beach here, watch the sailboats, and bask in the islanders' friendly welcome at the pub.

*Lunch:* **Port Browning Cafe** or **Pub** on the east coast of North Pender, off Hamilton Road. (604) 629–3493. The pub is known for its English-style fish-and-chips and Native decor; the masks and totems are part of a private collection. You can eat on the deck overlooking the marina. The cafe on a shaded slope around the corner also offers outdoor tables.

## Afternoon

Heading south, take Canal Road and cross the bridge to **South Pender.** Just past the bridge you'll see a path on the right that disappears into the woods above the shore. Take this trail for a lovely walk under tall cedars and madronas (arbutus), past ferns, moss, and mushrooms, to a rocky beach. Here, at low tide, spouts of water periodically shoot 2 and 3 feet from the holes of clams and worms—a cove-long cluster of miniature fountains.

Kingfishers dive for fish and break the quiet with their cries. Bedwell Harbour glimmers through the trees.

The trail continues along the coast to **Beaumont Marine Park,** one of the few underwater parks in the region and a favorite with divers. Hike as far as you wish; then turn back to the bridge and your car or bicycle.

Take Canal Road and Spalding to Gowlland Point Road, and proceed to the end. From the unmarked beach here, you have a good chance of observing orca (killer) whales. Perch on the boulders and watch the water's surface for spouts and the distinctive flukes of the great black-and-white mammals. You may see them swimming in pods of fifteen or so, an awesome sight. Another good whale-watching site is from the cove at the end of Higgs Road, also off Gowlland Point Road. You'll hear the steady moan of offshore buoys and the shrieks of seabirds as you search for whales.

A private path at the end of Higgs Road allows access to the beach and cove. Visitors are permitted to use it, as is often the case on the islands. Local residents know which landowners have granted permission for their trails to be used, and most will be happy to tell you where those trails are.

After you've sighted the orcas and relaxed in the sun, retrace your route to the bridge and North Pender. Drive to **Hope Bay** and one of the best lodgings in the islands, **Cliffside Inn On-the-Sea.** Ask about packages here; some have a minimum stay of two nights.

*Dinner:* Cliffside Inn On-the-Sea. Penny Tomlin serves a four-course dinner in The Conservatory, a glass-walled dining room in her inn. The candlelighted tables, superb food, and view across the water make this an evening to remember. For guests only, included in room rate. Monday, Wednesday, and Saturday only.

*Lodging:* Cliffside Inn On-the-Sea, North Pender Island, B.C. V0N 2M0. (604) 629–6691. A four-room inn of great charm and a hospitable hostess. Serene setting above Hope Bay, viewing Plumper Sound, Mayne and Saturna islands, and the Washington mainland with Mount Baker on the horizon.

# Day 2

## Morning

Rise early, and you may see the river otter that nests at the bottom of the cliff, the shorebirds of dawn, and the bald eagles that frequent the area.

*Breakfast:* Cliffside Inn On-the-Sea serves a full breakfast that includes fruits and berries from the garden.

This is a morning for relaxing in your island hideaway. Penny will lend buckets and shovels if you want to dig for clams. You can rent a boat or mountain bike at Bromley's Otter Bay marina. (Cliffside guests receive special rates).

Ask Penny about the unmarked trail to a secluded beach of crushed shells. From the inn it's a fifteen-minute walk over a country road and through a silent, enchanting forest of cedar to an old orchard and the beach.

Leave Cliffside for Otter Bay (2 miles) in time to catch the ferry bound for Sturdies Bay on **Galiano Island.**

Galiano's distinctive feature is its dense greenery. The island is 75 percent owned by MacMillan-Bloedel, a major timber company, and so has both logged-off areas and miles of Douglas fir forest. With 800 permanent residents, it's less developed and less rural than Pender.

*Lunch:* **Hummingbird Inn,** Sturdies Bay Road, Galiano Island. (604) 539–5472. A friendly, open pub with windows overlooking a grassy picnic area. Good soups and salads, several beers. Dart boards and a casual atmosphere.

## Afternoon

Drive the length of the island (18 miles or 29 km) on Porlier Pass Road toward **Coon Bay.**

When you reach Cook Road, near **Bodega Resort,** you're beginning 3 miles (5 km) of unpaved, deeply potholed road. This is a trip for a sturdy vehicle, but it's worth the effort. Along the way you may see bald eagles.

If you continue to the tip of the island, you'll arrive at **Dionisio Point Provincial Park** and the shore of **Porlier Pass Channel,** which separates Galiano and Valdes islands. The driftwood-strewn beach is ideal for contemplative strolls. Madrona trees and conifers cover a sandstone bluff with grassy paths that curve around the island's jagged edge to views of coves and a lighthouse.

The return trip on Cook Road seems easier, perhaps because you now know the puddles and ruts are passable. At the corner of Cook and Porlier Pass Road is Bodega Resort (604–539–2677). Experienced guides at the farm/resort offer one- and two-hour horseback rides on trails and logging roads. The well-trained horses carry you through sun-dappled valleys and along ridge tops that afford magnificent views of Georgia Strait and Trincomali Channel.

*Dinner:* **Woodstone Country Inn.** Fine dining in a small hotel restaurant.

*Lodging:* Woodstone Country Inn, RR 1, Georgeson Bay Road. (604) 539–2022. Twelve light, airy guest rooms furnished with wicker and antiques. Some fireplaces. Scenic setting.

# Day 3

## Morning

*Breakfast:* A hearty breakfast is included in the room rate at Woodstone Country Inn.

Drive to Sturdies Bay in time to board the ferry to **Village Bay, Mayne Island.**

Mayne, 4 miles (7 km) across, is the smallest of the islands on your brief tour, and it's the sweetest. Less developed than Pender, less forested than Galiano, its tone is softly pastoral. Open green fields and gardens surrounded with high wire fences (to keep the numerous deer out) characterize much of Mayne's landscape. Along the roadsides, Scotch broom bursts a brilliant yellow in spring, followed by summer's foxglove and lupine. As on the other islands, you'll see groves of madrona trees, with their distinctive, peeling red bark, along with towering firs.

Take Village Bay Road to **Miners Bay,** the local gathering spot and the island's commercial center. The picturesque bay was named after the many miners who stopped here in the mid-1800s on their way to the Fraser River/Cariboo gold rush.

At **Miners Bay Deli,** choose a thick sandwich-to-go; you can buy other picnic materials at **Miners Bay Trading Post** a few yards away.

Turn back on Village Bay Road to the entrance to **Helen Point Trail**. This walk through the woods to the beach takes about an hour each way. First it descends to a beach, then continues under trees, and ends on a mossy green bank above the light at Active Pass.

*Lunch:* Picnic at Helen Point.

## Afternoon

Hike back down the mountain and head southwest to Dinner Road. You'll be just in time for tea and check-in at **Oceanwood Country Inn.**

Williams Place is a short street off Dinner Road, ending in eleven-acre **Dinner Bay Community Park** and beach. After tea you might like to visit the sandy beach to search for shells, watch for bald eagles, and breathe the fresh, briny air.

*Dinner:* Oceanwood Country Inn. Prix fixe menu of continental dishes, specializing in fresh seafood and local ingredients imaginatively prepared. British Columbia house wines.

*Lodging:* Oceanwood Country Inn, C2 Leighton Lane, RR 1, Mayne Island, B.C. V0N 2J0. (604) 539–5074. Spacious, renovated Tudor-style inn overlooking a small bay. Gracious hosts Marilyn and Jonathan Chilvers welcome guests to rooms furnished with verve and style. Three have fireplaces and whirlpool tubs.

# Day 4

## Morning

*Breakfast:* The Chilvers serve a full breakfast—fruit, eggs, bacon, coffee, juice—in the pink stucco dining room at Oceanwood Country Inn.

Head for Miners Bay and gather picnic supplies. You might stop at **Mayne Street Mall** for Mayne Open Market's local produce and Manna Bakery Cafe, where sandwiches, soups, and baked goods are offered, as well as espresso and capuccino.

From Fernhill Road, turn northeast on Campbell Bay Road. As the road curves toward **Campbell Bay,** you'll see a grassy meadow and just beyond it a parking turnout. An unmarked trail borders the meadow. Walk this trail about ¼ mile, and you'll come to a wide, serene, protected beach, just right for sunbathing, beachcombing, and exploring the sandstone shelves that shelter brilliantly colored starfish.

Mayne Island has many attractive beaches, but Campbell Bay, with its deep, fjordlike bay, is one of the most appealing. It's the most popular swimming area on the island and a good, safe place to bring children.

*Lunch:* Picnic on the beach at Campbell Bay.

## Afternoon

Take Campbell Bay Road to Waugh Road and follow it to Georgina Point Road, headed toward **Oyster Bay.** At the tip of **Georgina Point,** on a grassy field with gnarled apple trees, is a lighthouse that is open to the public daily from 1:00 to 3:00 P.M. Originally built in 1885, **Active Pass Light Station** was replaced by the present structure in 1940, with a new tower opened in 1969.

After your lighthouse tour, take Georgina Point Road back toward Miners Bay. On the way you'll pass little **St. Mary Magdalene Church,** a historic structure built about 1898, and several turn-of-the-century homes.

In "downtown Mayne," see **Plumper Pass Lockup,** a minuscule jail that was built in 1896 to accommodate rowdy miners. (The story goes that it housed only one inmate—and he escaped.) Now it's a museum.

Overlooking the waterfront at the bottom of the hill is **Springwater Hotel.** Built in the 1890s, it's the oldest continuously operating hotel in British Columbia. The pub is a favorite local hangout, but the place to be on a sunny afternoon is the hillside deck. From your umbrella-shaded table, watch the boats and tourists go by as you quench your thirst.

After a few days of relaxing on "island time," your watch may seem irrelevant. But the ferry leaves Village Bay at 5:20 P.M. to carry you back to Tsawwassen. The 10-mile (16-km) ride will get you to the mainland by 6:40 P.M.

# There's More

**Archaeology dig.** On North Pender, a Salish Indian dig dating back 10,000 years. Occasionally open for summer tours.

**Arts and crafts.** Artery Studio, Oyster Bay, Mayne Island. Paintings and prints by Frances Faminow and other artists. Open afternoons.

Charterhouse, Charter Road near Bennett Bay, Mayne Island. Heather Maxey's home studio. Quilts, fine woolens, and enamels-on-copper. Open afternoons in summer, weekends in winter.

Greenhouse Studio, Village Bay, Mayne Island. Weavings and woodcrafts at studio of Ann and Brenan Simpson.

**Beaches and picnic sites.** Montague Harbour Provincial Park, Galiano Island. Waterside park; site of ancient Indian village. Sandy beach, picnic and camping sites.

Bluff Park, Galiano Island, 650 feet (200 m) above Active Pass. Grand view of Gulf and San Juan islands. Good spot for sighting eagles and orca whales.

Edith Point, Mayne Island. Near Campbell Bay, off Edith Point Road. One-hour hike to point with views of water, seals, and ferries on Georgia Strait.

Magic Lake Walk, southern end of North Pender Island. Loop path leading from Shingle Bay to Buck Lake and pretty Magic Lake.

**Boating.** Southwind Sailing Charters, Galiano Island, B.C. V0N 1P0. (604) 539–2930. Picnic cruises aboard a 46-foot catamaran, *Great*

*White Cloud.* Lunch includes smoked salmon, fruit, French bread, and wine.

Gulf Islands Kayaking, Galiano Island. (604) 539–2442. Guided sea-kayak trips available. No experience necessary. Office at ferry landing.

Island Charters, Mayne Island. (604) 539–5040. Cruises aboard a 33-foot sailboat; half- and full-day trips, the latter with lunch, available.

Mayne Island Kayak and Canoe Rentals, Seal Beach. (604) 539–2667. Ferry landing pickup and dropoff. Camping and showers available.

**Farmers' market.** Driftwood Centre, North Pender Island. Fresh local produce sold every summer weekend.

**Fishing.** Eagle Spirit Charters, Mayne Island. (604) 539–5540. Experienced guide specializes in salmon fishing; provides tackle and bait aboard 27-foot boat.

**Golf.** Galiano Golf and Country Club, Ellis Road, Galiano Island. (604) 539–5533. PGA-rated nine-hole course in quiet, wooded setting. (Tennis also available; rent rackets at clubhouse.)

## Special Events

**June.** Galiano Weavers Exhibit and Sale, Galiano Island.
**July.** Salmon barbecue and fish derby, Pender Islands.
**Mid-July.** Artists Guild Exhibition and Sale, Galiano Island.
**August.** Art Show and Fall Fair, Pender Islands.
**August.** Springwater Salmon Derby, Mayne Island.
**Mid-August.** Fall Fair, Mayne Island. Arts, crafts, photography, needlework, baking, canning, flowers, honey, wine, and produce exhibited in booths near the Agricultural Hall.
**November.** Christmas Craft Fair, Mayne Island.

## Other Recommended Restaurants and Lodgings

### Pender Island

Ashley Downs Bed-and-Breakfast, RR 1, Hoosen Road. (604) 629–6459. Half-timbered, Tudor-style country home near the golf course.

Cutlass Court Bed-and-Breakfast, Lot 8, Cutlass Court Road. (604) 629–6141. Log home with four guest rooms. Owner Doug Heath rents mountain bikes, canoes, and kayaks, and he skippers a 21-foot sailboat.

Driftwood Cafe, Driftwood Centre, Bedwell Harbour Road. (604) 629–6433. Casual meals in the island's only shopping mall. Tables indoors or on a brick terrace. Driftwood Centre also has a bakery, gift shop, pharmacy, liquor store, and garage.

## Galiano Island

Bodega Resort, Box 115. (604) 539–2677. Log cottages with kitchens on twenty-five pastoral acres of meadows and trees. Horses, sheep, hiking trails.

Chez Ferrie, Sturdies Bay dock. (604) 539–2033. Take-out wagon by the ferry landing. Hamburgers, fish-and-chips, snacks.

Galiano Golf and Country Club off Ellis Road. (604) 539–5533. Home-style cooking in a cafe setting; fixed menu of three-course dinners.

La Berengerie, Montague Harbour Road. (604) 539–5392. Restaurant nestled under the trees, serving Continental cuisine with an experimental (and expert) twist. Open nightly in summer, weekends in winter.

## Mayne Island

Fernhill Lodge, Box 140. (604) 539–2544. Outstanding inn and herb farm on a wooded hilltop. Gracious service, comfortable rooms, enchanting gardens, dinners geared to historical themes. Full breakfast included.

# For More Information

Galiano Island Visitors' Association, P.O. Box 73, Galiano Island, B.C. V0N 1P0. (604) 539–2233.

Tourism Association of Vancouver Island, Suite 302, 45 Bastion Square, Victoria, B.C. V8W 1J1. (604) 382–3551.

BC Ferries, 1112 Fort Street, Victoria, B.C. V8V 4V2. Vancouver (604) 669–1211, Victoria (604) 386–3431.

# Langdale to Lund

Desolation Sound Marine Park is world-renowned for its magnificent scenery.

## The Sunshine Coast

_____ 2 NIGHTS _____

Ferry rides · Scenic water views · Coastal villages · Unspoiled wilderness
Boat cruises · Fishing · Hiking · Beaches · Native arts

The 100-mile (160 km) stretch of British Columbia coastline between Howe Sound and Desolation Sound is said to bask under more sunny days than anywhere else in western British Columbia. The stretch lives up to its nickname, the Sunshine Coast, drawing visitors who are lured not only by the weather but by a wealth of outdoor recreation.

This itinerary provides a taste of the wilderness and seaside relaxation in a three-day escape to sheltered bays, fir-scented forests, and fish-filled waters.

# Day 1

## Morning

Board an early morning ferry at Horseshoe Bay, and travel north across Howe Sound to **Langdale,** a forty-minute ride. Under blue skies, the sea sparkles; if it's cloudy, with pewter skies and gray water, you feel that you're floating in a dream world of liquid silver.

Nearing the steep coastline, backed by massive, snow-cloaked mountains, you'll see private piers and cottages dotting the inlets.

From the Langdale ferry landing, it's a 2½-mile (4 km) drive into the village of **Gibsons,** where you can join hard-hatted workers for breakfast at **Harbour Cafe.** In this bustling local gathering place, the coffee pot is never empty and the pancakes and omelets satisfy the heartiest appetites.

Gibsons faces Shoal Channel and the Strait of Georgia. Descend the steps toward Gibsons Wharf, and you'll see a path edging the waterfront. This easy, level walk will provide you with a pleasant, ten-minute stroll and view of the boat traffic and sloping green hills around the harbor. Plaques posted along the route tell about Gibsons' founders.

**Elphinstone Pioneer Museum,** on Winn Road, houses Canada's largest shell collection as well as outstanding displays of historical items. Native stone hammers, spear points, cedar root baskets, knives, and arrowheads are on display, along with artifacts from pioneer life and the early logging, fishing, and canning industries. The museum is open daily in summer, and Sundays only from September through February.

**Soames Hill,** locally known as The Knob, lies off Bridgeman Road, between Gibsons and Langdale. A walk up this steep, 800-foot (245-m) hill will test your leg muscles with its many log steps, but it's a short hike (forty minutes round-trip) and presents you with a glorious view of Gibsons, Howe Sound, Gambier and Bowen islands, and the Squamish Mountains.

Return to Highway 101, the Sunshine Coast Highway, and drive north to **Sechelt.** You'll pass **Roberts Creek Provincial Park,** a waterside dell of dark cedars, sword fern, and bracken.

From the highway you seldom glimpse the water, since the view is blocked by forests so dense they form a virtually impenetrable wall. To enjoy the real flavor of this scenic country, you have to get out on the water—your afternoon excursion.

At the entrance to Sechelt, just off the highway, is the **Sechelt Indian Band Hall** and **Raven's Cry Theatre.** Standing like sentinels before the hall are twelve totem poles, each carved to record major events in recent Sechelt Indian culture. The band's carving house is open to the public.

*Lunch:* **Pebbles Restaurant** in the Driftwood Inn, Trail Avenue, Sechelt. (604) 885–5811. Savory seafood chowder, quiche, and salads served in an attractive dining room with a cheery atmosphere, overlooking the Strait of Georgia.

### Afternoon

Go to **Ocean Activity Centre,** 5644 Cowrie Street (604–885–9802). From here, experienced guides will take you sea kayaking or on an afternoon sight-seeing excursion around nearby islands. You'll see the waterways and coastline from a different, dramatic perspective. Cruises include a five-hour trip to the tidal rapids at **Skookumchuk Narrows,** an eight-hour sail up beautiful **Princess Louisa Inlet,** and an evening ride in **Sechelt Inlet.** Any fish you catch will be smoked and canned for you to take home.

*Dinner:* **Blue Heron Inn,** East Porpoise Bay Road, Sechelt. Quiet, romantic dining room with water view. Blue herons feed on the salt flats, while osprey and kingfishers swoop above. Fresh seafood includes lobster from the traps at the end of the inn's pier.

*Lodging:* **Driftwood Inn,** Box 829, Sechelt, B.C. V0N 3A0. (604) 885–5811. Modern Hotel with twenty-eight suites, some with water views and kitchenettes.

# Day 2

### Morning

*Breakfast:* Driftwood Inn.

Follow the highway north, passing moss-covered boulders, rocky outcroppings, and arbutus trees that twist at improbable angles over the sea bluffs. Scotch broom borders the roadside, its flowers bright yellow in spring.

Pass by the charms of **Half Moon Bay** and pretty **Secret Cove** and continue to **Madeira Park.** Stop at **Lowe's Resort** (604–883–2456), and board the boat for your scenic tour or fishing venture in **Pender Harbour.** Guides at this family resort are fishing experts. (You can rent a boat if you prefer.)

*Lunch:* Box lunch on your charter trip, provided (at additional charge) by Davina Morton, hostess at Lowe's Resort. Sandwiches, fruit, dessert, beverage.

### Afternoon

The salmon or cod you catch will be frozen and packed at Lowe's Resort.

North of Madeira Park, take Garden Bay Road to **Mount Daniel** trail. The former logging road, now somewhat overgrown, ascends about 1½ miles (2 km) to the western peak of the 1,545-foot (470 m) mountain, highest in the Pender Harbour area. Allow about an hour for the hike to the top. When you reach the summit, you'll have a panoramic view of lakes, islands, inlets, and Pender Harbour.

One of the lakes is **Garden Bay Lake,** which was considered sacred by the coast Salish Indians. Young girls, when they reached the age of puberty, would climb the eastern side of the mountain and spend four months there, communicating with the moon through circles of stone. When they returned to the tribe they were considered adult women. Evidence of their traditional rituals can still be seen on Mount Daniel.

Back on the highway again, drive to **Earl's Cove** and board the late-afternoon ferry to **Saltery Bay.** The ride around the tip of Nelson Island and across Jervis Inlet takes fifty minutes.

Drive another 18½ miles (30 km) to **Powell River,** through thick forests interrupted by narrow, shady side roads that wind enticingly down to the sea and private homes. The town is dominated by an immense pulp-and-paper mill, one of the world's largest. Signs at an overlook along the highway list events in the history of Powell River and the harborside mill that created it.

*Dinner:* **Beach Gardens Resort.** Comfortable dining room with a fine view and excellent food: tender salmon, spicy Cajun prawns, several seafood dishes, sizable salad bar.

*Lodging:* Beach Gardens Resort, 7074 Westminster Street, Powell River, B.C. V8A 1C5. (604) 485–6267 or (800) 663–7070. Cabins and sixty-six rooms with private balconies overlooking the marina. Stone-and-cedar buildings under the trees. Indoor pool, sauna, tennis courts, boat rentals.

# Day 3

## Morning

*Breakfast:* Restaurant at Beach Gardens Resort.

In Powell River, stop in at the historical museum, across from **Willingdon Beach.** The exhibit explains Powell River's origins as a logging town and displays offbeat artifacts, such as the first piano in the district, a vest made of fishnet, a mastodon bone, and a reconstruction of the unique cabin lived in by a eccentric hermit, Billy Goat Smith.

There are several art galleries along Marina Avenue. **Gallery Tantalus,** 3 blocks north of the ferry terminal, shows paintings, limited-edition prints, pottery, native carvings, jewelry, and glass works. **Paperworks Gallery** features hand-painted silk scarves, jewelry, and kites.

Visit the **Cranberry Lake Wildlife Sanctuary,** on the outskirts of Powell River, and you may see bald eagles and trumpeter swans eye to eye. Injured birds are brought to the lakeshore sanctuary for rehabilitation; it's a haven for migrating fowl.

On the southern shore of **Powell Lake, Pacific Coastal Air** keeps float planes available for business and tourist flights. For breathtaking views of the 30-mile (49-km) lake, the steep green slopes of **Goat Island** (inhabited by mountain goats), the untracked wilderness and its multitude of lakes, and the rugged mountains that surround them, an airplane tour is ideal.

A half-hour flight will buzz you over the cove-scalloped lake and forests, fish farms and log booms, to **Desolation Sound,** British Columbia's largest marine park. The area was named by Captain George Vancouver in 1792, when he explored here and was unimpressed with "not a single prospect that was pleasing to the eye." Today the sound and its many islands and inlets are considered jewels among the province's parks. The clear waters and rich undersea life make the area a favorite diving destination.

The plane flies above **Savary Island,** with its summer homes and miles of white sand beaches; passes the smoking sawmill; and circles back to land on Powell Lake.

*Lunch:* **Shinglemill Restaurant,** on Powell Lake. (604) 483–2001. Bistro and pub. Good chowder, pasta, sandwiches, seafood, and ambrosial desserts. Open, bright setting on lakeshore, near float-plane docks.

## Afternoon

Take the Sunshine Coast Highway as far as it will go, and you'll arrive in the outpost of **Lund,** about 17 miles (28 km) from Powell River. You've reached the northern end of Highway 101, a ribbon of road that stretches 10,000 miles from Lund to Puerto Montt, Chile.

Established in 1889 by the Thulin brothers, who named it after the Swedish town, Lund is a relaxed, friendly community, favored by boaters and lovers of peace and quiet.

Stop at **Carver's Coffee House** for espresso and cookies. The quaint cafe stands at the end of a boardwalk that extends over the water when the tide is in. Anne Steblyk and Keith Matthison, the owners, are hospitable folk who welcome visitors to their warm, inviting shop. Take your coffee to the deck, where you'll be joined by Skookum, the lovable Bernese mountain dog, and watch for the nesting eagles in the trees above.

**Debbie Dan Art Shop** near Lund is open Thursday through Sunday in summer. Debbie sells native artworks, portraits, wildlife paintings and photography, and carvings by the renowned Jackie Timothy, a local native artist.

Turn south now for the four-hour trip back to Vancouver. (The last summer ferry on Sundays and holiday Mondays departs from Langdale at 10:10 P.M. Check your ferry schedule for changes.) If there's time on the return trip, stop at one of the attractions you missed on the way up (see "There's More" for suggestions).

As you wend your way south on Highway 101 to Horseshoe Bay, it's a certainty that you'll be planning your next trip to the splendid Sunshine Coast.

# There's More

**Canoeing, kayaking.** Powell Forest Canoe Route travels a chain of eight wilderness lakes linked by portage trails with canoe resting racks and tent sites.

Ocean canoeing and kayaking are favorable in Jervis Inlet, Malaspina Inlet, and Desolation Sound Marine Park.

Pender Harbour and Three Lakes Circle Route is a 7½-mile (12-km) trip through Garden Bay, Mixal, and Lower Sakinaw lakes. You can see Indian pictographs at Sakinaw Lake.

**Diving.** Powell River, considered the diving capital of Canada, has numerous diving spots with colorful marine life and intriguing shipwrecks. Mermaid Cove, the "Iron Mines" on Texada Island, Saltery Bay, Scotch Fir Point, and Okeover Arm are favorites.

**Fishing and boating charters.** Captain Hook Sportsfishing Enterprises, P.O. Box 2699, Sechelt, B.C. V0N 3A0. (604) 885–3302. Complete packages for saltwater fishing: bait, tackle, guide, 28-foot boat with cabin, catch cleaned and packaged. Five percent discount for early bookings.

Blue Meaway, P.O. Box 2532, Sechelt, B.C. V0N 3A0. (604) 885–2862 or 885–5614. Sail a 37-foot cutter-rigged sloop, sight-seeing or fishing around the islands.

Sunshine Coast Tours and Charters, 449 Marine Drive, Gibsons, B.C. V0N 1V0. (604) 886–8341. Fishing charters, tours to Princess Louisa Inlet.

Coho Fishing Charters, 104 East Forty-ninth Avenue, Vancouver, B.C. V5W 2G2. (604) 324–8214. Fishing trips from Secret Cove, on 28- and 32-foot Fairlines. Yacht rentals available.

Sunshine Coast Charter Boat Association, Box 316, Madeira Park, B.C. V0N 2H0. (604) 885–5082. Half- and full-day fishing charters; all gear supplied.

**Golf.** Sunshine Coast Golf and Country Club, Highway 101, Gibsons. (604) 885–9212. Hillside nine-hole course above water. Non-members after 1:00 P.M. weekdays, after 3:00 P.M. weekends. Pender Harbour Golf Course, Highway 101, south side of Pender Harbour. (604) 883–9541. Nine holes. (Open daily.) Myrtle Point Golf Club, Powell River. New eighteen-hole championship course. (604) 487–GOLF.

**Pulp-and-paper mill tours.** Daily tours in summer of MacMillan-Bloedel pulp-and-paper mill, Powell River, are available. The minimum age is twelve.

**Hunter Gallery,** Marine Drive, Gibsons. Art gallery showing the works of more than one hundred local artists. Paintings, pottery, jewelry, scarves. (Open daily in summer.)

**Skookumchuk Narrows.** This is one of the West Coast's largest saltwater rapids. East of Earl's Cove, the tide turns in a narrow channel. There are cavernous whirlpools; on a 10-foot (3-m) tide, 200 billion gallons of water churn through the channel.

· **Princess Louisa Inlet.** This fjord lies in a majestic, glacier-carved gorge, with more than sixty waterfalls cascading down precipitous cliffs into placid inlet waters. Chatterbox Falls, at the head of the inlet, tumbles 120 feet (37 m); it's accessible only by sea.

**Inland Lake.** Unique to Powell River, Inland Lake is encircled by a wheelchair-accessible, 8-mile (13-km) trail. A wide, level, graveled path winds through cedar, fir, and dogwood and around a lake that contains native cutthroat trout. Log cabins, fishing piers, picnic tables, and overlooks are all designed for wheelchair use. (Open mid-April to mid-October.)

**Powell River Recreation and Cultural Centre.** This remarkable, top-quality community facility holds a 25-meter pool, sauna, whirlpool, leisure pool, exercise room, two regulation arenas, meeting rooms, and a 725-seat theater.

**Saltery Bay Provincial Park.** Sixteen miles (26 km) south of Powell River, this green park features ocean views, marine life, beaches, and campsites. You can swim, snorkel, and dive at Mermaid Cove, where a bronze mermaid rests 60 feet (19 m) beneath the surface.

**Silvertip Adventures,** Box 359, Powell River, B.C. V8A 5C2. (604) 483–4501. Adventure trips led by outdoorsman Brian Baldwin. (If you cancel all other plans and take one of Brian's excursions, you won't go wrong.)

**Raven's Coast Expeditions.** Guided Alpine hikes and other excursions. Rob Higgin, (604) 483–2149.

# Special Events

**July.** Sea Cavalcade, Gibsons. Salmon barbecues, parades, dances, log burling, boat races, long-distance swims.

**Early July (biannual, in even-numbered years).** Kathaumixw, Powell River. Week-long choral festival with choirs from around the world.

**Late July.** Sea Fair, Powell River. Parade, ethnic foods, pancake breakfast, outdoor music, folk dancing, Indian dancers, canoe jousting, navy ship tours.

**Mid-August.** Blackberry Festival, Powell River. Week-long celebration honoring the ubiquitous blackberry: baking contest, wine tastings, desserts, pancake feeds.

**August.** Festival of the Written Arts, Sechelt. Nationally renowned three-day gathering of authors, booksellers, journalists. Centered in Rockwood Lodge, restored heritage building with open-air pavilion.

**Early September (Labor Day weekend).** Sunshine Folk Festival, Powell River. Arts and crafts and music on outdoor stage.

# Other Recommended Restaurants and Lodgings

## Gibsons

Mariners Restaurant, Marine Drive. (604) 886–2334. Seafood, European-style cuisine, homemade desserts. Wide windows, stunning views. A local favorite. (Open daily.)

Bonniebrook Lodge, RR 4, S10 C34. (604) 886–2887. Former boarding lodge 3 miles (5 km) north of Gibsons, on Gower Point. Newly restored as small inn and fine restaurant, Chez Phillipe. French cuisine with West Coast influences.

Cedars Inn, Highway 101. (604) 886–3008. Modern motel near shopping center, forty-five rooms, outdoor pool, sauna, meeting rooms.

## Half Moon Bay

Jolly Roger Inn, RR 1, P.O. Box 7. (604) 885–7184. Fully equipped townhouses; kitchen, fireplace, television. Heated pool, views of beautiful little cove.

## Madeira Park

Lowe's Resort, Box 153. (604) 883–2456. Housekeeping cottages with one to three bedrooms, on cove of Pender Harbour.

## Powell River

Beacon B&B, 3750 Marine Avenue. (604) 485–5563. Centrally located across highway from beach. Four rooms, private baths, hot tub. Full breakfast.

McMaster's, 4448 Marine Avenue. (604) 485–9151. Pub-style restaurant with seafood specials. Overlooks the Westview ferry landing.

Herondell Bed and Breakfast, RR 1, Black Point 29. (604) 587–9528. Country home on forty wooded acres with creek, pond, and river, 8 miles (13 km) south of Powell River. Comfortable rooms, full breakfast.

# For More Information

Tourism Association of Southwestern B.C., Suite 204, 1755 West Broadway, Vancouver, B.C. V6J 455. (604) 739–9011.

Sechelt Chamber of Commerce, Box 360, Sechelt, B.C. V0N 3A0. (604) 885–3100.

Powell River Travel Infocentre, 6807 Wharf Street, Powell River, B.C. V8A 1T9. (604) 485–4051.

BC Ferries, 1112 Fort Street, Victoria, B.C. V8V 4V2. Vancouver (604) 669–1211, Victoria (604) 386–3431.

# Salt Spring Island

Ferries carry passengers daily to the Gulf Islands.

## Idylllic Island Retreat

_____ 2 NIGHTS _____

Scenic ferry rides · Panoramic views · Wooded, seaside park · Hiking
Horseback riding · Art galleries · Boutique shopping · Fine dining

It's the largest, most populated, most visited island in the Strait of Georgia, but Salt Spring retains its rural ambience and woodsy charm. This island is different from the others in many ways, beginning with its early history. Unlike most Gulf Islands, Salt Spring had no native Indian villages, though weddings and other important events were celebrated on its shores. The white shell beaches attest to centuries of shellfish feasting.

The first immigrants, who arrived in 1859, were black slaves from the United States, fleeing persecution. They were joined by pioneers of British, Portuguese, German, Japanese, and Hawaiian descent, the start of a multicultural community. As the island was more settled, agriculture became its mainstay, and then logging. Now, although orchards, dairies, and sheep farms can still be seen, Salt Spring's fame rests upon art and tourism.

Dozens of artists and craftspeople make their homes on the hilly, green island in a blue sea. Tourists come for the outdoor recreation, scenic beauty, and gallery browsing. All three are a part of this three-day visit to an extraordinary corner of Canada.

Avoid the summer crowds by visiting in spring or fall, if possible. The weather is warm, sailing winds are up, and there's far less traffic.

# Day 1

## Morning

In Tsawassen, south of Vancouver, board the ferry bound for the **Gulf Islands.** You're headed for **Long Harbour,** on **Salt Spring,** by way of Galiano, Mayne, and Pender islands. The trip takes about two and a half hours, a journey from mainland bustle into a world of calm beauty as you glide over the Strait of Georgia. The stillness is broken by the cries of gulls and the occasional bellow from the ferry's horn.

Cars, passengers, and bicycles are unloaded and loaded at each stop, until at last the ferry bumps against the splintered, barnacle-encrusted pilings of Long Harbour and you are on Salt Spring.

A ferry route that takes less time and has more daily sailings is from Tsawassen to Swartz Bay, on Vancouver Island; transfer ferries for the ride to **Fulford Harbor,** Salt Spring. (There's no additional charge for a transfer if you request it at Tsawassen.)

When you disembark, if you've taken an afternoon ferry, drive to your lodgings and check in. If you arrive earlier, drive to **Ganges,** a pedestrian-oriented village that is the island's major community. It's a festive place, full of shops and cafes, bobbing boats in the harbor, and an open-air **farmers' market** on Saturdays—all within easy walking distance.

At **The Fat Rascal,** on Fulford-Ganges Road, choose picnic items from the array of deli foods. Then head toward Cranberry Road and Maxwell Road (partially unpaved), which will take you up **Mount Maxwell** for a panoramic view of the island and its surroundings—a pleasant way to get your bearings. From the summit, the outlook encompasses the mountains of Vancouver Island, across Sansum Narrows, and the San Juan archipelago on the south. You'll see a log-sorting operation directly below, in **Burgoyne Bay.**

*Lunch:* Picnic on Mount Maxwell.

## Afternoon

Descend from Mount Maxwell and drive to **Ruckle Provincial Park,** at the far-southeast corner of the island. The park has an interesting history: settled in 1872 by Henry Ruckle, the land was purchased by the province in 1974, but Ruckle's descendants still live on the site. They run a 200-acre farm.

Several historic farm buildings in various states of repair stand in the park. One is the Ruckles' quaint, Victorian home, which can be seen from the road but is not open to the public.

Beyond the homestead is a campground with picnic tables and 6 miles (10 km) of hiking paths that wind through the thick forest of Douglas fir, cedar, maple, and ferns to secluded beaches. Walk the trails and you may see deer, raccoons, quail, and grouse.

A 2-mile (3.2-km) trail along the shore leads from the campground to the Ruckle farmhouse.

From the beach you may spot killer whales (orcas) in **Swanson Channel** and sea lions basking on the rocks. Cormorants, guillemots, and eagles fly above. The tide pools are full of mussels, oysters, crabs, anemones, and starfish.

Return to Ganges and purchase picnic foods for the next day. In Creekside, a complex of shops, you'll find rolls and other baked goods in Barb's Buns, and cheeses, produce, and organically grown foods in Mobile Market. Ganges' new Thrifty Market offers standard groceries.

*Dinner:* **House Piccolo,** 108 Hereford Avenue, Ganges. (604) 537–1844. Wide range of fine continental and Scandinavian cuisine in a small house on a side street. Known for asparagus, prawns, lamb, seafood platter.

*Lodging:* **Weston Lake Inn,** RR 1, 813 Beaver Point Road, Fulford Harbour, B.C. V0S 1C0. Bed-and-breakfast on ten-acre farm with lake views. Country charm, fireside lounge, three rooms with private baths, hot tub. Day sails on 36-foot sailboat available.

# Day 2

## Morning

*Breakfast:* Susan Evans serves a full breakfast at Weston Lake Inn.

Pack a picnic and drive out North End Road, passing the eastern shore of **St. Mary Lake,** to Southey Point Road, at the northern end of Salt Spring. Park your car near Sunset Drive, where you see a driveway blocked by a chain. Across the road there's a public access footpath to the beach.

A walk through the woods will take you to a pretty beach. At low tide, you can stroll the sand for several miles, beachcombing, relaxing, and enjoying the view of Trincomali Channel and Galiano Island.

For another pleasant country hike, park at the intersection of North End Road and Fernwood. Walk Fernwood to North Beach Road and turn north. The road above the shore proffers views of the beach and forests of Galiano, across the water. On the inland side are quaint cabins and large new homes.

Continue to North End Road; follow this road south to make the loop back to your car.

*Lunch:* Picnic on the beach.

## Afternoon

Follow Sunset Drive, the shoreside route to **Vesuvius Bay.** This is a region both pastoral and woodsy, with sheep grazing in open fields, stands of dark green firs, and madrona (arbutus) growing rusty red against the hills. The ferry to Crofton, Vancouver Island, sails from Vesuvius. There's a nice beach near the ferry terminal (though parking is limited). Like most Salt Spring beaches, it's accessible only when the tide is out. Tides reach 12 to 15 feet (4 to 5 m) on the island, and so beaches are often under water at high tide. Consult a tides table, printed in the local newspaper, as you make your plans.

Visit **Gordon Wales Pottery,** on Sunset Drive near Vesuvius, to see and purchase the artist's handiwork.

*Dinner:* **Vesuvius Inn,** at Vesuvius Ferry Dock, Vesuvius Bay. (604) 537-2312. Good Mexican food served in a pub with a convivial atmosphere.

*Lodging:* Weston Lake Inn.

# Day 3

## Morning

*Breakfast:* Weston Lake Inn.

See Salt Spring on horseback this morning, riding the wooded paths of the Mount Maxwell area. Make your arrangements through Salt Spring Trail Rides (604-537-5761). For an enjoyable alternative, arrange with Weston Lake Inn for a sailboat ride.

*Lunch:* **Tides Inn,** 132 Lower Ganges Road. (604) 537-1470. From fish-and-chips and pub-style finger food to entrees such as salmon Wellington with Stilton cheese. One of Ganges' best eateries.

## Afternoon

Close to half the island's 7,000 residents live in Ganges, a popular boating destination. Stroll by the busy harbor, watching the people and boats come and go, and browse through the town's interesting shops.

**Mouat's Mall,** in a 1912-vintage white-and-green frame building, has expanded and is linked by waterfront boardwalk to the renovated Harbour Building. Mouat's shops sell hardware, fashions, foods, toys, jewelry, and more, with the mall's lower floor devoted to thrift shops. Near the mall is Grace Point Square, a retail development and condos on the water.

Pegasus Gallery is one of the many **art galleries** on Salt Spring. Located in Mouat's Mall, it features the jewelry, carvings, and basketry of Northwest coastal Indian artists.

ArtCraft at Mahon Hall showcases the works of more than 200 artists in every imaginable medium: Weavings, paintings, jewelry, and batik work are a few. ArtCraft is open daily from June to September. Ewart Gallery displays fine art that includes oil paintings, watercolors, and sculptures by Canadian artists.

The Tufted Puffin, northeast of Ganges near the Long Harbour ferry terminal, shows David Jackson's wildlife sculptures.

Leave Long Harbour on the ferry in the late afternoon for the ride back to Tsawassen or take the ferry from Fulford Harbour to Swartz Bay, Vancouver Island, which runs much more often. From Swartz Bay you would ride another ferry to return to Tsawassen.

# There's More

**Bicycling.** Rent bicycles and mopeds at Spoke Folk, Gasoline Alley, Ganges. (604) 537–4664. A 62-mile (100-km) route circles the island. Some Salt Spring roads are hilly or graveled; Spoke Folk will give you information. They offer weekend guided bike tours.

**Fishing.** The island's lakes are stocked with trout and bass.

**Kayaking.** Rentals available at Salt Spring Kayaking, Fulford Harbour, and Sea Otter Kayaking, Ganges. Numerous small harbors and 77 miles (124 km) of shoreline offer interesting kayak ventures, such as this one:

Fulford Harbour to Musgrave Landing, an 18-mile (29-km) trip. Put in at the dock by the ferry terminal, and paddle down the bay and around Isabella Point. Pass Cape Keppel and continue northwest toward Musgrave Point and the little cove behind it. Fish for salmon, watch for seals and orca whales, and bask in tranquility.

**Hiking.** The Visitor InfoCentre has information on dozens of hiking trails. An easy walk is Beaver Point Park trail, starting next to the community center on Beaver Point Road. Old-growth forest, a rolling landscape, birds, and a pretty pond are among its attractions.

# Special Events

**Late May.** Sheep to Shawl, Ganges. Exhibition of wool process: sheep shearing, wool washing, spinning, dyeing.

**Mid-June.** Sea Capers, Ganges. Parade, clowns, dance, pancake breakfast, log jousting, sand-castle contest, sailboat race, tug-of-war, food stands, children's games, treasure hunt.

**July.** Festival of the Arts, Ganges. Month-long celebration of the performing arts. Dance and theater productions.

# Other Recommended Restaurants and Lodgings

## Ganges

Beach House Bed-and-Breakfast, Box 472. (604) 537–2879. Two units, consisting of a main house guest room and a private cottage on a cove on Samson Narrows. Three acres of gardens, 400 feet of waterfront, charter boat available for salmon fishing. Full breakfast, afternoon tea.

Hastings House, 160 Upper Ganges Road, P.O. Box 1110. (604) 537–2362 or (800) 661–9255. Expensive luxury and charm on a twenty-acre farm estate above Ganges Harbour. Twelve suites in several buildings, English country atmosphere, restaurant, superb service.

The Old Farmhouse, 1077 Northend Road, Ganges. (604) 537–4113. Restored, century-old farmhouse on three country acres. Idyllic setting, four rooms, full breakfast.

# For More Information

Salt Spring Island Tourist Information, Box 111, Ganges, B.C. V0S 1E0. (604) 537–5252.

BC Ferries, 1112 Fort Street, Victoria, B.C. V8V 4V2. Vancouver (604) 669–1211, Victoria (604) 386–3431.

# Whistler

Whistler Village is British Columbia's most popular ski resort.

## From Sea to Sky

_____ 2 NIGHTS _____

Wilderness scenery • Howe Sound • Ice-carved fjords
Rugged mountain peaks • Alpine meadows • Ski slopes • Boating, fishing
Hiking, bicycling • Waterfalls • River rafting

Canadians call the road that rises dramatically from British Columbia's coastal shore to inland peaks the Sea-to-Sky Highway. More prosaically known as Highway 99, it winds through forested hills and past immense granite blocks that resemble the California Sierras on its way from Vancouver to the resort village of Whistler. The cliff-clinging road is sometimes narrow and steep but is well maintained and kept clear in winter.

A nonstop drive takes about ninety minutes, but there are several worthwhile stops along the way.

# Day 1

## Morning

Travel north from Vancouver past Horseshoe Bay on Highway 99 as it edges Queen Charlotte Channel and then **Howe Sound.** The deep, blue-green waters of the sound, a fjord extending deep into the British Columbia mainland, reflect the astounding beauty around them—wooded islands, rugged cliffs, and snow-topped mountains.

On the drive you'll pass **Porteau Cove Provincial Park.** Right on the shore of the sound, this marine park is known for its scuba-diving facilities and waterfront campground.

At **Britannia Beach,** 30 miles (48 km) north of Vancouver, stop for a guided tour of the **B.C. Museum of Mining** (open daily; 604–688–8735). The largest producing copper mine in the British Empire was located here. In addition to tours, the museum has working displays, a rock and mineral collection, and a gift shop. You can even try your luck at panning for gold; equipment is supplied.

When you reach the north end of Howe Sound, you'll see **Shannon Falls Provincial Park.** This grassy, tree-shaded park has nice picnicking areas and a replica of an 1820 sawmill waterwheel on display. Be sure to walk the path, boardwalk, and stairs leading to the waterfall. In sensational cascades, Shannon Falls drops more than 1,000 feet down a rocky cliff.

**Squamish,** 40 miles (64 km) from Vancouver, is a town of 10,500 people and a deep-water port that was settled in 1888. Its name means "mother of the wind" in Salish. Rock climbers come to Squamish for the challenge of **Stawamus Chief,** an imposing piece of granite that is the second-largest monolith in the world. Sight-seers like the **charter flights** that provide close-up views of glaciers. And sailboarders come for the winds that make Howe Sound known as "Gorge North." (The Columbia River Gorge, between Washington and Oregon, is reputed to have the best sailboarding conditions in the world.)

Leaving Squamish and Howe Sound, the next stop on this scenic route is **Garibaldi Provincial Park,** a stretch of virgin wilderness with clear lakes, alpine meadows, glaciers, and twisted lava formations. Lava flows and extinct cinder cones are reminders of the powerful forces that created the Coast Range 15,000 years ago. The famous Black Tusk, thrusting 7,598 feet (2,330 m) skyward, is an example of the unsual geography of the area. Garibaldi is webbed with hiking trails and is popular with cross-country skiers in winter.

The **Diamond Head** area, often blanketed in 16 feet of snow, has trails for experienced Nordic skiers.

Continue on to **Brandywine Falls** parking area. From here a ¼-mile path through the trees will lead you to an observation point. Brandywine Falls drops an impressive 211 feet (65 m), crashing into an immense volcanic bowl.

Everyone who returns to **Whistler Village** after being away for even a short time is amazed at its growth. Since 1980, when the resort community opened, explosive development has taken place. There are more than 2,700 hotel rooms, with more to come, but the European-style pedestrian village retains its intimate, relaxed atmosphere.

Whistler, 75 miles (120 km) from Vancouver, lies at the foot of America's two largest ski mountains, **Whistler** and **Blackcomb.** It has become Canada's busiest winter tourist destination, with 1.3 million skier visits annually. On Blackcomb, you can ski in the summer, as well.

*Lunch:* If you didn't picnic along the way, try **Original Ristorante,** in the Brandywine Building at the base of Whistler lifts. The Italian cafe serves pizza and pasta in a congenial atmosphere. (604) 932–6408.

## Afternoon

If you're a skier, winter or summer there's no question as to how you'll spend the rest of your time in Whistler. The numerous lifts rising to scores of ski runs are beckoning, and you'll be happily occupied.

If it's summer, and you're not skiing, take the **express gondola** up Whistler Mountain, rising almost 4,000 feet (1,157 m). Tickets are available at Carleton Lodge Sports and McConkey Sport Shop. At the top, in an exhilarating alpine setting, walk the gentle trails and admire dazzling views of the snowcapped mountains, blue lakes, wildflowers, and forests. You might observe wildlife.

Later, descend for a game of golf at **Whistler Golf Club.** The 18-hole, Arnold Palmer course, a three-minute walk from the village, offers both golfing challenge and scenic splendor. (604) 932–4222. Or play the 18-hole Chateau Whistler Golf Course. (604) 938–8000.

If golfing's not your pleasure, try an hour's horseback ride on wilderness trails. **Layton Bryson Outfitting and Trail Rides** is glad to oblige with horses and guides. (604) 932–6623.

Other recreational choices include hiking, tennis, sailboarding, canoeing on Alta Lake (the lake's water is warm enough for swimming, and there are three public beaches), or simply relaxing at your hotel.

*Dinner:* **Chez Joel,** on the village square. (604) 932–2112. Warm, rustic atmosphere and excellent French cooking. Specializes in fondues and French alpine cuisine. Lobster and crab tank, Sunday-afternoon raclette, après-ski bar.

*Lodging:* **Chateau Whistler Resort,** 4599 Chateau Boulevard, Whistler, B.C. V0N 1B0. (604) 938–8000; in Canada, (800) 268–9420; in the United States, (800) 828–7447. Deluxe ch_teau-style resort hotel close to the high-speed lifts of Blackcomb Mountain. Restaurants, bar, health club, 343 guest rooms.

# Day 2

## Morning

*Breakfast:* **The Wildflower Cafe,** Chateau Whistler. Buffet breakfast, not included in hotel room rate.

At 9:00 A.M. your two-hour **white-water rafting** trip begins. The safe, exciting ride runs the roaring rapids of the **Green River,** a seven-minute drive from the village. For reservations, contact a guide company such as **Whistler River Adventures,** Box 202, Whistler, B.C. V0N 1B0 (604) 932–3532. (Longer trips are available.)

Back in the village, stop at **Hatto's Corner Deli** for a picnic basket. Call ahead, and it will be waiting for you (604–932–8345).

Pick up a trail guide at the Whistler Activity and Information Centre, located at the front entrance of the Conference Centre, and hike to **Lost Lake,** a short, easy walk. A large wooden map near the municipal hall points out all the Lost Lake trails. The **Valley Trail network,** running through the entire Whistler Valley to Green Lake, is paved and provides another easy, scenic walk.

If you'd like something more challenging, in higher country, take the gondola up Blackcomb or Whistler and hike to an alpine lake for lunch.

*Lunch:* Picnic at Lost Lake or other lakeshore.

## Afternoon

After your mountain hike, return to the hotel for a swim in the indoor or outdoor pool, a relaxing sauna, and a massage to ease the muscles.

An aperitif in the château's **Mallard Bar** provides the perfect capper to the afternoon. The bar is a tranquil hideaway, with its estate-library atmosphere and wildlife theme. Canadian folk artists were commissioned to create colorful, three-dimensional works with a bird motif.

*Dinner:* **Rim Rock Cafe and Oyster Bar,** Highway 99, Whistler. (604) 932–5565. Outstanding seafood and a fine wine list in a lively, candlelighted restaurant 3 miles (5 km) south of the village. Sunday-night jazz until midnight.

Top off the evening with a decadent dessert by the fireside at

**Planters Lounge,** in Listel Whistler Hotel. (604) 932–1133.
*Lodging:* Chateau Whistler Resort.

# Day 3

## Morning

*Breakfast:* The Wildflower Cafe or, for a change, **Myrtle's,** in the Timberline Hotel.

After breakfast take your choice from Whistler's extensive recreation menu. You can rent a canoe or rowboat and go boating on Alta Lake or learn to sailboard from Whistler Outdoor Experience Company (604-932-3389).

You might prefer instead to rent a mountain bike (available in several village shops) and explore backcountry roads or marked forest trails. Or take your bike in the gondola up Whistler and bounce and skid all the way down (this is part of a tour package; for information call 604-932-3434). You can also bike on the Valley Trail Network.

*Lunch:* **Twigs Restaurant,** Delta Mountain Inn. (604) 877–1133. Continental menu, buffet on weekends, Sunday brunch.

## Afternoon

Return from sky to sea on Highway 99. If you missed Garibaldi Provincial Park or Brandywine or Shannon falls, this is your chance to see them and perhaps take a last walk in the woods before driving on to Vancouver.

# There's More

**Whistler activities.** Flight-see, heli-hike. Explore meadows and peaks around Rainbow Mountain. Paraglide off Blackcomb Mountain. Skateboard in the village's skateboard bowls. Hike to Cheakamus Lake to see giant fir trees (an easy hike, but you have to drive a bumpy logging road to get to the trailhead).

**Royal Hudson.** Take a steam-train ride up Howe Sound to Squamish. Coach tours continue from Squamish over Cheakamus Canyon to Whistler. Return on a different route to North Vancouver. (604) 683–0209.

**Guided bike tours.** Whistler Backroads Mountain Bike Adventures offers custom-tailored day trips into the backcountry. (604) 932–3111.

**Ski lessons.** Instruction for all ages and experience levels, available all year. Ask at your hotel or the visitors' center for information.

**Lillooet Express**. Day-long train trip to gold-rush country. Includes lunch, gold panning, sight-seeing. Phone Sea to Sky Tours and Cruises at (604) 984–2224.

# Special Events

**March.** World Cup Downhill, Whistler.

**April.** Saudan Couloir Ski Race Extreme. Ski competition on Blackcomb.

**June.** Great Snow, Earth, and Water Race, Whistler.

**July.** Squamish Open Golf Tournament.

**Mid-July.** Whistler Country and Blues Festival.

**Late July.** Squamish Days Logging Show, Squamish. Clowns, ax-throwing, log rolling, tree climbing, Timber Queen Pageant, Truck Loggers Rodeo, music, bicycle race, pancake breakfast, parade, and Loggers Stomp Dance.

**August.** VSO on Whistler Mountain. Vancouver Symphony Orchestra performs on the mountain.

**Mid-September.** Whistler Fall for Jazz Festival.

# Other Recommended Restaurants and Lodgings

## Whistler

Il Camineto di Umberto. (604) 932–4442. Exceptional Italian food, plus seafood, duck, and reindeer. Festive atmosphere in the heart of the village.

Le Deux Gros, Twin Lakes Village, south of Whistler Creek. (604) 932–4611. Top-quality French fare.

Val d'Isere. (604) 932–2112. Memorable French meals.

Wainwright's, in Nancy Greene's Lodge. (604) 932–2221. Pleasant, airy restaurant, serving Canadian cuisine.

Chalet Luise, Box 352. (604) 932–4187. Chalet-style bed-and-breakfast outside village. Austrian theme.

Delta Mountain Inn, 4050 Whistler Way, Box 550. (604) 932–1982 or (800) 877–1133. One of the largest village hotels. Swimming pool, whirlpool tubs, tennis courts, exercise room, restaurant, fireplace lounge, ski rentals, underground parking. Adjacent to Whistler Mountain lifts.

Durlacher Hof, Box 1125. (604) 932–1924. Hospitable bed-and-breakfast outside village. Light, tasteful Austrian country decor. Bountiful breakfast.

Haus Heidi, Box 354. (604) 932–3113. Bed-and-breakfast with four rooms. Alpine motif, two tower rooms, sauna, full breakfast.

Hearthstone Lodge, P.O. Box 747. (604) 932–6699; in British Columbia and the United States (800) 663–7711. On village square, suites with kitchens, fireplaces. Condos sleep up to ten.

## For More Information

Squamish Chamber of Commerce, P.O. Box 1009, Squamish, B.C. V0N 3G0. (604) 892–9244.

Whistler Central Reservations: in Vancouver, 685–3650; toll-free in the United States and Canada, (800) WHISTLER.

Whistler Activity and Information Centre, Whistler Convention Centre, Whistler, B.C. V0N 1B4. (604) 932–2394.

# The Okanagan

The restored Okanagan Post Office and General Store at O'Keefe Ranch.

## Peach Blossoms and Wine

———————————— 3 NIGHTS ————————————

Sunshine · Orchards · Lakes · Wineries
Museums · Stern-wheeler cruise · Luxury resorts

British Columbia's Okanagan country, rich in fertile valleys, clear lakes, and frontier history, has one more enviable attraction: sunshine. People say there are more sunny days in this region than in any other part of Canada. Penticton proudly proclaims that while Tahiti receives 453 hours of sunshine in July and August, and Bermuda basks under 584 hours, the southern Okanagan Valley gets 598.

Thus it's not surprising that fruit orchards and vineyards flourish and oudoor recreation is a way of life in the Okanagan-Similkameen. Much of the area focuses on the water, for Lake Okanagan stretches up the valley for 80 miles (128 km), and there are dozens more lakes and streams nearby. Three major ski areas draw thousands to the dry powder that falls east of the British Columbia Cascades.

Bicycling, boating, fishing, and sports events make the Okanagan an active vacationer's dream. This four-day itinerary adds other points of interest—such as museum tours, wine tastings, and a tour through ranching country—to the recreational fun.

# Day 1

## Morning

Pack a picnic lunch and drive Trans-Canada Highway 1 east from Vancouver to Hope, 90 miles (144 km). Turn south on Route 3 to **Manning Provincial Park.**

Manning is a vast, green playground for nature lovers. There are boat launches, campsites, hiking trails, calm mountain lakes, wildlife, and wildflowers. Hike into Alpine Meadows in summer, and you'll walk among carpets of colorful blooms.

*Lunch:* Picnic in Manning Park.

## Afternoon

Continue north on Route 3, along the Similkameen River, to Princeton, where the road turns south toward **Keremeos.** Stop here for a look at the **Old Grist Mill,** on Upper Bench Road (604-499-2888). Built in 1877 and still operating, it's one of the best-preserved water-powered mills in Canada. Take a tea break in the mill's restaurant, and then turn northeast on Route 3A.

You're in the heart of the **Okanagan,** where volcanic mountain ranges shelter a series of valleys, creating a unique microclimate. It ranges from arid desert in the south to a dry and mild environment in the north.

When you reach **Penticton,** on the southern edge of **Lake Okanagan,** check in at **The Coast Lakeside Resort at Penticon.**

Stretch your legs with a shoreside stroll to the **Rose Garden**, where a miniature golf course full of castles and windmills may tempt you into a game; or take a cruise on the *Casabella Princess.* The fifty-passenger stern-wheeler, which began service in Penticton in 1986, sails daily from the beach at the Coast Lakeside Resort. Penticton has another stern-wheeler, the *SS Sicamous,* built in 1914, that plied the lake's waters for three decades. Now it rests on dry land, as a museum with displays showing the history of paddlewheelers on the lake.

*Dinner:* **Theo's,** 687 Main Street. (604) 492-4019. Greek food in

Mediterranean atmosphere. Tables in courtyard with hanging bougainvillea and indoors under open beams and copper pots.

*Lodging:* The Coast Lakeside Resort at Penticton, 21 Lakeshore Drive West, Penticton, B.C. V2A 7M5. (604) 493–8221 or (800) 663–9400. Full-service resort at water's edge. Swimming pool, tennis courts, fitness center, sandy beach, restaurants, 204 guest rooms.

# Day 2

## Morning

*Breakfast:* **Peaches and Cream,** Coast Lakeside Resort. A cafe off the open, airy white lobby, with lake view.

Drive north on Route 97 along the western shore of Okanagan Lake. On your left are high, eroded cliffs and pillars, while the ground slopes to the blue lake on the right. Small parks dot points of land beside the water. At the sign pointing to the **Summerland Research Station,** turn left and ascend the hill, through vineyards and fruit trees, to the agricultural center, where new varieties of grapes and other fruits are developed. There's a lovely garden here, with flowers identified, and a picnic area.

Continue north on 97 to **Peachland** and **Westbank** and watch for the signs to **Okanagan Butterfly World.** This outstanding exhibit, which has a coffee shop and wheelchair access, is well worth a stop. In exotic botanical gardens, hundreds of butterflies flutter. One species has a wingspan of 7 feet. There are streams, birds, and a butterfly breeding area.

From here cross the bridge to **Kelowna,** a town on the east side of Okanagan Lake. Since this is orchard country, where most of British Columbia's apples, peaches, apricots, grapes, and cherries are grown, this is the place to see a working orchard and vineyard.

Drive out KLO Road to Dunster Road and **Appleberry Farm,** 3193 Dunster Road. (604) 868–3814. On this working farm, which has a restaurant and gift shop set in a small orchard, tours show visitors how orchards are run.

*Lunch:* **McCullough Station,** on KLO Road. (604) 762–8882. The pub/cafe, built to resemble an old-time railway station, is adorned with historic photos of the Kettle Valley Railway. You can sit outside in the orchard or indoors by the fireplace.

## Afternoon

Another tour, this time exploring the wine industry, is next on the agenda. Head for **Calona Wines,** 1125 Richter Street (604–762–3332).

Calona, established in 1932, is the oldest and largest commercial winery in the Okanagan.

With a unique microclimate and soil of volcanic ash and clay loam, vineyards flourish in the region. Calona, known for its riesling, gewürztraminer, and chardonnay wines, has garnered more than 145 medals in international competitions over the past ten years. It's noted for blended table wines, especially the popular Schloss Laderheim, a crisp white wine introduced in the mid-1970s. The winery offers tours, tastings, and souvenirs daily in summer and weekdays in winter.

In downtown Kelowna, at the foot of Bernard Avenue, you'll find lakeside symbols illustrating the Okanagan spirit: a soaring sculpture, *Sails,* by Dow Reid; an old-fashioned paddle wheeler, the *M.V. Fintry Queen;* an inviting green park with a public beach; and a whimsical statue of *Ogopogo,* Okanagan Lake's legendary sea serpent. The *Fintry Queen* offers lunch and dinner cruises daily. Beyond this is **Kelowna Waterfront Park,** with lagoons and walkways, adjoining the Grand Okanagan Resort, a large resort complex.

Purchase gifts and boutique items in Kelowna's quaint shops (with names like Teddy Bear Crossing and Scalliwag's) on **Tutt Street.** You might take tea here, in The Gathering Room.

Turn east at this point to Benvoulin Road, where the **Pioneer Country Market and Museum** is located. The old-fashioned market stands where fields of onions once grew, planted by the pioneering Casorso family. The Casorsos grew produce and tobacco and ranched cattle, sheep, and hogs. John Casorso's great-granddaughter now operates the remarkable store, displaying antiques and heritage photos, as well as a wide variety of preserves and country crafts. It's a good place to buy locally made gifts and souvenirs.

Nearby, also on Benvoulin Road, is the **Father Pandosy Mission.** Father Charles Pandosy was the first white man in the valley. He set up a mission in 1860 and began Okanagan's fruit industry by planting the first apple tree. The home, church, schoolhouse, and blacksmith shop on the carefully maintained heritage site are open for tours. (604) 860-8369.

*Dinner:* **Hotel Eldorado.** Lakeside dining in a light, upbeat atmosphere. Emphasis on seafood prepared with imagination (prawns with fresh papaya, three seafood mousses baked in puff pastry, salmon with saffron). Fresh seafood menu daily. Homemade *gelatos* and tempting pastries.

*Lodging:* Hotel Eldorado, 500 Cook Road, Kelowna, B.C. V1Y 4V4. (604) 763-7500. Small, elegant country inn with twenty rooms, most with views of Okanagan Lake. Antiques, Jacuzzi tubs, original art, live music in the lounge, and an art deco flavor.

# Day 3

## Morning

*Breakfast:* In the Hotel Eldorado sun room. Try the toasted brioche with fresh fruit and syrup.

Drive north beside several small lakes for 28 miles (45 km) to Vernon. You'll leave sagebrush-covered ridges to climb green, rolling hills, finally descending to a lush valley with mountains rising in the distance.

**Vernon** is a small, rural town with lakes on all sides. Okanagan, Kalamalka, and Swan lakes all have beaches and parks and offer good boating, fishing, waterskiing, and swimming.

Seven miles (11 km) north of town, on Highway 97, is **O'Keefe Ranch,** a significant piece of Okanagan history. On the sixty-two-acre site are ten buildings dating from the late 1800s. Each brings the past to life, through outstanding displays, demonstrations, and exhibits.

The General Store holds an array of merchandise from yesteryear: high-button shoes, harnesses, butter churns, bolts of calico. In the blacksmith shop, the big bellows keeps a fire blazing while the blacksmith forges tools (some are for sale in the ranch's gift shop). St. Anne's, a simple wooden church, was the first Catholic church in the Okanagan. Its first service was held in 1889.

The O'Keefe mansion illustrates the opulence of ranch life at the turn of the century, in contrast to the humble log house that was the first home of Cornelius and Mary Ann O'Keefe. The ranch the O'Keefes founded was run by the family until the 1960s.

Leaving Vernon and Okanagan Lake, drive north toward **Armstrong,** a Spallumcheen Valley town known for its cheese production, and **Enderby,** which lies in the shadow of the highest cliffs in the Okanagan. You're traveling through a peaceful, pastoral land, about to turn toward the dry hills of ranch country.

Past Enderby, take Route 97B to Highway 1 and turn west toward **Salmon Arm.** This attractive small town lies at the southern end of one of **Shuswap Lake's** many arms. Just before reaching Salmon Arm you'll see the sign to the **R. J. Haney Heritage House and Park.** Stop here for a tour of the eighty-year-old farmhouse, which stands on forty acres of pastoral beauty. The wooded park has walking paths, bridges, benches, and picnic tables. In addition to the house, other heritage buildings have been brought to the park and are now being restored to create an authentic replica of a nineteenth-century pioneer village.

Continue on to Salmon Arm.

*Lunch:* **The Eatery,** 361 Alexander, Salmon Arm. (604) 832–7490. Take a sidewalk table, fenced by petunia-topped lattices, and watch the strollers go by as you enjoy lunch at this casual spot. Good soups and sandwiches.

## Afternoon

Walk through Salmon Arm's compact, revitalized downtown area, where hanging flower baskets, colorful awnings, and ornamental street lighting create a pleasant shopping area. There are more than eighty stores within a few blocks' radius.

**Waterfront Park** is the village's marine park, wharf, and float-plane base. Its Promenade Pier, at 990 feet (300 m), is one of the longest freshwater piers in Canada and is a good spot for bird-watching. Rental houseboats are moored here, and the *Phoebe Ann,* a classic stern-wheeler, leaves the marina twice a day on Tuesdays and Saturdays to cruise Salmon Arm Bay.

The highway from Salmon Arm twists north and then southwest, occasionally touching the shore of Shuswap Lake and then following the **Thompson River.** You're headed for **Kamloops,** a major recreational center in British Columbia's sunny interior.

Alternatively, if you wish to make this a shorter trip, take Route 97 west after you leave Vernon. The 48-mile (78-km) drive will lead you to Monte Cristo; from there it's 16 miles (26 km) west to Kamloops.

Cool off in **Riverside Park,** a stretch of greenery along the Thompson River near downtown Kamloops. The park has an outdoor pool, a lawn bowling green, several tennis courts, playground equipment, and a long, sandy beach with lifeguard supervision. There are an old steam locomotive on display and a Japanese garden honoring Kamloops's sister city, Uji, Japan.

Back when water transport was used to reach British Columbia's mountainous interior, there were more steam-driven paddle wheelers on its lakes and rivers than anywhere else in the world, including the Mississippi River. Those days are long gone, but Kamloops has a boat that evokes nostalgic memories. The *Wanda-Sue* is a one-hundred-passenger stern-wheeler, hand built by a local retiree in his backyard several years ago. Two-hour cruises now travel the scenic waters of the Thompson rivers (604–374–7447 or 374–1505).

Take Route 5A south from Kamloops, through a long stretch of rugged, mountainous terrain, to **Quilchena,** on the shore of Nicola Lake.

*Dinner:* **Quilchena Hotel.** Hearty ranch food in a quaint country inn.

*Lodging:* Quilchena Hotel, Quilchena, B.C. V0E 2R0. (604) 378–2611. Hotel built in 1906 on a 66,000-acre cattle ranch. Fourteen rooms share two baths. Victorian parlor, restaurant, peaceful setting. Fishing, sailing, horseback riding, and golf available.

# Day 4

## Morning

*Breakfast:* Quilchena Hotel restaurant.

Join the Coquihalla Highway at **Merritt,** and drive south. It's 72 fast miles (120 km) from Merritt to Hope, with one stop at the toll plaza (the current toll is $10). The freeway drive is both speedy and scenic, with craggy peaks rising high above the forested ridges on either side of the road. Waterfalls stream down steep, rocky ravines, while snow-fields glisten on the mountainsides.

When you reach **Hope,** cross the **Fraser River** to Highway 7, bound for **Harrison Hot Springs.** Many visitors are surprised to learn that **Harrison Lake** is the largest lake in southwestern British Columbia. It offers hiking trails, boat cruises, helicopter touring, fishing, and bird-watching, as well as the famous hot springs.

*Lunch:* **The Black Forest Restaurant,** 180 Esplanade Avenue, Harrison Hot Springs. (604) 796-9343. Bavarian chalet facing Harrison Lake. Steaks, schnitzels, German specialties. Lunch served in summer; dinner served year-round.

## Afternoon

Stroll the esplanade in the landscaped park bordering the lake shore. It's an easy, 1-mile walk from Harrison Hot Springs Hotel to the boat launch and lagoon. Going the other direction, toward the west end of the lake, you can walk along the dike and trail that leads to Whippoorwill Point and see the hot springs bubbling up from their source. Two springs emerge from the mountain base, each with a different temperature and chemical content. You can bathe in the mineral water in an indoor pool in the center of the village; it's open to the public for a fee.

After a relaxing soak in the pool, make the return trip to Vancouver. From Harrison Hot Springs, it's a ninety-minute drive.

# There's More

**Red Bridge,** Keremeos. This 1911-era covered bridge was left from the days of the Great Northern Railway. Mountain goats are sometimes seen nearby.

**Okanagan Game Farm,** Penticton. (604) 497-5405. Open daily, 8:00 A.M. to dusk. Exotic animals roam 560 acres of land above Skaha Lake, 5 miles (8 km) south of Penticton.

**Wineries.** Cedar Creek Estate Winery, 9 miles (15 km) south of

Kelowna. (604) 764–8866. Landscaped grounds overlooking Okanagan Lake. Tastings daily, tours in summer.

Gray Monk Cellars, Okanagan Centre (between Kelowna and Vernon, off Highway 97 in Winfield). (604) 766–3168. Tours and tastings daily.

Lang Vineyards, Naramata (north of Penticton). (604) 496–5987. British Columbia's first farm winery, with wines produced from grapes grown on-site. Small winery with limited acreage and production. Open for tastings and sales on afternoons, except Sunday and Thursday.

Mission Hill Vineyards, south of Kelowna in Westbank. (604) 768–5125. Daily tours and tastings.

Sumac Ridge Estate Winery and Golf Course, Summerland. (604) 494–0451. Tours, tastings, and golf daily in summer.

**Kettle Valley Railway.** Hike and cycle on the old railway; rails and ties have been removed between McCullough Lake Resort to Myra Canyon at Kelowna, and through to Penticton. There are fine views from sixteen trestles, all safe to cross.

**The Lloyd Gallery,** 598 Main Street, Penticton. (604) 492–4484. Centrally located art gallery with more than 2,000 square feet of exhibition space. Works by noted Canadian sculptors and painters.

**Munson Mountain,** Penticton. Drive up the mountain on the edge of town, and walk the last few yards to the summit for a view of the long lake. It's touted as the "$100 view" because the scene was once depicted on the $100 bill.

**B.C. Orchard Industry Museum,** Ellis Street, Kelowna. One hundred-year history of fruit industry in the valley.

**Kalamalka Lookout,** south of Vernon. Hike or bicycle to the lookout for a striking view of Kalamalka, the "Lake of Many Colours," which shimmers in brilliant hues of green and blue.

**The Galloping Goose Gift Gallery,** 3316 Thirtieth Avenue, Vernon. (604) 545–7606. Named for an early-day passenger train, the gallery showcases pottery, porcelain, weavings, raku, stained glass, painted silk, and other works by local artists and craftspeople.

**Davison Orchards,** west of Vernon off Bella Vista Road. (604) 542–7840. Family farm market selling numerous apple varieties and other produce. Orchard tours available.

**Fishing.** Hundreds of lakes in the Okanagan and Shuswap regions offer good fishing for kokanee, Dolly Varden, and the world-famed Kamloops rainbow trout. Ask at Visitors InfoCentres for local information.

**Golf.** Gallagher's Canyon Golf Resort, Kelowna. (604) 861–4240. Eighteen-hole course under ponderosa pines, beautiful views.

Predator Ridge Golf Resort, Vernon. (604) 542–9494. Challenging eighteen-hole, world-class course.

Salmon Arm Golf Course, Salmon Arm. (604) 832–4727. Eighteen-hole, championship course in Shuswap Lake country.

Aberdeen Hills Golf Club, Kamloops. (604) 828–1149. Challenging eighteen-hole course. Hillside views of Kamloops and the river valley.

**Skiing.** Apex, Penticton (forty minutes' drive from town). (604) 493–3200. Hilly course for the intermediate and advanced skier. Four lifts, thirty-six runs. Condo rentals available.

Big White, Kelowna (forty minutes' drive). (604) 765–8888; in western Canada, (800) 663–2772. Highest ski resort in British Columbia. Warm temperatures, dry powder snow on 7,606-foot (2,319-m) mountain. Forty-five runs, eight lifts (two high-speed quads), 25 kilometers of Nordic trails. Numerous accommodations and restaurants.

Silver Star Mountain, Vernon. (604) 542–0224 or (800) 663–4431. Ideal powder conditions, usually sunny November through April. Resort village in Old West style; ski shop, restaurant, saloon, condo rentals. Seven lifts, thirty-five runs. Summer chair lift to summit, 6,280 feet (1,915 m), for wide view of Monashee Mountain Range.

**The Caravan Farm Theatre,** Armstrong. (604) 546–8533. Unique theater of marionettes, masked musicians, and actors at home and on the road.

**Armstrong Cheese Factory,** Pleasant Valley Road, Armstrong. (604) 546–3087. Watch world-famous cheeses under production. Includes tasting.

**Penticton Museum,** 785 Main Street. (604) 492–6025. Considered to have the largest collection of western Canadiana in the British Columbia interior.

**B.X. Falls,** Vernon. Off Silver Star Road, a gorgeous waterfall and picnic area.

**Kamloops Wildlife Park,** Kamloops. (604) 573–3242. Largest non-profit wildlife park/zoo in British Columbia. Exotic and British Columbia wildlife in natural surroundings, miniature train, picnic areas, concession stand.

**Secwepemc Museum,** Kamloops. Exhibits portraying all aspects of the culture of the Secwepemc Indians (European newcomers abbreviated the name to Shuswap).

# Special Events

**February.** Vernon Winter Carnival, Vernon. Largest festival of its kind in western Canada, with a parade, dances, sleigh rides, ice sculpture, and stock-car races on ice.

**Early July.** Harrison Festival of the Arts, Harrison Hot Springs.

Nine-day event celebrating visual arts, music, theater. Juried craft market, workshops, entertainment.

**Early July.** Rendezvous and Display, O'Keefe Ranch, Vernon. Musket shooting, tomahawk throwing, teepee living, country dancing, rifle show.

**Mid-August.** Penticton Peach Festival. Ten days of music, contests, carnivals, parades, puppet shows, peach feasts.

**Late August.** Ironman, Penticton. Qualifying events for Hawaii Triathlon.

**Mid-September.** World Championship Sand Sculpture Competition, Harrison Hot Springs.

**Early October.** Wine Festival, Okanagan Valley. Twenty-five wineries participate in tastings, special dinners.

**October.** Suds and Cider Festival, Vernon. Bavarian bands, foods, tastings of local ciders and brewery products.

**October.** Salute to the Sockeye, Adams River, Salmon Arm. Honors the salmon's return to spawning grounds. Interpretive signs and tours explain the migration cycle.

# Other Recommended Restaurants and Lodgings

## Kaledan

Ponderosa Point Resort, P.O. Box 106. (604) 497-5354. Twenty-six snug log cottages and A-frames on Skaha Lake. Nicely furnished and immaculately clean. Shaded green lawns, pine trees, peace and quiet.

## Penticton

Country Squire, Naramata (north of Penticton). (604) 496-5416. An experience in fine dining. Leisurely, multicourse meal, with a walk around the scenic grounds between salad and entree. Set in a heritage house on Okanagan Lake's east shore.

Granny Bogner's, 302 Eckhardt Avenue West, Penticton. (604) 493-2711. Half-timbered former private home on landscaped grounds. Fine cuisine.

Munchee's, Courtyard Lane, next door to Theo's on Main Street. (604) 492-5063. B. D. Ellis prepares home-baked goods with flavors from her native Uruguay. She'll make up a picnic basket if you call ahead.

Riordan's, 689 Winnipeg Street. (604) 493-5997. Ivy-covered, brick-and-stucco home of charm, serving lunch and tea Tuesday–Saturday, dinner Friday and Saturday.

## Hatheume Lake

Hatheume Lake Resort, P.O. Box 490, Peachland, B.C. V0H IX0. (604) 767–2642. Open June to October. Log cabins on mountain wilderness lake, famous for fly fishing. All meals provided.

## Kelowna

Earl's on Top, 211 Bernard Avenue. (604) 763–2777. Across the street from the lake and *Fintry Queen* landing. Outstanding food and unique art deco atmosphere, with lots of glass and plants.

Lake Okanagan Resort, P.O. Box 1321, Station A. (604) 769–3511. Full-service lakeside resort offering golf, tennis, boating, horseback riding, dining, 193 rooms.

## Vernon

Castle on the Mountain, S.10, C.12, RR 8. (604) 542–4593. Bed-and-breakfast and art gallery on Silver Star Road. Three guest rooms, use of kitchen, whirlpool tub on outdoor deck, barbecue area, spectacular view of lakes and valley.

Demetre's, 2705 Thirty-second Street. (604) 549–3442. Steakhouse; well-spiced Greek foods.

Intermezzo Restaurant, 3206 Thirty-fourth Avenue. (604) 542–3853. Small place serving excellent Italian entrees. Veal, pasta, chicken, seafood. Take-out available.

Squires Four Public House, Stickle Road (off Highway 97 north of Vernon). (604) 549–2144. Multilevel pub with oak trim and hanging plants. Lunch and dinner daily. Traditional English dishes, daily soup-and-sandwich specials, chicken, pizza.

Windmill House B&B, 5672 Learmouth Road. (604) 549–2804. For the adventurous, a room in a windmill home. Three rooms share one bath; one room with private bath. Country setting, full breakfast.

## Salmon Arm

The Peppermill Deli, 230 Ross Street. (604) 832–4262. A wide variety of deli foods; good stop for picnic makings.

Orchard House, 720 Twenty-second Street NE. (604) 832–3434. Local favorite for steak, seafood, prime rib.

## Harrison Hot Springs

Harrison Hot Springs Hotel. (604) 521–8888; in the Pacific Northwest, (800) 663–2266. Long-established resort hotel on the lakefront, recently expanded. Restaurant, pub, outdoor swimming pool, mineral hot pools, saunas, and steam baths.

The Springs Cafe, 130 Esplanade. (604) 796–2731. Clean, bright, friendly cafe serving breakfast all day, plus homemade soups and sandwiches.

The Swiss Gourmet, 270 Esplanade. (604) 796–9339. Creative Swiss and West Coast cuisine. An international mix: salmon, schnitzel, linguine, Zurich bratwurst.

## For More Information

Okanagan Similkameen Tourism Association, 104–515 Route 97 South, Kelowna, B.C. V1Z 3J2. (604) 769–5959.

Kamloops Travel InfoCentre, 10 Tenth Avenue, Kamloops, B.C. V2C 6J7. (604) 374–3377.

Harrison Hot Springs Chamber of Commerce, P.O. Box 255, Harrison Hot Springs, B.C. V0M 1K0. (604) 796–3425.

# Southeast Vancouver Island

The luxurious rooms at the Aerie overlook Finlayson Arm on Vancouver Island's east coast.

## Native Art and Edwardian Luxury

———————————— 3 NIGHTS ————————————

Ferry rides · Scenic water views · Native art · Intriguing murals
Fine cuisine · Nature trails · World-famous gardens
Country mansions · Luxury lodging

A rich mixture of British Columbia history is clustered around the bays and lakes of Vancouver Island's southeastern shore, in the Duncan/Cowichan region. Here you'll find settlers' farmhouses and rich men's mansions, proud displays of Native art, wooded paths by quiet streams, and clear-cut hillsides that once were forest. This itinerary covers them all. Since the area covered is within a 50-mile radius and distances between stops are short, mileage is only occasionally included.

Bring outdoor clothes and a dress-up outfit; this is a journey of contrasts.

# Day 1

## Morning

Board a morning ferry at Tsawassen, south of Vancouver, headed for Swartz Bay (there are twenty round trips daily in summer). The 24-mile ride takes an hour and thirty-five minutes, with the ferry cruising through the scenic **Strait of Georgia** and among the **Gulf Islands.** In spring and fall you'll see bald eagles and thousands of shore birds, as well as sea lions and possibly orca whales.

From Swartz Bay terminal, head south on Highway 17 and follow the signs to **Brentwood Bay** and **Butterfly World,** located at the intersection of Highway 17A and Keating Cross Road. When you enter the 12,000-square-foot conservatory that houses Butterfly World, you're in an exotic garden far removed from the Northwest. Here hundreds of multicolored butterflies live in tropical greenery. (Open daily 10:00 A.M. to 5:00 P.M. May to October, 10:00 A.M. to 4:00 P.M. other months; admission charged.)

You might choose to see Butterfly World on your return trip, allowing more time to enjoy the nearby **Butchart Gardens.** It takes at least two hours to explore the gardens, fifty acres of plantings carved from a former limestone quarry. This site is a must for any traveler who appreciates floral beauty and imaginative landscaping.

*Lunch:* **The Dining Room,** Butchart Gardens. (604) 652–5256. A charming restaurant, once the home of the estate's owners, serves lunch, afternoon tea, and dinners in summer. Less expensive meals are offered in the casual, plant-filled Blue Poppy Restaurant.

## Afternoon

Catch the Brentwood Bay–Mill Bay ferry that crosses Saanich Inlet. After the twenty-five-minute ride on the little ferry, a contrast to the behemoths that ply the Strait of Georgia, turn north to follow Mill Bay Road, edging to the shore. You'll have views of the water, beaches, and Saanich Peninsula on the east.

When you reach the village of **Mill Bay,** you'll see a shopping complex, Mill Bay Centre, which has several interesting shops. **Asian Imports** sells intricate carvings and puppets from Indonesia, baskets, beaded shoes, and bags. **The Flying Pig** is filled with whimsical gift and kitchen items, cards, and stationery. Mexican and Guatemalan imports, pottery, and watercolors are displayed in **Excellent Framing Gallery and Handcrafts,** while **Third Addition** is a browser's delight, selling toys, linens, gifts, and cards of high quality. The Centre has a sizable grocery market and an ice cream shop, **The Creamery,** where you might settle at an outdoor table for coffee or ice cream and dip into the book you purchased at **Volume One Bookstore.**

From here take Trans-Canada Highway 1 north to Cowichan Bay Road, turning northeast toward the pretty bay where the Cowichan and Koksilah rivers join in marshlands at the northern tip of the inlet. The Cowichan Indians gathered here long before Europeans arrived, clamming and fishing for cod and salmon. Fishing is still a major attraction. **The Maritime Centre,** home of the Cowichan Bay Wooden Boat Society and School, is open for tours. Its cedar buildings, set on a 300-foot pier, have exhibits showing the area's settlement and gradual change from agriculture and fishing to a recreational community.

At the Centre you can watch students build and restore traditional and contemporary wooden boats. The **Marine Ecology Station** offers marine educational programs to schools and groups. (Open daily in summer, weekends other months. 604–746–4955.)

Next to the Centre is a tiny art gallery, **The Red Door,** where pottery and weavings are displayed and sold.

Nearby **Hecate Park,** on the waterfront, has a boat ramp and picnic facilities. Look across the harbor and you'll see Mount Tzouhalem, crouching like a huge stone frog—transformed from a living frog, according to a Cowichan legend.

Past Hecate Park on Cowichan Bay Road is Theik Reserve Footpath, a choice place for flowers and birds. It has picnic tables and is close to a shore bird habitat. You may see otters.

Turning inland on Cowichan Bay Road, you'll see myriad birds in the wetlands near the South Cowichan Lawn Tennis Club. In winter they swarm with trumpeter swans and bald eagles.

Continue north on Cowichan Bay Road to Tzouhalem Road, which winds through the Cowichan Indian Reserve. Notice the old stone church on a hill on your left. It's empty and vandalized now, but retains the quaint look of a stone country church built with care.

At Lakes Road, turn north to check in at **Grove Hall Estate,** where you'll probably arrive in time for tea and appetizers and a walk around the tranquil lakefront grounds.

On your way to dinner, stop at **Art Kinsman Park** on Quamichan Lake to see the flocks of swans, ducks, and Canada geese. The park has a grassy area, playground and boat launch.

*Dinner:* **Quamichan Inn,** 1478 Maple Bay Road. (604) 746–7028. Tudor-style restaurant on the east side of Quamichan Lake, noted for its continental cuisine in a linens-and-candlelight atmosphere.

*Lodging:* Grove Hall Estate, 6159 Lakes Road, Duncan, B.C. V9L 4J6. (604) 746–6152. Stately, half-timbered manor house on seventeen scenic acres. Three spacious rooms furnished with Oriental art and antiques.

# Day 2

## Morning

*Breakfast:* Grove Hall serves a full English breakfast in the dining room overlooking the lawn and lake.

Just north of Duncan on Highway 1 is the **Somenos Marsh Wildlife Refuge.** Here you'll see herons, ducks, geese, and other waterfowl in the fall, winter, and spring. There are observation points along the road and more under development.

Continue north and stop at the **British Columbia Forest Museum,** where one hundred acres are dedicated to the history of forestry and logging. You can ride an authentic steam train once used on a logging operation and watch demonstrations of logging skills along the way. (604–746–1251, open May to September.)

Continue north on Highway 1, turning east on 1A to reach the village of **Chemaninus.** The "Little Town That Did" is a mile off the main highway and well worth a detour. Thirty-two scenes of the area's history, painted by Canadian, European, and American artists, cover the walls of Chemainus's buildings. In the early 1980s the townsfolk decided to rescue their dying economy by embarking on a program that would attract tourists. They chose historical murals.

Their plan worked. Visitors now flock there to follow the painted yellow footsteps, which guide you past the murals to busy art galleries, quaint gift shops, and ice cream parlors. See **Waterwheel Park,** the **Chemainus Valley Museum,** century-old **St. Michael & All Angels Church** (open to tourists 1:00 to 4:00 P.M. Wednesday, Friday, and Saturday in summer), and **Locomotive Park.** Kin Park has a beach, a playground, and a boat ramp.

The big sawmill on the edge of town is a reminder of the area's logging history. Tours of the mill are available on Tuesday and Thursday afternoons in summer (604–246–3221).

On Oak Street tour the **Mechanical Music Museum,** with its display of historical music boxes and phonographs. Shop for souvenirs, cards, and kitchen items in the **Chemainiac Shop** on Willow Street (604–246–4621). **Sa-Cinn Native Enterprises, Ltd.,** features jewelry, carvings, pottery, prints, and other fine-quality Native arts and crafts. At **Images of the Circle,** a working studio on Chemainus Road, you can watch the artists at work and purchase carvings, paintings, and jewelry.

*Lunch:* **Harp and Heather Tea Room,** 9749 Willow Street, Chemainus. (604) 246–2434. Fresh salads, soups, and sandwiches, generously portioned, served indoors or at umbrella tables on the terrace.

## Afternoon

Drive south on Trans-Canada Highway 1 to **Duncan,** the commerical hub of the region. It's easy to find the **totem poles** the city is famous for. There are about eighty throughout the city, especially in the downtown district, made by Native carvers.

The Totem Pole Project, which began in 1985, honors an ancient Northwest Coast tradition and art form. Guided tours are available; check at the **Travel InfoCentre,** 381 Highway 1, Duncan. (604–746–4636). Several totems stand near the Duncan Railway Station, which houses the **Cowichan Valley Museum.** It contains pioneer possessions, a typical turn-of-the-century general store, and a gift and souvenir shop. (Open Monday to Saturday in summer, Thursday to Saturday in winter. Hours vary; phone 604–746–6612.)

On Craig Street, **Judy Hill Gallery** is a small shop with good-quality Native carvings and jewelry. Stop for espresso or cappuccino at Gallows Glass Books on Canada Avenue, near the railway station museum; then take Cowichan Way south to the **Native Heritage Centre,** a complex of buildings where you can see how the famous Cowichan sweaters are made, watch a totem carver at work, and purchase fine Native crafts. This is an exceptional visitors attraction, not to be missed. Owned by the Cowichan Indians, the largest tribe in British Columbia, it represents a rich and proud culture.

One mile south of Duncan on Highway 1 is **Hill's Indian Crafts,** one of several Hill's stores selling unique totems, ceremonial masks, leather moccasins, and Cowichan handknit sweaters.

Return to Grove Hall for afternoon tea and a game of tennis or a stroll on the lawn.

*Dinner:* **Bluenose Steak and Seafood House,** 1765 Cowichan Bay Road, Cowichan Bay. (604) 748–2841. Prime rib and seafood in a pleasant setting on the water.

*Lodging:* Grove Hall Estate.

# Day 3

## Morning

*Breakfast:* The menu varies daily at Grove Hall. You might have bacon and eggs cooked as you like them, or pancakes with local berry syrup.

From Duncan, take Koksilah Road south to **Bright Angel Provincial Park.** Walk the suspension bridge that hangs above the Koksilah River, hike the trails that wind through fir and cedar trees, and enjoy the rocky, riverside beach. You can swim (a convenient rope swing hangs from a tree limb, over the water) and fish.

Take Koksilah Road east to join Trans-Canada Highway 1 and turn south; past Dougan Lake, branch west on Cobble Hill Road. Driving through this rural area you'll pass a farm selling raspberries and blueberries in season. When you reach the little community of **Cobble Hill,** look for the Crafty Old Lady and Cobble Hill Country Furnishings, antiques and craft shops that have a combination of antiques, collectibles, and locally made handicrafts.

Purchase a picnic lunch at the snack shop in Cobble Hill Country Furnishings and walk across the train tracks that lie at the base of Cobble Hill. Just behind the railroad shelter a trail begins into **Quarry Wilderness Park.** Follow this trail (there are several offshoots; just keep going upward) to the top of the hill, and if it's a clear day you'll enjoy a sweeping view of the countryside. It takes about two hours to climb the hill. There are picnic tables on the summit.

*Lunch:* Picnic on Cobble Hill.

## Afternoon

After ambling back down Cobble Hill, you might take a refreshment break at the ice cream bar in Cobble Hill Country Furnishings or in Cobblestone Inn, a Tudor-style pub with a full bar, darts, and evening entertainment on weekends. Then head south on Shawnigan Lake Road.

The country road goes to **Shawnigan Lake Village,** where you can check to see if the **Auld Kirk Gallery** is open. The gallery, in a former church on Wilmot Avenue and Walbank Road, sells the pottery and textiles of local artisans. It's open weekend afternoons in winter and daily in summer. Phone (604) 743–4811.

Continuing on East Shawnigan Lake Road, you'll come to Recreation Road, a right turn. At the end of the road is **Old Mill Community Park,** site of a former sawmill. In the early 1900s, when logging seemed unlimited, the mill handled 80,000 to 100,000 board feet a day. The last mill burned in 1945 and was never rebuilt; now there are few remnants left among the trails that wind through the woods and along the lakeshore.

East Shawnigan Lake Road continues south to join Highway 1. At the juncture, turn north on the highway to Whitaker Road. Travel less than a mile on Whitaker and you'll come to **Spectacle Lake Provincial Park,** a quiet, pretty park centered around a lovely lake. It takes about thirty minutes to walk completely around the lake. Part of the path is wheelchair accessible.

**The Aerie** is near Spectacle Lake, off Whitaker Road, and is your destination for the night.

*Dinner:* The Aerie. Expensive, fine cuisine in a spectacular setting with forest, mountain, and water views. Try the pheasant in almond

crust or rack of lamb with herbs, and save room for the heavenly chocolate-rum truffles. This is a special place for special occasions.
*Lodging:* The Aerie, P.O. Box 108, Malahat, B.C. V0R 2L0. (604) 743–7115. Luxurious, Mediterranean-style villa on a hillside above Finlayson Arm, with grand mountain and forest views. Twelve rooms, some with Jacuzzi tubs and fireplaces.

# Day 4

## Morning

*Breakfast:* A full breakfast, included in the Aerie's room rate, is served in the dining room with fine china and silver.

Head north on Trans-Canada Highway 1 to the ferry landing south of Mill Bay. If you have time to explore, drive into **Bamberton Provincial Park** for a last walk in the woods.

Catch the ferry to Brentwood Bay. Take Highway 17 north to Swartz Bay and board the ferry bound for Tsawassen.

# There's More

**Boating.** Heritage Sailing Cruises offers cruises on the *Meriah*, a 50-foot sailing yacht. Contact Inn at the Water, Cowichan Bay. (604) 748–7374.

Pacific Coast Diving Services, (604) 746–4188, offers guided kayak trips in sheltered waters and an introductory pool session. Each trip has a focus on wildlife, botany, the shoreline, water currents, or another theme befitting the area.

**Centennial Park,** at the end of First Street in Duncan, has a playground, tennis courts, and lawn bowling.

**Chemainus Theatre,** Chemainus. (604) 246–9820 or (800) 565–7738. Dinner theater, arts-and-crafts gallery.

**Cowichan Lake,** west of Route 18. Inland lake with fishing, picnicking, and hiking trails (much of the forest has been logged off, however).

**Diving.** Pacific Coast Diving Services, 6683 Beaumont Ave., RR 1, Duncan, B.C. V9L 1M3. (604) 746–4188. Instruction and equipment available for diving charters in Maple Bay. Expert guides take you down to swim among the teeming marine life; see octopus, wolf eel, scallops, and abalone.

**Golf.** Mount Brenton Golf Course, Chemainus. Eighteen-hole course with fir trees and several lakes and creek crossings. Easy to walk but challenging. (604) 246–9322.

**Hiking.** Cowichan River Footpath follows the scenic, wooded south bank of Cowichan River. The trailhead is shown on the large map at the Community Hall of Glenora, southwest of Duncan, off Indian Road. It's a 6-mile hike in to Sahtlam Lodge (see Other Recommended Restaurants and Lodgings).

**Fishing.** Beachcomber Charters, P.O. Box 51, Cowichan Bay, B.C. V0R 1N0. (604) 748–8733. Insured, professional guides offer charters for salmon, steelhead, and bottom fish. All gear supplied.

**Shawnigan Lake Marina,** 2346 East Shawnigan Lake Road, (604) 743–1364, rents canoes, paddleboats, rowboats, and motorboats. Marina also has jet skis and fishing licenses.

**Zanatta,** in Cowichan Valley, is a farm gate winery, which means that the wine is sold at the farm. (604) 748–2338.

## Special Events

**May.** Mill Bay Country Music Festival, Mill Bay.

**June.** Cowichan Wooden Boat Festival, Cowichan Bay.

**July.** Cowichan Band Canoe Races at Indian Beach.

**Mid-July.** Duncan-Cowichan Summer Festival.

**July through October.** Festival of Murals, Chemainus. Outdoor theater, parades, puppetry, street music, folk dancing, food, music, swap meet, and arts-and-crafts demonstrations and sales.

**Mid-August.** Original Traditions, Chemainus. Weekend celebration of contemporary fine crafts, showcasing artisans from around western Canada.

## Other Recommended Restaurants and Lodgings

### Chemainus

Bird Song Cottage, 9909 Maple Street, Chemainus V0R 1K0. (604) 246–9910. Three suites in a light and airy home decorated with fanciful floral stencils. Hospitable innkeeper, cozy sitting room, vegetarian breakfast included.

Chemainus Bakery, 2875 Oak Street, Chemainus. (604) 246–4321. Sandwiches and pastries in a bright, cheery space that's flooded with sun on clear days. Good chewy walnut cookies. Morning doughnut and coffee, $1.00. Closed Sunday and Monday.

Saltair Pub, north of Chemainus on Route 1A. (604) 246–4942. Casual country restaurant in a rural, woodsy setting.

## Cobble Hill

Heron Hill Bed-and-Breakfast, 3745 Granfield Place, V0R 1L0. (604) 743–3855. Three bedrooms in a country home with views. Casual, homey, family choice. Guest sitting room with fireplace, refrigerator, and microwave.

## Cowichan Bay

The Inn at the Water, 1681 Botwood Lane, V0R 1N0. (604) 748–6222. Waterside hotel with fifty-six one-bedroom suites. Kitchenettes, a pool, and restaurant with ordinary food but great view of the bay.

Masthead Restaurant, 1705 Cowichan Bay Road. (604) 748–3714. Seafood and prime rib in waterside setting.

Rock Cod Cafe, 1759 Cowichan Bay Road. (604) 746–8006. Inexpensive spot with nautical atmosphere and marina views. Fish-and-chips and specials such as honey Dijon halibut with rice and salad.

## Duncan

Fairburn Farm Country Manor, 3310 Jackson Road. (604) 746–4637. A working bed-and-breakfast farm with seven rooms, set on 128 secluded acres. Homegrown vegetables, fresh eggs and butter, and freshly baked bread.

Oak and Carriage Neighbourhood Pub, 3287 Lake Cowichan Road, Duncan. (604) 746–4144. English-style pub with comfy couches by the fireplace. A good place for lunch (generous hamburgers) and a game of darts.

Pioneer House, 4675 Trans-Canada Highway. (604) 746–5848. Large log restaurant with friendly, prompt service and well-prepared steak, ribs, seafood, and chicken.

Sahtlam Lodge and Cabins, 5720 Riverbottom Road, Duncan V9L 1N9. (604) 748–7738. Charming, old-fashioned lodge and rustic cabins scattered among woodland and gardens on the Cowichan River. Excellent meals; dinner served to the public, breakfast and lunch for guests only.

## Maple Bay

Brigantine Pub, above the bay. (604) 746–5422. Eat outdoors on the deck at this friendly pub. A local favorite, it has the usual dart board and television. A good spot for a light, flavorful meal; the mushroom soup is top-notch.

## Mill Bay

Friday's, on Highway 1. (604) 743–5533. Lively spot with a youthful clientele. The most popular item is pizza, cooked in open brick ovens.

Pine Lodge Farm, 3191 Mutter Road. (604) 743–4083. Antiques-filled country inn with gardens, pastures, seven guest rooms, and an impressive stone fireplace. Full bacon-and-eggs breakfast included.

### Shawigan Lake

Marifield Manor, 2309 Merrifield Lane, V0R 2W0. (604) 743–9930. Spacious Edwardian home with three rooms, lake views, and hospitable hosts. Full breakfast included.

## For More Information

B.C. Ferries, 1112 Fort Street, Victoria, B.C. V8V 4V2. Vancouver (604) 669–1211, Victoria (604) 386–3431.

Chemainus InfoCentre, Box 575, Chemainus, B.C. V0R 1K0. (604) 246–3944.

Duncan-Cowichan Chamber of Commerce, 381 Trans-Canada Highway, Duncan, B.C. V9L 3Y2. (604) 746–4636.

Tourism Association of Vancouver Island, Suite 302, 45 Bastion Square, Victoria, B.C. V8W 1J1. (604) 382–3551.

# Bellingham and Lummi Island

The *Whatcom Chief* makes regular daily runs between the mainland and Lummi Island.

## Historic Charm by the Bay

### 1 NIGHT

Living history homestead · 1890s street scene · Museums · Art galleries
Outdoor sculpture · Rural island · Sandy beaches · Bay cruise · Fine dining

More than a century of Northwest history is covered in this brief, two-day sojourn across the border. Past cultures can be seen in exhibits and in living interpretations. Modern-day art, theater, shopping, and recreation mingle with a rich history that is still in the making.

## Day 1

**Morning**

Drive south from Vancouver on U.S. I–5 to Ferndale exit 262, about 60 miles (100 km). **Ferndale,** set on the banks of the **Nooksack**

**River,** has the quiet atmosphere of a small rural community. It's surrounded by corn and berry fields and pastures, yet much of its economic base rests on the local oil and aluminum refineries.

For a sense of Ferndale's roots, turn on Nielsen Road to the **Hovander Homestead,** 5299 Nielsen Road (206–384–3444). This enterprise, listed on the National Register of Historic Places, allows visitors to experience life as it was on a turn-of-the-century farm, not just in the Ferndale area but throughout the Northwest.

The Scandinavian-style farmhouse on the sixty-acre grounds houses the visitors' center. A red barn as big as a cathedral holds the well-used tools of another era: corn chopper, root cutter, stud cart, grain thrasher. Around the now-silent, rusting equipment, swallows swoop from their nests high in the dusty eaves.

The farm animals—pigs, chickens, cows—are favorites with youngsters. There's a vegetable garden on this working farm, and there's even a small weed patch that identifies various common weeds. Trails lead into the surrounding woods and to the neighboring **Tennant Lake Natural History Interpretive Center.**

One-half mile of boardwalk trails wind through the 200 acres of marshy wildfowl habitat at Tennant Lake. You can climb a bird-watching observation tower; visit **Nielsen House,** an early homestead in use as the interpretive center; and wander through the unusual **Fragrance Garden,** where the scents of lavender, bee balm, pineapple mint, and nutmeg geranium fill the air. The garden's paths are wide and paved, accessible to wheelchairs. The center offers naturalist programs and classes all summer. For information, call Whatcom County Parks at (206) 592–5161 or 733–2900.

From Tennant Lake, drive to **Pioneer Park,** 2 blocks south of Main Street on First Avenue in Ferndale. The green park beside the Nooksack River contains seven log cabins built by early settlers of Whatcom County. All are filled with pioneer relics and are open for afternoon tours, May through October. The hand-hewn cedar buildings, standing in a grove of tall, western red cedar, include the first church built in Whatcom County.

Pioneer Park is not just a museum. It's full of life, with softball games, Frisbee tosses, and family picnics taking place on warm evenings and weekends. The Old Settlers' Pioneer Picnic is held here every July.

From Ferndale, rejoin I–5 and continue south to exit 250, following Old Fairhaven Parkway west to Twelfth Street. Turn right toward Harris Street in **Fairhaven, Bellingham's** historic district.

The streets of Fairhaven are lined with brick buildings from the 1890s that now house restaurants, gift shops, coffee houses, and theaters. The appealing human scale of the district draws visitors and locals alike to shop, listen to street musicians, play chess in cafes, sniff vendors' flowers, and dine al fresco when the weather allows.

Down the hill at the foot of Harris Street, cruise ships dock on their way to or from Alaska. Near the **Alaska Terminal** is **Marine Park,** a corner of waterside greenery with views of sailboats and ships entering Bellingham Bay.

The **Fairhaven Marketplace,** 1200 Harris Avenue, holds twenty-four specialty shops in one building—the former Mason Block, built in 1890. An early-day shopping mall, it housed Fagan's Dry Goods, Great Northern Express Company, and the Cascade Gentlemen's Club, among others. If they could see the place today, those first patrons would be impressed with the vitality of their "mall," which was restored in the 1970s with four tiers of banistered balconies, staircases finished in finely carved woodwork, high ceilings, and glass. Shops offer contemporary art, flowers, country gifts, antiques, jewelry, scarves, and worldwide imports. Musicians entertain on weekends on the elevated stage in the building's atrium-style center.

**Artwood,** a gallery on Harris Street, displays wood designers' sculpture, carvings, and furniture. It's open Wednesday through Sunday.

A block away, on Eleventh Street, there's a rambling, two-level bookstore, **Village Books.**

*Lunch:* **Colophon Cafe,** 1210 Eleventh Street, Bellingham. (206) 647–0092. Casual cafe with good seafood chowder and a few exotic specialties. Adjoins Village Books.

## Afternoon

Driving along South State Street, you'll edge busy **Bellingham Bay,** a deep-water port and center for pleasure boats. When you reach Cornwall Street, you're near **Civic Center,** in the heart of Bellingham's downtown district. Colorful awnings, sidewalk flowers, specialty shops, and restaurants make this an inviting area to explore. **Whatcom Creek** winds through the downtown district, flowing into Bellingham Bay.

Take Holly Street to Prospect and visit the **Whatcom Museum of History and Art,** 121 Prospect Street (206–676–6981). Open from noon to 5:00 P.M. Tuesday through Sunday, it is Bellingham's architectural and historic landmark and the centerpiece of a museum complex. The brick, gabled, towered building, built in 1892, stands on a bluff with a commanding view of the bay. It was the city hall until 1939. Restored, it now holds permanent exhibitions of Northwest art and history, as well as changing displays.

A few doors from the Whatcom Museum is the **Children's Museum Northwest,** 227 Prospect (206–733–8769). This hands-on museum is a great place for traveling children to blow off steam. There are firefighting equipment, a television studio, a dental center, a puppet theater, a science center, and an exploration corner for toddlers. Also part of the complex are the **Syre Education Center,** with logging dioramas, and the ARCO Exhibit Hall, which has rotating shows of contemporary art.

Around the corner, at 304 West Champion Street, is **The Elements Gallery,** a cooperative fine arts exhibition space. The gallery showcases a wide variety of works by local artists (206–734–1689). It's open from 11:00 A.M. to 4:00 P.M., Monday through Saturday.

Follow Indian Street to Highland Drive, turning on West College Way, and you'll spot the visitors' center at **Western Washington University.** The hillside campus overlooking the city and Bellingham Bay covers 180 wooded acres. Paths wind through its wide lawns, passing graceful brick buildings to a central courtyard where a fountain plays.

Much of Bellingham's notable collection of **outdoor sculpture** is on the campus. An *Art Map* that will guide you to sculpture throughout the city is available from Bellingham Municipal Arts Commission, 210 Lottie Street, Bellingham, WA 98225.

Travel west on Holly Street, which becomes Eldridge Avenue, to **DeCann House** and check in. You'll have time before dinner to browse through the inn's sizable library or to play a game of pool in the parlor. The innkeepers will provide a walking-tour map of the **Eldridge Avenue Historic District,** if you'd like a closer look at some of the classic homes in the neighborhood.

*Dinner:* **Il Fiasco,** 1308 Railroad Avenue, Bellingham. (206) 676–9136. Superior Italian food at Bellingham's top restaurant. High, skylighted ceilings, Italian prints on the walls. Fresh seafood, imaginative pasta dishes, roast duck, steak. Extensive wine list.

After or before dining, step into the lobby of the **Mount Baker Theater,** 2 blocks from Il Fiasco on Commercial. The theater is a fine example of ornate Moorish/Spanish decor and architecture.

*Lodging:* DeCann House, 2610 Eldridge Avenue, Bellingham, WA 98225. (206) 734–9172. Turn-of-the-century bed-and-breakfast home a block from the harbor. Two guest rooms, heirloom furnishings, friendly and casual atmosphere.

# Day 2

## Morning

*Breakfast:* The full breakfast at DeCann House includes egg specialties and homemade blackberry jam.

**Squalicum Harbor Marina,** the second-largest marina on Puget Sound, is a short distance from DeCann House. At the marina, you can walk the promenade of **Harbor Center,** which is ideally suited for watching the water traffic, launching a boat, and attending special events and boat shows. This is the new forty-eight-acre Squalicum Harbor development area.

At the wharf, board a charter boat for a scenic cruise around the bay.

*Lunch:* **The Marina,** 985 Thomas Glenn Drive, Bellingham. (206) 773–8292. Stylish waterside restaurant with bar and outside patio. Located at the jetty entrance where boats come and go.

### Afternoon

From Eldridge Avenue, turn north on Marine Drive to Ferndale Road. Follow Ferndale to Slater Road; then turn left, and left again on Haxton Way. This is the **Lummi Indian Reservation,** on a peninsula that forms the northwestern boundary of Bellingham Bay and points toward your next destination, **Lummi Island.**

The mountainous island was once used as a summer camping ground by the Lummi Indians. The Lummis left their camp because of raiding tribes that came in from the North by canoe to capture slaves. Today, the Lummi tribe's fishing fleet is considered the Northwest's largest. The tribe operates a sizable aquaculture plant on the reservation, along with seafood processing, net making, and shellfish harvesting.

It's a ten-minute ride on the quaint ferry *Whatcom Chief* from Gooseberry Point at Fisherman's Cove, across Hale Passage to Lummi Island.

You may spy eagles in the trees as you drive north on Lummi to **The Willows Inn.** After checking in, go for a hike or a bicycle ride on the quiet, tree-shaded country roads, or relax in the gorgeous garden for the rest of the afternoon.

*Dinner:* The Willows Inn. Gourmet dinner (set menu) in a dining room overlooking the colorful gardens and the sea. Friday night meals are served family style. Saturdays are reserved for romantic, multi-course dinners at candlelighted tables. Reserve early; Victoria Flynn's cooking is justifiably renowned. Expensive and very special.

*Lodging:* The Willows Inn, 2579 West Shore Drive, Lummi Island, WA 98262. (206) 758–2620. Country inn set on a slope above the sea amid gardens profuse with summer flowers. Four guest rooms plus honeymoon cottage.

# Day 3

## Morning

*Breakfast:* Hot Irish soda bread and coffee or tea are brought to your room; later, a three-course breakfast is served in The Willows dining room.

This is a morning for relaxation, enjoying the scenery and the peace and quiet. You might visit one of the island's many art studios (open by appointment), where weaving, pottery, pewter jewelry, fine woodwork, and sculptures are created.

To see a unique activity on Lummi, drive to **Legoe Bay,** at Village Point on the west side of the island. Here the Lummi Indians fish for salmon with reef nets, an ancient skill they developed for pulling fish into the boats anchored in Legoe Bay.

Return to the ferry landing, purchase picnic foods from the deli, and take the ferry back to the mainland. Drive Haxton Way to Slater Road, turn west onto Terrell Road and north, onto Kickerville Road, through farming country bounded by tree-covered hills. Curve around **Lake Terrell,** and head west on Birch Bay Road to **Birch Bay State Park.**

*Lunch:* Picnic, Birch Bay State Park.

## Afternoon

**Birch Bay** is a resort community facing Georgia Strait. It's known for its wide, sandy beaches and water that, because it is shallow and protected, is sun warmed for swimming and wading. There's a lot to do at Birch Bay: dig clams, go roller skating, rent a bicycle, ride the waterslide, play miniature golf.

Later, follow the shore north on Semiahmoo Drive to **Semiahmoo Spit,** a protective arm between Semiahmoo Bay and Drayton Harbor, directly across from Blaine and the Canadian border. This place was the last port of call for Alaskan sailing fleets bringing their catches to the cannery on the site. Early, restored buildings are now part of a county park and used as the **Semiahmoo Interpretive Center.** The center tells the history of fishing and canning here on the Northwest corner of the United States and describes Native American life as it was on the spit.

Walk the beach or play a round of golf on the superb, Eighteen-hole course at The Inn at Semiahmoo.

*Dinner:* **Stars** restaurant, The Inn at Semiahmoo, 9596 Semiahmoo Parkway, Semiahoo Spit. (206) 371–3000. Perfectly cooked seafood, veal, prime rib, and chicken, plus menu of reduced-sodium and -cholesterol dishes. Quiet, attractive restaurant with waterfront views.

From Semiahmoo, it's a one-hour drive across the border to Vancouver.

# There's More

**Bloedel Donovan Park,** 2214 Electric Avenue, Bellingham. Sailing, waterskiing, and swimming are available in this lakeside park.

**Chuckanut Drive.** This famous road, State Route 11, edges the sandstone cliffs above Chuckanut Bay, south of Bellingham, for 21 miles (34 km). Along the scenic route are restaurants of charm, art galleries, and overlooks.

**Golf.** Lake Padden Park, 4882 Samish Way, Bellingham. (206) 676–6989. Tight, hilly eighteen-hole course, considered one of Washington's best.

Semiahmoo Golf and Country Club, Blaine. (206) 371–7005. Eighteen-hole course, seaside setting.

**Hiking.** Larrabee State Park, 245 Chuckanut Drive, Bellingham. The first state park in Washington, Larrabee has myriad trails, sea views, and lookout points. Find tide pools on the seaward side of Chuckanut Mountain. An enjoyable, easy hike is to follow the Interurban Trail 6 miles (10 km) into Bellingham, where it emerges near Fairhaven Park.

**Kayaking.** Fairhaven Boats, (206) 647–2469, rents sea kayaks and other small boats. Kayak in the bay, off Gooseberry Point, and in other nearby waters.

**Maritime Heritage Center,** 1600 C Street, Bellingham. (206) 676–6873. Outdoor rearing tanks and indoor displays can be seen at this salmon-life-cycle facility and learning center.

**Whale-watching and charter cruises.** Island Mariner, 5 Squalicum Esplanade, Bellingham, WA 98225. (206) 734–8866. Cruises through the San Juans on the 83-foot *Rosario Princess*. Wildlife, sunset, mystery, and party cruises; Sunday brunch on Rosario cruise.

See Squalicum Harbor from the eighteen-passenger *Zephyr* (summer only). Gray Line Cruises, (800) 443–4552.

## Special Events

**Last weekend of May.** Ski to Sea Festival, Mount Baker to Puget Sound. Parades, carnival, street fair. Main event is the race from Mount Baker—skiing, running, canoeing, bicycling, and sailing.

**Late May.** Lummi Stommish, Lummi Island. Indian water carnival—war canoe races, arts-and-crafts sales, salmon bake, Indian dancing, drumming, games.

**Third weekend in August.** Maritime Heritage Festival, Boulevard Park, Bellingham. Classic sailing-vessel races, salmon bake, Art Day at the Bay, West Coast Chowder Challenge.

## Other Recommended Restaurants and Lodgings

### Bellingham

Cliff House, 331 North State Street. (206) 734–8660. American menu in a restaurant with a view of the bay. A good place to watch the sunset.

La Belle Rose, 1801 Roeder Avenue. (206) 647–0833. Intimate restaurant in a courtyard by the harbor. Mostly seafood prepared with French flair.

North Garden Inn, 1014 North Garden Street. (206) 671–7828. Large, dramatic Victorian home on a hillside with seven guest rooms and mostly shared baths. Two grand pianos, musical hosts, full breakfast.

Pepper Sisters, 1055 North State Street. (206) 671–3414. Colorful cafe with southwestern decor and menu. Delicious sopapillas and burritos, and outstanding Southwest Pizza: chiles, pine nuts, tomatoes, and cheese on a cornmeal crust.

## Blaine

The Inn at Semiahmoo, 9865 Semiahmoo Parkway. (206) 371–2000; in the United States, (800) 854–2608; in Canada, (800) 854–6742. Resort with 200 guest rooms, two restaurants, extensive fitness facility, 18-hole golf course, 250-slip marina.

## Lummi Island

Loganita, 2825 Westshore Drive. (206) 758–2651. Estate on landscaped grounds with panoramic views. Nightly and weekly rentals in tastefully furnished suites. Warm, hospitable innkeeper. Continental breakfast included.

West Shore Farm, 2781 West Shore Drive. (206) 758–2600. Handbuilt octagonal home, two guest rooms, congenial hosts. Breakfast served, other meals available: "natural enough to be healthy, gourmet enough to be interesting."

# For More Information

Ferndale Chamber of Commerce, 5640 Riverside Drive, Ferndale, WA 98248. (206) 384–3042.

Bellingham/Whatcom County Visitor and Convention Bureau, 904 Potter, Bellingham, WA 98226. (206) 671–3990.

# Lake Whatcom/Mount Baker

Mount Baker and its surrounding wilderness are a spectacular sight.

## Backroads and Byways
## to a Classic Mountain Peak

_____ 1 NIGHTS _____

Dutch-style village · Lake Whatcom · Waterfalls · Rural countryside
Steam-train ride · Wine tasting · Mountain views

This three-day getaway will take you from a Dutch-style village to a luxurious lakefront retreat, and from a peaceful green valley to the end of the road on a snow-cloaked volcano.

Lake Whatcom, east of Bellingham, is Washington's fifth-largest lake. Fifteen miles long, shaped roughly like a leaping fish, it's edged with fir and cedar trees, pebbled beaches, shoreside homes, and a developing county park. At the southwest end is Sudden Valley, a resort community on 1,800 acres of waterfront and forestland.

East of the lake are Whatcom County's backroads and byways, where quiet villages nestle in a picture-book valley against the foothills of the north Cascades.

Farther north, along the Nooksack River, is the Mount Baker Highway, leading to Mount Baker's wilderness areas.

# Day 1

## Morning

Drive south across the Canadian/U.S. border and take I–5 to Birch Bay–Lynden Road (exit 270). Head east toward **Lynden.**

Dominated by its Dutch heritage, Lynden calls itself "a little bit of Holland" and has maintained the old traditions through its architecture, shops, and landscaping. Dutch farmers settled here because the land and climate reminded them of the Netherlands.

Until 1881, when steamboats took over, access to Lynden was by canoe on the Nooksack River. Logging was major employment; in the late 1800s the county had 110 shingle mills, where the workers earned $3.00 per day.

Today a four-story windmill (a restaurant and inn) marks the entrance to the downtown **Dutch Village Mall.** Under one skylighted roof the mall re-creates typical scenes from Holland, including an Amsterdam sidewalk cafe, a cobblestone walkway, and a 150-foot canal. Dutch provincial flags flutter above eighteen shops selling almond pastries, wooden shoes, laces, and other ethnic goods.

Tour **Lynden Pioneer Museum,** 217 Front Street (206–354–3675), one of the largest of its kind in Washington. Its rare collections include horse-drawn buggies and wagons, Indian artifacts, military memorabilia from the Spanish-American War to the Korean War, and Chevrolets dating from 1914 to 1931.

*Lunch:* **Hollandia,** 655 Front Street, Lynden. (206) 354–4133. Restaurant in a windmill. Pleasant setting, standard soups and sandwiches, and authentic Dutch dishes.

## Afternoon

From Lynden take Meridian south, joining I–5 at exit 256, just past Bellis Fair Mall. Continue south to exit 253, and drive east on Lakeway Drive to Electric Avenue.

Enter **Whatcom Falls Park,** 1401 Electric Avenue. The 241-acre park on **Whatcom Creek** has hiking trails, barbecue pits, tennis courts, a playground, and picnic shelters. The ponds of a fish hatchery are close to the parking lot. Take the trail down to a bridge over the creek for a view of the falls. Fir-needled paths web the forest from here; choose one, and hike along the creek or through the woods, eventually looping back toward the parking area.

From the park, take Electric Avenue to Northshore Drive. The drive skirts the northern tip of Lake Whatcom and its eastern shore, ending where a county park with an extensive trail system is under construction. No road completely encircles Lake Whatcom.

Check in at **Sunrise Bay Bed-and-Breakfast** and relax by the pool or on the beach.

*Dinner:* **Sadigih's,** 921 Lakeway Drive, Bellingham. (206) 647–1109. Fine Continental dining between downtown Bellingham and Lake Whatcom. Candlelight and classical music. Closed Tuesday.

*Lodging:* Sunrise Bay Bed-and-Breakfast, 2141 North Shore Road, Bellingham, WA 98226. (206) 647–0376. Remodeled home on the lake. Private entrances to guest rooms in separate cottage. Light, bright, and airy, with skylighted private baths. Swimming pool, friendly hosts, quiet lakeside district.

# Day 2

## Morning

*Breakfast:* A full breakfast is served in the glass-enclosed dining room at Sunrise Bay.

Circle Lake Whatcom from east to west, joining Lake Whatcom Boulevard. Head toward Route 9 and **Wickersham.** This is the boarding place for the old-fashioned steam train that will take you on a one-hour excursion through the countryside. Engine 1070 puffs clouds of steam and sounds a melodic chime whistle as it pulls the coaches on this nostalgic ride. (Lake Whatcom Railway, P.O. Box 91, Acme, WA 98220; 206–595–2218. Reservations recommended.)

When your train trip is over, drive north on Route 9, crossing the **Nooksack River** at **Acme.** Stewart and Homer mountains rise on your left and the Cascade foothills on your right, backdrops to the rolling fields and picturesque barns of this peaceful farming valley.

At the little community of **Van Zandt,** check out the merchandise in **Everybody's Store.** Jeff and Amy Margolis carry an eclectic assortment of goods, from Chinese herbs to well-priced Washington wines and, a major claim to fame, nickel pickles. They sell bulk grains, raw honey, field guides, cards, Skagit Indian baskets, and smoked German sausage.

Buy picnic goods at Everybody's—the regional cheeses are tasty—and continue on Route 9, recrossing the Nooksack, to join 542 (Mount Baker Highway). Just past **Deming,** known for its splashy iris fields and annual logging show, you'll reach **Mount Baker Vineyards** (4298 Mount Baker Highway, Deming, WA 98244; 206–592–2300).

The winery, surrounded by vineyards, produces several varietals and such specialty wines as Madeline Angevine and Müller Thurgau. Plum wine is made in the Japanese style, with fruit from the farm's own plum trees. Tastings are offered Wednesday through Sunday afternoons.

*Lunch:* Picnic on the terrace at Mount Baker Vineyards while you sample wines and enjoy the view of the vineyards, weathered barn, and low mountains in the distance.

## Afternoon

Take Route 542 north along the **North Fork Nooksack River** as it rises from the valley floor into wild, hilly country. Foxglove, daisies, fireweed, and buttercups grow in profusion along the roadside. At Kendall (your last chance to buy gas), turn east. All along Mount Baker Highway you'll be treated to captivating scenery: waterfalls, tumbling streams, and thick forests, with the looming presence of snowcapped **Mount Baker** behind them.

The great volcano was born a million years ago and still shows a little eruptive action now and again. Always mantled in white, it contains one of the largest glacial systems in the continental United States.

When you reach **Glacier,** stop for a coffee break at Graham's, 9989 Mount Baker Highway (open daily July and August; weekends the rest of the year). Fix a make-it-yourself sundae at the ice cream bar in this unique cafe and tavern, or just sit back and enjoy the offbeat atmosphere of whimsical fun. You're sure to hear about Clark Gable's visit to Glacier in 1934, when part of *The Call of the Wild* was filmed in the area.

Cross the road to **Milano's** (206–599–2863) to pick up a pastry treat and coffee for the following day's breakfast. The new market-and-deli is a light, open cafe with arched windows and a patio. Its focus is Italian foods: fresh pasta daily, minestrone, lasagna, *biscotti.* (There's also a grocery store near your night's lodging site.)

Pick up maps and information on trail conditions at the **Glacier Public Service Center** (ranger station) in Glacier (206–599–2714). The center, built in 1939 by the Civilian Conservation Corps, has had recent improvements, such as a plaza with informational kiosks, a public phone and washrooms, and interior remodeling. It's worth a visit just to see the new exhibits and the large topographical map of the Mount Baker area. Ask about free interpretive programs on the botany, history, and wildlife of Mount Baker.

A mile east of Glacier, turn right on Road 39 for a 9-mile side trip up to the best view on the mountain. The road follows **Glacier Creek** to **Mount Baker Vista,** which is as close to the summit as you can get by car.

Trail 677 begins here, leading 6 miles to **Heliotrope Ridge.** This is the usual approach trail for climbers. It travels through dense forest and over cold, babbling creeks to open meadows and finally to the base of **Coleman Glacier,** at 5,800 feet. The outlook is stunning, encompassing immense glaciers, the Black Buttes, the Nooksack Valley below, and the lofty mountain summit.

Assuming you're not on the trail for the next four hours, return to Route 542 and drive on to **Nooksack Falls.** This dramatic cascade of rushing water is a short distance off the highway; the turnoff is Wells Creek Road.

Next, continue on Route 542, which winds through national forestland and up the northeast flank of Mount Baker, ending at **Heather Meadows,** on the border of Mount Baker Wilderness. Above you, the long, icy finger of **Mazama Glacier** extends from the 10,778-foot summit. To the east is **Mount Shuksan,** at 9,038 feet another major peak.

Baker, which the Indians called *Komo Kulshan* ("white and shining"), was renamed by Captain George Vancouver. When he sailed into Puget Sound in 1791, the still-active volcano on the mountain was spewing steam and smoke. Vancouver named it for a junior officer of his fleet.

Heather Meadows, the mountain's most popular ski area, has been the recent focus of extensive replanting. The natural alpine vegetation was replaced and new, self-guided interpretive trails constructed.

On winter weekends and holidays, this part of the mountain bustles with ski action. Mount Baker has the longest ski season and the earliest snow in the state. Heather Meadows is equipped with a day lodge, eight chair lifts, one rope tow, two warming huts, and a ski shop. Snowboarding and cross-country skiing are also very popular.

After drinking in the view and walking the mountain paths, descend to Glacier.

*Dinner:* **Innisfree,** 9383 Mount Baker Highway, Glacier. (206) 599–2373. Creative use of Northwest ingredients, including produce from the owners' organic garden, results in a memorable cuisine. Northwest wines, fresh fruit desserts, and a wicked espresso truffle pie with raspberry sauce. Inviting dining areas include a solarium with a woodsy view.

*Lodging:* **Glacier Creek Motel,** P.O. Box A, Glacier, WA 98244. (206) 599–2991. Cabins (one wheelchair accessible) and motel units in the cedar trees by Glacier Creek. Kitchens, barbecues, outdoor hot tub, gift shop, coffee shop. Owners have a list of suggestions for day hikes.

# Day 3

## Morning

*Breakfast:* In your cabin, or picnic by the creek.

Drive Route 542 west to **Maple Falls,** and turn north on Silver Lake Road to **Silver Lake Park.** The 411-acre park surrounding a blue lake is unusually beautiful, even in this strikingly scenic area. On the property are a former private resort, homestead, and old logging site. There are boat launches and rentals, a food concession, campsites, stable and bridle trails (bring your own horse), and cabins.

From the park, South Pass Road curves up to brush the Canadian border, then turns southwest. Where the road meets Route 547, a group of potters operate a working studio, **Cloudy Mountain Pottery.** They welcome visitors to watch them work and see their functional porcelain and stoneware pottery.

Drive Route 547 north to Sumas.

*Lunch:* **Sumas Mountain Village,** 819 Cherry Street, Sumas. Comfortable, casual family restaurant in a log lodge. Varied menu, substantial lunches, convenient location.

## Afternoon

Cross the border into Canada. **Abbotsford,** north of the border, is known as the home of North America's largest air show, the **Abbotsford International Air Show,** held yearly in August. Begun in 1961 with 16,000 visitors, the show now draws crowds of more than 300,000.

Another nearby attraction is the **Vancouver Game Farm** in Aldergrove, 8 miles (13 km) west of Abbotsford. Here eighty-five species of animals in danger of extinction, among them lions, tigers, and zebras, are bred and cared for on twenty acres of fields and woodlands. Phone (604) 856–6825; in Vancouver, call (604) 261–0225.

Return to Vancouver, 79 miles (127 km) on Trans-Canada Highway 1.

# There's More

**Berthusen Park,** Lynden. This 236-acre forested park has hiking trails, a playground, and picnic areas. On the grounds are Berthusen's Barn, built in 1913, which holds old sleds, boats, bellows, and other relics.

**Bloedel Donovan Park,** Bellingham. Twelve-acre park on Lake Whatcom. Swimming, boating, picnicking. Paddleboat and canoe rentals.

**Boating.** Nooksack Valley canoeists like to paddle the South Fork of the Nooksack River. You can rent a canoe in Bellingham (Bellingham Boat Rentals; (206–676–1363) and put in at the Acme Bridge for a scenic, ninety-minute river trip under the branches of cottonwood trees. Fish for salmon or steelhead and observe eagles as you paddle past Mount Baker Vineyards, finally leaving the river at Nugent's Corner.

**Hiking.** The Hannegan Pass Trail is one of several long, enjoyable hikes on or near Mount Baker. Usually free of snow by late summer, the 10-mile trail goes up Hannegan Pass, through a valley, and over a ridge where blueberries and heather grow. You can see two lakes and magnificent views of Mount Shuksan and Mount Baker.

## Special Events

**Early May.** Holland Days, Lynden. Wooden-shoe races and dancing, street-scrubbing ceremony, arts-and-crafts sales, Dutch art show, international foods, parade, games, horse-and-buggy rides.

**May.** Ski to Sea Race, Mount Baker. Relay teams ski, run, bicycle, canoe, and sail from Mount Baker's ski area down the Nooksack River, across Bellingham Bay to Fairhaven.

**Mid-June.** Deming Logging Show, Deming. Celebrates a major industry in the region. Salmon barbecue, equipment displays, breakfast, and logging competition: choker setting, ax throwing, and speed tree climbing are a few.

**Mid-August.** Northwest Washington Fair, Lynden. Old-fashioned country fair, with farm animals, baked and canned goods, tractor pulls, entertainment.

## Other Recommended Restaurants and Lodgings

### Bellingham

Eleni's Greek Cuisine, 1046 Lakeway Center. (206) 676–5555. Simple atmosphere; top-quality souvlaki, moussaka, and other Greek dishes. Open for lunch and dinner daily except Sundays.

Schnauzer Crossing, 4421 Lakeway Drive. (206) 733–0055. Two guest rooms in lovely private home with lake views. Private tennis court, full breakfast, outdoor hot tub, hospitality.

Sudden Valley Resort, 2145 Whatcom Boulevard. (206) 734–6430. Condos available in a full resort community on the water. Tennis courts, swimming pools, walking trails, 18-hole golf course, restaurant.

Anderson Creek Lodge, 5602 Mission Road. (206) 966–2126. Spacious inn on sixty-five secluded woodland acres. Five guest rooms, large living room with stone fireplace, full breakfast, swimming pool, walking and skiing trails.

## Deming

The Logs at Canyon Creek, 9002 Mount Baker Highway. (206) 599–2711. Five rustic, two-bedroom log cabins in the forest, at the confluence of Canyon Creek and the North Fork Nooksack River. Stone fireplaces, kitchens, swimming pool.

## Glacier

Mount Baker Lodging and Travel, P.O. Box 472. (206) 599–2453; in Vancouver, (604) 241–0074. Agent for wide range of cabins and chalets in Glacier. Kitchens, wood stoves or fireplaces; some saunas, hot tubs, and televisions.

## Lynden

Dutch Village Inn, 655 Front Street. (206) 354–4440. Hotel in a 72-foot windmill. Six rooms, three in the windmill and three in an adjoining annex. Quaint, clean, and nicely furnished. Breakfast included.

# For More Information

Lynden Chamber of Commerce, 444 Front Street, Suite 252, Lynden, WA 98264. (206) 354–5995.

Bellingham/Whatcom County Visitor and Convention Bureau, 904 Potter, Bellingham, WA 98226. (206) 671–3990.

Mount Baker–Snoqualmie National Forest Service and National Park Service, 2105 Highway 20, Sedro Woolley, WA 98284. (206) 856–5700.

# Index

## A

Abbotsford, 311
Ainsworth State Park, 56, 77
Airplane excursions, 202, 226, 270
Aloha, 73
American Camp, 207
Anacortes, 147, 150
Anne Hathaway's Cottage, 216
Antiques, 8, 15, 17, 26, 71, 88, 110, 113, 135, 139, 141, 155–56, 167, 188, 189, 193, 215, 279, 293
Ape Cave, 42
April Point Lodge, 225
Ark, 112
Armstrong, 280
Arterberry Winery Cellars, 71
Art galleries, 8, 14, 17, 27, 64, 72, 87, 97, 104, 110, 112, 121, 133, 136, 139, 145, 162, 188, 193, 206, 222, 234, 251, 257, 258, 260, 267, 283, 291, 300, 301, 304
Arthur D. Feiro Marine Laboratory, 124
Ashford, 178
Astoria, 6–7, 11
Augustine's 75
Aurora, 88, 91

## B

Bainbridge Island, 181
Bay City, 16
B.C. Museum of Mining, 270
Beach Gardens Resort, 257
Beacon Rock, 62
Beaumont Marine Park, 247
Bedford Hotel, 215
Belknap Crater, 96

Bellingham, 298–305, 312
Bell Point Trail, 206
Bend, 102, 106
Benham Falls, 103
Bicycling, 124, 163, 208, 244, 267, 273
Big Four Ice Caves, 168
Big Four Mountain, 167
Bilbo's, 199
Bingen, 63
Bird Haven, 86
Black Butte, 104
Black Butte Ranch, 107
Black Crater Trail, 104
Black Forest Restaurant, 282
Blackman House Museum, 167
Blaine, 305
Blue Heron, 232
Blue Heron Inn, 256
Boating, 9, 72, 112, 124, 171, 201, 208, 217, 251, 259, 294, 312
Bodega Resort, 248
Bonneville Dam, 56, 62
Box Canyon, 174–75
Bremerton, 132, 184
Bridal Veil, 59
Bridal Veil Falls State Park, 55–56
Bridge of the Gods Park, 35
British Columbia Forest Museum, 291
Broken Group Islands, 232
Brownsville, 48, 96
Bush House, 87
Bush House Country Inn, 159
Butchart Gardens, 289
Butterfly World, 234, 289

## C

Cafe Bissett, 206
Cafe de la Mer, 14

Cafe Langley, 146
Calona Wines, 278–79
Campbell River, 224, 228, 239
Campbell River Museum, 224
Camping, 44, 130
Canby, 88, 91
Cannon Beach, 13, 20
Cape Disappointment, 109
Cape Falcon, 15
Cape Flattery, 122
Carnation, 155, 156
Carson, 66
Carson Hot Mineral Springs Resort, 63
Casa del Sol, 140
Cascade Head, 17
Cascade Lake, 199
Cascade Locks, 35, 59
Cascade Mountain Inn, 168
Cascades Dining Room, 33
Cashmere, 160, 164
Castle Rock, 40
Cathedral Grove, 231
Cathlamet, 6, 10
Champoeg State Park, 512
Chateau Benoit Winery, 71
Chateau Ste. Michelle Winery, 159
Chateau Whistler Resort, 272
Chelan County Historical Museum, 161
Chemainus, 291, 295
Chetzemoka Park, 121
Chez Joel, 271
Chief Lelooska Living History Presentation, 44
Chinese Tree of Heaven, 120
Chinook, 109, 113
Clallam Bay, 122
Clallam County Historical Museum, 121
Clatskanie, 5, 10
Clear Lake, 96
Cliffside Inn On-the-Sea, 247

Cloud Cap Inn, 34
Cloverdale, 21
Coast Lakeside Resort at Penticton, 277
Colophon Cafe, 300
Columbia City, 5
*Columbia Gorge* dinner cruises, 35–36
Columbia Gorge Hotel, 57
Columbian Cafe, 8
Columbian White-tailed Deer Refuge, 6
Columbia River Gorge
    Oregon, 33, 35, 54–60
    Washington, 61–67
Common Loaf Bake Shop, 233
Comox, 239
Comox Valley, 222
Cooley's Gardens, 89
Cougar, 43
Coupeville, 146, 150
Courtenay, 223, 228
Cove Palisades State Park, 101
Cowichan Bay, 296
Coxcomb Hill, 7
Crab Bar, 234
Craigdorrach Castle, 215
Cranberry bogs, 111, 112
Crown Point, 55
Crystal Mountain, 178

**D**
DeCann House, 301
Deception Falls, 159
Deception Pass State Park, 147
Deepwood Estate, 87
Deer Harbor West, 201
Deming, 308, 313
Denman Island, 242
Deschutes Brewery and Public House, 102
Deschutes Historical Center, 102
Deschutes River Canyon, 81, 101

Desolation Sound, 258
Discovery Pier, 224
Diving, 235, 259, 294
Dr. John C. Brougher Museum, 72
Doe Bay Village Resort, 200
Duck Brand Cantina, 171
Duck Soup Inn, 207
Duncan, 292, 296
Dundee Wine Cellar, 71
Dungeness Spit, 124

**E**

Eagle Creek Trail, 57
Eagle's Nest Inn, 146
Eastsound, 198, 202
Eatery, 280
Eliot Hiking Trail, 111
Elochoman Slough Marina, 6
Elphinstone Pioneer Museum, 255
Emmons Glacier, 174
Empress Hotel, 215
Enderby, 280
End of the Trail Interpretive Center, 85
Englishman River Falls Provincial Park, 231
Errington, 231
Eugene, 22, 29, 94, 98
Eyrie, 71

**F**

Fairhaven, 299
Fall City, 152–57
Father Pandosy Mission, 279
Ferndale, 298–99
Fidel's, 64
Fifth Street Public Market, 23, 94
Fishing, 9, 18–19, 36, 82, 97, 112, 124, 141, 171, 201, 217, 224, 226, 235, 252, 256, 259, 267, 283, 295

Flippen House, 5
Flower Ridge Trail, 241
Forest Grove, 70, 74
Forks, 129, 131
Forks Timber Museum, 130
Fort Canby State Park, 109
Fort Cascades National Historic Landmark, 62
Fort Casey Sate Park, 149
Fort Clatsop National Memorial, 7
Fort Ebey State Park, 146
Fort Rodd Hill National Historic Park, 216
Fort Stevens State Park, 8
Fort Vancouver National Historic Site, 62
Fort Worden State Park, 120
Fountain Cafe, 121
Fragrance Garden, 299
Friday Harbor, 205, 209
Front Street Cafe, 211
Fulford Harbour, 264

**G**

Gaches Mansion, 188
Galiano Island, 248, 253
Ganges, 264, 268
Garden Bay Lake, 257
Garibaldi, 16, 20
Garibaldi Provincial Park, 270
General Store, 26, 97
Gere-a-Deli, 149
Gibsons, 255, 261
Gig Harbor, 192–96
Gina's Cafe, 243
Glacier Creek Motel, 310
Glenwood, 66
Goat Island, 258
Goldendale, 64
Goldendale Observatory State Park, 65
Golden Hinde, 239
Golfing, 19, 28, 52, 59, 72, 112,

124, 136, 141, 156, 163, 195, 218, 227, 235, 252, 259, 271, 283–84, 294, 304
Goosie's, 140
Granary, The, 187
Grays River, 6
Greenbank, 146
Greenery, 122
Greystone Manor, 223
Grove of the Patriarchs, 174
Gulf Islands, 245–53, 264, 289

**H**
Half Moon Bay, 256, 261
Hall of Mosses, 129
Hang gliding, 25–26
Harp and Heather Tea Room, 291
Harrison Hot Springs, 282, 286–87
Hatheume Lake, 286
Hayes Oysters, 16
Haystack Rock, 14
Hebo, 21
Helicopter rides, 44
Helliwell Provincial Park, 243
Herbfarm, 155
Heron and Beaver Pub, 110
Herons, 222
High Desert Museum, 102
Hiking, 28, 98, 104, 124, 177, 201, 227, 267, 295, 304, 312
Hoh River Valley, rain forest, 127–31
Hollandia, 307
Honeywood Winery, 88
Hood Canal, 128, 133
Hood River, 35, 37, 60
Hood River County Historical Museum, 58
Hood River Hotel, 57
Hood River Valley, 34, 57
Hoover-Minthorn House, 72

Hope, 282
Hopkins Hill, 44
Horseback riding, 65, 105, 162, 171, 271
Horse Heaven Hills, 65
Hotel Eldorado, 279
Hot springs, 98, 235
Hovander Homestead, 299
Hummingbird Inn, 248
Hurricane Ridge, 124

**I**
Il Fiasco, 301
Illwaco, 109, 113
Independence Pass, 42
Index, 159
Inn at Cooper Spur, 34
Innisfree, 310
Inspiration Point, 34
Issaquah, 155, 156, 163

**J**
Jack's Sporting Goods and Restaurant, 43
Jefferson County Courthouse, 120
Jefferson County Historical Museum, 119
Jewell, 9
Judith's Tea Room, 181

**K**
Kaledan, 285
Karsten's, 184
Kayaking, 200, 208, 235, 242, 252, 259, 267, 304
Kelowna, 278, 286
Keremeos, 277
Kitsap Peninsula, 180
Kitsap State Memorial Park, 183
Klickitat County Historical Museum, 64

Klipsan Beach, 111
Knudsen Erath Winery, 71
Koosah Falls, 96
Kopachuck State Park, 194
Kwaguilth Museum and Cultural
  Center, 225

# L

La Conner, 187, 190
Lafayette, 71
Lahar Viewpoint, 43
Lake Crescent, 123, 128
Lake Crescent Lodge, 123
Lake Ozette, 122
Lake Wenatchee State Park, 160
Lake Whatcom, 306–13
Landfall, 119–20
Langdale, 254–62
Langley, 145, 150
La Petite, 148
Latourell Falls, 55
Laurel Ridge Winery, 69
Lava Butte, 102
Lava Cast Forest, 105
Lava River Cave, 105
Lazy Susan Cafe, 14
Leaburg, 94, 98
Leadbetter Point State Park, 111
Leavenworth, 158–65
Leeward Pub, 239
Leeward Pub and Brewery, 223
Lewis and Clark Interpretive
  Center, 109
Lewis and Clark State Park, 41
Lillooet Express, 274
Lime Kiln Point State Park, 207
Lincoln City, 17, 21
Linn County Museum, 97
Little Italy West, 130
Little Mount Si, 154
Laube Orchards, 74
Loft, The, 233
Log Cabin Inn, 95

Lone Fir Resort, 43
Long Beach Peninsula, 108–14
Longmire, 176, 178
Lopez Island, 198, 202
Lummi Indian Reservation, 302
Lummi Island, 298–305
Lund, 254–62
Lynden, 307, 313

# M

McCullough Station, 278
McKenzie River Highway area,
  93–99
McLoughlin House, 85
McMinnville, 74
Madeira Park, 256, 261
Majestic European Country Inn,
  148
Makah Indian Reservation, 122
Manning Provincial Park, 277
Manor Farm Inn, 182
Manzanita, 15, 20
Margison House, 217
Marina, The, 302
Marine Park, 35, 300
Marquam Hill Vineyards, 89
Marten Rapids, 95
Maryhill Museum of Art, 64
Marymere Falls, 123
Maury Island, 138
Mayne Island, 246, 249, 253
Mazama Country Inn, 170
Meares Island, 233
Meeker Mansion, 177
Mertie Stevens House, 85
Meta Lake Trail, 41
Miller Tree Inn, 129
Miners Bay, 249
Mink Lake Trial, 128
Miracle Beach Provincial Park,
  224
Mission Mill Village, 87
Molalla River State Park, 89

Mom's Pies, 95
Monroe, 165
Montinore Vineyards, 70
Moran State Park, 199
Morning Star II, 18
Morton, 41, 45
Mossyrock, 41
Mount Adams, 56, 63
Mount Angel, 89
Mount Baker, 187, 200, 306–13
Mount Baker-Snoqualmie National Forest, 167
Mount Hood area, 31–38
Mount Hood Meadows Ski Area, 33
Mount Hood Railroad, 36, 59
Mount Jefferson, 101
Mount Rainier Loop, 173–79
Mount Rainier National Park, 174
Mount Rainier Scenic Railroad, 176
Mount St. Helens area, 39–45, 56
Mount Storm King Trail, 123
Mount Young, 206
Moyer House, 97
Multnomah Falls Lodge, 56
Museums, 6, 16, 23, 41, 47, 50, 51, 62, 64, 66, 79, 85, 88, 90, 97, 101, 102, 133, 149, 161, 167, 171, 181, 183, 188, 193, 195, 198, 215, 223, 225, 234, 270, 283, 284, 291, 292, 300, 307
Mushroom collecting, 36
My Mom's Pie Kitchen, 111

**N**
Nahcotta, 111
Neah Bay, 122
Neahkahnie Mountain, 15
Nehalem, 15
Neskowin, 17
Netarts Bay, 21

Neva's, 65
Neville's Shoreline, 194
Newberg, 74
Newberry Crater Obsidian Trail, 103
New Day Seafood, 181
Newhalem, 169
Nick's Italian Cafe, 70
Nisqually Glacier, 175
North Bend, 154, 157
North Cascades area, 166–72
North Central Washington Museum, 161
North Kitsap Peninsula, 180–85
Northwest Trek, 176

**O**
Oak Bay Beach Hotel, 216
Observatories, 65, 105
Obsidian flows, 103
Ocean Park, 111
Oceanwood Country Inn, 249
Octagon Building, 88
Of Sea and Shore Museum, 183
Okanagan, 276–87
O'Keefe Ranch, 280
Old Aurora Colony Museum, 88
Old Bell Tower, 120
Old House Restaurant, 223
Old Mahle House, 235
Old Settlers Museum, 41
Olga, 200
Olympic National Park, 122
Olympic Peninsula, 119
Oneonta Gorge Botanical Area, 56, 77
Orcas Hotel, 201
Orcas Island, 197–203
Orchard Hill Inn, 63
Oregon City area, 84–92
Oregon Coastline Express, 19
Otis, 18
Otis Cafe, 18

Oxbow Salmon Hatchery, 35
Oysterville, 111

**P**

Pacific Crest National Scenic
    Trail, 33
Pacific Rim National Park, 232
Pacific Sands Beach Resort, 232
Pacific University, 70
Packwood, 179
Palmer Glacier, 33
Panorama Point, 35, 58, 175
Panther Creek, 71
Paradise, 174
Paradise Inn, 175
Paradise Park, 33, 175
Parksville, 222, 229, 234
Parliament Buildings, 215
Peaches and Cream, 278
Pebbles Restaurant, 256
Pender Islands, 246, 252–53
Penticton, 277, 285
Perdition Trail, 56
Peterson Rock Garden, 105
Pillars of Hercules, 55
The Pillars Bed and Breakfast, 194
Pine Mountain Observatory, 105
Pine Tavern Restaurant, 103
Pioneer Museum, 16
Pioneer Park, 86, 299
Pioneer Village Museum, 167
Planters Lounge, 273
Portage, 140
Port Alberni, 231
Port Angeles, 121, 122
Port Browning Pub, 125, 246
Port Gamble, 183
Port Ludlow, 125
Port Madison Indian Reservation,
    181
Port Townsend, 119, 125
Poulsbo, 181
Powell River, 257, 262

Promenade, 13
Puget Island, 5
Puyallup, 176, 179

**Q**

Quadra Island, 225
Qualicum Beach, 222, 229
Quilchena, 281
Quilchena Hotel, 281

**R**

Rainy Lake National Recreation
    Trail, 169
Ramona Falls, 32
Ram's Head Bar, 33
Rex Hill Vineyards, 71
Rhododendron, 37
Rialto Beach, 130
Riffe Lake, 41
Rim Rock Cafe and Oyster Bar,
    272
Robson Bight Ecological Reserve,
    226
Rockaway Beach, 15
Rock climbing, 105
Rockport, 168
Rosario Resort, 200
Ross Lake, 169
Round Butte Dam, 101
Royal British Columbia Museum,
    215
Ruckle Provincial Park, 265

**S**

Sadigih's, 308
Sahalie Falls, 34, 96
Sailboarding, 58
St. Helens, 5, 10
St. Helens Cafe, 5
St. Josef's Weinkeller Winery, 89
Salem, 86, 87, 91

Salish Lodge, 154
Salmon Arm, 280, 286
Salmon hatcheries, 6, 35, 59, 155
Salmon Point Marine Pub and
    Restaurant, 224
Salmon River Valley, 225
Salt Cairn, 19
Salt Creek Recreation Area, 122
Salt Spring Island, 263–68
Sand Island, 9
Sandy, 32, 37
San Juan Island, 204–9
San Juan Island Historical Mu-
    seum, 205–6
San Juan Island National Histori-
    cal Park, 206
Sankey Park, 48, 96
Santiam River, 86, 96, 104
Saturday market, 28, 94
Scappoose, 9
Sea Breeze Lodge, 242
Seagull Factory, 17
Sealand of the Pacific, 216
Seaside, 13, 20
Seaview, 110, 114
Sekiu, 122
Semiahmoo Spit, 303
Serenity's Restaurant, 63
Shafer Museum, 171
Shafer Vineyard Cellars, 69
Shelburne Inn, 110, 112
Shoalwater Restaurant, 110
Silver Falls State Park, 86
Silver Lake Park, 311
Silverton, 85, 90
Silverton Country Museum, 86
Sisters, 103, 107
Skagit County, 186–91
Skagit Wildlife Recreation Area,
    189
Skamania County Historical Mu-
    seum, 63
Skamokawa, 6, 11

Skiing, 33, 159, 163, 171, 177,
    270–71, 273, 284
Skykomish River, 159
Slip Point, 122
Smith Rocks, 104
Snohomish, 167
Snoqualmie Falls, 152–57, 163
Snoqualmie Valley Historic Mu-
    seum, 154
Sokol Blosser Winery, 71
Sol Duc Hot Springs Resort, 128
Soleduck Falls, 128
Soleduck River, 123
Sooke, 216, 219
Sooke Harbor, 217
Sooke Harbor House, 217
Sound Food Restaurant and Bak-
    ery, 139
Southeast Vancouver Island,
    288–97
South Pender, 247
South Vancouver Island, 214–20
South Whidbey Historical Mu-
    seum, 145
South Whidbey State Park, 149
Spelunking, 105
Spirit Lake, 42
Springtree Eating Establishment
    and Farm, 205
Springwater Hotel, 251
Spruce Railroad Trail, 124
Squamish, 270
Stanwood, 189
State capitol, 87
State House Bed and Breakfast,
    86
Stayton, 86, 91
Stevenson, 62, 66
Stevens Pass, 159
Stonehedge Inn, 57
Stonehenge replica, 65
Strait of Juan de Fuca, 118–26,
    128

Strathcona Park Lodge, 239
Strawberry Island, 233
Sumas Mountain Village, 311
Sumner, 179
Sunriver, 103, 107
Suquamish Museum, 181
Sweet Home, 48, 96

# T

Tahlequah, 141
Tamanawaus Falls Trail, 34
Tatoosh Island, 122
Terwilliger Hot Springs, 95
Three Creeks Lodge, 64
Three Fingered Jack, 101
Three Rivers Winery, 58
Three Sisters, 101
Thunderbird Park, 215
Tides Tavern, 195
Tillamook, 16, 20
Tillamook Bay, 16
Tillicum Park, 130
Timberline Lodge, 32, 33
Tofino, 232, 237
Toutle River, 40
Trail of the Cedars, 169
Trail's End Heritage Center, 85
Trail of Two Forests, 42
Treasure Island, 240
Tribune Bay Provincial Park, 242
Troutdale, 60
Trout hatchery, 94
Trout Lake, 66
Taulatin Mountains, 72
Taulatin Vineyards, 69
Tudor Room, 216
Tunnel Falls, 57
Turtleback Farm Inn, 199
Tweten's Lighthouse, 136
Twigs Restaurant, 273

# U

Ucluelet, 236–37
Umbrella Falls, 34

# V

Vancouver Island
    northeast coast, 221–29
    west shore, 230–37
Van Zandt, 308
Vashon Island, 138–43, 193
Veritas Vineyard, 72
Vernon, 280, 286
Vesuvius Bay, 266
Victoria, 215, 219
Vida, 99
Vineyards, 69–75, 89, 309
Vista House, 55

# W

Wahkiakum County Historical
    Museum, 6
Waikiki Beach, 109
Walking tours, 6, 8, 72, 97, 106
Wallace Falls State Park, 159
Wallalute Falls, 34
Warm Springs, 107
Washington County Museum, 69
Washington County vineyards,
    68–75
Water Board Park, 97
Waterfront Park, 160, 281
Water Street, 120
Waves, The, 14
W.B. Scott's, 195
Weedle Bridge, 96
Welches, 32, 37
Wenatchee, 161

West Coast Trail, 219, 232, 235
Westport, 5
Whale Museum, 205
Whale watching, 19, 27, 207,
    226, 233, 304
Whalewatch Park, 207
Wheeler, 15, 20
Whidbey Island, 144–51
Whistler, 269–75
White River, 33, 82
White Salmon, 63
White water rafting, 28, 64, 81,
    98, 105, 162, 163–64, 272
Wickersham, 308
Wildflower Cafe, 272
Wild Ginger Trail, 240
Wildlife preserves, 6, 14, 24, 111,
    176, 284
Willamette Falls, 85
Willamette Valley area, 104
Willapa National Wildlife Refuge,
    111

Willingdon Beach, 257
Willows Inn, 302
Wilson Glacier, 175
Windy Ridge Viewpoint, 42
Wineries, 8, 24, 37, 58–59, 71,
    88, 89, 159, 278–79, 282–83
Winthrop, 170, 172
Wolf Rock, 95
Woodland, 44
World War II blimp hangars, 18

**Y**
Yamhill, 74
Yamhill County Historical Society
    Museum, 71

**Z**
Zigzag, 32

# About the Author

Marilyn McFarlane is the author of *Best Places to Stay in the Pacific Northwest* and *Best Places to Stay in California.* Her extensive writings on travel include a weekly column, "Northwest Discoveries," for *This Week,* an Oregon newspaper. McFarlane has lived on the West Coast all her life and has explored almost every corner. She now resides in Portland, Oregon, with her attorney husband, John M. Parkhurst, and three cats.

# Also of interest from The Globe Pequot Press

*Alaska's Southeast,* 4th Edition   $12.95
Touring the scenic inside passage

*Best Bike Rides in the Pacific Northwest*   $12.95
50 beautiful rides in Western Canada and the U.S.

*Driving the Pacific Coast: Oregon & Washington,* 2nd Edition   $12.95
Scenic driving tours along coastal highways

*Seattle Guidebook,* 8th Edition   $11.95
The ultimate reference to a favorite city

*Short Bike Rides in Western Washington*   $12.95
Fabulous rides in the Puget Sound region

*Guide to Western Canada,* 3rd Edition   $12.95
Comprehensive guide to its great cities

*Montana: Off the Beaten Path*   $9.95
A guide to lesser-known spots of interest

*Oregon: Off the Beaten Path*   $9.95
A guide to lesser-known spots of interest

*Washington: Off the Beaten Path*   $9.95
A guide to lesser-known spots of interest

## Other Titles in this Series

*Quick Escapes in Southern California*   $13.95
*Quick Escapes from Chicago*   $12.95
*Quick Escapes from San Francisco*   $13.95

Available from your bookstore or directly from the publisher. For a free catalogue or to place an order, call toll-free 24 hours a day 1–800–243–0495 (in Connecticut, call 1–800–962–0973) or write to The Globe Pequot Press, P.O. Box 833, Old Saybrook, Connecticut 06475-0833.